For a LIBERATORY
POLITICS *of* HOME

For a LIBERATORY POLITICS *of* HOME

Michele Lancione

Duke University Press   *Durham and London*   2023

Project Editor: Michael Trudeau
Cover designed by Matthew Tauch
Typeset in Portrait Text by Westchester Publishing Services

Library of Congress Cataloging-in-Publication Data
Names: Lancione, Michele, author.
Title: For a liberatory politics of home / Michele Lancione.
Description: Durham : Duke University Press, 2023. | Includes
bibliographical references and index.
Identifiers: LCCN 2023001578 (print)
LCCN 2023001579 (ebook)
ISBN 9781478025306 (paperback)
ISBN 9781478020523 (hardcover)
ISBN 9781478027423 (ebook)
Subjects: LCSH: Homelessness—Political aspects. | Home—Political
aspects. | Homeless persons. | Sociology, Urban. | Marginality, Social. |
Human geog-raphy. | BISAC: SOCIAL SCIENCE / Sociology / Urban |
SOCIAL SCIENCE / Poverty & Homelessness
Classification: LCC HT151 .L26 2023 (print) | LCC HT151 (ebook) |
DDC 305.5/692—DC23/ENG/20230508
LC record available at https://lccn.loc.gov/2023001578
LC ebook record available at https://lccn.loc.gov/2023001579

Cover art: Photo by author

Contents

What if the solution to *homelessness* is not *home*? What if home is not worth going back to, and one instead needs the constitution of a more radical beyond? What kind of epistemic and material liberation is needed for thinking and doing that?

In this book, I try to provide an initial response to these questions by transcending a binary reading of home and its other. Conventionally, home is longed for as a place of ontological security and belonging; its loss defines what it means to be home-*less*. What follows is a political and affective charge to "go back home": to fight homelessness as the deviation from an otherwise worthy path. Entire economies of the homely, large industries of salvation and even instances of housing activism are founded on this oppositional reading of home and its less. Contrary to this, my proposal is to conceive home and homelessness as matter of the same. This is not about discarding traumatic experiences conventionally conflated in the latter but to affirm that home contains in itself the possibility of not being at home: for one can be made to inhabit a space of the less without requiring home to alter its parameters. This is what I call the impossible possibility of home: a salvation designed around its annihilation; a tension sitting very much at the heart of what is made to count as other and how that is governed, recursively so, from the level of individual subjection through the diagram of global boundaries.

I aim to explore these tensions, moved by the belief that current conceptual frameworks of home and homelessness are inadequate and dangerous. They are inadequate because they reduce homelessness to the realm of exceptionality and thereby (re)produce it rather than solve it. And they are dangerous because they sustain particular ideologies of home, hence foreclosing other ways of inhabiting the world. The proposition I bring to the fore is radically simple: homelessness cannot be solved without dismantling our current makings of home. There is no possible adjustment, no innovative intervention, and no salvation if we do not crack through the ceiling of home itself. This means many things, including challenging scholarship and policies on the matter and intersecting with cognate struggles against patriarchy, the financialization of housing, and the violence of racial capitalism. But above all, it means retrieving and then building upon the desire for liberation that constantly unfolds, and lingers through, the interstices of home and its foundational "lessness." The book provides a concrete propositional politics in such a sense (part III). To get there, it offers a conceptual grammar to navigate the constitutive threshold of home/homelessness (part I), and it grounds the argument locally (taking up the case of Italy) and in the West (part II). Through this journey, the ambition is to offer just one possible way of thinking for a liberatory politics of home: a praxis to move beyond current modes of homing the world.

I want to be clear about the inescapable limitations of this volume. I say *inescapable* because these are limitations related to my journey. I have been able to care for, and struggle with, friends, comrades, and research participants fighting for another way of homing for a while, but I do not assume I can speak for them. Although all the arguments in this book have been discussed and validated through many years of engagement, they remain mediated by my trajectory. I am a white bisexual man, born into a very modest working-class family from a tiny industrial village in the northern periphery of Italy.[1] The making of this subjectivity grants me a limited view of the world, which impacts how I see, feel, and make sense of things. My journey as an adult has questioned and added to this, but this book can only offer partial accounts of the individuals rendered in its pages. These are people whose experiences come with their historical freight and specific violence. I have tried to account for these complex histories but have probably failed. The same goes for the geographies of reference: this text is grounded in my Italian ethnographic work, with connections to the Anglo-Saxon worlds of the UK and North America. It knows little of other contexts and does not presume to speak about them. However, I hope that its methodological, conceptual, and political grammar may be helpful to those fighting entrenched understandings of home elsewhere in the world, too.

Given these limitations, the following aims to provide a transversal pathway to the land of lessness, where some are supposedly at home and others are not. I aim to account for the fact that, in immanent terms, many lack a way of dwelling joyfully, and there is much to be gained in recentering thinking from that standpoint. I believe that a critical approach to what I call home(lessness) provides access to broader and more radical framings. Hopefully, this book indicates a way to experiment with those, dismantle convention where necessary, and expand understandings and struggles affirming thousands of liberated kinds of homes.

I had been working on this book, on and off, for more than a decade. This means much life and many projects intersected its development, and I will never be able to give justice to all of it in only a few lines. So I focus here on the most immediate entanglements.

The European Research Council supported the substantive development of this book through my project Inhabiting Radical Housing (grant no. 851940). At the same time, core ideas were nurtured at Durham University (during my PhD) and, years later, at the Urban Institute in Sheffield. I am indebted to these institutions for providing me with the time and resources for this work. But these wouldn't mean much without the attentiveness and intellectual stimuli colleagues have shared with me along the way. Thank you to Francesca Governa, without whom I wouldn't have had the chance of becoming an academic; Ash Amin, who showed me how to love intellectual labor with great patience, care, and insight; Colin McFarlane, from whom I have learned much intellectually and around the job of being an academic; Stewart Clegg, for providing me the space to pursue my ideas in my time at the University of Technology of Sydney; Tatiana Thieme, for a sisterhood that comes back anew every year; and then, with much love to them, thanks to my colleagues at the University of Sheffield, who provided a shared sense of purpose and the confidence to experiment and explore. My gratitude to John Flint, Ryan Powell, Beth Perry, Vanesa Castán Broto, Jon Silver, Simon Marvin, Aidan While, and all the early career postdoctoral fellows for what we shared and built together. Along a similar line, I want to thank the members of the Beyond Inhabitation Lab at DIST, Polytechnic of Turin, the PhD candidates I advise in the UK and Italy, and the team of postdoctoral researchers currently working with me. I am privileged to share intellectual and political labor with all of you.

An early version of this book benefited from the comments of some of the colleagues listed here, and ideas were tested in several academic and activist settings across the years. I am thankful to those who provided invitations and engagement. I want to recall a few in particular. The first thank you goes to the late Josie Jolley, an incredibly talented PhD scholar with whom I had the fortune of discussing ideas around "home" and learning from her own writing. The second goes to my friend Kiera Chapman, who proofread a very different version of this book but gave me the crucial confidence to fully embrace a way of thinking beyond binaries. Then, to Katherine Brickell, for her meaningful writings on (un)homing, home violence, and their multiscalar politics, and for her generous and insightful reading of my work. A special thank you to Ananya Roy: beyond what I have learned from her scholarship and her direct actions, and beyond the daily inspiration she provides with her doings through the Unequal Cities Network, I am thankful to her for pushing me hard to reconsider ideas, to rewrite, to commit further. All errors remain mine, but without Katherine and Ananya, I would have liked this book less. Thank you to production editors Liz Smith and Michael Trudeau, editorial associate Laura Jaramillo, copyeditor Karen Fisher, book designer Matthew Tauch, and the marketing team at Duke. A special thank you note to my wonderful editor, Courtney Berger, who believed in the core ideas of my proposal, supported me throughout, and gave me the confidence to pursue this work.

Much of my thinking around housing politics is derived from grassroots experiences, to which I hope this book will contribute. I am indebted to houseless friends and research participants in Italy and beyond, and in particular, for the ideas developed in this book, thank you to Amos and the late Paolo and Pancrazio—who many years ago made Turin's streets and their biopolitical diagrams legible to me. Gratitude also goes to my *Radical Housing Journal* comrades, particularly Melissa Fernández Arrigoitia, Mara Ferreri, Melissa García-Lamarca, and Erin McElroy, with whom we shared much work to envision, construct, and nurture a new global infrastructure for emancipatory housing knowledge. Similarly, thanks to my comrades in the Common Front for Housing Rights in Bucharest (albeit the struggles we shared are not part of this volume, I am thankful for what I have learned with you) and thanks, too, to those individuals and groups, all across Italy and beyond, who support direct actions and organizing to keep Frontex out of our universities, and those who fight, on an everyday basis, to abolish it altogether. Liberating home in Europe today also requires that.

Finally, a line of something more profound than gratitude goes to my brother AbdouMaliq Simone because, since the end of my PhD, he has always been there—physically, emotionally, intellectually—with concrete gestures of care in an academic realm often spurred by those, without expecting anything in return. But Maliq needs to be also thanked for his intellectual project, a politically charged but soft-spoken relentless search for those nonapparent surrounds where life is rendered possible and impossible, those interstices where one can trace the insurgence of lives beyond what the pastiche of sociological thinking has made of them. Thank you for those storylines, brother.

Grazie to Marina and Antonio for your unconditional love and unbounded sacrifices. *Grazie* to Leo, for putting up with me, for shaking my depression when it needs to be shaken, for pushing me to write this thing, for nurturing the tempo of our becoming, for just being there and being you. I dedicate this book to my nieces Bianca and Laura and my sister Silvia—inspiring women affirming their liberation.

INTRODUCTION. The Problem of *Lessness*

"Sans" is a short story in French, written in 1969 by Samuel Beckett, later translated into English under the title "Lessness." It is composed of sixty sentences, ordered into paragraphs that, according to Beckett, follow a random structure.[1] The result is a narrative in which chunks can be reordered at pleasure without the whole losing its meaning; a story that still conveys its effect when it is messed up. The text depicts "a small grey upright body standing among the ruins of a refuge in an endless grey expanse."[2] The body does not do much but is charged by fragments of passing light, by the beats of a heart, by a landscape of sand, ash, and holes, even by a "blank mind."[3] In encountering it, in reading "Sans," we are charged too: the effect produced is one of anguished fear, an expanded tension arising from the way a body dwelling in a vast gray plateau is affected by the elements.

Little body same grey as the earth sky ruins only upright. No sound not a breath same grey all sides earth sky body ruins. Blacked out fallen open four walls over backwards true refuge issueless.

No sound no stir ash grey sky mirrored earth mirrored sky. Grey air timeless earth sky as one same grey as the ruins flatness endless. In the sand no hold one step more in the endlessness he will make it. It will be day and night again over him the endlessness the air heart will beat again.[4]

The claustrophobic experience of "Sans" can be lived and felt over and over again, no matter how its structure is aligned. Even though its sentences can be rearranged in more than 8.3×10^{81} permutations—and an online project allows a reader to do this—the effect produced will always be the same.[5] Here are three sentences randomly arranged by myself:

No sound no stir ash grey sky mirrored earth mirrored sky. It will be day and night again over him the endlessness the air heart will beat again. Light refuge sheer white blank planes all gone from mind.

"Sans" is crisscrossed by a diagrammatic power in which the arrangement of things is the source of happenings. Yet, through the recurrence of its key repertoire of phrases and its obsessively fragmented syntax and schizoid tempo, happenings in "Sans" always stay the same. This is a particular type of inertia, playing at the level of affect: it is different in kind from the logic of the *Gattopardo*, where an incredible amount of purposive effort is made to "change everything so that nothing changes."[6] Despite being strategic in its outline (it is, after all, the output of a writer's pen), "Sans" is able to acquire a life of its own, an ability to affect others that stays the same despite huge possibilities of variation. In encountering it, we bypass the logic of traditional narrative, with its forward propulsion, to be charged and rewired by its permeating lack, by its engraving of hollowness on our bodies. Ultimately, the diagrammatic power of "Sans" is about subsuming all possibilities of becoming in its endless recurrence, and, for the ones who get into its arrangement, it is about becoming subject-of that exhaustive becoming too.[7]

The upright gray body populating the "Lessness" plateau seems lost. In there, right in the middle of a land that does not provide but only takes, one is hardly in a place one could call home. Beckett speaks of "scattered ruins," of a "refuge" that is long gone. The subject of "Lessness" is folded inside out, rounded in—as if the individual is subsumed and completed in—the formation of the vast gray plateau they inhabit: "all sides endlessness earth sky as one no stir not a breath. Blank planes sheer white calm eye light of reason all gone from mind." In such an arrangement, *lack* is not the missing property of a mind, of a subject or a land; instead, it becomes the constitutive power-to and power-from; in other words, it is both what is produced and what produces, what is offered and what is taken. In "Sans" there is no escape, not because something is holding the gray body from escaping but because (ontologically) there is nowhere else to go. "Lessness" reproduces its infinite possibilities and permutations to always serve the same finite outcome: excruciating exposure to hollowness, on a plateau that sometimes might get easier (milder wind, fewer fragments, easier prose) but ultimately always folds into its enduring reproduction of lack.

In this book, I am interested in taking the problem of lessness seriously and in treating it as Beckett does: not as a province of an otherwise functional plateau, but as a plateau of life in and of itself. This means conceiving of lessness and of its diagrammatic power beyond dichotomous understandings of possession. In such a reading, lacking something is not a status opposite to having that thing but part of a peculiar instantiation of life, where having can be subsumed into lacking and vice versa: a plateau where the underlying grammar through which things are arranged speaks of subtraction, annihilation, extraction, no matter what its provisional arrangements smell or look like. Such an understanding is contrary to what we are commonly used to in thinking about lessness. In the English language, *less* is always *less-than*: an appendix defining a status opposed to a fuller extent. You are, you own, you do, you look, you dream, or you mean *less* than that—*less* than the next person. The status of the less in its common acceptations (well beyond English) is one of opposites— that is, one squarely rooted in binary thinking. Less, understood in the common way, knows little of the ways in which Beckett wrote about it in "Sans." If the latter is a nonescapable diagram, the former implies a possibility of betterment, even if only ideally so.

In the following pages, I am interested in challenging this common understanding of the less, and in reading lessness as an entire world of its own: a world populated with binaries rather than a binary itself. In sneaking through the (un)makings of lack in this way, I aim to reapproach important couplets of our times such as home/homeless, saved/lost, and possession/dispossession, not as inherently alternative one to the other but as coherent expressions of a wider sphere founded upon a shared affective and political economy (a lessness, as I explain later, rooted in the functions of expulsion and extraction). The common resolution of those couplets—the moving, for instance, from dispossession to possession—does not bring one outside lessness but unfolds within it, and it is functional to the maintenance and reproduction of its power equilibrium and internal reproduction. In thinking about lessness in this way, I aim to challenge the common resolution of those couplets but also to indicate that a genuine politics of liberation from lessness needs unavoidably to go beyond lessness itself. This might seem obvious. But for the most part, in the immanence of our collective dealings with matter and subjects of lack, current solutions to lessness are crafted within its expulsive and extractive logic—not beyond them. The upright gray body Beckett speaks about is helped, loved, and cared for (in the best instances, of course) still within diagrams of subtraction, control, and extraction: in lessness, becoming less and being helped out take forms and praxis squarely mirroring the annihilating diagrammatic politics of that plateau.

The only possibility for liberation, in this context, would be for the gray subject to go beyond lessness tout court and, in doing so, to go beyond itself too: it would mean to arrange for another plateau, to become another subject. The book, therefore, does not propose adjustments but argues for walking away from the table: opening up a drawer, taking up a new slate, writing a different story; one defining its characters not in an oppositional reading to lessness but in their capacity to extend beyond their supposed otherness. Such a move requires the deep intensification, rather than the resolution, of collective struggles. As I argue at a later stage, echoing anarchist sensitivities, this means conceiving a revolutionary process necessary to encompass lessness as the end on its own, rather than conceiving the termination of lessness as the end point of revolution. In other words, the book argues that cracking through lessness will never be completed, and it must never be completed: liberation from it lies within our collective capacity to constantly fight beyond—in an affirmative way and not simply against—its reinstantiation. One, in this sense, will never really put the word *end* in writing a story without lessness: to be cracked, the diagram must be left open beyond sixty options and their thousands of painfully equal permutations.

There have been important contributions in recent years advocating for similar all-encompassing, yet forcefully processual, redrawings. For the likes of Escobar on design, Gago on feminist politics, Ferdinand on decolonial inhabitation, Rolnik on financialized housing, Roy on poverty politics, or Gilmore on racialized incarcerations, the concern is not just around (policy) solutions to a defined set of issues but to transcend entire systems of oppression and related modes of thinking, theorizing, and discussing. Intersecting these conversations, I situate my contribution at a particular nexus, one where the binaries of lessness are particularly salient and have, perhaps, become even more so in the aftermath of the COVID-19 pandemic. The book focuses on the constitutive crossroads of home and its defined other, homelessness.[8] As I expand upon later, I do not conceive of lessness as limited to this juncture. The affective and political economy of constituting others as subjects of lack—what I refer to as expulsion—and the related appropriation of a varied set of values from it (extraction) well encompass what generally and most commonly is defined as home and homelessness. Yet I find this particular juncture important in its capacity to offer a privileged access point, both to explore the logic of lessness at the heart of most people's concerns (home) and to propose a radical politics of inhabitation arising from the embodied experiences of those currently defined as unhomed.

At the most basic level, in common discourse, to be homeless is to lack something: a permanent and secure abode, but also social respectability, ontological security, and the material and relational means allowing one to flourish in life. Homelessness, to go back to Beckett, seems equal to the plateau of "Lessness": a land defined by intersecting sociocultural and economic factors that profoundly affect bodies, reproducing seemingly endless stories of agony and loss. The sand, light, and ash of Beckett's story become phenotypical and material orderings—that is, racial, gendered, and economic classifications—of bodies defined as other, as home-less. The vast gray plateau of "Sans" is replaced with the neoliberal city, where dispossession takes place under the shadow of broken refuges, of thousands of lost, more secure pasts. These homes have vanished in financialized schemes, and all that is left are ruins, violent racialized orderings, "ash grey sky mirrored earth mirrored sky." As in "Sans," on the plateau of homelessness, things do not stay still, and yet they remain the same. The terrain shifts, according to the way that the story is rearranged. Homeless individuals are studied, helped, depicted, moved, placed, intervened upon, medicalized, jailed, and freed. Yet they are not lacking in agency: they too do all sorts of things. Being upright, in their circumstance, means dealing with both the orderings intersecting their lives and with the governmentalities of their context. Their stillness is of an active kind, as they respond to new permutations of their experiential conditions and new arrangements of their story. This is at least how many homeless men and women have described their lives to me: as a perennial struggle and trauma to endure and cope with their condition of lack, a state where things never seem to change, where energies get lost in complex and detached mechanisms that nonetheless substantively impact on personal experience. The number of individual permutations a life can follow in this state of homelessness is infinite, but violence and trauma are common and permanently present.

And yet sometimes, some people do get out—or so we are told. Some do get better. Some do get back home. This getting home is supposed to be the line of flight, the breakthrough. It is the moment in which the upright gray body moves at a different tempo, when their chains break and they leave the plateau to the notes of John Denver's "Take Me Home, Country Roads." The road cutting across the plain fades to black, the sound of a roaring engine, rolling credits, The End. From there, we are told, they will enter into a different life arrangement, another story made of alternative orderings and governmentalities. They will be on a plateau different from that which Beckett writes about, in a narration that is not included in the sixty diagrammatic sentences of his story. They will seek, and perhaps succeed in their pursuit of, happiness, like Will Smith in the homonymous movie: moving from *absence of* to *presence of*; from homelessness to home. The affective and replete presence of home, where sweet memories dwell, "dark and dusty, painted on the sky," is there to comfort them, and all of us, in that transition. Here I am not talking of the return to the home one might well have escaped from, but the idealized portrayal of a home one can project oneself toward. That home is made possible because the many oppose its psychological, political, economic, and social impossibility. That home exists because its absence is to be fought as the negation of a desired state, a loss of security, the lack of a form of care that is supposed to ground who we are into the world. That home is conceived as the way out of lessness, the solution to it. But is it? In this book, I essentially argue that that home is not a solution to anything; instead, it is the problem. That happiness, unless it fundamentally alters the parameters upon which mainstream ideals of home are founded, shares much with lessness rather than departing from it. In this book, I argue that, under current conditions, there is no walking out of the plateau of lessness, no transition: just a violent home that encloses its supposed negation in individualized narratives of salvation.

Choosing the tensioned binary of home/homelessness as my point of departure is strategic: in discussing it, my goal is to explicitly go beyond what is currently made of this couplet, in a methodological attempt to break through its power and signal liberatory formations. The thesis is that there is no home worth going back to and no salvation for the homeless within the current understanding of home. In this volume, home and homelessness are not opposites but matter of the same. This entails reading Beckett's "Lessness"—as one among many possible metaphors offered by art—as a representation of home as a whole, of home and homelessness, or, to introduce a term I rely upon to signify the concomitant reading of the two, of home(lessness).[9] This logic enables two important moves. First, in home(lessness) there is no return home from homelessness and, crucially, no capacity to become homeless. Being at home is conceptually on a continuum with not being at home. There is only one plateau. Second, the factors intersecting the upright gray body (violent sociocultural and racialized histories, economic inequalities, the urban biopolitical machine and its various ruins) do not concern the few but the many (which is different than saying their violence is experienced by the many; see below). Following this, the capacity of the diagram of home(lessness) to (re)produce lack would affect all its dwellers, shaping everybody who is assembling life through its means. Lessness moves from being a metaphor for a condition affecting a particular population (the gray bodies) in certain spaces (an exceptional plateau) to becoming an affective predisposition of the general arrangement of things, a capacity that resides in all kinds of worldly arrangements.[10] The only way to get rid of homelessness, in this case, would be to imagine and construct a completely different story of home.

Would Housing All the Homeless in the World Be Enough to End Homelessness?

Globally, housing futures do not look bright. As UN-HABITAT and other international agencies report, each year millions of people face forced eviction from their homes. A staggering 1.6 billion people are inadequately housed.[11] Forecasts that consider the increase in global population and rising urbanization suggest that housing precarity will continue to grow in scale, while commentators and scholars alike agree that urban and housing crises—in the form of massive displacement, gentrification, and uneven development—are the new normal.[12] As Natalie Osborne reminds us, "our cities are increasingly inequitable and precarious places," and this tendency is only likely to increase in years to come.[13] What does it mean, then, to think and to write about the binaries of home and homelessness, or the insurgent power of housing precarity, when our present condition seems to foreclose possibilities of sustainable provisioning and resistance? Would it not be more serious to reinforce the message of housing for all, and to fight that battle, instead of arguing for a broader reenvisioning and a more radical outline?

I am writing this book convinced that the only way forward—in the sense of being the only way to stay meaningfully alive—is through a global fight for housing justice. And yet I also believe that a radical fight for housing justice, in order to achieve its goal, needs to recenter the question of the kind of home it is fighting for. This is a thin and difficult line to navigate, because it brings with itself questions around the meaning of housing justice and, more fundamentally, questions around the meaning of thinking of home and homelessness beyond their conventional binary reading. After all, if people are rallying behind policies like Housing First, it is because they want to end homelessness and provide homes. If organizers are occupying, stopping evictions, and advocating for public housing, it is because they want to stop precarity and poverty when it comes to dwelling. From these perspectives, stating that being at home and being homeless are matter of the same would seem to be a neoliberal fantasy: a narration spurred by the entrenched suffering and traumas of living in precarious dwelling conditions. But a deeper reading is possible: a transversal approach inviting one to stay close to the interstices of home(lessness), where the makings of home and its supposed other are somewhat fuzzier, dangerously slippery, and, therefore, productively unstable. In what follows, I expand on the meaning of this by clarifying three core tenets of this book: its treatment of housing precarity; its effort to experiment with a renewed grammar of home(lessness); and its ethnographic approach.

ON PRECARIOUS HOUSING

It is of crucial importance to clarify one thing straight away. In refusing to see home and homelessness as distinct, the book does not dismiss the different ways in which their same foundation is experienced—that is, the ways in which home(lessness) is lived and felt. The experience of living rough, or in a violent household, or under the constant threat of eviction, has experientially nothing in common with the privilege I currently have as a white man, typing this book in the comfort of the apartment I live in, in shared love with my partner, with a working heater and a relatively stable mortgage, backed by a secure salary. These experiences are not only temporally and spatially specific, but they also have much to do with longer structurations intersecting forms of violence, extraction, expulsion, and embodiments. Encompassing the home/homelessness binary is not about flattening what Robert Desjarlais has called the sharp "cultural, historical, political and pragmatical forces" shaping the experience of housing precarity.[14] The making of that precarity needs to be carefully centered, not only to avoid its epistemic annihilation and desubjectification, but also because that experience provides the foundation for its own liberation (see below, on the minor).

Thinking about home(lessness) does not mean we are all homeless in the canonical sense of the world. Far from it. It means we are all at home, and the home is really violent and needs to be burned down. Not adjusted, not solved, not fixed—but burned down. It means to say that the sharpest experiences of home(lessness), including but not limited to sleeping rough, living in camps, prisons, violent households, gendered and cisnormative spaces, and racialized lives, are not taking place in realms separated from the idyllic pastures of safe homes unless the latter are conceived and lived entirely beyond lessness—that is, outside racial capitalism, patriarchy, heteronormativity, nationalism, financialized housing, settler colonialism, and other common forms of expulsion and extraction (chapters 1 and 2). Those experiencing the harshest intensities of lessness are very much part of the same logic sustaining mainstream ideologies and the practice of home; they are very much part of the same affective political economy. What we currently conceive as homelessness takes place well within the logic supposedly there to solve it or offered as a solution to it (home, sweet home!).

The distinction between the experience and the substratum of that experience is fundamental here. I do not experience housing precarity, but I am very much part of the mechanisms perpetuating it. For instance, I own a credit card, and I have a mortgage—both tools fueling a logic of financialization around housing that, ultimately, is a source of much precarity. Even replacing both, I would not distance myself too much from the reproduction of precarious dwelling under contemporary racial capitalism. I would still be salaried to do a job within a whitening institution structured around forms of epistemic privilege that have colonized, and medicalized, the other of home—creating forms of professionalization and expertise that, ultimately, extract their sustenance from someone else's struggles. Also, five years ago, my partner and I decided to marry in a civil union for the bureaucratic advantages it brought us as economic migrants. Notwithstanding our everyday shared queer politics, in doing so, we validated a cultural institution founded upon patriarchal structures that do so much in shaping the violent experiences of precarious homes. I could go on. But also, I could find alternatives around my credit card; I could leave academia; and my partner and I could divorce, while still being together. The key question is not if these things could happen—because they might indeed happen—but to ask: what is the other plan? In other words, the key question is not to solve these as isolated tensions, as a series of problems/solutions locked in their binaries (the neoliberal quest to ameliorate oneself). The key question is rather how to go beyond those couplets, how to break them, how to push beyond their role in reproducing far more excruciating lives in home(lessness).

The trauma of "continuous displacement," as Catherine Robinson puts it, and the entrenched forms of dispossession structuring it, are not equal to the common meaning of being at home; however, the latter is founded upon perpetuating those logics.[15] Put simply, home is not extraneous to displacement and dispossession, but possible because it displaces and it dispossesses (see chapter 2). Navigating this fine line across experiences and their substratum is difficult, especially if done from the standpoint of the academy, which has done much to colonize all experiences, to reduce them to pastiche for sociological analysis, and, as a number of decolonial thinkers have powerfully argued, for extractive representation. And yet I take the risk of navigating this line precisely because in recentering the common substratum of home(lessness), I aim to recenter the political within its most traumatic experiences. Advancing a joint understanding of the two means to decolonize homelessness from home as well as imagining a home that does not need an otherness to be defined. By refuting the way in which we have been made to think about home and homelessness as a binary, my goal is to resist the depiction of the trauma and suffering of precarious dwelling as abnormal. Instead, I want to argue that through the intensities of home(lessness), a terrain of resistance is already in the making, as a contestation that points toward more than bare survival and fights for autonomous ways of thinking and doing home. The aim of this book is to work with the liberatory politics of those experiences, as defined by their own tempo and their own becoming(s).

ON A GRAMMAR FOR HOME(LESSNESS)

Others have pointed at the need to rethink the relationship of home and homelessness from the ground up.[16] Peter Somerville has provided some helpful provocations in this sense, albeit without showing how certain functions of home are reproduced and maintained through the othering of homelessness.[17] Lindsey McCarthy has taken an inspiring step closer, and her careful work shows how a sense of home can be constructed in homelessness, and vice versa, problematizing binary readings of the two terms.[18] Earlier geographical work from the 1990s on rough sleeping and street life, such as that of Veness and Ruddick, along with the later work of Blunt and Dowling and especially of Katherine Brickell, has shown how a sense and praxis of home can be attained and upheld in unconventional circumstances, challenging any clear conceptual distinction between homelessness and home.[19] April Veness, in particular, explicitly called for a renewed understanding of the two terms in order to look at "the personal worlds of marginal people without assuming that these people and the places where they live must fit prevailing definitions of home and homeless."[20] But recognizing that there is something problematic about the ways in which these two terms relate is not, on its own, liberatory. It is also necessary to explore how the prevailing definitions of home are not only produced but coconstituted and maintained through the home/homelessness binary.

A critical account along these lines was proposed by anthropologist Craig Willse in his 2015 book *The Value of Homelessness*, where he brilliantly shows the role played by both social services and social sciences in the reproduction of the "homelessness industry" in the United States (a term used to indicate that broad spectrum of professionals, and their institutions, working around homelessness). Similar accounts can be found in other contributions pushing conventional homelessness thinking, from anthropology (in the works of Robert Desjarlais, Vincent Lyon-Callo, and especially Teresa Gowan) to geography (in Ananya Roy's work on dispossession, Raquel Rolnik on financialized housing, Catherine Robinson on the trauma of displacement, and AbdouMaliq Simone on the uninhabitable), social psychology (Kim Hopper's critique of institutionalization, echoing the works of antipsychiatrists such as Franca Ongaro and Franco Basaglia, which are relevant to the Italian context I explore in this book), political theory (for instance, Hagar Kotef on settler-colonial homemaking), and philosophy (such as in Judith Butler and Athena Athanasiou's conversations on the embodiments of dispossession).[21] Most of their concerns resonate with mine, and in the coming pages I intersect a heterogeneous set of critical and liberatory literatures to expand on these contemporary debates. The conceptual grammar emerging from this journey is explored in chapter 1, but it can be summarized here in three points.

First, the book explores the constitutive makings of home(lessness), focusing on two functions underpinning, and reproducing, the home/homeless business: expulsion and extraction. The first part of this volume illustrates how mainstream ideas of home depend on the expulsion of the other and the ways in which this is the basis for the extraction of a sense of security, entitlement, and belonging. This othering is not merely conceptual but practical: it is managed and reproduced by cultural, economic, political, and knowledge industries that depend on these twin functions. In an effort to stay close to the production of the home/homeless divide, this book follows Ash Amin's call to critique not only the "framing" of the other but the "bordering practices" that surround them, an approach powerfully extended by the work of Mezzadra and Neilson, and their notion of "borders as method."[22] When it comes to the plane of home(lessness), borderings that signify the home/homeless dichotomy comprise both violent understandings of home (of multiple types, e.g., anthropocentrism, racialization, heteronormalization, and capitalization) and mainstream cultural understandings of homelessness as they unfold in institutional policy, charitable management, knowledge production, and expertise.

As will be clearer in a second, I use the Italian case to ground and present this critique.

Second, the book argues that at the intersection of home(lessness), there is a concrete chance to articulate a renewed and liberatory politics of home. What does it mean to work with the notion of home(lessness) not only critically, but radically: as a way to stay with the problem and do something concrete about it? How to rethink the intensities of home(lessness) beyond the limits of conventional ideas of destitution? The book draws on housing movements around the globe to show that the fight for housing is populated by more than a mere request for shelter. The latter is present, of course, but it is often not reduced to a manageable endpoint: what is being demanded is something beyond the standard idea of home. Instead, many are already using the housing question as a radical starting point through which to articulate a different way of dwelling in the world. Being able to see how these fomentations become political—that is, how they become a shared matter of concern through which thoughts and actions are articulated—is an epistemological problem: a problem of how one sees and makes sense of what it means to inhabit the world. It is a matter of learning how to read home(lessness) in an affirmative fashion, beyond the narrow and repressive interpretations of the homelessness industry. The book therefore offers a micropolitics of inhabitation, which is presented in chapters 6 and 7, and is recalled in the remaining parts of this introduction.

Finally, thinking through home(lessness) is about considering the (re)production of expulsive and extractive praxis that not only keeps the other at bay, but constitutes the other as the only possible way to constantly (re)constitute home itself. Such a critique is at the same time a conceptual, empirical, and political exercise. The grammar instantiated by this book is therefore an attempt at signaling a praxis, or at least a method of inquiry and of action: it is about dealing with how to think, enact, and change home(lessness), not simply to reconsider how one can study it. In chapters 3, 4, and 5, where I ground the discussion ethnographically, I aim to illustrate how a set of ideals of home is reverberated and made operational, both in everyday localized practices of poverty management in Italy (chapter 4) and in the global discourse bolstering new solutions to the problem of homelessness (chapter 5). But the journey from home to its other is not a circular progression that will bring the reader and this writer back home—that is, to an evaluation of shortcomings that can be fixed in order to instantiate more progressive homelessness policies. The journey is a departure from home through the back door of homelessness: it is about undoing home via the gateway of its home-less other, to put aside the shared diagrammatic politics of the two and imagine anew. This is why, ultimately, I see the grammar of this book as a form of praxis, a point to which I dedicate chapter 7.

ON A MINOR ETHNOGRAPHIC APPROACH

I am convinced that the diagrams of home(lessness) cut through many locales and histories. And yet, it is only through a discussion attentive to specific formations that a critical form of translocal theorizing can come to the fore: expulsion and extraction, and their related processes of subject formation, are temporal and context specific. For this reason, the ethnographic discussion presented at the core of this book focuses mainly around a loosely defined geographical and historic signifier—Italy—and, for the more detailed ethnographic narration, a slightly more specific locale, the city of Turin.[23] From there, I will connect to translocal aspects of the diagrams of home(lessness) across the Atlantic and beyond. Ultimately, Italy or Turin are no more representative of a trend than any other place I spent time investigating homelessness in. The choice of this starting point is simply strategic: it has to do with my ability to unfold some of the salient boundary formations with a minimum degree of grounding and detailing.[24] Most of my recent work has been focused on Romania and Bucharest—which will serve as the ground to expand the arguments proposed here, in a separate book—however, I have decided to go back to Italy also to confront the uneasiness I feel around my own experience of being at home. This being said, the book does not offer a comprehensive sociology of home, housing, and related assemblages (such as the family) in the peninsula, but a profiling of the home(lessness) machinery in the country, a narration that aims to showcase a method of inquiry around the colonies of home and its subjects, rather than providing an exhaustive critique of the case.

Central to such a method of inquiry—which is discussed at length in chapter 6—is a minor understanding of socio-ethnographic critique and of its political project. The minor, here, is not understood as the minoritarian or the small but as a method through which established configurations are challenged from within. In this sense, homelessness is not the minor—not only is it not that numerically, but it is not even in the sense of being a matter of marginalized groups. Homelessness is, on the contrary, what Deleuze and Guattari would call a "molar" formation: a configuration belonging to the majoritarian, to institutional power (which, in this case, is also a power of knowledge production), through which biopolitical processes of subject formation occur (what the two philosophers called "segmentation"). On the face of this molarity, the minor would be the endeavor of cracking through those processes of subject formation from their interstices, or their inner makings. For the feminist geographer Cindi Katz, thinking through the minor does not lead to a theory explaining, or attempting an explanation of, matter such as structure/agency, or center/margins.[25] Rather, the minor is a way of looking at the problem of how one deals—conceptually and pragmatically—with violent molar formations cutting across different strata of life. Does the minor advocate for a reform of the molar or, instead, is it about finding a language and a pathway to cut across the molar itself and go beyond it?

Deleuze and Guattari wrote that the minor "no longer characterizes certain literatures, but describes *the revolutionary conditions* of any literature within what we call the great (or established)."[26] For them, the minor is a method to embrace and boost those conditions, which, as Hardt and Negri remind us, are multiplicitous: there is not a single minor but a series of struggles that can intersect, and work together, in a minor fashion (a point made, albeit with a different conceptual grammar, also by Nash).[27] But how does one actually define the "fight from within"? For Deleuze and Guattari, the three key tenets of a minor approach are, first, for a minority to work with "a major language"; second, for "everything in [that effort to be] political"; and third, for "everything [in that effort to have] a collective value."[28] What I take from their exposition of the minor is an invitation to stay close to what Katz has called the "interstices" of theory making and of action, and to use those as a way to work through experiences, assemblages, and their power, which need to be understood as a collective matter, even when they are reduced to individual manifestations.[29] It is important to stress that in this context, the minor is not only a method of inquiry but also a method of action: it is both the analytics used to ethnographically investigate the home(lessness) land and the milieu upon which the political proposition of the book is advanced. And it could not be otherwise: the sole use of these concepts is to do some work, not to explain and enclose.[30]

I expand on this use and understanding of the minor in chapter 1, since it is strictly connected to the search for a grammar of home(lessness). Here, I would simply like to stress some nuanced differences this modality of thinking bears vis-à-vis a more conventional political-economy analysis of homelessness and home. The importance of situating processes historically and spatially, and of grounding analysis within them, is inescapable for both.[31] But if, as Amin and I have recently argued, a certain attention to the ground of social processes has always been central in critical spatial thinking, the minor distinguishes itself in its strategic positioning—that is, in its attempt at staying close to borders and liminalities to theorize, to propose, and to execute its political plan.[32] Such an orientation implies three things. First, it means to advocate for an analysis of expulsion and extraction attentive to following what Simone and Pieterse call "storylines"—that is, stories connecting different places and lives.[33] In ethnographic terms, this is about centering experiences in their going beyond themselves (in their collective formations) at the core of the ethnographic project. The difference with a more conventional political economy analysis of everyday life is the tendency of the latter to subsume experience into wider social facts and molar structurings. Staying with the minor means to conceptually and empirically focus on how a storyline unfolds. The hypothesis, in such a move, is that the latter will point, often implicitly so, to places other than the molar. In relation to the focus of this book, I follow Simone in his call to occupy a middle terrain, between the conventional way of looking at home/homelessness and a position that would normalize the uninhabitable: "How can we operate somewhere between the tightening standardization of habitation—with all its pretenses of producing and regulating new types of individuals—and making the uninhabitable a new norm, where value rests in what can be constantly converted, remade, or readapted? Such a middle is not so much a new regime, imaginary, or place; rather, it is a way of drawing lines of connection among the various instances and forms of habitation, in order to find ways of making them have something to do with each other beyond common abstractions."[34]

Second, notwithstanding what I have just said, a critical approach to minor ethnography always has to return to the molar. This is coherent with the broader attempt of Deleuze and Guattari to write a processual political economy of subject formations within contemporary capitalism (an effort that has clear limits too; see chapter 1). For them, "molecular escapes and movements would be nothing if they did not return to the molar organizations to reshuffle their segments, their binary distributions of sexes, classes, and parties."[35] This of course mirrors the Marxist project, with a perilous caveat: the minor ethnographic effort can more easily and problematically slip into the romanticization of those "molecular escapes." Both within the realm of conventional ethnographic detailing of the urban margins (think, for instance, of Duneier's *Sidewalk*) and within literatures more explicitly inspired by notions of assemblage (especially in Anglophone human geography), a critical return to the molar is rarely there.[36] In staying close to the interstices and struggles of everyday life, minor ethnography can easily lose track of its own path—that is, it can lose track of its project, which necessarily must be political (returning to the molar) and collective (because politics is a matter of being concerned about processes of subject formation, which are always a collectivity—see chapter 1).

To fight the romanticization of relative deterritorializations and escapes, processual minor thinking needs to reconnect more profoundly and explicitly with other forms of critical thinking, with which it has much to share. In doing so, and therefore in recentering its orientation toward the molar while holding its micropolitical ground, minor thinking can then fully exert its third distinctive point—that is, an invitation to read the minor (the interstitial, the liminal, the in-between) not only as an analytical and a lived and felt locus of human suffering but also as a concrete, immanent ground for a form of revolutionary becoming that proposes its standalone affirmation. Here, I believe, the minor breaks with the historic and scalar entrapment of Marxism, because it does not seek staged transitioning, nor does it focus on replacing the molar (even if just momentarily so). The aim is to stay and perdure in between, to use the interstices as a way to, prefiguratively, construct our future present in the here and now, affirmatively so. The minor embraced in this book is therefore of an autonomous kind, being defined in relation to contextual histories and subjects but also transversally rooted in a micropolitics of liberation (chapters 6, 7).

In this book, working with the minor means situating much of the empirical discussion in Italy and in Turin, which are some of the grounds relevant to the writer and therefore apt for embodied reflection and theorization. But it also means to bring into productive conversation a feminist sensibility of the embodiment of housing precarity, a processual take on the assemblage of the social, and an autonomous political outlook to challenge conventions on where to look for, and how to enact, solutions for the home(lessness) problem. The approach proposed here is not a tout court alternative to cognate fights that aim to encompass the makings of lessness, but it does have its own specificity, which may or may not intersect other political projects, as I clarify in the concluding chapters of this book.

The Horizon of the Housing Political

I agree with Madden and Marcuse when they state that "a truly radical right to housing . . . would not be a demand for inclusion within the horizon of housing politics as usual but *an effort to move that horizon*."[37] In the book, I argue that, in order to envision such a new horizon and to imagine new housing futures, one needs to get closer to housing precarity anew. Only then will it be possible to widen the scope of our struggle from housing to home. But getting closer to housing precarity is not a self-explanatory endeavor. It is, on the contrary, fraught with violence of its own. If home(lessness) is really a matter of shared underlying processes of expulsion and extraction, a renewed way of looking within its most intense experiences of dispossession must know nothing of current sociologies of homelessness, of current approaches to solving it or saving its subjects, of current interventions to patch it up. Getting closer to housing precarity means to take the minor politics of the latter seriously, to get beyond the (epistemic and material) framework currently entrapping the insurgent power of that politics within the home/homelessness binary. Billions of urbanites worldwide challenge the entrenched homely habitus around them on a daily basis. Their resistance consists in their shifting, frail, and continuous struggle with forms of (cultural, material, economic) bordering, a struggle that is about finding a (literal and metaphorical) space to become, without having to fit in with a system that so obviously does not work. This is not about being resilient in a given status quo but about articulating modes of being that involve mundane acts of resistance and care and thereby question prevailing forces and modalities. Moving the horizon of the housing political is about finding nonextractive ways of working with those interstitial forms of radical care and to consider them political—a concern of and for life—beyond prevailing definitions of politics.

Defining what kind of home one envisions beyond home(lessness) is a task that pertains to collectives, not a writer like myself, in the isolation of my room. So I am careful, in this volume, to avoid a checklist of what an ideal liberated home would look like, a benchmark that, by all means, would simply reproduce the entrapment of a totalizing sense of home and would stay too uncomfortably close to lessness. After the exposition of why and how home and homelessness are made of the same, which takes place in parts I and II of the book, in part III I focus on the wider meaning of liberating home rather than on its form. Coherently with the need to produce affirmations in order to get beyond the binaries of lessness, I define *liberated* as that capacity to allow for emancipatory desires of habitation to emerge and take place in the world. Such a capacity is not the end point of the revolutionary effort but the ongoing struggle to affirm, from the interstices of home(lessness), that another way of inhabiting the world is possible. So, liberating home, in this book, is situated within the intense experiences of housing precarity (it starts from there, from its embodiments), and it is about allowing for emancipatory assemblages to emerge. Once again, the form and content of those arrangements is not for me to enlist. Focusing on the liberatory as a capacity that needs to be excavated and enabled, rather than defined a priori, is coherent with an understanding of the minor as method: the minor is a way to write from within, not a specification of what should be written.

At the same time, as we have seen, the minor must entail an attack on the molar. Seeing liberation as a process—more precisely, as a way of enabling formations that do not need to be enclosed in their definition—is about saying that if the home needs to be burned down and rewritten again, the most pressing thing to do is to strategize on how that can happen. How can one enable a liberatory capacity to instantiate another kind of home? Staying closer to my departure point—the intensities of housing precarity under home(lessness)—in chapter 7, I illustrate what an initial strategy in this sense might entail. Three movements are discussed. First, deinstitution through the praxis of striking. The focus here is on deinstitutionalizing and fighting against the industries currently caring for the "other" of home, which include much of the current service provision for the homeless, as well as knowledge production around them. Second, reinstitution through radical caring. Here the focus is on allowing ourselves to relearn how to care for inhabitation and its struggles, and to constitute, on that basis, a universal approach to housing focused on dwellers' control. The apparent resonance of this point with some current progressive policies—most notably, Housing First—is demystified in chapter 5, while its grounding in autonomous practice, with potential links to current Black organizing for housing justice, is unpacked in chapter 7. Third, institution through affirmation, which is focused on considering occupation and grassroots organizing as a viable alternative to interventions focused on policy change. Institution is therefore about bypassing state inertia and prefiguratively enacting a liberatory politics of home in the here and now. Deinstitution, reinstitution, and institution work toward the liberation of a desire for a thousand different homes to emerge, rather than proposing a new home. Their potential multiplicitous ends are the core of their liberatory affirmation, also evoked by the suffix *-statuere*: to put in place, to establish, to cause, to stand. The shared ethos of these moves reverberates the politics of thinkers such as Colin Ward, for instance, when he said that one shouldn't really make plans about housing but develop "an attitude" that "will enable millions of people to make their own plans."[38]

What people will do, once that attitude is liberated, needs to stay unspecified, but, crucially, the ways one liberates attitudes provide not only a stand but also a clear sense of direction. As I clarify in the book, deinstitution, reinstitution, and institution propose and enact moves that explicitly counter expulsion and extraction. The first is about a deinstitutionalization of homelessness, to counter the routine maintenance of the other of home (expulsion), through which appropriation and value taking can be enacted (extraction). The second is to make such deinstitutionalization a decolonization too, which again can be done only affirmatively, through a different kind of reinstitution of housing policy and politics back to dwellers. The third is about crafting other diagrams of home away from institutions of power (which are necessary for the first two moves). In this last move, collective and autonomous forms of radical care are centered to institute an everyday praxis spurred by the functions of lessness. The plateau emerging from these moves, arranged right through the interstices of our shared home(lessness), knows nothing of the latter.

Outline

The remainder of this book is composed of seven chapters that follow storylines across the land of home(lessness). The most empirical chapters are grounded, as I said, in ethnographic work I undertook in Turin for my PhD as well as in continuous research that I have been doing in the past decade on housing, homelessness, and notions of home in Italy and across the Atlantic. They are written in a way that mixes anecdotes, social media analysis, ethnographic insights, and theory, because I am conscious that the community of people interested in homelessness is varied, with different interests and languages. This calls for heterogeneous approaches and experimentation, not for specialization and dogmatism.

Chapters 1 and 2 provide a basic relational lexicon to first navigate and then go beyond the binaries of home(lessness). Lessness is discussed as an affective becoming and a political economy, reproducing subjects that are considered and managed as less than the normal other, while at the same time being functional to the reproduction and sustenance of that homely normality. The grammar proposed in the two chapters is a first step toward the explanation of why providing housing to all the homeless in the world would not be enough to end homelessness and, as well, to sketch what the politics of home that needs to complement that effort is. Concretely, the chapters discuss notions of borderings, of the extractive and expulsive diagrams constituting those, and of their power to (re)produce subjects and normative becomings (the concept of ritornello is deployed to illustrate the circulatory linkage between home and homelessness). These concepts are presented before the ethnographic material simply for the sake of analytical clarity, but they do not emerge from a place other than the encounters with people living in precarious housing conditions, and the struggles I have encountered in the past decade or so. I am presenting them as tools allowing me to think with the recursiveness of certain subject formations and the politics cracking through those, better than is done by what the heavily compromised catalog that the sociology of home and homelessness currently has to offer.

Chapters 3, 4, and 5 explore how our current modalities of governing homelessness are really no different from those governing our homes. Chapter 3 explores two diagrams of home in Italy: patriarchy and racial capitalism. Discussing the formation of these diagrams and how they fueled the central ideology of home in the country, the chapter provides grounding to discuss how these diagrams and their power are linked to particular ways of managing the other of home (chapter 4), which ultimately reverberate beyond Italy (chapter 5, where I also discuss the ways in which my proposal differs, substantially, from Housing First). Taken together, chapters 4 and 5 stress how current approaches to end homelessness sit squarely in the reproduction of the ritornellos of home(lessness) highlighted in chapter 2. This second part of the book concludes with a renewed call for a more daring plan: to think of homelessness not as the other of home, and not as a problem to be fixed in the light of home, but to follow and support those that are already, in the everyday of their precarious dwelling conditions, trying to get beyond that binary.

Chapter 6 focuses on why starting from homelessness to liberate home not only makes sense but also might be a viable way to complement other approaches that are trying to radically reform our ways of inhabiting the world. Central to this endeavor is an epistemological task: seeing the political within everyday experiences of housing precarity; staying close to the collective concerns about home emerging from there; finding ways of coming together as accomplices; and tracing paths that are transversal to what is taken as the given projection of home, starting from within these interstices. Conflating attention to these precarious becomings with a romanticization of poverty is a desperate attempt to safeguard the violent epistemic knowledge granted by forms of specialization and expertise, which is founded on the silencing of the poor. If one takes the trauma and suffering found in the intensities of home(lessness) seriously, then no such silencing is possible: instead of bringing subjects back home, it becomes imperative to recognize that many don't want any such return. Instead, they want to demolish the systemic violence of home and build anew. Grasping this requires us to go beyond the matrix of help, salvation, and building individual capacity (radically beyond, in a sense, what institutional approaches advocate for).[39] It requires an understanding of the use value of housing as multiple and fundamentally open to forms of becoming. This is, as intersectional housing movements recognize, a question of retrieving the experience and knowledge of those precarious dwellers who are already using housing struggles as a gateway to more profound changes: it entails micropolitical attention to the ways in which one dwells in the world and to forms of inhabitation that are detached from, and opposed to, the expulsion and extraction structuring current ideals of home.

Chapter 7 addresses the question of how to work with the micropolitics the previous chapter ended on. How to work from the interstices, and, from there, how to get beyond the binaries of lessness? It illustrates the political proposition of the book, covering the three parallel moves of deinstitution, reinstitution, and institution of which I have spoken. The chapter also discusses how, in signaling these moves, the book does not aim to reinvent the wheel. Each one of these is, in one way or another, already present in the struggle for housing justice across geographies in the world. Deinstitution has been on many progressive homelessness practitioners' minds for a long time; reinstitution is there in the quest to care for more just ways of living on the planet; practices of institution are foundational to collective grassroots organizing worldwide. And yet the articulation of these three is not usually brought to the fore as a way to end homelessness via ending home. These moves are for the most part taken and thought of in isolation from one another. In chapter 7, I try to work with them together, and I discuss how the isolated take of one over the other lends itself to being subsumed by the ritornellos of home(lessness), as shown, for instance, by the common dismissal on behalf of radical housing movements of the plights of the nonpoliticized urban poor. The conclusion provides a summary of the main propositions and returns to the necessary work of accompliceship to be carried forward by those holding the epistemic privilege around notions and policies of home and homelessness today.

Part I

I

THE SUBJECT AT HOME

"Home" is founded on local and global histories of neglect, entrapment, exploitation, and expulsion, which intersect with other entrenched forms of embodied violence at the level of gender, race, ecology, and class. As the COVID-19
pandemic showed, home can be read as a juncture where many of the inequalities of our time come and are held together structurally; yet, at the same time,
home maintains an attractive lure to itself, as a place one is called to defend
or to work toward, in order to be freed from subjections that seem to render
home impossible in the first place. In this chapter and in the next, my aim is to
stay close to this only apparent contradiction, which I would like to name the
"impossible possibility of home." With this notion, I want to interpret the unjust and violent foundations of home not as opposite to, but as foundational

to, its capacity to allude to one's own betterment in terms of belonging, security, and care. This means to say that the lure of home as a space of belonging is emerging from the foundations of home itself, rather than being a means toward salvation from its violence. The impossible possibility of home lies in home's capacity to sell a diagram of liberation as a line of flight, a breakthrough from its unjust underpinnings, while in immanent, lived, and felt terms, that diagram is a very powerful function of those.

Here it is important to stress the difference between my usage of the term *home*—with which I conceive a wide set of cultural, ideological, political, and material arrangements—and the notion of housing. If the latter can be understood, rightly so, as more than the material expression of the former (indeed, as I discuss in chapter 6, housing can be a gateway to the liberation of home), at the same time home is also and always more than housing. As anthropological scholarship by the likes of Daniel Miller has shown, home is an assemblage of aspirations, of their material manifestation, of their politico-economic structuration, as well as a logic of inhabitation, a modality of dwelling.[1] How the components of this assemblage are aligned to one another is always history and context dependent, and this is why a critical analysis of home and homelessness needs to be situated (part II of this book). However, the baseline dynamics of home in contemporary capitalism cut across geographies. Around the world, individuals and communities struggle for the betterment of their home. They are driven by aspirations and demands that guide a thousand fights to transition from unjust current homes to newer, freer, safer, more emancipatory ones. What unites these struggles is, at a bare minimum, the idea that attaining a betterment of life in this world is possible, and that individual and collective inhabitation of planet Earth and its communities is key to succeeding at that goal. Such a shared affect is, in many cases, structured within the diagrams it wishes to fight and contest. It is educated and organized within them. It inhabits as much as it wishes to combat them.

This is not to say that genuinely emancipatory struggles aren't possible. It is simply to say that they are very rare, precisely because home is possible in allowing for its impossibility to perdure, to stay close by, to be matter of the same assemblage, not an otherwise. Thinking of home in this way means to distinguish between the enormity of efforts put in place to at least nominally challenge or change our ways of inhabiting the world and those that are factually progressing toward radical change. As I have clarified in the introduction, the expansiveness of the notions of home and inhabitation immediately lends itself to connections across fields and concerns. Thinking about the impossible possibility of home means to think of and around war, of and around racialization, of and around neoliberalization, of and around colonization, of and around extraction ecologies, of and around relations among those, and much more. Ultimately, my broader aim is to illustrate a method of inquiry, which starts with what I have called home(lessness) but can be extended well beyond it to intersect with other liberatory ways of thinking and organizing.

To begin this exploration, I focus on the home/homelessness binary, first, by introducing a basic relational lexicon to think "home"; second, by focusing on the productive nature of that binary as a form of epistemic and material bordering; and third, by discussing what it means to be at home, or to be a subject of home, through a language of relational ontologies. From these conceptual groundings, I then introduce the two baseline functionings of the diagram of home(lessness) across geographies, expulsion and extraction. These are explored further in chapter 2, where I provide illustration of how expulsion and extraction work as a ritornello defining and reproducing home(lessness) in contemporary global capitalism. My hope is that these two chapters taken together will offer the reader a clearer idea of the analytics proposed in the book, which is then put to work in the second and third parts of the volume.

Thinking Home Relationally

Before tackling the constitutive relationship between home and homelessness, I want to recall three insights that I consider particularly important. First, home is never just a thing but an arrangement of things, and, consequently, it is never just created but always in creation. As banal as it might sound, one is never at home, but always ongoing with and through it. Focusing on the processual becoming and unfolding of home means highlighting how its normative instantiations are never just a given, no matter how powerful they are. Instead, they are constantly maintained and therefore open to contestation. But here I aim to highlight such processual features of home in an epistemological sense, even before I turn to a counterpolitical analysis. In such a view, the process of constructing home as an assemblage of things involves the intersection of an imaginary with material forces, cutting through, and yet holding together, individual and collective scales. To use Filip De Boeck's metaphor, it is in the knotting among the strings of these relationships that one's own known reality of homing—being as becoming at home—emerges.[2] As Blunt and Dowling put it, "home is a relation between material and imaginative realms and processes, whereby physical location and materiality, feelings and ideas, are bound together and influence each other, rather than be separate and distinct. Moreover, home is a process of creating and understanding forms of dwelling and belonging. Home is lived as well as imagined. What home means and how it is materially manifested are continually created and re-created through everyday home-making practices, which are themselves tied to spatial imaginaries of home."[3]

If we accept the multiplicity of home, and its state of constant becoming, as our point of departure, then the things that are most frequently associated with homemaking (housing, belonging, affections, social reproduction, family relations, and matters of ontological security more widely) can only be approached in their unfolding, too. A processual focus on home invites us to read home and its becoming beyond supposed adherence to a static, ideologically grounded status quo.[4] Again, this might sound banal, but it is very different from the mainstream reading of home as the place, the salvation, the opportunity to seize. It invites instead, to follow geographer Katherine Brickell, an attention to what she calls "home un-makings," that is, home as the process of making and unmaking it.[5]

Second, and continuing along similar lines, home is never just contained or designed. A plurality of complex relations design it for us and through us. Here, I am inspired by the relational understanding of place, space, and belonging offered by Doreen Massey and by the ontological take on design proposed by Arturo Escobar. For Massey, "a large component of the identity of that place called home derived precisely from the fact that it had always in one way or another been open; constructed out of movement, communication, social relations which always stretched beyond it."[6] That sense of place we call home is relationally constituted by things that have apparently little association with it; yet they are there in the "ever-shifting geography of social relations present and past" making up what we consider to be home. For Massey, this always involves unequal geometries of power. Noting these broad processes that make home allows us to understand it as a concept and a practice that is (re) produced and situated in evolving transscalar power geometries: if home is a place, its placement becomes apparent not by pointing to its physical, and even ideological, location in space and time, but only by tracing the constitutive extensiveness of the relations making up its location. Home, in other words, can only be constantly traced and never really captured.

Moreover, to expand on this, it is not only that home is a place because of its being situated in networks of power relations, but it is also that those relations fundamentally design what home and its inhabitants ultimately are, and become, at home. As Arturo Escobar proposes in his ontological understanding of design: humans design their world, but the world designs us back.[7] When it comes to home, this designing is not only concerned with homely comforts and material accessories but is a matter of ideologies, ecologies, economies, histories, and governmentalities that mold the wider assemblage of home, including its subjects. Home, in such a view, becomes a spatially and temporally diffuse production of subjectivities. Being at home in the world means becoming within, and reproducing, a number of intersections across nature and culture that are not given but continually crisscrossing (and rearranging) a variety of pluriverses. Ultimately, a relational ontology of home alerts us to the fact that its multiplicity is not only produced by its material and imagined components but in turn produces what it means to dwell in the world at large. As Escobar puts it, "it contributes to shaping what it is to be human."[8]

But if home is a multiple assemblage that is always becoming in a vast field of relations, then how can one deal with it, critically, practically, and radically? How can one pin it down, even for just a moment? The third, fundamental notion here is around the intersectionality of home. If the assemblage of home is structured through intersecting relational ontologies, a critical reading of its becoming can only be situated at those busy intersections where diagrams of power structure, individual and collective experiences, embodiments, and relational position and possibilities meet. It is not sufficient to appreciate how home is constructed through a plurality of apparent and nonapparent relations, if one does not also account for the ways in which power constitutes, and is constituted by, the becoming of home. I am conscious that this proposition may sound obvious to critical scholars and activists, but a dichotomous reading of home/homelessness depends precisely on a failure to understand—or to acknowledge—this two-way relationship and the intersections it carries beyond itself. Theory, practice, and policy have maintained the mainstream, technocratically inflected home/homeless binary by refusing to see both the complexity of the material and ideological relationships that surround them and the power relations that ensure that what we call homelessness emerges from and stays within the rotten substratum of home.

An intersectional reading of home would be one in which we connect the dots. Going back to Hill Collins, "as opposed to examining gender, race, class, and nation, as separate systems of oppression," we need to show "how these systems mutually construct one another."[9] That would mean exploring how systems of oppression reinforce and reproduce normative ideologies of home and show how they do so by a process of othering the homeless. I return to the fundamental work of feminist thinkers and cognate queer readings of home throughout the book. For now, it suffices to stress how the importance of this multilayered and situated reading of home is not only conceptual but fundamentally political. For example, it refuses to see domestic violence as an episodic manifestation of deviance, for which incremental solutions and adjustments can be proposed, and instead insists that it is inextricably part of the deeper unjust functionings of what I am calling home(lessness). Similarly, Catherine Baker has argued that the "home-centric" response to the COVID-19 pandemic in many Western countries pivots around a patriarchal and heteronormative understanding of home that is oblivious to the dangerous inequalities that are inherent in that concept.[10] Thinking through a more relational approach would oppose a reading of home as a thing one can fill, come back to, pin down easily, or instrumentalize. Instead, it invites us to trace how (i.e., through which intersecting power dynamics and structurations) home is made, as a material and imagined assemblage of crisscrossing ontologies.[11]

Talking of home(lessness) is a way of taking the complex relationalities of home seriously. It is not that violence is sometimes perpetrated at home or through it, with the concept (and mainstream idealization) of home remaining separate and unsullied by this. Home and violence are constitutively related, and this is their impossible possibility: the relationship between them cuts through the ways in which families are structured, through normative ideas of community and belonging, and through the attempts to govern or change these. Thinking of home(lessness) means therefore to think of a multiplicity of troubles that most of us are embroiled in, though at different individual degrees of intensity. To go back to Beckett's plateau, home and its negation must be seen in a way that shows that they are of the same: a milieu where everything can be made less by processes of bordering that enact types of expulsion, which in turn allow the extraction of multiple forms of value. These fundamental functions of home(lessness) are discussed in the remainder of this chapter.

Homely Borderings

Home is an exclusionary act, an act of seclusion. It is made of walls and doors, which create forms of control and allow the policing of flows. It is made of social relationships based on emotional bonds, which are carved out through exclusion (in a mainstream understanding, there is no bonding if there is no exclusion of others). It is constructed, in its material form, thanks to accumulations of capital that emerge from, and reproduce, systems of oppression. As many have shown, home also has internal exclusions, in gendered power relationships and heteronormative modes of breeding. In its material guise as housing, home can quite easily be turned into an exploitative machine and used as a means of capital accumulation that has effects not only on tenants but also on land values, urban development, and financial markets. As a construct, it cuts across multiple dimensions of human life; as a machine, it is capable of abstracting from those domains a conceptual and ideological auton-omy that enables it to reproduce itself materially in the longer term, convert-ing the plurality of ways to be in the world into dogmatic forms of existence for the purposes of specific sets of extractive endeavors. Capitalist, neoliberal, and financialized forms of housing work through this conceptual and material structure, and, in doing so, they accelerate and intensify the extractions that found home. However, homely precarity cannot be reduced to these processes alone; it extends beyond them, through many domains of life. Focusing exclu-sively on one of them will not show how homely precarity cuts through, or the ways in which it is a matter of diffused, yet entrenched, intersections.

Can one move a step closer to an analysis of home and homelessness en-abling one to see, and work through, their coconstitutive relationship? How to work, in other words, beyond the dominant dichotomous reading and reap-proach the problem as one of fundamental home(lessness)? The place where to locate such a processual, relational, and intersectional analysis sits at the margins of the dominant formulation, where home is maintained and practi-cally reproduced. Such a place is the border, the threshold where the bound-ary of home/homelessness is defined. I follow Mezzadra and Neilson here, in their tripartite understanding of borders as a relational matter, as devices that design worlds and as analytical tools or methods.[12] This means, first, that the border between home and homelessness is not just a device to isolate, to mark a division in the terrain. Such a view is reductive: it "does not allow us to grasp the flexibility of this institution [of the border]," because it suggests a clear-cut, in-and-out, split.[13] Instead, borders are the outcome of bordering practices, which are relational: the border is not an invisible line between what is in and what is out; it is a series of processual relations, a practice. Second, borders do exclude, but that exclusion involves a definition, and therefore a production of knowledge and power relations. As Mezzadra and Neilson put it, "insofar as it serves at once to make divisions and establish connections, the border is an epistemological device."[14] Naturally, the border is not just an epistemological device, but its practice and governance are deeply linked to its epistemological function. This understanding of bordering connects well with the relational ontologies of home sketched above: the border, to go back to Escobar, designs. With home/homelessness, the border constructs a set of ideal homely *agence-ments*, from which the homeless (and the various others of home) are excluded as other. In the process, the latter are defined as objects for intervention, as re-cipients of love and hate, as subjects of knowledge production and, ultimately, extraction.

Third, Mezzadra and Neilson's understanding of bordering offers a powerful way of approaching the becoming of home from a relational and situated perspective too. It invites us to place our analytical viewpoint at the intersection where borders are made and maintained, and thereby to question their production. This methodological approach is also immediately "a question of politics, about the kinds of social worlds and subjectivities produced at the border and the ways that thought and knowledge can intervene in these processes of production."[15] Crucially, in order to work with and through borderings, a suspension of our everyday approach to epistemology is needed. We need "to recall a phenomenological category, the set of disciplinary practices that present the objects of knowledge as already constituted."[16] When it comes to the border between home and homelessness, the only possible starting point lies in the suspension of our normal definitions of both, preliminary to investigating "the processes by which these objects are constituted."[17]

Similarly, Ash Amin and I have advocated for "postcategorical thinking" as a fruitful approach to questions of urban life and politics, and to question the ways in which urban categorizations and political tools are structured by particular forms of epistemic power.[18] Approaching borders as a matter of relations, of world design, in the spirit of postcategorical analytics, allows one to see them as "a site of struggle," which is why Mezzadra and Neilson call their understanding of borders a "method": it offers an access point to the mechanics of what goes on within their makings.[19] In other words, there is a politics in the making and maintenance of borders, and the goal is to access that without silencing its possibilities. I expand on the epistemological importance of such a minor understanding of the political at length, in chapter 6. Here I just want to stress a crucial aspect of the relational understanding of bordering: its capacity to diagram the assemblage of ways of being at home into the world is not just done to subjects, but must be read as a matter of embodiments, of coconstitutive relationship between those border machinations and individual and collective subjectivities.[20] As Mezzadra and Neilson also note, such a concern resonates well with a feminist reading of belonging and bordering, for instance in the work of Gloria Anzaldúa, where neither the border nor its subjects are a thing but an intensity to be lived through.[21] But such an understanding is even more prominent in the work of bell hooks and in her invitation to read the margins not just as a site of relegation (the other site of the border, the other site of home) but as a site of resistance constructed through the inhabitation of the threshold.[22] The borders of home(lessness) are, in this fashion, read as sites where home(lessness) itself—including the home/homelessness binary— is reproduced in institutional, as well as mundane, embodiments and politics, but also as offering the relational place from which liberation can be assembled and come to the fore.

The Subject at Home

Thinking around and of home(lessness) is perilous. At each point, in blurring the distinction between home and homelessness, the risk of flattening experiences and their trauma is very real. Can one say that owning multiple properties rented out through Airbnb is the same as queuing at 5 a.m. to get a serving at the local soup kitchen, after having spent all night in a car? Most certainly this is not the argument carried forward in this book. These experiences are not the same, and, needless to say, the former bears decisive powers in the definition of the latter. And yet, I believe it is worth approaching these experiences as matter of the same. The distinction is not only semantic but has to do, as I have mentioned in the introduction, with how one analytically distinguishes the experience and the substratum of that experience. The former is highly situated in individual and collective embodiments: it is the process by which becoming becomes lived and felt, a process dependent upon entrenched structures, historical lineages, and power geometries activated through intersecting bordering processes. However, the latter do not emerge from a vacuum but are expressions of functions ultimately working in a certain direction—that is, defining what is home and what is homelessness in a certain way and not another.[23] In this assemblage, being matter of the same means being entangled in that sense of direction: it means to become—to dwell in the world—while being enclosed in a definition of inhabitation that can't do without its -less. That sense of direction is the same inhabited by those at home and those homeless in current mainstream framings of home today, albeit in very different experiential ways.

But what is the value of thinking along these lines? Wouldn't the provision of housing for all ultimately challenge the expulsive and extractive nature of what I've called lessness, altering the structuring, lineages, and power geometries currently designing home in its relationship to homelessness? Thinking about home(lessness) introduces a different way of analyzing the problem of home/homelessness and enables one to articulate a radical political proposition around it. Such a proposition would answer "no" to the last question. No: housing won't be enough to counter our current home because, if home and homelessness are matter of the same, then the only possible proposition is to encompass home altogether in order to break its current ritornellos, its current sense of direction. Providing housing to all is fundamental for that breaking through to succeed, but if the "horizon of housing politics," as Madden and Marcuse put it, stops at housing provisioning and policy reform, that won't cut it: the proposition of home(lessness) is to more fundamentally alter how home and its other are mutually constituted.[24]

To further unpack the value of thinkings along these lines, consider the following question. In the current global moment, can one think of home without homelessness? I am not simply asking if we can house all the homeless in the world (that would mean to reduce home to housing). The question is ontological: what is home without its otherness? Can one think of ontological security without thinking of ontological insecurity? Of belonging without alienation? Of being housed without rooflessness? Of security without fear? Can one think of home without having constantly to enclose in its definition the possibility that, within itself, things can be impossible, untenable, and become -less? The current substratum uniting those at home and those in a condition of homelessness in contemporary global capitalism does not encourage such an envisioning, because it is forged around the impossible possibility of a home that cannot be thought of, and practiced, without its otherness. What would home be if homelessness were not only to be solved but were fundamentally impossible to think and to make? A home without homelessness requires a politics beyond current framings: it requires an affective and material political economy beyond lessness. That home would be a home within which there is no possibility to be made -less, because that procedure is not scripted in its diagram. Such a home would not base its possibility on the refusal of its impossibility, which as we have seen is a negation that is also an acceptance of the need for the existence of another home. Rather, it would be a home that exists in itself, a home that is possible in the affirmation of its possibility. It would be a home that does not need a binary to be defined, but a new device cutting through all binaries to reemerge, on the other side, with a differential tempo of worldly inhabitation.

Asking if such a home is possible clarifies the distinction between the experience and its substratum. No matter how one experiences it, the substratum of a home defined by its impossibility is a shared plateau of capitalistic extractions and other bordering practices across humans and nature, genders, racialized matters, and epistemic knowledges that, taken together, instantiate and reproduce the home/homelessness binary and its power (chapter 2). The imbalanced power relationship between those experiences is not flattened in revealing their common foundation in lessness. On the contrary: a mere focus on experience, even when situated within the careful reconstruction of histories of oppression, can lose track of the fact that incremental adjustments are not enough to fight that shared plateau, and, ultimately, it reduces the power of resistance coming from its margins. Focusing on home(lessness) means to say that if, at points, the way out of traumatic life experiences might be individualized, the cracking of their substratum requires a more profound and diffused collective redesign. The latter is a revolutionary movement. Getting beyond home(lessness)—to liberate home—is about displacing the homelessness question as a problem to be fixed in order to get home right and seeing instead both home and homelessness as coconstituted problems. One requires a conceptual lexicon to enable excavation of their shared substratum, without losing sight of the politics of their experiences.

On top of a relational understanding of home and of the productive nature of its bordering with homelessness, a further step in this sense consists in a processual reading of the subject of home. This means to encompass seeing those at home and the homeless as enclosed by their respective experiences. Rather, it would require the work of tracing how their experiences are coconstituted as part of a broader set of intersections that seem to be functional to the maintenance of a substratum of lessness, of a peculiar set of rhythms, of a shared becoming. On one level, this still means to take situatedness and the embodiment of experience as the cornerstone of analysis. But on a different analytical level, this means to show how the production of subjectivity in lessness is both, at the same time, an end point and a reinstantiation: constitutive both of experience and of its underlying structuring. Another way of saying this is that on the first level of analysis, one is accounting for the experience of dispossession—at both ends of the stick—while on the second, as Butler and Athanasiou remind us, one is trying to deal with the fact that, in lessness, we are all constantly and ceaselessly dispossessed, and we all dispossess.[25] Considering the latter does not diminish the politics of the former, it enables us to investigate how subjectivities are not just the end points of histories of violence but also assemblages of the baseline functioning allowing for that violence to emerge and perdure (as beautifully illustrated most recently by Kotef's accounts on home in Israel/Palestine in *The Colonizing Self*, to which I return in chapter 2).

To clarify, this is not an evocation of nomadism and open subjectivities. It is not that the subject is not anchored, and not defined, by histories and processes. Of course there are subjects that bear greater responsibilities than others in the making of the intensities of lessness. But at the same time, notwithstanding the expression of their experience and of the power structuring it, the subject is always a collective enterprise, and never just an individual matter.[26] The subject is a becoming assembled through two concomitant and mutually constituting processes: one manifested in the ongoing crafting of experience, the other shared at the substratum of collective machination. Thinking processually about subjectivity means to account for both processes. It follows that, analytically, the subject at home can be individuated at best as a provisional and ongoing cartography of experience and of underlying rhythms constitutive of their becoming, a cartography exceeding what the experiencing self, or external observation, can make of it. This does not deny the cognitive and emotional capacities of any human being, but it decenters those abilities, to understand humans as Amin and Thrift proposed, building on Lazzarato, as "dividuals": "who most of the time are simply part of a combination of bodies or parts of bodies, resonating around a particular matter of concern."[27] Subjectivity encompasses both subjection and affirmation, and what self-reflection makes of it.

If at the first level, home(lessness) is populated by selves, with their stories and differential power, at the second there is no self and no singular story to be told: just a tempo of dispossession, defining the conatus of that life in that home. Both processes are subjective, and a processual analysis takes these two analytical levels at its core, at the same time. As Judith Butler also contends, thinking of subjectivity in this way means both to "talk about how a self struggles with and against the norms through which it is formed" and "tracing how a certain forming of the formed takes place." "In this way," she continues, "we might think the 'I' as an interval or relay in an ongoing process of social crafting," a dividual (although she does not use Lazzarato's term), "who crafts oneself [but also who] is already formed by social relations and norms that are themselves in the making, that is, in process, open to crafting."[28] Talking of the experience and its substratum is a way, surely among others, to hold together, conceptually and analytically, the processual dividual nature of subject formation in a way that is attentive to varied agencies and affections, without falling into the trap of conflating the existence of the self with the latter and vice versa. What matters is to trace the relational cartography enacting the subjective experience and the collective becoming, holding it together, in a productive act of (re)production that is about both the experience and its wider sense of direction.

As Simon O'Sullivan states in his On the Production of Subjectivity, thinking about subjectivity in this vitalist way matters because the process of its production becomes, in itself, "the site and locus of a kind of battle against the homogenizing powers of capitalism, and especially its reduction and standardization of heterogeneity."[29] Lessness can be read as a system of decoding, creating situated axioms of experience (first level) underpinned by a shared affect, tempo, and direction (second level). The subject cuts through both: it is the map of relationships between both. A processual reading of subjectivity is key to cracking through the system of decoding of lessness precisely because one process of the subject is always collective; it is always of-the-machine and cannot be reduced to the space of their experience. Humanitarianist and economicist narratives of the subject—dominant in current progressive service provisioning for the homeless (chapters 4, 5)—are not able to capture this complexity because, in the best cases, they are too preoccupied with colonizing the other, to save it by placing it squarely in its given experience, as if the other were really something different from the one who does the saving. At the level of struggle, which includes the power one bears toward that other, such difference is definitely there and must be kept well in sight (chapter 6). But at the same time, the substratum of the experiences activated in that relationship— between the savior and the saved, between home and homelessness—is matter of the same: a diagram keeping a tempo of homely dispossession through ritornellos of anthropocentrism, heteronormativity, racialization, capitalization, and epistemic violence that situate all parties, and their subjective cartographies, well within home(lessness) (chapter 2). The maintenance of their detachment is functional to the reproduction of home, and not a means to liberate one another.

If understanding the subject as a cartography of relations is an analytical maneuver, its task is political. It is a method—surely one among many others— to illustrate how, in home(lessness), there is no salvation in thinking that some can save some others. And this is where, ultimately, my project differs from the revival of the humanist in recent post-structuralist thinking (what Honig has called "mortalist humanism").[30] The problem, as Danewid correctly argues, is in asking what mourning, and therefore suffering, does.[31] Notwithstanding the importance that Butler's work has had in my own way of understanding the embodiment of housing precarity, the grounds upon which I structure the political proposition of this book are not around a straightforward recognition of the other's—of home's—suffering. Rather, I am interested in showing how the other's suffering is foundational to my nonsuffering, and also in showing how my nonsuffering is structured around expulsive and extractive logics that render violence and the potential to be rendered less not a threat but a condition of life. The political, here, cannot be grounded in recognition—a gesture that seemingly portrays a humanitarian vicinity but factually maintains a colonizing relationship to the one to be recognized and saved. The political, here, is about tracing the ambivalent workings of structures of violence and in revealing how suffering itself has been colonized and its potential propositional politics silenced (chapter 6). As Danewid puts it, "mourning does something more than simply mark the loss of certain lives: It makes possible certain forms of politics while obfuscating others."[32]

The final proposition of this book is that desires for inhabitation must be freed, epistemically and materially, from their constitutive relationship with their negation. Ultimately, it is not enough to house all the homeless in the world to end homelessness because the ritornellos structuring it are transversal, cutting through subjectivities across the land. A liberated desire for a liberated kind of home must go beyond the diagrams of lessness: "it is not a question of adapting it, socializing it, disciplining it [or saving it, governing it, housing it], but of plugging it in such a way that its process not be interrupted in the social body, and that its expression be collective."[33] Before moving there, I will open a brief parenthesis to further clarify the ontological premises enabling this thinking through diagrams, relational ontologies, and transversal becoming. Strictly speaking, the following section is not needed to navigate the land of home(lessness)—I've put it here just to unpack things further for those interested in these kinds of debates. If you aren't, please feel free to skip to the "colonies of home" in chapter 2.

A Note on Immanence

Before turning to extraction and expulsion in more detail, here is a final note on the ways in which I understand the construction of the borders I am discussing. Foregrounded in these pages is an understanding of home/homelessness, and of the ceaseless bordering needed to keep it afloat, as a process that is both more than what humans make of it and more of what its expression seems to indicate. This is to say that home/homelessness cannot be reduced to experience, as I have already made clear, but also, and simultaneously, that the (re)production of its borders always contains in itself the possibility for other productions to come to the fore. Following Deleuze's work, the machinic production of borders is real in being both actual and virtual. In other words, if the process of bordering is something that is made of very material practice but cannot be reduced to what experience makes of it, at the same time, its expression is only one among the many it could take. This is not simply about saying—neoliberally so—that change is possible. Rather, it is to say that that which exists (the actual) already also contains, in the cartography of its processual assemblage, the potential for all of the many permutations of its becoming (which are understood as being virtually present).[34]

As Elizabeth Grosz reminds us, the virtual realm is therefore much larger than the actual one: it captures the possible alternative ways in which we could think about power, ethics, and relations—and it captures them by stating they are not a possibility but an immanent reality.[35] As much as saying that the expression of an experience is not the same at its substratum, stating that the virtual is real is not about forgetting the various reasons why only some of its forms become actual. Rather, it is to account in full for those reasons, in reminding us that injustice is not only a foreclosure on the actual—in its being a violence bringing to the fore particular forms of experience—but a much more profound act of ontological violence: the silencing and controlling toward becomings that are already in the here and now, lingering (virtually so) in the real, but cut off in their actual codification. The counterpolitical, therefore, cannot be about incrementally fixing the actual but must be about dismantling its capacity to diagram the future of its virtual presence: it must be about liberating the expression of its immanent possibility and enabling for their affirmative assemblage. Translated into the concerns of this book: home is the diagram silencing the liberatory politics of its own becoming, via codifying itself in lessness, while at the same time maintaining the potential for a thousand other articulations to emerge. A radical form of housing justice means not to fix but to liberate the latter, because inhabitation already is—in its immanent potential being—more than its constant annihilation.

This understanding of the actual and the virtual as both real is key to the later works of Deleuze, particularly in his attack, with Guattari, on the Oedipal structuring of desire as something rooted in lack.[36] To "liberate desire," as Guattari argues, the first task is to read it not as the expression of an absence but as a force that actively produces the world. Desire is not an individual thing but a connection between desiring-machines that are both actualized and virtual; it extends beyond our human capacity to map it. These desiring-machines are what Deleuze and Guattari called *agencements*, assemblages, or arrangements of things that are held together not as an expression of a particular desire but as a form of desire in themselves. Desire, in other words, is alive because it is capable of creating—mapping—real connections across multiple domains of life (both actual and virtual). The core of this thinking is a vitalist one, in which the focus is not the form of being human (which is just a territorialized desiring-machine among others) but on something that unites: a life in which anything bears the capacity to affect and be affected.[37] Desiring-machines are therefore powerful in an affective sense or capacity: they design the world, though the world also has the capacity to shape desire (simply because the world itself is nothing other than a sum of desiring-machines).

If I have expanded on this vitalist capacity of things elsewhere, here I am more modestly interested in highlighting two points.[38] First, how every desiring-machine is both a product and producer of other desiring-machines. The political, in this view, is something that emerges as being of concern in the process of these makings, and not what is announced as such (see chapter 6). Second, desiring production creates repetitions in time and space, leaving traces that become ingrained, and thus structuring both the actual and virtual domain. These repetitions are diagrams that operate almost like a Foucauldian *dispositif*, but for Deleuze and Guattari they are more than a matter of literal utterances.[39] They emerge, instead, as molar forces cutting through the spaces and times through which the production of desire-machines takes place, thus affecting the assemblage of everyday life among other things, diagramming (codifying) its becoming. In the context of this conceptual grammar, stating that humans are a matter of desiring-machines does not mean to flatten social difference but to look for analytics of difference inviting us to a reading of social processes (such as the instantiation of historic violence and enduring inequalities) understood as transversal codifications of actual/virtual maps across multiple planes of life that have the capacity to take on a life of their own.

In Deleuze and Guattari's own words, "every machine functions as a break in the flow in relation to the machine to which it is connected, but at the same time is also a flow itself, or the production of a flow, in relation to the machine connected to it. This is the law of the production of production."[40] By organizing this production of production, the two conceive capitalism as a very powerful diagram (a machine-of-machines that emerged historically and spatially) that ultimately is able to axiomatize almost every domain of our lives.[41] However, because this production of productions is constantly in becoming, and because its actuation is always exceeded by its virtual potentiality, ruptures and reshuffling are not only possible but inscribed in the bare mechanics of things. As Claire Colebrook put it, "life is a plane of potentialities or tendencies that may be actualized in certain relations but that could also produce other relations, other worlds."[42] Capitalism, of course, knows this very well, and ultimately this is a reason why it works by constantly breaking apart. But everything—everybody—in this cartography of affections works by constantly breaking apart: producing, or codifying an assemblage, is about interrupting a flow, territorializing its actualization from its immanent potential. Approaching the social paying attention to how power—the assemblage of desire—is dispersed across the map of those repetitions allows for a nuanced reading of its effects. The subject at home is never just the end point of a process—the experience of it—but also, at the same time, the arrangement through which a broader cartography of desire is put in place and held together, across a life, an immanence, underpinned by its own vitalist capacity to go beyond itself.

Deleuze and Guattari offer a set of relational ontological tools to think with. However, I don't buy every affirmation of theirs, and I think their lack of engagement with cognate liberatory literatures ultimately reduces the disruptive potential of their claims. Indeed, there are a number of serious problems with the ways in which Deleuze and Guattari wrote about the differential becomings they were most interested in (what they call "schizoid" becomings). The first has been a tendency to oversimplify the rupture emerging from the micropolitical, which is mostly evident in *A Thousand Plateaus* and, especially, in countless commentaries arising from that book. The stress on the line of flight that has the capacity to deterritorialize the oppressive diagrams of life and to produce, therefore, a form of body without organs has often been oversimplified. This is especially true in Anglophone debates, where the appropriation of their concepts has sometimes been superficial. On a closer reading, Deleuze and Guattari were alert to several kinds of deterritorialization (relative, absolute-static, absolute-positive), but only the latter is a real (in their sense) breakthrough. It is also, as they contend, the most unattainable. Second, their processual and vitalist approach has also been misread as a way of explaining or enumerating things, a gross misappropriation of so-called assemblage approaches that fails to grasp not only the anarchic insurgency of assemblage-thinking but its intersectionality, which are the very things I find useful for unpacking the complex relationalities uniting home and homelessness. Third, and perhaps most importantly, there are some serious limitations in Deleuze and Guattari relating to the ways in which schizoid becomings could be attained. As many feminist scholars have noted—most notably, Spivak—their description of the liberatory journey entails a becoming-woman that essentializes (and therefore, forecloses the possibility of emancipatory becoming for) women themselves.[43] The same goes, as Erin McElroy notices, for their becoming-nomad, which is once again an essentializing, flawed, and ultimately racist logic.[44]

To me, these are fundamental points that should be forefronted when approaching Deleuze and Guattari critically—which is, after all, what I believe they would have preferred, too. But there is value in staying close to their conceptual grammar. A critical appreciation of their work offers tools to encompass the binaries of contemporary sociological thinking and can be appropriated in rather radical, very practical, ways.[45] If there are many ways to think relationally about space, place, and various social structurations—some of which I have presented in this chapter—their vitalist lexicon has enabled me to expand on those and focus on, first, the immanence of change; second, an understanding of subjectivity as a machinic, collective endeavor; and third, an understanding of the social beyond its facts, to focus on its micropolitical assemblage. When it comes to the issues of home and homelessness, such a conceptual grammar has invited me to consider how the micropolitics of inhabitation in contemporary capitalism is a matter of arrangements coming out of (in their language, desiring) their own repression and, therefore, to think of radical politics as that proposition—the becoming of a desiring-machine—which goes beyond negation. In other words, liberating home starts with thinking about it through a positive ontology of life.

Working with the tools presented in this chapter is about tackling the micropolitics of the assemblage of home and of its supposed other, by stepping out of its diagrammatic ritornellos, to affirm home beyond current schemes. Ultimately, navigating the borderlands of home(lessness) is an act of epistemological care toward that social field, one in which recursive violence is perpetrated through different means, in order to (re)produce and maintain a false sense of security for the many.[46] But beyond repression, at times a desire for liberation is assembled within the interstices of home(lessness). In searching for the immanent potential of another home, one needs to start from the most intensified experiences of the current one. Within those subjective cartographies, the desiring-machine (or the assemblage) for a home beyond its lessness is already experimented with, by necessity; however, this necessity is not reducible to the expression of its plight, but it extends beyond itself: it reaches into the virtual, sketching the formation of its own salvation and of its own liberation. It is within precarity, and not elsewhere, that forms of desires elaborating alternative actual and virtual propositions to expulsion and extraction take place, and it is these that I shall trace in the second and third parts of this book, with the help of literatures attentive to the counter power of the micropolitical. For now, however, I want to return to the ways in which the functions of expulsion and extraction have diagrammed home.

2

EXPULSION AND EXTRACTION

In this chapter, I refer to the notion of "colonies of home" to indicate the affective and political economies rendering home a machine of expulsion and extraction. I refer to these as colonies because home works—in its makings and unmakings—as a colonial project. Saying that home is a colonial project does not mean to flatten the discourse around settler colonialism, which maintains specific connotations in terms of land grabbing, occupation, and control of territories. At the same time, it is possible to recognize how the fundamental diagrams at play through the latter are key to the inner constitutive dynamics of home, too. As Said reminded us, for a colonial project to exist, something and someone needs to be occupied and, therefore, to be constructed as worth being occupied.[1] The bordering of the homely enterprise works precisely in this sense. It is a diagram doing what Said has talked about, through two concomitant moves: first, it carves out a space for itself by defining an alterity; second, while keeping that alterity at bay, it constitutes a violent relationship with it, through which values—in the various forms taken by cultural standing, sustenance, security, profit, and belonging—can be extracted and become essential for the reproduction of home. This is colonial in the sense of what Grosfoguel has called the "colonial situation," that is, "the cultural, political, sexual, spiritual, epistemic and economic oppression/exploitation of subordinate racialized/ethnic groups by dominant racialized/ethnic groups with or without the existence of colonial administrations."[2] At home, questioning this colonial situation means to ask questions such as: What is home—in contemporary capitalism—without its otherness? How can its mainstream security, its belonging, its ecological, economic, gendered, racial, and vitalist affordances be maintained, if one breaks through the definition, and management, of alterity at its core? Would home even stand, if confronted with its violent foundations?

In this chapter, I expand on the idea that homely extractive grounds impede not only the realization, but even the simple envisioning, of home as an affirmative project that can stand on its own to be and become. Feminist considerations around the structural violence linking homes with patriarchal and patronizing structurings have highlighted similar relationalities. Most recently, this is what the work of theorist and activist Veronica Gago has brought to the fore, with its reinvigorating critique of affirmative feminist action in the context of Latin America (to which I return in chapter 7).[3] Even more explicitly, Hagar Kotef has moved in the direction of critiquing home and homing practices at their colonial roots.[4] For Kotef, home is a matter of colonies because it is through the colonization of what needs to be kept at bay that home is instantiated as a safe harboring for the settler. Through this kind of homing, racialized assemblages are reproduced; gendered violence is instantiated; and the notion of family and nationhood pivots around the creation (through the creative process of expulsion) of what is not nation, and what is not familiar. If Kotef is looking at home in the settler-colonial state of Israel, she is not reducing the colonial violence of home to occupation, although that is a quintessential part of it, as it is also in part of the history I am going to outline in the second part of this book pertaining to the Italian home. Rather, the idea is to look within what links the intimate and the state, as well as the cultural, the religious, and the economic, to produce a narrative of home that reveals how violence is not the exceptional force from which home protects but the structure of the homely. In Kotef's words, such an approach shifts the focus on the homely violence: "it no longer works inward, but rather outward; it is no longer the intimate violence in the home, but mass violence that occurs through and by the means of homes—their movements, their logics of expansion, the national forms they come to take as homelands."[5]

In a sense, the reasoning I am presenting in this book through the colonies of home(lessness) complements Hagar's specific focus around the violence of the settler-colonial home. If she is interested in the violence that takes place in the home, looking outward, the reading that I am proposing sits on the threshold between the inward and the outward violence of home. It is situated at the threshold allowing home to reproduce itself as a machine cutting across, and uniting, a number of bordering practices and discourses between what is supposedly homely and what is not. Through this reading, there is nothing as an inside or an outside of home as such but a terrain of repetition through which a differentiated, and yet always occurring, violent mode of inhabiting the world is instantiated and reproduced. Tracing such repetitive moves is about lifting the veil of ignorance around home, albeit not to arrive at a Rawlsian consensus on how to adjust the framing of what might be possible for everyone, everywhere, and at the maximum level of abstraction.[6] Key to this process is to conceive home as a nexus where what Kotef calls various "objects of violence" come together, to then imagine multiple renewed form of inhabitation beyond such foundations.

But how do the bordering practices which conceal the unitary nature of home(lessness) get operationalized? How is the violent logic of home reproduced, and how does that reproduction create a sort of propulsive sense of direction (which we could also call an affection) that carries a particular mode of being at home forward? What is the "descriptive statement," to paraphrase Sylvia Wynter, of being at home in contemporary neoliberal capitalism in the West?[7]

Answering this question requires identifying the affective and political economy of home(lessness) more precisely. The task is to appreciate what reverberates through the (re)production of multiple homely borders. From such a transversal viewpoint, cutting across the power geometries giving rise to the instantiation of singular events, an extensive land of subjectivities that are made not to fit and then reappropriated to maintain unjust, and dogmatic, boundaries of home and their industries becomes apparent. Hundreds of bordering practices are frantically operating across this vast gray plane. One can see that what they do is not necessarily connected, one to the other; however, altogether they form a coherent—if brutal—lessness whole. I propose to read what cuts across this land and its bordering practices not as a specific variable, or relation, definable from a theory or explanation. Rather, it is more a matter of attuning to the machinations uniting domains, of sensing and registering the ritornellos arising from their inner operations. What cuts across lessness is the sound of something expelled and yet kept close; the rhythm of a machinic movement that can change its forms, content, and expression, but ultimately maintains a procedural, operational tempo across several forms of bordering regimes to sustain the home/homelessness paradigm. That ritornello, or violent refrain, speaks of a logic working without specification: a sort of diagrammatic infrastructural layout, a substratum cutting through several planes of life, upon which home is founded and becomes apparent. At a bare minimum, the key feature of such a diagrammatic refrain seems to revolve around two baseline functions, which are recursively operationalized to sustain and (re) produce the home/homelessness divide and its permeating logic of lack. In this book—echoing traditions spanning from Marxist to feminist and critical race thinking—I identify these functions using the notions of *expulsion* and *extraction*.

These functions are not in themselves sufficient to explain the violent becomings of home, or, to put it differently, this is not the reason why I focus on them. Rather, I understand expulsion and extraction as a form of becoming, a diagram holding home(lessness) together. This is a diagram providing a transversal—because cutting across multiple and intersecting domains of lives, as Guattari would have it—infrastructure through which home itself, and its subjects, can be reproduced.[8] These are functions shared across the board, dictating the tempo of home for the many, across experiences and geographies. In this sense, they are not just operations—with clear instruction and identifiable forms, but more realistically refrains: patterns that can be operationalized through bordering practices, sustaining and reproducing the home/homelessness binary, in various ways and forms. Their use is to maintain the terrain they have historically emerged from—home(lessness)—as safe and valuable for those who are aligned with its power. The scope of focusing on these inner transversal functions is to highlight how home and homelessness are founded upon the same tempo: it is about taking home(lessness), and its relational production of borders and subjectivities, in a situated and therefore politically attentive way.

Expulsion denotes a double-faced segmentation. It is a cutting off of the other, which entails its creation as other (a process beautifully discussed, among others, by Sarah Ahmed in her *Strange Encounters*). On the one hand, expulsion creates a normative assemblage via selectively deciding what belongs and what is made to fit. On the other hand, it engages in a process of othering, silencing, and erasing that which doesn't fit, which comes to be defined against the exclusionary norm. This is not a simple matter of selecting subjects or groups allowed to enter and others kept at bay. In a more nuanced gloss, expulsion works through segmentations that intersect multiple planes of subjectivity; in simple terms, this means that one individual can be segmented and made homely in a number of concomitant ways. This is similar to the Foucauldian production of the abnormal, a subject who is defined using specialized knowledge but also material politico-economic relations, silencing their multiple becomings to a manageable segment (or segments), for various purposes including being loved, being governed, being kept in check, or being a gateway for other forms of extraction.[9] For instance, the "rough sleeper" is created by reducing an entire life to a codified experience, which is in part expelled from home (hence contributing to the affirmation of a logic of ontological security for those at home) and in part, and at the same time, made available for further operations. As the book will show, once again, this does not mean to say that the intense experience of sleeping rough, with all its trauma and material harshness, is a simple epistemological creation. Rather, it means to say that, throughout that experience, an epistemological colonization takes place, which is also a political act: it is about the codification of that complex experience into a diagrammatic politics that reduces its complexity to a given quantity, from which the extraction of value can take place. What is made not to fit is not, in expulsion, simply trashed or conceived as redundant marginality devoid of consciousness waiting to be re–plugged into the industrial machine, but actively constituted as a foundational other.

On this threshold, *extraction* is operationalized. The bordering of home is not something that finishes with the creation of homelessness and its like; it is maintained and reproduced through the appropriation of that alterity for strategic types of appropriations. In this sense, extraction creates value from expulsion, where value is understood in the largest possible sense, as encompassing but also moving beyond Marxist definitions of use value, exchange value, and socially necessary quanta of labor. The value that is extracted through expulsion includes a broad set of social, cultural, and economic assets that are made to count as valuable by the individuals, collectives, or enterprises operationalizing expulsion for their own ends. These can include social affirmation, parental authority, moral justification, accrual of epistemic privilege, and sexual pleasure, alongside good old-fashioned profiteering. Expulsion and extraction are those two functions operationalized across the land of lessness in order to maintain and reproduce home in its current fashion: an impossible possibility founded in defining its otherness and in extracting legitimacy and power from it. I call the various operationalizations of expulsion and extraction a ritornello because they are recursive, and then also because they are not simply a script.

The way they take place, their form, and the expression of their experiences changes vis-à-vis the subjective maps, histories, and geographies they interlace with. But a sense of direction in their instantiation is maintained, across domains, allowing for the usual homely song to be sung by the many.

Others have argued that extraction of value from the homeless forms a pivotal mechanism sustaining the homelessness industry, including (most recently and powerfully) Craig Willse.[10] I expand on their understanding by connecting this extraction of value to the broader processes that constitute and reproduce what I am calling home(lessness). Expulsion (the reductive segmentation and production of the other) and extraction (the varied assemblages gaining societal, cultural, and economic forms of value from expulsion) are there not only to reproduce the homelessness industry but to create and maintain a larger series of power relations centering on the home/homeless binary and so, centering on the foundational becoming of our dear home under contemporary capitalism. It is not only the rough sleeper who is dispossessed, expelled, and extracted from, but also each and every one of us—even those benefiting from the rough sleeper extraction—who partakes in the fictional division of home and homelessness, and the alterity that this creates. Entire economies of poverty management and everyday reaffirmations of authoritarian control are extracted in a manner that feeds back into mechanisms of expulsion. In this way, a whole range of power relations are operationalized and reproduced: from the level of city-homeless-swipes or fencing migrants out of a country to that of a father reproducing in speech and action heteronormative and patriarchal practices vis-à-vis his wife and kids.

I am conscious of the rather abstract presentation of these concepts. But they come out of situated practices of thinking and writing about home and its struggle, which will hopefully become more apparent in the second part of this book. If the reader will stay with me a bit longer, before turning to Italy, I will now briefly provide a preliminary discussion of four ritornellos of home(lessness), which I have selected because of their paradigmatic importance in structuring formations of home and lessness under contemporary capitalism. The four overlapping violent ritornellos are those of anthropocentrism, racialization, heteronormalization, and capitalization. In the context of this short chapter, these should be read as concepts signposting a wider, hectic, intersectional grammar to approach and discuss the colonies of home(lessness), rather than the descriptors themselves. In a sense, these are for me basic coordinates toward a nonbinary study of homelessness and home: a minimum analytics to hear out, and then investigate, the tempo of expulsion and extraction across the land of home(lessness) in the remainder of this book.

Transversal Borderings

At its most basic level, the first border through which home(lessness)—the affective and political economy of expulsion and extraction founding mainstream ideas of home—reproduces itself is of an anthropocentric kind. With this term, I aim to highlight dominant conceptions positing home against nature, in a discursive sense but also through concrete material and affective workings around that which is to be expelled and that which is to be retained. Positing home against nature is grounded in an expulsive logic—the carving out of a space by maintaining a relationship of alterity with what has been carved out—which activates at least three well-studied kinds of extraction. First, it distinguishes a terrain of human and cultural belonging (the made) against the wilderness of nature; second, it allows selective extraction and circulation of refined natural resources to sustain the infrastructure of housing; third, it expels the foreign, the wild, and the strange from space, thereby extracting a sense of security and territorialized control.

The anthropocentrism of home consists in the creation of a Cartesian geography through which a wild other is defined and tamed in order to extract pleasure, energy, security, and all those circulatory regimes of accumulation that political ecologists have lucidly identified and commented upon.[11] I say *Cartesian* because there is a particular kind of anthropomorphism at play in the construction of such a boundary: man (white, heterosexual, male) becomes the foundation from which a particular project is conceived and executed. "Cogito, ergo sum" is here more than a form of inward-looking certainty, through which a particular kind of subjectivity is affirmed; it is a profound exercise in mapping the world from the making of that subjectivity.[12] A different anthropocentrism would have created and managed a different kind of boundary between home and nature, as illustrated vividly by the feminist animist thinking of Anzaldúa, but also by relational ecological thought, schizoanalytical thinking of the subject, or by the cyborg proposition of Donna Haraway, which aims at imagining a different bordering between humanity and nature, "where the one can no longer be the resource for appropriation or incorporation by the other."[13]

In the anthropocentrism of home, the expulsion of a natural state that is not made to fit is the basis for the reconstitution of a wild otherness that is made to fit through confinement, exploitation, and uncaring practices. Expulsion creates a foundational other to home that can then be appropriated: the nonhuman is alive only to a lesser degree in Cartesian logic. Such a form of bordering bears profound consequences for how all ecologies are made to inhabit home(lessness). Maria Kaika has explained this very well: "excluding socio-natural processes as 'the other' becomes a prerequisite for the construction of the familiar space of the home. The inside becomes safe, familiar and independent not only by excluding rain, cold and pollution, but also through keeping fear, anxiety, social upheaval and inequality outside."[14] Through these operationalizations, one (white, male) ecological understanding is made to flourish both at the expense of all others and through the active reproduction of this inequality. This anti-ecological, or uni-ecological, way of being at home is a primordial bordering. It is the product of a singular vision and produces a multiplicity of issues: "By reconstructing the invisible material and social continuity that exists between the production of nature and the production of the modern home, it is shown that, although natural and social processes remain invisible and are scripted as 'the other' to the modern home, they are in fact the precondition for the home's very existence and always remain part and parcel of its inside."[15]

In this sense, the climate catastrophe we are currently inhabiting is made at home, in at least two ways: first, as Vanesa Castán Broto has shown, through the technologies that (re)produce the home/nature border, most obviously at the level of housing and its technocratic management; but also at the level of wider infrastructural networks encompassing housing and structuring urban lives at large, as revealed, for instance, in the work of Matthew Gandy and others attentive to the interplay of ecological infrastructures in our cities.[16] Second, climate change is made at home because its underpinnings are to be found in the patriarchal project of managing (operationalizing) the border of home/nature. Referring to the work of Claudia von Werlhof, Escobar reminds us how patriarchy has designed the uni-ecological bordering of home across the last five thousand years of Western history, at the expense of a matriarchal conception of life that is "not based on domination and hierarchies, [but] respectful of the relational fabric of all life." Through Western history, and at the hands of men, the alchemy of life became "a practice of destruction, the fragmenting of the elements of matter to eventually produce, out of the isolated elements, what was considered most valuable, such as gold or the philosopher's stone. Destruction progressively became the program to be advanced, contradictorily in the name of creating life; eventually, with modernity and the dominance of the machine, the program transmuted into the search for endless progress and the promise of a ceaselessly better world."[17]

The kind of contradiction Escobar highlights in this passage is not just simply, and generally, anthropocentric, but profoundly racialized, too. Racialization is a tempo of becoming—a life emergent in its repetition—that has been of fundamental importance to sustaining the anthropocentric project of home of which I have just spoken. Among others, the rhythmic link between anthropocentrism and racialization has been well discussed by the French political ecologist Malcolm Ferdinand in his *Une écologie décoloniale*. For Ferdinand, the racial other has been constituted—as an ecology of inhabitation—through the anthropocentrism of a white and colonial bordering between culture and nature. Attacking what he defines as the "double fracture coloniale et environmentale de la modernité," Ferdinand aims to show the links between colonial history and the history of environmental exploitation.[18] In doing so, he attacks the ways in which specializations founded in white epistemic privilege generate knowledge production in each area, in a manner that ensures that an extractive environmental logic, and a repressive ecological discourse, reinforce the racial foundation of the colonial project.[19] This is what he calls an "écologie coloniale" or "habiter coloniale," and he counters it with the proposal of an "écologie décoloniale" founded on *une libération* of the "condition d'esclaves coloniaux," mapping a radical, decolonial inhabitation (therefore, as I recently argued with AbdouMaliq Simone, a form of inhabitation beyond the colonies of home).[20]

Ferdinand is interested in a total change, *une quête de monde*, a conquering that is about a redesigning of the actual from the cracks of its tensioned, racialized, and colonial history. He argues that we need to get out of the racialized and colonial diagramming of our mainstream inhabitation of the world:

> In addition to the genocide of Indigenous peoples and the destruction of ecosystems, this colonial inhabitation has transformed the lands into jigsaws of factories and plantations that characterize this geological era, the *Plantationocene*. This is an era that has led us to lose matriarchal relationships with the Earth: *matricides*. The recourse to the transatlantic slave trade and to colonial slavery, confining specific human and non-human beings in the hold of the world [for Malcolm this is a metaphor for the hold of the ship], the "Negroes," also qualify this geological era as the *Negrocene*. Following this history, disasters such as the regular cyclones that ravage the American coasts have only repeated these fractures of colonial inhabitation and prolonged the enslavement of the dominated, turning the ecological storm into a veritable *colonial cyclone*.[21]

In this short passage, which introduces some key ideas of his analytical repertoire (including the Négrocène and the matricidal loss of relations to the Earth), Ferdinand is linking the expulsion and extraction of the slave plantation to a particular kind of industrialization and, then, to the segregated and spatially zoned housing market of poor Black communities in the American metropoles, who are also those most affected by environmental disaster (the implicit city of reference being New Orleans). Evidently here Ferdinand builds on, and he is joined by, a number of critical thinkers who have shown how the racial logic of the plantation is transposed, in time and space, into spatial planning and, most notably, into contemporary regimes of incarceration in the United States.[22] What emerges in these accounts is the maintenance and reproduction of a particular logic of dispossession pivoted around the construction of the Black others, reduced (through an operation of expulsion) to a simulacrum, a segment, and made therefore a manageable object from which extractions of all kinds can take place.[23] The latter include economic profiteering from the new carceral plantation, but also a more profound cultural legitimization of white privilege, the structuring of entire cities to extract perceived safeness and protection from the Black poor, and much more. Far from being confined to North America, the ways in which expulsion and extraction have been operationalized through race have been foundational to the political construction of home in Europe, albeit arguably scholarship on this side of the Atlantic has tended to remain attached to a taxonomic reading of ethnicity and diversity that reproduces, instead of fighting, *l'habiter colonial* (Brar and Sharma, but also Hawthorne, offer a productive account linking Black critical studies across the Atlantic, to which I have also contributed with my work on racialized dispossession in postsocialist Romania; Picker provides a good study of how European colonialism is deeply linked to the racialization of its most notorious others, the Roma).[24]

I am only brushing the surface of the ways in which racism is materially structured here, and I will expand on these arguments when I discuss the Italian case. What is evident, however, is that when it comes to matters of inhabitation, racialization is a process through which expulsion and extraction are not only operationalized but reproduced to map a particular white, anthropocentric form of dwelling into the world, of being and becoming at home in it. To get even closer to home, we can look at the work of Heidi J. Nast, who has unpacked these concerns by focusing on the familiar communitarian and intimate work of social and biological reproduction. What I found particularly helpful in her work is her focus on the unconscious reproduction of racialization at home. Crucially, for Nast the unconscious is not a hidden thing to be discovered and mapped through the lens of lack, or a place that "speaks univocally to oedipal familiar desire."[25] Instead of the unconscious staging things and then interpreting them in arcane spectacle, the unconscious is a machine that is produced, maintained, and assembled, always in a state of immanent actual/virtual becoming. For Nast, following Deleuze and Guattari, "the unconscious is not a theatre, but a factory."[26] Two points are key here: "First, the *system of biological reproduction* was contained ideologically and sociospatially by the nuclear familial unit. This geographical arrangement allowed fatherhood and patriarchy to be scripted and enabled through the *biologized familial home*, a system of containment dependent on and libidinized through private property and nationhood. Secondly, racialized black bodies and lives were not the stuff out of which imaginary-symbolic ideals of the (white) oedipal family were shaped and encoded. Bodies of color, especially black bodies, were rendered animalistic and childlike, requiring that they be held at sociospatial bay."[27]

Both points entail a structuring expulsion followed by a diagramming extraction. First, there is a particular anthropocentrism of home, a modality that segments family along patriarchal lines, allowing a libidinal extraction (among others) to take place. Second, the Black other needs to be constructed as such via the expulsion of a multiplicity of becomings, a silencing that allows both the reappropriation of the ideal of home and a series of further extractive practices. Nast shows how this operationalization of racialization has been encoded in the unconscious diagram of home/homelessness throughout the last three hundred years of American history. Home is a desiring-machine actively maintained through the infantilization of the Black other (for instance, the denial of a surname to enslaved Black men); the maintenance of a domesticated "white female as iconic of pure motherhood" from whom the Black other is kept at bay as a potential rapist; the spatial actualization of a keeping-at-bay in residential restrictions operating in slave quarters, city planning more broadly, and redlining housing restrictions; the "lynchings and castrations of black 'boys'" after the Civil War, indicating "white anxiety and rage over the possibilities of a black paternal"; and the invention of a new language of crime that conflates deviancy with blackness, allowing "disciplinary procedures against African Americans to be taken, this time under discursive cover of 'preventing crime'" and so on.[28] Ultimately, "racistly oedipalized dreams, fears, and desires [are] mapped onto colonial-familial relations that are instrumental to plantation and industrial capitalisms. The oedipal myth and theories work precisely because they are made to carry out work," that of maintaining a familiar home, through the continuous expulsion of and extraction from the other.[29]

Crucially, such an operationalization is territorialized through our unconscious selves, where it reverberates not only with anthropocentrism but also with another key ritornello structuring home(lessness): heteronormalization. The white episteme articulating mainstream ideas of home is designed from and for a specific kind of man: a desiring machine diagrammed through the heterosexual and patriarchal strata. Feminist scholarship, and in particular

Black feminist scholars, have done much to illustrate these foundations of home. *Expulsion* here defines a particular kind of femininity (which is clearly at play in the makings of racializations), from which all sorts of violent extractions take place. The latter are diagrammed with the social reproduction of home at their core. Historically, as Dolores Hayden has shown, this is not only a matter of normatively understood forms of care but also of the material forms homes have taken across much of the West (most obviously in the traditional form of North American suburban housing, which, as Alison Blunt and Robyn Dowling illustrated, "exacerbate the amount of work required of women because they privatize or individualize domestic labour" and because "home depends upon a myriad of nurturing activities, also undertaken by women").[30]

More recently, Juanita Elias and Shirin Rai have expanded upon traditional feminist concerns around everyday social reproduction and home, sharpening understanding of both. Their contribution invites us to read social reproduction and the everyday as one and the same: a process carried out through "spatial, temporal, and violent social regimes" that is "sustained as well as challenged through agency exercised in different scales and registers."[31] Social reproduction ("the socially necessary work that is central to the production of life itself") is the everyday: an everyday of spatial relations, temporalities, and systemic violence through which a particular kind of (re)production can emerge and can be repeated over space and time.[32] Their attentiveness to the notion of the everyday as constitutive of social reproduction is close to the understanding of subjects and cartographies of homely colonial violence advanced in this book, which traces how the everyday embodiments of housing precarity are both a product and a producer of the "housing political" (chapter 6). When it comes to the notion of home, this is equivalent to saying that there is no way of reading its production, maintenance, and reproduction—the embodiment of its lived and felt everyday life—in dissociation from the wider intersections structuring those experiences. Therefore, there is no chance of reading home, housing, or homelessness as policy or a technical problem. Home is always beyond its containment, always more than its dichotomous reading, always about multiple situated troubles—about the repetition of lessness across the board.

Concerning heteronormativity, expulsion and extraction work through the construction of a normative subject with two faces—one pointing inward, to homing praxis, the other reverberating out of it. The first face is diagrammed by cisnormativity: the possible becomings of a body are made to fit into a binary construction, forcing superficial gendered appearances into a dichotomous cultural paradigm and rejecting more indeterminate forms of gender identity.[33] This enables the creation of a home where the gendered other can be expelled in its creation (segmentation) and therefore governed. Second, like other operationalizations of expulsion and extraction, cisnormativity plays from, through, and beyond home: it suffices to say that the legal possibility to identify oneself, on a voluntary basis, as nonbinary is available in less than a dozen countries in the world.[34] The institutionalization of cisnorms into key domains of social reproduction, which have direct links with homemaking, closes the circle of the heteronormative (patriarchal) household project. As Affrica Taylor and Carmel Richardson have shown, schools play an important role here, since "the trope of appropriateness, drawing its authority from a Western-scientific paradigm, is firmly located within a moral regime that is inextricably bound up with prelapsarian (or sexually innocent) and heteronormative conceptualisations of childhood."[35] Adherence to social customs reproduces a heteronormative culture from infancy onward, at an individual and collective level. This entwines with the other primordial becomings sketched in this chapter: the silencing of nondichotomous genders sings its song of expulsion and extraction via anthropocentrism (what the queer other can or cannot do with the wild otherness of home), racialization (reinforcing cultural and societal bordering of identity formations), and capitalization (both in the sense of extracting value from the nominal acceptance of diversity and by making it work for someone else's good).

A queer way of thinking helps to navigate the intersections of these homely borderings. I am conscious of the fact that the word *queer* emerges from an explicit critique of the normalization of heterosexuality by the gay community.[36] Yet I am also inspired by what queer thinking can do to disrupt othering and queering norms beyond sexuality. In such a reading, to follow Natalie Oswin, the heteronormative becoming of home can be read not only as the "universal policing of a heterosexual–homosexual binary" but also as "the geographically and historically specific coincidence of race, class, gender, nationality and sexual norms."[37] Queering home becomes about understanding these issues relationally and then fighting those policing, silencing, and expelling to entrench entitlement, power, and security via a heteronormative ideal of home. I expand on this in the third part of this book. For now, it suffices to say that queering the border of home and homelessness is about ceaselessly fighting the institution of dichotomous binaries, which, to follow Will McKeithen, reduce plurality, keeping "concerns of sexuality, kinship, and heteronormativity largely divorced from questions of nature-society and human-nonhuman relationships."[38] The question, then, becomes not only to account for queer experiences of homelessness (a fundamental and liberatory practice of its own), but also to transcend our given heteronormative home altogether: in the theory of home(lessness) and the praxis of its liberation.[39] Is it possible, as Anne-Marie Fortier has it, "to conceive of being 'at home' in a way that already encounters/engenders queerness, but without deploying an originary narrative of 'home'?"[40] The task of fighting for a liberatory politics of home must confront this question, and I return to it in the second half of this volume.

The working of the three ritornellos that I have briefly sketched is not a given. In themselves, without their affective interlacing and reciprocal sustenance, they would not have maintained the capacity for their reproduction and expansion across space and time. Key to this process are the continued and renewed affordances offered by the specific mode of production and consumption instantiated by contemporary capitalism. More precisely, it is the logic of proprietorship at the core of the latter that matters. Within contemporary racial capitalism, there is no possession outside of proprietorship, which is to say, no possibility of claiming one's own economic (broadly understood) place in the world unless that space of relations is individualized, inscribed in the singular (as shown by Robert Nichols), and therefore grounded in the subtraction—or bordering—from, and of, the other.[41] It is in this context, in which possession is diagrammed as proprietorship, that capitalism is able to work within and through racialized logics, to (re)produce, following Cedric Robinson, a "world system . . . dependent on slavery, violence, imperialism, and genocide," to which one could add anthropocentric and cisnormative concerns, too.[42]

The attachment to objects of violence is one of the key tenets of capitalism. As Kotef, following Berland, reminds us, "in capitalism we find mechanisms of attachment to objects of violence—objects whose production necessitates violence—and a continuous attachment to these objects even after this violence becomes apparent."[43] This is not by chance: it is because of the attachment to, and the reproduction of, objects of violence—such as a violent household; the foreclosure of a home; the gendered nature of homely spaces and their cultural representation—that the economy of lessness, and its transversal tempo of dispossession, is held together, maintained, and expanded upon. The proprietorship here is not just around goods but around the foundations of possession. It is about who can expel whom, in order to extract its own sustenance and the capacity to endure its position. Where capitalization comes into play is in the ability of the market and its agents to open up relational spaces where proprietorship can be assembled through breaks, crisis, creative (re)productions. This last ritornello, here, provides the connective tissue with all others, not only in its dialectical grammar, through which a material political economy is provided for anthropocentric, racialized, and heteronormative conceptions and practices of home to endure, but also, crucially, in its affective capacity to generate a lively orientation to proprietorship. This is possibly the biggest achievement of the *Capitalism and Schizophrenia* project of Deleuze and Guattari: their reading of capitalism as a plateau of machines, grounded in a specific mode of production, but not exhausted in it. Each juncture works as a hinge to affect the passage or the blockage of further arrangements, through which powerful extractive capacities can be diagrammed and take on a life of their own (sometimes entirely abstracting from history, space, and time, and then returning to impact on the future).

Such an assemblage, or ontological reading, of capitalism points to concrete material formations (the political economy part) and their external capacities (or affective relationships).[44] Here, the key assemblage for the discussion in the remaining parts of this book is obviously housing, because it is through that specific arrangement of economies—material and affective—that many of the ritornellos of home(lessness) are (re)made in the everyday for the many. At its most basic level, housing is a vehicle for capitalization. In her book on the neoliberalization of housing in the global north, Sarah Glynn summarizes the problem: "At the heart of today's housing crisis is the prioritization of the house as investment rather than as home, that is, of its exchange value over its use value."[45] The 2008 financial and housing crisis has exposed the extent of capital's reach within housing and land markets across the globe. As the work of David Harvey and others has shown, land has been turned into a nodal point through which a particular modality of financialized profit making has flourished.[46] Involvement of the state in housing policy and provision has been strategically reduced, leaving space for the advancement of private estate investment, including global financial circuits of capital and translocal speculation.[47] Crisscrossing these high-level circulations, mundane terrains for capital extraction and accumulation have come to the fore, from technocratic rent management to the subtraction of units from the long-term housing market in the name of short-term, high-return, profit making (the clearest example of the latter being the extensive Airbnb-ization of dwellings in tourist areas worldwide). These processes are, of course, geographically and contextually specific in their structures and dynamics. Think for instance of the epochal transformation of housing in the so-called postsocialist context from state provision to an explosion of private ownership, and of the ways in which the latter needs to be understood through its own history and logic to avoid further colonization.[48]

When it comes to housing, then, capitalization hinges on processes of expulsion and extraction at many different levels. It works by ordering social and material relations, all the way from the intimate private realm to the highly relational and digitalized world of financial speculations: from a small rented room without windows in a shared London flat to total return swaps on real estate derivatives. What unites these operations around housing is, as Raquel Rolnik has argued, "the ideological and practical hegemony of a specific model of housing policy: one based on the promotion of home ownership through market purchase via credit loans."[49] In more detail:

> Through the finance of private home purchase, global capital market expansion was based on private indebtedness, establishing an intimate link between individuals' biological lives and the global process of income extraction and speculation. Therefore, the channelling of capital surplus flowing into residential property also has a lived dimension: mortgaged lives, namely the generation of people in debt—a new subjectivity produced by the disciplinary mechanisms that subject life itself to debt servicing. This became evident when the real-estate bubble burst, and all risks and onus fell on those who had borrowed. . . . It is important to note that it would not have been possible to expand the mortgage market on this enormous scale had other housing access options not been blocked or rolled back to a residual level.[50]

But on top of this, if one wants to embrace a transversal reading of the expulsion and extraction cutting across and uniting the logic of being made and being extracted in lack, in lessness, there is more. Housing must be approached not just as an object of content, with its own market value and its own use value that can be approached and critiqued as such, but more fundamentally it needs to be read as a wide cartography, linking up bodies and markets, histories and thresholds, resolutions and times. This is a cartography where subjects are made or not to fit, and through which extraction or liberation—beyond current inhabitation and its proprietorship—can be forged (see part III). The invitation is to read housing, in the broader affair of home(lessness), as a machine of machines acting on multiple planes of life—not only that of the market or that of the ontological security it can grant to its members. As much as I am trying to expand on that which pertains to homelessness, including ritornellos of violence that are traditionally kept separated, the same goes for housing, to avoid falling back into the trap of considering it the solution, the technical fix, to a multiplicity of troubles that so very clearly at the same time encompass, and yet crisscross, it.

Expulsion and extraction are hence put to work throughout the current market/housing diagram, operationalized via daily routines of evictions, removals, and foreclosures that are then reappropriated through the extraction of value in financial markets, and in the political sphere, where the reaffirmation of right-wing politics reinforces the interests of the elite while mobilizing the popular vote on the basis of diffused discontent. But most importantly, expulsion and extraction are operationalized by neoliberal housing markets in a manner that cuts through the other types of expulsion I have mentioned above. In this sense, capitalization falls last in my list of the colonies of home(lessness) not because it is the least important, but because an appreciation of its effects requires a genuinely relational lens.[51] A focus on housing markets and/or claims around housing rights is necessary to appreciate how capitalization structures home(lessness), but not sufficient. Here I follow Hardt and Negri, when they say that "no one structure of domination is primary to (or reducible to) the others," which translates for me on reading the intersections operationalizing housing in contemporary capitalism on multiple fronts.[52]

This means the capitalization of home(lessness) and its housing cuts through several "economies of dispossession," including anthropocentrism, racialization, and heteronormatization, and surely many more. As Byrd et al. conceived, it is not simply "accumulation by dispossession," a concept that "preserves an analytical separation between the practices of primitive accumulation . . . such as colonization and Indigenous dispossession in the Americas, and those practices of accumulation by dispossession . . . such as the post-1970s crises of capitalist overaccumulation."[53] It is about understanding the dispossessive power at the core of the kind of proprietorship fueling contemporary racial capitalism, and its ritornellos, as "an ontological proposition" structured around and structuring some "primary conditions of possibility," which include "colonization, Indigeneity, racialization, and chattel slavery and its afterlives, along with the heteropatriarchal household economy."[54] In this view, dispossession is not only something to be traced in history but is viewed as the de facto diagram of life in conditions in which "propriety" becomes the core function of individual and collective relations, as also illustrated by Butler and Athanasiou. When, to follow Byrd et al. again, such a "conception and practice of the proper" becomes the structuring form of collective life, "the logic of appropriation instantiated through dis/possession works in tandem with the production of colonial, racial, gender, and sexual categories that change over time."[55]

This is a form of foundational violence, the diagram at the core of the colonies of home, which "enact and disavow racial and colonial violence *by constituting people, land, and the relations of social life as translatable into value form, making incommensurate histories, experiences, and forms of social being commensurate by reducing them* to their meaning and value within 'the capital relation,' placing them within the ontology of dis/possession."[56] Such a relational constitution through what Byrd et al. call "incommensurate reduction" in order to "accrue value via dis/possessions" is close to what I have tentatively identified as the functions cutting across the plane of home(lessness). Through those operationalizations—which is to say, following Best and Ramírez, through the "continual organizing of bodies, technologies and things, producing legal regimes that uphold and reproduce the extraction of value from people in place"—there is nothing like being at home or not being at home, just inhabitation through multitudes of expulsions and extractions operating through Cartesian, racialized, cisnormative/heterosexual becomings, accelerated, and co-opted too, by the inner logics of racial capitalism.[57]

A Note on Scholarship

Policies dealing with housing precarity and experiences of homelessness know little of the intersecting processes I have just sketched above. Their preoccupation is not around the transversal tempos of expulsion and extraction cutting through, and reproducing, the land of home(lessness). Rather, the focus is opposite: it is on a binary reading of home and its other, therefore allowing the management of both into scientifically separated realms of policy and action. Mainstream policy and scholarship, being for the most part direct expressions of institutions deeply entangled in the reproduction of the dispossessive logics evoked in this chapter, have no interest in such an oeuvre. The effort is put into the maintenance of separateness, or segmentation: into the construction of the illusion of home/homelessness. But this comes with great effort. For if there is a certain degree of complexity in dealing with the plane of lessness, and in maintaining a relational and intersectional outlook on its formations, it is undoubtedly also very complex to force specialist readings; to implement myopic, surgical interventions; and to reproduce the belief that incremental policy adjustments can offer radical change. So why this is done? Why, or better how, is it possible to think that the problem of housing precarity can be solved without tackling histories of racialized dispossession, patriarchal violence, and ecological extractivism? How is it that housing and homelessness policy still pivot around narrow concerns and focuses rather than embracing a wider and more profound reading of both structures of homely violence and their experiences? How is it that the expulsive and extractive functions structuring mainstream ideas of home are constantly maintained rather than challenged in policies addressing home and its other?

The specialization of interventions around homelessness, housing, and home at large resides in the (positivist) idea that social problems can be dealt with in specialized, technical, and therefore ultimately detached ways. Even the most nuanced interventions (such as Housing First, see chapter 5) do not break away from a linear logic, and they do not challenge the ritornellos of expulsion and extraction sketched above. Such an avoidance is strategic. On the one hand, it serves to maintain the foundational distinction between home and homelessness, upon which the bare idea of helping or saving somebody is founded. As Didier Fassin and other critical scholars of humanitarianism showed, there is no saving without the colonizing constitution of an other to be saved, and therefore the latter needs to be maintained.[58] On the other hand, such a maintenance does not require full awareness or enunciation to work at the level of everyday policy practice: it is enough for the parties involved to do their given jobs. There is an inertia at play in the remaking of a ritornello. To go with its flow, to follow its tempo, it is sufficient to carry on duties and avoid—sometimes purposely—linking things up and advancing questioning.

Within this scheme of power—where lessness becomes indistinguishable from its subjects—scholarship has been instrumental in reproducing the expulsive and extractive logics of home(lessness). Just focusing on what is canonically discussed as homelessness, the sheer amount of science produced every year is staggering. The Scopus database lists more than 850 scientific studies on homelessness produced in 2020, more than two peer-reviewed academic publications per day. And this is only the tip of the iceberg, since it does not include policy reports, NGO and charity publications, or newspaper articles and blog posts written by researchers and practitioners alike. There is obviously much of interest in these works, some of which are able to grasp multiple facets of the heterogeneous experiences of precarious dwelling. But despite variety and nuances, homelessness scholarship still refuses to see a direct link between the foundations of home and its supposed other, offering instead understandings and policy recommendations that squarely pivot around the idea that homelessness can be solved, or tackled, as a problem in itself. This is not just a question of balancing carefully between individual characteristics and "structural causations" of homelessness but of changing the entire outlook on the matter at stake.[59] It is not about conceiving it as a social problem but about conceptualizing, and dealing with, a wider and foundational dispossessive logic of proprietorship.

Despite much calling for critical, relational, and even intersectional approaches in homelessness studies, scholarship for the most part pivots on descriptivism (of conditions of otherness) and prescriptivism (of interventions and solutions). Here expulsion and extraction seem to work through a logic of what I already referred to as *segmentation*, a term coming from marketing studies, and pointing to the ways in which a market of potential customers is divided into groups, based on characteristics that are defined from above. In policy, the homeless are often referred to as the clients of a service, segmented as users of a series of resources. In scholarship—in the silencing scheme of knowledge production—they are identified as a question in need of an answer, a subjectivity that needs to be addressed in manageable ways. The immanence of life needs to be segmented into parts, in order to produce the homeless as the raw matter on which scholarship can go to work. The residue of this process, that which exceeds segmentation, is a series of inarticulable and unnameable desires, structured by systemic oppressions and yet outrunning those too. These cannot be contained, explained, or narrated in ways that easily fit within the urge of the disciplinary field to describe, to prescribe, and to illustrate.

Segmentation is the founding act of a form of scholarship constructed around Durkheimian principles: we (the bearers of knowledge and *technē*) are confronted with a world of social facts that require our intervention, our action. The challenge here is not to understand how things are formed, to evoke Gabriel Tarde, but to find ways to contain given formations within increasingly elaborate categories and modes of calculation (the obsession to quantify the homeless is a clear signal of this).[60] In this highly medicalized field, the homeless are segmented in order to be fitted in, in a manner that evolves ever more refined forms of subcategorization and specialization. From the very beginnings of the field of study, scholars have proposed elaborate definitions and conceptualizations of homelessness, in order to foster a more reliable collection of homelessness data, so that they can shape policy, often in ways that cause only small disruptions to an existing institutional landscape.[61] The basic idea is that if scholarship gets better at counting, naming, identifying, recollecting, and comparing, then it can get better at informing policy and at ending homelessness. Segmentation therefore continues, not as a side effect of scholarship but as its main founding principle and its main proposition. Defining homelessness in order to be able to work with it: a violent parcellation of life.

For example, the following table shows how leading scholars of homelessness across the Atlantic (UK–United States–Europe)—Volker Busch-Geertsema, Dennis Culhane, and Suzanne Fitzpatrick—who are all working with their own respective national governments, are proposing to develop a global framework for conceptualizing and measuring homelessness. Who's who, and what is expelled, in order to extract what can be contained, in such powerful framings? These fragments of life are what we can extract as the homeless, after having expelled the rest:

1. People without Accommodation

1(a) People sleeping in the streets or in other open spaces (such as parks, railway embankments, under bridges, on pavements, on river banks, in forests, etc.)

1(b) People sleeping in public roofed spaces or buildings not intended for human habitation (such as bus and railway stations, taxi ranks, derelict buildings, public buildings, etc.)

1(c) People sleeping in their cars, rickshaws, open fishing boats and other forms of transport

1(d) "Pavement dwellers"—individuals or households who live on the street in a regular spot, usually with some form of makeshift cover

2. People Living in Temporary or Crisis Accommodation

2(a) People staying in night shelters (where occupants have to renegotiate their accommodation nightly)

2(b) People living in homeless hostels and other types of temporary accommodation for homeless people (where occupants have a designated bed or room)

2(c) Women and children living in refuges for those fleeing domestic violence

2(d) People living in camps provided for "internally displaced people" i.e. those who have fled their homes as a result of armed conflict, natural or human-made disasters, human rights violations, development projects, etc. but have not crossed international borders

2(e) People living in camps or reception centres/temporary accommodation for asylum seekers, refugees and other immigrants

3. People Living in Severely Inadequate and/or Insecure Accommodation

3(a) People sharing with friends and relatives on a temporary basis

3(b) People living under threat of violence

3(c) People living in cheap hotels, bed and breakfasts and similar

3(d) People squatting in conventional housing

3(e) People living in conventional housing that is unfit for human habitation

3(f) People living in trailers, caravans and tents

3(g) People living in extremely overcrowded conditions

3(h) People living in non-conventional buildings and temporary structures, including those living in slums/informal settlements.[62]

Recognizing the central role played by segmentation in scholarship, as the founding act of a certain way of looking at the world and, therefore, of a certain way of acting upon it, is central to approaching home and homelessness differently. Again, here the problem is not to reduce the harshest intensities of home(lessness) to a mere epistemological problem but precisely to address the violent epistemologies colonizing those experiences in order to unravel the politics of the latter, the life that has been segmented out. The objection that is usually raised by those corners, when presented with such critique, is that in focusing on a transversal reading of home and homelessness, I am avoiding a clear definition of the latter and therefore become unable to do anything about the problem of people sleeping on the street, in temporary accommodation, in inadequate housing, or in violent households. But such a unidirectional way of looking at those life experiences is not the only possibility; it is also possible to refuse segmentation and to address the multiple troubles making up precarious lives as a whole. In segmenting subjects as in the above quote—and related policy frameworks—we resolve homelessness only in the sense of reducing its structural violence to the manageable racket of home/homelessness, and, in so doing, we engage in the social and epistemic control of a defined deviance. A game that not only is foundational to an entire homelessness industry—critiqued, as said by scholars such as Gowan, Willse, Lyon-Callo, and Hopper—but that also reproduces the cultural paradigms through which the maintenance of home/homelessness continues, undisturbed.

By taking the power of categories seriously, and rejecting the work that goes into maintaining them, I do not deny the lived reality of experiences of houselessness and deprivation; instead, such a move opens up the possibility of taking them and their politics seriously, on their own terms, without the conceptual and material constraints of current sociological grammars. As critical poverty thinkers such as Sarah Elwood, Vicky Lawson, Ananya Roy, or Gautam Bhan—to cite just four who have done much to reimagine ways of talking relationally of urban and housing precarity—remind us, questioning dominant epistemologies is the first starting point if one wants to avoid the essentialization of experience in the name of knowledge.[63] To an extent, thinking through home(lessness) is the antisociology of both home and homelessness: an invitation to focus less on their containment and more on the tempo of their wider structurations, as expressed in situated experience.

Grounding the Analysis

Our current mainstream ideologies of home are founded on unecological, racist, patriarchal-heteronormative, and capitalized becomings. The explanatory force of these becomings lies not in their individuality but in their status as bordering practices and their productive intersection. As Neferti X. M. Tadiar has noted, it is through racial, sexualized, classist, and other powerful categories and assemblages of difference that the "contemporary contradictions between state and capital, nation and state, [and, I would add, home and homelessness] are 'resolved,' put to use toward ends that only exacerbate the inequalities of our times."[64] Perhaps at the risk of oversimplifying, I found that the diagrammatic logic operating at the core of this resolution lay in its tensioned making of the other of home through expulsion, in order to accrue value from it, via extraction. Perhaps there are more of these functions at play (indeed, in the coming chapters I discuss mechanisms of exposure in this matrix). But the context- and time-specific operations through which ideologies and material cultures of home/homelessness are maintained in the West reveal a constant selective creation of otherness from which extended and varied forms of value are appropriated.

It is important to note that in this chapter I did not aim for comprehensiveness on the becomings of home. Many other factors are at play in reproducing the expulsive and extractive plane of home(lessness), such as medicalization, aestheticization, and, perhaps above all, urbanization (on which I've expanded elsewhere).[65] Migration is also critical to the ways in which home(lessness) is managed in today's cities, and I will suggest its significance at relevant intersections throughout the book.[66] In this part of the book, however, my intent has been more modest: to outline a basic relational grammar of home; to show how the border between home and homelessness is a porous, constitutive, intersectional matter, which can be turned into a method of exploration; and to sketch some of the ways that bordering is (re)produced through colonizing mechanisms of expulsion and extraction, which enact a rhythmic form of homely violence.

On this premise, I can now move on to the second part of this book, where I wish to illustrate a transversal method to explore the harshest intensification of home(lessness): one replacing a conventional language and logic of deviance and relegation with a functional insistence on expulsion and extraction. I focus on the loosely defined geographical signifier of *Italy* to discuss stories of homing and of precarious housing, first, questioning the foundational violence of the making of home in the country, and then by looking at how those same foundations percolate throughout to the management of their otherness in a specific Italian city. I then expand further, to show how the terrain of home(lessness) is wider and further reaching than a city, or a country, particularly at the level of cultural representations and policy travel, at least within the West. Throughout the second part of the book, my aim is to set the terrain for the question tackled in the third and final part of the volume. If one embraces the home(lessness) epistemology, can housing be a gateway for radical change? How can one liberate homelessness through a renewed kind of home? Before arriving at that, turning to Italy will allow me to clarify and ground the political proposition of the book.

Part II

3

ITALIAN RITORNELLOS

In this chapter, I am grounding the home(lessness) epistemology in the specific geographical signifier of Italy. I use this term to signal my intention to move freely, in the entire second part of this book, both historically and geographically, to trace how mainstream notions of home and of its supposed other have emerged in the recent history of the country across coloniality, migrations, religion, political and economic power, the law, and the media, focusing on the last 150 years. My intention is not to provide a comprehensive analysis of such an emergence, but to show a method of inquiry around the boundary making of lessness and its related violence in the home. How are the ritornellos emerging from the colonies of home at play in Italy? What can an analysis holding together the homely and its negation, as part of the same, tell us about their constitution and their reproduction? Can an appreciation of the unjust formation of home(lessness) tell us something more on how to get beyond it? This chapter provides the grounds to appreciate how the expulsive and extractive formations of home expand toward the homeless of our time, both locally (chapter 4) and globally (chapter 5). The third part of the book builds on the conceptual works of the first part and the empirical evidence of the second to fully unpack its epistemological (chapter 6) and political propositions (chapter 7 and conclusion).

Critical scholarship on housing, home, and homelessness is relatively minor in Italy. There are few meaningful works on homeless service provisions; few, but excellent, emerging readings of old and new housing struggles, policy, and problematizations; as well as critical scholarship looking at migrations and housing issues.[1] Beyond a couple of other minor exceptions—mostly coming from the grassroots and from scholars trying to situate the Italian housing spectrum within the international debate—housing-related scholarship in Italy is written for the most part in mainstream tones to serve mainstream attitudes.[2] This does not mean, however, that the housing question is not relevant in the country. Quite the contrary: it has been and still is one of the crucial aspects around which state policies have gathered since the early twentieth century. Yet these interventions have very rarely tackled the issue of housing provisioning in meaningful ways but have always touched upon its inherent intersectionality to sustain, in turn, regressive family policies; conservative takes on migrations and citizenship; dubious transitions to a greener economy; and the reproduction of classist segmentations of Italian society. To provide further context, there are essentially three recent historical moments through which the continuous reaffirmation and reworking of a certain kind of home has taken place in the country. These are rough periodizations; however, they might be helpful for the international reader to situate what I discuss in this chapter.

The first includes the birth of the nation-state (formally announced in 1861, then transformed roughly into its present state in 1870) and the time when the Fascist regime had its grip on the whole country (1922–43). Then, for around forty years after World War II, Italy was governed by the biggest Catholic party in Europe (and possibly the world), Democrazia Cristiana (Christian Democracy); interestingly, at the same time, its opposition party, the Italian Communist Party (PCI), was the biggest communist party in Europe. During these years, Italy was firmly within the grip of US geopolitical plans and maneuvers, which heavily influenced politics and everyday life, including the constitution of a paramilitary organization to combat the expansion of communist power in Italy and in Europe (Operation Gladio).[3] This is a time characterized first by the economic miracle and demographic boom (1950–60), then by increased social unrest during the 1970s—the so-called *anni di piombo* (years of lead)—led by extreme left-wing groups (notorious for killing police officers, entrepreneurs, and high-profile politicians) and neofascist organizations (who organized a failed coup d'état and carried out major terrorist attacks in public squares and train stations, as well as targeted assassinations). Toward the end of the century, the country entered a new phase, characterized by the decreasing significance of the Democrazia Cristiana and a major restructuring of national power, especially in the 1990s, which included terrorist attacks and killings perpetrated by the Sicilian Mafia across the country.[4] What emerges from this time is conventionally referred to as the Second Republic, and it is characterized by a mostly bipolar political system, in which Silvio Berlusconi was one of the key players both politically (being prime minister three times from 2001 to 2011) and culturally, due to his vast financial and media empire, and flamboyant public persona. In the aftermath of his political decline post-2008, Italy's political landscape has been characterized by technocratic governments imposed in the name of financial security and austerity, by the rise of the populist and antiestablishment Five Star Movement, and by the reaffirmation of far-right parties such as Lega Nord (Northern League) and Fratelli d'Italia (Brothers of Italy).

I did not choose Italy to ground my conversation on lessness because I aim to elevate this case as a sort of paradigmatic example above others. More modestly, I have chosen it for practicality and relevance. This is the country where I was born, but I have spent much of my adult life being an economic migrant outside of it. For family reasons, in 2021 I had to relocate back to Italy, and in going back, much to my dismay, I found a country lost in racist, neglectful, peripheral, and fearful understanding of the world. It is not that I deem the other (anglophone) countries I had lived in any better. However, in Italy, the violence of patriarchy, sexism, dogmatic and institutional Catholicism, rightwing predatory capitalism, ecological extractivism, historical ignorance, importing cultural models and references without understanding them, lack of care for the other, and, generally speaking, extremely low-quality intellectual debates combined with a white (masculine) self-referential attitude (particularly evident within academic circles) has struck me with quite some power. Whether for my understanding of the cultural references in place or for linguistic reasons, I found the Italy I had returned to, to be repressive, ignorant, and dangerous. The danger here is not toward me as a person but in the power that such a country has in terms of its economic and cultural standing, and in how it uses such power to make the lives of many expendable. This is evident against migrants and asylum seekers, the elderly, nonaligned citizens, and, by and large, against its women and nonbinary population. I refer later to how some of these troubles came particularly close to home for me, but even beyond my personal experience, Italy remains a very interesting case to explore the (un)makings of home(lessness). Next I provide some grounds to the housing question in the country, before expanding on the expulsive and extractive nature of its take on home.

Situating the Italian Housing Question

Data available tells us Italy's housing stock is for the most part owner occupied (around 70 percent), with some private rentals (14–18 percent) and a residual component of public housing (about 3.8 percent). The last figure is one of the lowest of the European Union, comparable to those of other southern European states such as Spain, Portugal, and Greece and only marginally better than some eastern European settings (where housing privatization was rampant in the postsocialist period), but considerably worse than comparable economies such as France (16 percent). There are historic, societal, and geopolitical reasons at play in the differences across housing structures in southern, western, and eastern Europe, some of which have been explained and narrated, reproducing semicolonial legacies and understandings of the world.[5] Without the need for too much detail, at a bare minimum it is clear, thanks to the numbers above, that Italians show a preference for homeownership as the cornerstone of their individual aspiration and national policies. Not unlike other Western countries, the ideology behind this is an evolutionary assemblage bringing together a traditional take on family and the household (to reproduce patriarchal power first and industrial labor second) and a contemporary evolution of housing markets (where the extraction of financialized value meets individual aspirations, to produce what García-Lamarca and Kaika have poignantly called "mortgaged lives").[6]

In this context, there are at least three intersecting processes forging the contemporary Italian housing context. The first is undoubtedly the financialization of housing, which here, as elsewhere, has become a major structuring force of markets and subjects. From the 1990s, the Italian state has willfully contributed to the opening of new opportunities for financial actors in the housing sector, most notably by easing access to home and consumer loans. In particular, as Filandri and Paulì have shown, the process was boosted in the early 2000s by the introduction of new legislative measures aimed at easing the creation of real estate investment funds, which grew from less than 50 in 2000 to more than 150 in 2015.[7] In 2020 only, according to the Italian Tax Agency, the total value of the home mortgages released in the country was 78 billion euros, equal to roughly 5 percent of the Italian GDP for that year.[8] The level of individual exposure has grown, too. If in 2013 someone taking out a mortgage was asking for 63 percent of the total value of the house, by 2018 that increased to 70 percent, while during COVID-19 the state pushed this further, introducing a measure allowing citizens to take mortgages up to 100 percent of the property value.[9] On top of this, in 2005 Italy also introduced the *prestiti vitalizi ipotecari*, better known in the anglophone world from which they originated as lifetime mortgages. Now, people over sixty can reverse mortgage their house in order to access immediate credit, risking, however, the loss of their property as a result of the reverse interest rate.[10] These new tools, in addition to an expanding remit of consumer credit options, make the average Italian household increasingly financially exposed to lenders and their predatory tactics.

Such a state-driven push toward the financialization of housing, and the related support offered to homeownership, has gone hand in hand with the second process: the explosion of the real estate sector and of its economic and symbolic power in the country. According to the work of sociologist Massimo Baldini, in the early 2000s, 8.3 percent of the total working population was occupied in the construction industry, which made up 13 percent of the total industry in the country.[11] If in the post-2008 years these numbers decreased, in recent times they have started to grow again, boosted by massive state investments in the sector, which now account for at least 4.5 percent of the total national GDP.[12] The importance of real estate industries in the country is reflected in the power they have at the level of major metropolitan areas, where a few families can dictate the fate of urban planning and are responsible for its unequal social consequences (it is worth recalling that the most powerful man in recent Italian history—Silvio Berlusconi—made his fortune as a real estate entrepreneur in Milan, before turning into a media mogul).[13] A recent example of the power held by the real estate sector in the country lies in the measures launched by the Italian government to boost the economy in 2020, the so-called Superbonus 110 Percent.[14] Wrapped in the thin veil of green economy, from 2021 to 2026 the state will invest a massive 31.77 billion euros in this plan in order to reimburse homeowners' expenses (through tax credits) to improve the energy efficiency of their houses (in certain cases, the state increases the reimbursement by 10 percent of the total costs incurred in the renovation work, hence 110 percent). Given the lack of any low-income threshold to access these measures, the scheme has benefited only middle- and upper-class dwellers, who are the only ones who can incur the expenses in the first place. This is not only going to exacerbate housing injustices but has shifted the power balance even more toward the housing markets and its entrepreneurs, who have increased their gatekeeping power, have been able to delay the completion of projects, and—according to some—have ultimately speculated on pricing.[15]

At the intersection of these state-led and privately executed housing plans, the increased pauperization of low-income dwellers shows up as the third process. As Baldini reports, "whereas in 1977, only 6 percent of households paid more than 30 percent in rent, [by 2010] that share has risen to a quarter of all renters (about 1.2 million households), and to nearly 40 percent for low-income renters."[16] Today, statistics show that 9.4 percent of Italians live in absolute poverty (growing from 7.7 percent in 2019) and that 43.1 percent of all poor families live in rentals (compared to around 18 percent of all families, as seen before).[17] Moreover, 27.4 percent of Italian families live in conditions of "severe housing distress" (defined as either lack of sanitary facilities, leaking roof, or excessively dark housing): a stark number compared with 7.4 percent for France, 7 percent in Germany, and 5.5 percent in Spain.[18] These conditions expose poor dwellers to more housing precarity due to low-quality dwellings, rent arrears, and financial exposure, while at the same time condemning them to live under continuous threats of eviction.[19] In 2018, before the partial suspension of displacements imposed in response to the COVID-19 emergency, in Italy, 56,140 eviction hearings took place, of which 49,290 were for arrears.[20] In other words, 90 percent of the evicted population cannot afford to pay their rent, often after already having incurred a number of intersecting debts in the form of small private loans and taxing financial schemes.

But if these pressing facts are pointing to a renewed centrality of the housing question in the peninsula, the history of progressive state reforms and wider mobilization around that same question is not new. It is worth recalling the most salient moments of the housing question, because they allow me to ground the discussion that follows. I rely here on the excellent publication of Italian thinker and trade union organizer Giancarlo Storto, who has written the most up-to-date and critical history of housing policy for Italy's capital, Rome. In his book, *La casa abbandonata*, Storto lays out a number of national laws and grassroots mobilizations that have considerably shaped Italy's contemporary housing history. These can be organized into three main groups by theme.

The first group consists of the foundation, and then morphing, of the state's public housing framework. The stepping stone was the creation of the Istituto Autonomo Case Popolari (IACP) in 1903, a national framework that allowed the creation of local institutes to build and manage public housing. The Fascist regime, through the Testo Unico sull'Edilizia Popolare Economica in 1938, expanded the construction of public housing and the operative framework of the IACP. To finance the construction of post–World War II public dwellings, the state launched the INA-CASA plan, which was arguably the biggest investment of its kind ever made in Italy, leading to the construction of more than 350,000 units by its end in 1963.[21] At that point, the scheme was replaced by a fund called GESCAL, with which houses were constructed directly with the investment of the workers that were going to be the beneficiaries.[22] In 1973, GESCAL was closed, and its remaining funds were transferred to the IACP, whose control was, in the meantime, decentralized from the state to the regions. According to Storto, at that point, the system ceased to work well, due to poor political and managerial ability, and following IACP's tendency—rampant in Europe in the 1980s—to sell its stock on the market.

The second thematic group includes a number of laws that have played a significant part in the recent history of the country in expanding housing rights for all. For the most part, these laws came after a time of very intense mobilization around housing, which saw its peak with the—now legendary—national housing strike of November 19, 1969, the biggest housing strike in Italy to date (a mobilization that started in Quarto Oggiaro, a big public housing estate neighborhood in northwestern Milan, and expanded throughout Italy, organized by trade unions and activists).[23] According to Storto, this is a time in which "the struggles for the right to housing are part of the more general process of civil awakening that shakes national society. The feminist movement, the student movement and the workers' movement intertwine and fight the battles for work, school, and women's rights, intersecting the issue of housing, raising the level of confrontation and opening a new season of unparalleled demands." Such an intersectional approach to the housing question brought to the fore the first rental strike in the country, leading to the 1969 mobilization and to the creation of new forms of organization, such as the Unione Inquilini (Tenants' Union). "In that year," Storto continues, "a completely new vision of the urban question and of social struggles emerged; theories began to be elaborated on the extension of the domination of capital over urban areas and the affirmation of an awareness of exploitation even outside the factories."[24]

As argued by Monica Quirico, housing in those years became the strategy through which groups like Lotta Continua (Continuous Fight) linked class and inhabitation struggles, in their case through strategies of occupation.[25] On the wave of this mobilization, the Italian state passed a number of fundamental laws, including the right to expropriate private lands to build public dwellings (865/1971); the Bucalossi Law (10/1977), which further strengthened the role of the state in the construction of private and public housing (dividing the right to own from the right to build); the so-called *legge sull'equo canone* (392/1978), which provided protections for tenants and factually established a rent cap based on the kind and state of dwelling; and Law 457/1978, or the Ten-Year Plan, which granted regions major powers and certain economic resources over ten years, to develop plans for public housing and (for the first time) granted specific resources for the requalification of the existing stock.

This level of meaningful public engagement in housing was never to be repeated. By the turn of the 1980s, we see the emergence of the last group of reforms, which consist of what another Italian scholar, Vezio De Lucia, called *controriforma* (counterreform). In introducing Storto's analysis, De Lucia argues that the counterreform of the 1980s is "a change of historical significance and planetary extension, determined in particular by the neoliberal philosophies of Margaret Thatcher and Ronald Reagan, which spread throughout Europe, and in Italy also contaminated the political culture of the left. In a short time, one by one, the achievements of the previous twenty years were cancelled, and as the years went by, they increasingly took on the connotations of a lost golden age. Bucalossi's urban reform, the rules on expropriations and those for the containment of rents fell, until the substantial dissolution of public housing."[26] At that point in time, the neoliberal and individualistic turn is consolidated, and public housing exits the scene. The state, at that point, focuses entirely on boosting families' access to private loans (the Amato credit reform in 1990), in deregulating access to financial markets, in dismantling the protection granted with previous interventions (the *equo canone* was scrapped in 1998), and in advancing a series of *condoni edilizi*, or building amnesty, which allowed one to obtain amnesty for construction carried out without a license or building permit (arguably encouraging an individual—and classist—fix for the lack of a universal housing framework).[27] The effective withdrawal from public investment in housing and rolling out of the new neoliberal framework have not been mitigated by state interventions to support tenants on the private market.[28]

These recent processes intersect other challenges in the Italian economy, which has arguably been stalling for many years (showing a negative or just above 1 percent GDP growth for the past two decades), as well as broader structural changes in the demographics of the country, which is simultaneously ageing (being one of oldest countries in the world) and becoming an incoming migrant destination (from 1.3 million legal migrants in 2001 to 5.3 million in 2019).[29] Yet, crucially for the home(lessness) approach I am taking in this book, there is more to these processes than the sociology of numbers can reveal. The housing question in the country is more than a problem of affordability, state disinvestment, and financialization, although these are, of course, very much part of the lessness tackled here. The question needs to be around how housing, in its wider assemblage, contributes to the maintenance of a specific political and affective economy of home—an economy founded not on the emancipatory potential of its liberation but on its being constantly faced with the possibility of its annihilation. Is there, in the history sketched above, a moment, beyond the time of collective organizing (see part III), where the homely plans of the state are allowed to break free from its racist, patriarchal, anthropocentric, and capitalist underpinnings? Is there a point in which the multifaceted liberatory potential of housing is allowed not only to challenge, but also to dismantle and design anew, the expulsive and extractive mechanisms allowing for violent homely grounds to exist and endure across time?

Focusing just on the political economy of housing and its history is limiting and problematic, because it ends up assuming that certain forms of mass provisioning and protections (such as the ones devised in Italy during the 1960s and '70s) are the ultimate horizon of what Madden and Marcuse have called the "housing question."[30] Most definitely, the baseline housing rights granted by the Bucalossi Law are incomparable, in their offering of material and ontological security, to the dismantling measures brought to the fore by the Amato or Berlusconi governments from the mid-1990s onward. And yet, what kind of inhabitation was (re)produced throughout all these reforms? Is there something uniting the Fascist call for public housing, the tenant protection law advanced by Catholic-communist alliances, and the efforts to push the many into a financialized form of existence? Or, to say it better, what kind of subjects are emerging from the inhabitation of these spaces? The question, here, becomes one of interrogating the use value of housing as emerging from the colonizing functioning of its becoming into the world (chapter 2). In asking such a question, one encompasses the entrapment of provisioning (either one is at home or not at home), to center housing as that nexus where the grounds of inhabitation are laid out for all, both housed and unhoused. If having a mortgaged home in a mortgaged house is exponentially better than living in a perennial move from state shelter to state shelter, the grounds making both lives less are matter of the same and must be investigated as such.

It is clear there are two stories to be told here in order to unpack home(lessness) in Italy, and they go hand in hand. The first is the story of how an era of housing struggles has lost its battle, and how the entire framework of reference has shifted—decree after decree—to the current market-driven scenario, one in which the state has explicitly withdrawn from universal provisioning. Many, including Storto in Italy, tell this history with much nuance and rigor. The second is the story I am going to tell. It's the story of the reproduction of the colonies of home in recent Italian history, through the expulsive and extractive logics sketched in part I of this book. I focus here on two ritornellos that are particularly important for the country: patriarchy and racial capitalism. In selecting these, beyond direct experience, I am following a suggestion brought to the fore by the late Umberto Eco, when he introduced and discussed the notion of "Ur-fascism" or "eternal fascism."[31] For Eco, the Italian Resistenza won the battle against the Fascist regime, but not against a much wider and deeper cultural fascism that, in his opinion, underpins the recent history of the country. For Eco, the Ur-fascism of contemporary Italy is defined by "a series of characteristics including machismo, cult of tradition, appeal to the frustrated middle classes, fear of difference, contempt for the weak."[32] These, to me, are forms of violence speaking the lexicon of patriarchy and racialized class/capitalist formations. I am now going to unpack them, staying close to their bordering works at the threshold of the Italian home.

Patriarchy, or: *La famiglia cristiana* (the Christian Family)

The patriarchal—and hetero, cisnormative—ritornello is constituent of the Italian way of life. It is ingrained in public discourse, in public space, in history, and in the way history is told. It is instantiated on the bodies of women, men, and those not identifying with either, as well as in the body of the economy, the law, and representative politics. To appreciate its role in the making of the average Italian home, one has to focus in particular on the intersection between the family, the state, and the church. This could well be the setting of an Italian B movie, featuring all of the above and a lover; or it could be Fellini's *La dolce vita*, with Marcello and Sylvia climbing up St. Peter's Dome watched by paparazzi, an angry fiancé, and a *carabiniere* passing by. In real life, things are a bit less glamorous, yet they remain equally sexist. The clearer manifestation of this—as highlighted time and time again by feminist thinkers—has to do with who bears the costs of reproductive labor. By creating the figure of a female subject responsible for care—through a process of creative expulsion rejecting everything else such a subject can be—a productive extraction of value takes place to sustain the household and, crucially, to sustain also a wider patriarchal ritornello cutting through it. The effects of this diagram of power are listed below: lack of civic rights, unjust economies, gendered killings and hate, the unchecked masculine and sexist political class, and so on. Contrary to what the media narrative proposes on a daily basis in Italy, this kind of lessness is not a manifestation of deviance. Rather, its structures run deeper and across discontinuous times and spaces to reaffirm their power in and beyond the homely.

This is, of course, a common feature of Western societies. As Nast clearly laid out: "The white-oedipal or nuclear family of industrial times, culturally specific and economically and politically conservative, was (and is) overdetermined, many social structures shoring it up and reaping meaning and benefit from it. Over the past three centuries, many social groups have been invested in sustaining its imaginary-symbolic form, especially those invested in colonial and industrial economies of desire."[33] In Italy the intersection of the family, the state, and the church is crucial in this sense, starting from the ways in which the last has always based its power in the first, with the state maneuvering in between. The family and the household are, in this context, the means through which the particular societal order of each time gets reproduced.[34] The three historic periodizations with which I began the chapter are situated in the longer unfolding of the Christian-Catholic roots of Italy, which is central to the definition of the patriarchal structuring of the main idea of the familiar and the homely. Without the pretension of exhaustiveness, I will recall the salient points of this structuring, showing how they have been reworked through the time periods I mentioned in the beginning to reach today's situation.

Families and their reproductive ability have been always at the center of Roman Catholicism, not only in a general pronatalist sense, but as one of the cornerstones through which God's love and power are believed to be reflected on the Earth. According to the current pope, Francis, "The ability of human couples to beget life is the path along which the history of salvation progresses. Seen this way, the couple's fruitful relationship becomes an image for understanding and describing the mystery of God himself, for in the Christian vision of the Trinity, God is contemplated as Father, Son and Spirit of love. The triune God is a communion of love, and the family is its living reflection."[35] Given its prominence as a locus for eternal love and secular power, it is perhaps surprising that the most significantly explicit intervention of the church on how to govern families is relatively recent. I am referring to the Concilio di Trento (Council of Trent) (1554–63), where the church enacted the so-called Counter-Reformation, in response to the Protestant Reformation, and where, in 1563, it defined the "widest and most important dogmatic definition" of the holiness of Catholic marriages.[36] As historians report, beyond the definition of the ceremonial dogmas that are, for the most part, still in place today, the Council of Trent defined the absolute indissolubility of sacramental marriage, meaning that—even when divorced, or even in case of adultery or death—the "holy trinity" of marriage was never to be separated.[37] Such a decision came to shape Catholic family structures for centuries to follow. This is true not only at the level of faith and religious dogmatism but also at the level of social control and economic power (influencing matters such as social status or heritage). At the center of this indissolubility, unsurprisingly, there is the man: the husband who has to provide for his family, while the woman is relegated to reproductive and care labor.

If the patriarchy was not invented in Trent, the structuring of the familiar abode along—indissoluble—patriarchal lines imposed the tempo at which all future family/church/state dances had to be performed. Even in changing societal and cultural conditions, the church always tried to maintain a strong grip on the family. For instance, in 1880, in response to the rise of modern industrial society and the spread of socialist ideas, Pope Leo XIII promulgated an encyclical in which he argued for the apparent parity of roles between man and woman in the Christian family. At the same time, he argued that women should not be participating in the workforce and should stay at home, complying with their traditional role of caring for the household's well-being and the education of their kids.[38] These directives were taught in compulsory religious classes at school, repeated in well-attended sermons at mass, and ingrained in the everyday fabric of hiring procedures in the emergent industries of the time. Their echo trickled down, in Italy, almost to our present day. It was very common for working-class families throughout the second half of the twentieth century to precisely reproduce this scheme, with men at work in the factory and mothers at home with their kids. The latter might have been working before their pregnancy but had to give up their jobs to tend to the household. Even in cases common in the late 1980s and the '90s—the home I grew up in is an example—where public preschool was a possibility, many lower-working-class households still played by the old rules, in a mix of inertia and reproduction of patriarchal power. In these contexts, monies were never enough, so, sooner or later, the women had to go back to work; however, having lost years of employment, they were often reduced to precarious, noninsured, and non-pension-accruing jobs on the black market (e.g., cleaners, elderly caregivers, and the like).

The expulsion of women from full ownership of their own lives and of the household has been the place of extraction of patriarchal power within the walls of the average Italian home and well beyond. This dynamic became even more evident at the turn of the twentieth century, with the birth of the Italian nation-state and the increased intervention of the latter in the family sphere. According to Italian family sociologist Chiara Saraceno, throughout the twentieth and into the twenty-first century, the family in Italy, "with its division of tasks and responsibilities along gender and generation lines, far from being ignored by the state, comes to constitute the explicit partner of the Italian welfare state."[39] The state invests the family with responsibilities at the educational level, but also at the level of care for the elderly, for mental health, and when it comes to dealing with matters of housing precarity (chapter 4), not by accident but through a clear design that pivots on the historical and cultural importance given to the family unit in the peninsula.

But the more the state intervenes in, and cares for, family structures—bringing those into its legislation, for instance, through the institution of civil marriage (1865)—the more that space brings the state into a potential conflict of power with the other big player in the triad, the church. The latter responds to these tensions in two ways: first, by reclaiming its role in defining how the parties involved in the marriage have to behave within the household and the relationship of the latter with the changing society (as seen with Pope Leo XIII); and second, by increasingly shifting its attention from the family as such to its biological domain. It is through the latter, as historian Emmanuel Betta states, that "Catholic morality has sought and found in biology the opportunity to recover an authoritative and influential public presence, building itself as an authority on the human and living, actively present in the confrontation with biomedical sciences and their practices."[40]

In the recent history of the country, the point at which the domains of biology and the family were most highly contested by the church and the state were surely during the rise, and then the affirmation, of the Fascist regime. On the one hand, you have a regime that is centered on its rural roots. Mussolini and the early Fascists are not urbanites, or fine intellectuals, but soldiers coming home from World War I, poor and destitute, returning to their rural lives in Emilia Romagna, where Il Duce was born. There—in a land heavily influenced by the church before Italian unification—the family is structured around strong patriarchal lines, infused with nationalist sentiments that were going to bear a major weight in the formation of the action squads that led to the march on Rome (1922).[41] When Mussolini gained power, one of his goals was to create the new "fascist man," dedicated to the country and to its imperialist goals. Thanks to his rural roots, and fascinated by the patriarchal intellectuals of his time (such as Ferdinando Loffredo), Mussolini makes the concept of family one of the cornerstones of this strategy.[42]

The regime invests heavily in the education of youngsters and their militarization through the formation of the Balilla groups and advances a pronatalist agenda to fulfill the expansive military goals of the nation. In his famous "Discorso dell'Ascensione" (Ascension Day speech, 1927), where he provides an overview of his ideas for the country, Mussolini is quick to criticize the liberal view of the family brought to the fore by "modernity," "homosexuality," and "Bolshevism," which are, in his opinion, undermining the "health" of the nation. He therefore limits the freedom of women outside of the family by restricting their roles as teachers in public schools (1926) and cutting their salaries in half by law (1927)—and then launches his *battaglia demografica* (demographic battle), introducing pervasive pronatalist propaganda, a tax on celibacy, grants for families with numerous kids, and a fight against contraceptive methods and abortion (which later, with the infamous Codice Rocco [Rocco Code] in 1930, became completely illegal).

Although Mussolini is essentially playing along the same lines as the Vatican, the latter is threatened by the increasing power of the state in its family affairs. The response is therefore to increase its already rigid approach and to expand, as said, its influence beyond the procedures, virtues, and meaning of Catholic marriages. Pope Pius XI took two decisive steps in this sense. First, he tried to reassert the importance of Christian education and morale with the encyclical "Divini illius magistri" (The divine teacher, 1929), in which he wanted, according to Betta, "to challenge Mussolini's claim to a monopoly on the education of young people, which . . . was manifested in a contrast of Catholic youth organizations, primarily Catholic Action."[43] But then, he went all-in with the strongly worded—and very influential—"Casti connubii" (Of chaste wedlock), one of his most famous encyclicals, promulgated in 1930. In it, he fiercely condemns abortion and birth control, and, crucially, he departed from Leo XIII by refuting the equality of the spouses and insisting on the submission of the wife to her husband. In the "Casti connubii," according to Betta, "Any hypothesis emancipating the role of women—in terms of property, work, administration—was rejected, with the affirmation of the need for the state to put 'every father of a family' in a position to provide for the support of his wife and children."[44]

It is through the expulsion and extraction exercised on the female body, through the familiar and the household, that the Fascist regime and the church found, after a moment of apparent tension, their common ground and their respective roles. The patriarchal home becomes both a means for religious salvation and a way to articulate the imperialist policy of the emergent Fascist state; through this assemblage, both are reaffirming their respective power, which is a reverberation of their shared violent patriarchal genealogy. To echo Nast, such a ritornello is put to work in schooling, propaganda, sermons, and state laws, producing long-term effects. For instance, the following is a short excerpt of the *decalogo* (a list of precepts), which every girl from eight to fourteen years old had to comply with, as part of their compulsory enrollment in the Piccole Italiane (Young Italian Girls) organization (note that the *decalogo* was often also reported in the books used in the teaching of Catholic religion in schools and church oratories at that time).

Little Italian, these are some precepts by which you must be inspired:
Do your duty as a daughter, sister, schoolgirl, friend, with kindness, joy, even if the duty is sometimes heavy.
To serve the Fatherland as the greatest Mother, the Mother of all good Italians.
To love Il Duce, who has made the Fatherland stronger and greater.
To joyfully obey one's superiors.

. . . .

Little Italian, this is the decalogue of your discipline:
Pray and work for peace, but prepare your heart for war.
Every disaster is mitigated by fortitude, work and charity.
The Fatherland is also served by sweeping one's home.
Civil discipline begins with family discipline.

. . . .

During the war, the discipline of the troops reflects the moral resistance of the families over which the woman presides.

. . . .

Il Duce has rebuilt the true Italian family: rich in children, sparing in needs, tenacious in fatigue, ardent in the fascist and Christian faith.
The Italian woman is mobilized by Il Duce to serve the homeland.[45]

Of course, many years have passed since the Fascist regime, but as Eco contended, a sort of Ur-fascism has been maintained throughout the second half of the twentieth century and into the next. Feminists had to work hard, alongside working-class-led struggles, to fight the normative entrapments of the Fascist era, and much work still needs to be done. Italy promulgated a law to legalize abortion only in 1978, but even today there is no year in which far-right and Catholic groups have not tried to undermine its validity. A law on divorce was passed in 1970, but it is still very costly and troublesome today to reach the final legal status of divorced, and many still make do with de facto separations, which offer fewer protections and rights. Only in 1975 did the state pass a comprehensive reform of the family, where for the first time in the history of the country it was stated that the man is not the *capo*, or chief, of the family unit. Yet it was only in 1981 that mitigating circumstances for honor killings were scrapped, and it was only in 1996 that rape was defined as a penal crime against the person (previously, it had only been considered a crime against individual freedom).[46] And yet, even with these important reforms, the cultural and societal patriarchal blueprint defining the mainstream Italian home are still in place.

The structural damage had been done. Violence against women and non-binary individuals is rampant in the country. For instance, in 2021 there were 114 *femminicidi* (killings of women), one every three days, mostly perpetrated within the household, by partners.[47] Moreover, following an analysis by the Italian National Institute of Statistics (ISTAT), by 2014, "31.5% of 16–70-year-old women . . . have suffered some form of physical or sexual violence in their lifetime; 20.2% . . . have suffered physical violence; 21% . . . sexual violence."[48] In this context, both the state and the church continue to express strong views on the sanctity of marriage and have supported very clear anti-LGBTQ+ propaganda (with former pope Benedict XVI saying that gay marriages will endanger the "future of humanity").[49] This is, ultimately, the context in which the sexist views and public demeanor of Berlusconi—and other politicians including the leader of the progressive Five Star Movement—have found space.[50] To unpack this a little further, we can look at one of the latest workings of the homely through the family/church/state assemblage in Italy.

A recent case of this long history is represented by Pope Francis's *Amoris laetitia* (The joy of love), a 2016 apostolic exhortation that came out after two Synods on the Family held in Rome in 2014 and 2015.[51] The exhortation is relevant because the pope, in a very clear and detailed fashion, condemns violence perpetrated against women in the domestic sphere, but also because of an apparently minor, yet controversial, footnote he added when discussing the topic of "Accompanying, Discerning and Integrating Weakness." The pope essentially argued that—although strictly forbidden by the church's canons—priests should consider offering the sacraments of Reconciliation (through the practice of confession) and Eucharist (by receiving consecrated hosts at mass) to people who live in "irregular situations," that is, divorced individuals who have civilly remarried.[52] This proposal was welcomed with suspicion by parts of the church and with open hostility by a number of bishops, overall creating much noise and scandal across the international Catholic community.[53] However, what is interesting about these two elements of *Amoris laetitia* is not their apparent absolute progressiveness, but their only relative importance. Vis-à-vis the historic role of women and divorced couples in the framework of the Council of Trent's defined holiness of the family union, one could rightly argue that Pope Francis's exhortation is moving. However, when reading between the lines, the move stays close to its home, and it reflects—and reverberates into—the wider sentiments of the country.

In the same text, Pope Francis is quick to reassert his hold on the important biological terrain that has been so central to the power of the church in the contemporary era. There are at least two important elements in this sense. The first relates to procreation and reaffirms a mantra very dear to the Catholic Church, that of welcoming large families and of being against any forms of contraception and abortion. The message is clearly focused on the Catholic family, but given the changes in who has control over whom in the contemporary era (as discussed above), the pope is also clearly pointing at the state: "the church strongly rejects the forced state intervention in favor of contraception, sterilization and even abortion. Such measures are unacceptable even in places with high birth rates, yet also in countries with disturbingly low birth rates we see politicians encouraging them."[54] The second important element concerns gender. It is worth quoting at length what the pope had to say on this topic:

> Another challenge is posed by the various forms of an ideology of gender that denies the difference and reciprocity in nature of a man and a woman and envisages a society without sexual differences, thereby eliminating *the anthropological basis of the family*. This ideology leads to *educational programs and legislative enactments* that promote a personal identity and emotional intimacy radically separated from the biological difference between male and female. Consequently, human identity becomes the choice of the individual, one which can also change over time. . . . It needs to be emphasized that biological sex and the sociocultural role of sex (gender) can be distinguished but not separated. . . . It is one thing to be understanding of *human weakness and the complexities of life*, and another to accept ideologies that attempt to sunder what are inseparable aspects of reality. Let us not fall into the sin of trying to replace the Creator. We are creatures, and not omnipotent. Creation is prior to us and must be received as a gift. At the same time, *we are called to protect our humanity, and this means, in the first place, accepting it and respecting it as it was created*.[55]

This is not the book to fully unpack what this series of very problematic statements means for the life of many around the world, who find themselves living in secular contexts deeply governed by these violent readings of what life (and its power to create) is and can be. But even in a (fairly) postsecular context such as Italy, these assertions do play a major role in structuring the possibility of some kinds of homes to exist and precluding the emergence of others. As is clear from the sentences I have emphasized, the Roman Catholic Church here is speaking directly to the state (educational programs and legislative enactments), telling it to be wary of touching upon the "anthropological basis of the family," which needs to be respected for how it was "created." These indictments speak directly to the politicians sitting in the Italian Parliament, who represent secular constituencies or who are more prosaically using (extracting from) the Catholic construction of the gendered other as a means for their political ends.

The consequence of these heteronormative tunes—played along the lines of *Amoris laetitia*—are deep and felt by many. Without considering the East for a moment, Italy is practically the only country in the whole of Europe that still refuses to allow same-sex marriages. Civil unions were allowed only in 2016, but the country is still lacking a framework for same-sex adoption.[56] This is in a context in which many other Catholic European countries, including southern nations such as Spain and Portugal, introduced similar legislation in the early 2000s. Recently, even a relatively minor, yet important, law decree to combat discriminatory practices and violence based on sex, gender identity, sexual orientation, and disability was rejected by the parliament and led to months of heated discussion across the country. The Zan decree, from the name of its proponent, was blocked in the higher chamber with 153 no votes (against 133 yes).[57] After the voting, a standing ovation, with senators clapping their hands and exchanging high fives, ensued.[58] It is clear that *Amoris laetitia* and the Zan decree are not the same, and they are not even explicitly referring to one another. And yet they are a matter of the same patriarchal, cis- and heteronormative ritornellos underpinning the formation of a very peculiar kind of home, and the power transversally working through it, in Italy.

In this sense, in the brief historic excursus just outlined, I do not mean to give to the church the role of mastermind behind the patriarchal and heteronormative underpinnings of the Italian home. Yet in a country where, for hundreds of years, the church was a major secular power; where Christian-devoted parties have been, and still are, major players in the national political arena; where much of its population self-defines as Catholic, and even people who do not identify themselves this way have received, in one form or another, a Catholic-infused education (like this writer); and where one of the most-watched TV series of the past two decades is a show called *Don Matteo*, featuring the adventures of a good-looking and crime-fighting priest—in this context, it is relevant to acknowledge the ways in which such an institution has rendered the family a de facto patriarchal and heteronormative space, substantiated by a state that has repeatedly channeled its power along similar lines.[59] The kind of familiar belonging emerging from the ongoing restructuring of the family/

church/state triad in Italy worked and continues to work, to quote Nast, "precisely because it has a lot of work to do, its cellular triadic structure emanating out from the family and home to embrace science, nation, and, in Christian contexts, God—the Father and the Son."[60] Such a patriarchal substratum, as we have already seen, goes hand in hand with nationalist and racial capitalist ritornellos, to which I now turn.

Racial Capitalism, or: *Italiani brava gente* (Italians, Good People)

The modern Italian nationalist project is one centered around expulsion and extraction. In a crude and simplistic way, it is about a population claiming a ground against another population, which is constructed, in its otherness, as the enemy through which the nationalist claim can stand.[61] Although not usually counted among the prominent imperial powers of the nineteenth and twentieth centuries—mostly because the Italian empire was a failure, even in military terms—the country has been nonetheless deeply shaped by processes of internal and external colonization. In what follows, I sketch how today's Italian home is indebted to the colonial sentiments structuring the birth of the nation and how the latter structures its racial capitalist grounds. In order to sketch these connections, I start by discussing how colonial and Fascist legacies are trickling down to today's management of the home/homeless boundary, focusing in particular around the diagram of citizenship. Then, I move onto two interlaced processes that I consider to be central in order to understand the racist ritornellos cutting through the contemporary Italian home: the maintenance of racialized economies and the EU and national governmentalities protecting the Italian (and European) home from the Black African other, and from the figure of the asylum seeker.

As I recalled earlier, the country was established, as a unified kingdom of Italy, in 1861; however, it had to wait until 1870 to include Rome and the extended Vatican possessions of that time. The process of unification saw the Savoy king and his government (based in Turin) foster the military operations of Garibaldi and his revolutionary army, who fought against the Bourbon kings (based in Naples) in the southern regions. The latter became a tensioned geographical space in the aftermath of the 1861 declaration. Groups of so-called *briganti* (bandits), defined as such by the Savoy rhetoric, started to enact forms of resistance and sabotage against the new ruling power. What ensued is traditionally taught in public schools across the peninsula as *brigantaggio* (brigandage)—a sum of indiscriminate terrorist acts perpetrated against the good plans and good doings of the unification process. Critical historiographers have, however, offered a different picture, which was already summed up by Antonio Gramsci in his mid-1920s writings on the "Southern Question": "The Northern bourgeoisie has subjugated the South of Italy and the Islands, and reduced them to exploitable colonies."[62] Gramsci is referring not only to the brutal killings perpetrated against the *briganti* and their families by the northern king's army but to a different interpretation of the unification process altogether. According to Gramsci, as reported by Conelli, "the southern masses were viewed by northern industrialists and southern landowners as being in 'a position analogous to that of colonial populations.'" Always, according to Conelli and other historiographers like Verdicchio, through unification, "as the West has done with the East, the [Italian] South is constructed as 'other,' under the banner of a historicist colonial discourse, in which the North and Europe embodied the ideas of progress and European civilization and the South the opposite, a matter of extreme backwardness and barbarism."[63]

The legacy of these northern views on the Italian south had stayed very strong until just a generation ago and have not yet been completely eradicated. Southerners are often referred to as *terroni*, which literally means "of the earth," which mocks their supposed peasant roots. In the booming industrial north of the 1950s, '60s, and '70s, it was very common to find signs that read "We do not rent to southerners," and an entire political party (the Northern League, who now refer to themselves simply as the League) made its first foray into politics by advocating for the division of the country along these racial lines. Needless to say, the industries of the north and the racist politics of the League have found their fortunes precisely by extracting value—economic and political—from the southern Italian other. But even if these dynamics, and the multiple value extractions attached to them, are key to the contemporary history of Italian society, the Southern Question is still today very rarely debated and studied as one of colonization. The question has for the most part been downgraded to a matter of eradicating corruption, fighting economic underdevelopment, and strategies to boost—also through EU funding—local growth and modernization. The matter has been reduced to disparities between the north and the south, precisely to avoid dealing with the racial foundation of the unification (and then industrialization) problem. To tackle those, one has to confront what Camilla Hawthorne has called "a potent repertoire of racist practices, imagery, and modes of socio-spatial organization" cutting through Italy's internal and external colonialism.[64]

It is not my intention in these pages to cover the extent of Italian settler-colonial violence in Albania, Dodecanese Aegean islands, Eritrea, Ethiopia,

Libya, and Somalia. Suffice it to say that the history of the Italian empire was one peppered with concentration camps, use of chemical weapons, mass killings, systemic rape, and deportation. This sits contrary to the (in)famous saying *Italiani brava gente*, translatable as "Italians, good people" or "the good Italian people." The saying was generated from, and repeated through, wartime propaganda, from fascism to contemporary wars such as that in Iraq, essentially arguing that Italian soldiers are among the most welcome in war contexts because of their supposed humanity and care. The myth has been busted by the careful and fundamental work of contemporary critical historians such as Angelo Del Boca,[65] who have painstakingly shown the systematic violence perpetrated in the making and running of the Italian empire. For instance, during the Fascist regime, and in particular during the so-called reconquering of the Cyrenaica in Libya (1928–32), Italians were among the first to use concentration camps as a strategic weapon for their imperialist ends.[66] According to Federico Cresti, in the Gebel campaign, "it is estimated that at least 80,000, but most probably more than 100,000 people (roughly half of the total population of Cyrenaica at the time in which the [Italian] conquering began) were deported into concentration camps" and also that "at least 50,000 Cyrenians died during this time."[67] The systematic use of chemical weapons, aerial bombardments, and the indiscriminate killing of civilians, as well as the disruption of local economies of agricultural and pastoral sustenance, contributed to the massive destitution of the Libyan (but also of the Somali, Eritrean, and Ethiopian) population in the years of Italian control.

One key aspect of the fascist colonial plans was related to the creation of a sense of national pride, based, according to Mussolini, on a renewed Italian influence on the international sphere, bringing the country to the same level as the big colonial powers of the time (above all, the enemies France and the UK). The creation and sustenance of this sentiment was very much crafted through the use of the home, and the colonial home in particular, to construe and affirm the new fascist man and his family. Italian settler colonizers were sold the dream of fertile new African lands where they could own their house and pasture, and where the regime was going to provide schooling for their kids and a beautiful kitchen for their wives. As simplistic as these dreams seem today, they were quite moving for the average Italian peasant classes, impoverished by World War I, without much hope for the future, and with a new international conflict rising on the horizon. Sold the dream of a prosperous future—and invested with the manly responsibility of making Italy a great nation—hundreds of thousands joined the settler-colonial enterprise during the fascist years, only to find themselves facing dreadful living conditions, constant warfare, and death. A crucial part of this process was not only the construction of a sense of attainable well-being but the constitution of shared affect around the ultimate rightfulness of the whole enterprise (references to the transcendental destiny guiding the creation of the fascist empire were common in Mussolini's propaganda).

To assemble this generalized affect, the colonized other had to be constructed as inferior, underdeveloped; in other words, not as human as the white Catholic bearer of fascist modernity. In this process, the fascist patriarchal home comes then to the fore with a strengthened double foundation. On the one hand, epistemically, there is the opportunity of making it stronger and prouder through the nationalist affect for the empire, while on the other, materially, there is the opportunity of expanding its space beyond the peninsula, through settler violence against the racialized African other. The constitution of such a shared racial affection is foundational to the renewed fascist family, and it is therefore inscribed into state propaganda, military training, and teaching of the young *balillas*. In school, the Black other is portrayed as the salvage ground upon which the new fascist home can rightfully stand, instantiating its civilizing mission, and being allowed to do so violently and with full determination. As Luciana Caminiti reports, "Whatever their social condition, through their school notebooks the pupils were guided . . . to enter the nation and to feel proud to be part of it. The message on identity was even more appealing because it did not stop at the territorial boundaries of the nation, but went conceptually beyond, placing Italy, represented as white, civilized and economically developed, within the area of the most advanced countries in Europe and with hegemonic presence in the Mediterranean."[68]

Racial diagrams for the creation of the new Italian were intersected with, and reinforced by, the aforementioned ritornello of patriarchy. Mussolini built on the works of one of his favorite intellectuals, Ferdinando Loffredo, a fascist Catholic sociologist and demographer, writer of the influential *Politica della famiglia* (Family politics) in 1938. In this book, Loffredo made the link between race and gender the cornerstone for the national and family identity question. As Poidimani recalls, "Loffredo provided the regime with an overall project of the family as a function of the 'homeland' and of 'race.'"[69] In Loffredo's own words (cited in Poidimani): "Female emancipation, as contrary to the interests of the family, is contrary to the interests of the race. Intellectualism, professional equality, sexual freedom, impudence, promiscuity, and sport masculinize women, and thus ridicule their aptitude to be a good ruler of domestic government and a mother of numerous and healthy children [which is key for the development of the race]. . . . The politics of race and politics of the family require woman to be woman only: prepared for the highest tasks to which her spirit and her body are called."[70] As much as the constitution of a Black other was crucial to the definition of the colonial home, the preservation of whiteness was equally important for the same end. These words did not remain mere intentions but trickled down into cultural beliefs and social behaviors, through the regime's constant interventions in the governance of Italian families and households. As Valeria Deplano recalls, following the "declaration of the Italian empire in May 1936, . . . new rules were introduced that sought to avoid any possible 'contamination of the race' by colonial subjects, and to maintain the 'body of the nation' intact. All marriage between Italians and Africans was prohibited, and from 1940 legal recognition of children with African mothers and Italian fathers was also banned."[71]

It is at the intersection of the patriarchal and racialized/colonial ritornello that the purity of the Italian nation, and of its families and households, became a matter of everyday exclusionary praxis. These logics were inscribed in Fascist laws, including those regulating citizenship that remained essentially the same from 1912 until 1992, when the new Italian citizenship law was introduced. Even after the demise of the Fascist regime, the state reaffirmed that legal belonging was possible only on the basis of *ius sanguinis*—by which citizenship is transmitted only from a parent, or ascendant, in possession of citizenship themselves—therefore providing for the continuation of the whitening principles inscribed by the racial colonial state to date. Following Deplano, "by maintaining the same inclusion and exclusion criteria devised in 1912, with all their racist undercurrents, the nascent Republic of Italy became a state that was still heavily imbued with colonialist culture."[72] In this sense, in the aftermath of World War II and throughout the second half of the twentieth century, "Italian authorities continued to maintain a very restrictive and inflexible concept of who could and could not be considered Italian, and who could or could not be granted full rights to live in the country: although it was never made explicit, both having black skin and generic cultural differences (as in the case of the Libyan Jews) were considered incompatible with Italian citizenship."[73] Crucially, the changes brought to the fore by the 1992 citizenship reform did not alter these logics but possibly reinforced them, this time in the light of rising levels of immigration into the country. According to Camilla Hawthorne, the new 1992 law "reinforced the principle of *ius sanguinis* from the original 1912 Italian citizenship law: it simultaneously became easier for Italians in diaspora who had never set foot in Italy to re-acquire citizenship, and more difficult for immigrants and their Italian-born children to naturalize."[74]

The changing demographic profile of the country is key to appreciating the violence of this racial logic in the definition of who can call themselves at home in Italy. According to contemporary historian Michele Colucci, the non-Italian population went from 356,159 in 1991 to 1,334,889 in 2001, respectively 0.6 percent and 2.3 percent of the total population.[75] There has been a visible change in Italian society, felt at all levels. For instance, in terms of schooling at the primary and secondary levels, the country has gone from 6,104 students without Italian citizenship in the school system in 1983–84 (when I was born) to 826,091 in 2016–17 (when my own child could attend school if I had one). The increase in the arrival of asylum seekers on southern Italian shores adds to these demographic changes, not only numerically but also in terms of providing a further layer for their racial codification. Despite being characterized by a discontinuous trend, the far right and the most conservative (even religious) element of Italian society had an easy time creating a discourse of fear around the *sbarchi* (landings) and connecting them to the ongoing changes in the demography of the country. According to Colucci, "The trend of arrivals by sea fluctuates from year to year: in 2012 they fall to 13,267, in 2013 they rise to 42,925, then increase again, becoming 170,100 in 2014 and 153,842 in 2015. They reach the highest peak in 2016, with 181,436 arrivals, while in 2017 they drop again to 119,247."[76] Grounded in its colonialist and racist lineage, and assembled through whitened ideas of how Italy should be inhabited, the state answer to asylum requests does not surprise: "38.8% of applications rejected in 2013, 39.2% in 2014, 58.4% in 2015, and 61.3% in 2016. Thus, the vast majority of asylum claims from 2015 are rejected." This contrasts, for instance, with trends in Germany where, always according to Colucci, "in 2016, 68.8% of the 765,455 applications received are accepted."[77]

The racialized link between land, law, and blood becomes the structure of today's Italian homes and a means to defend their definition of security vis-à-vis the wilderness of the other (chapter 2). This is a bordering process through which, as Camilla Hawthorne has argued, "African bodies are (re-)marked as iconic signifiers of illegitimate belonging, represented for instance in media images of packed fishing vessels entering the country clandestinely through southern maritime borders, and in tropes of itinerant street peddlers and prostitutes, suggesting that their very being in an Italian place threatens the moral purity of the nation state."[78] Crucially, it is not only that all Black others are banned but that their selective inclusion takes place through an act of expulsion: if they can accept the racial script, leaving out what is not needed, homely Italian belonging might be enjoyed. Hawthorne also adds, "the incorporation of Black migrants and their families as potential citizens is contingent upon the extent to which they can blend seamlessly into a mixed Italian populace, shedding their difference entirely or reworking it into something that can be considered a 'contribution' to the dominant national culture."[79] Such expulsion is of course productive. In contemporary Italy, it allows for at least three kinds of extraction: the possibility of reinforcing a particular, whitened, discourse around nationhood (never really challenged by the Italian parliamentary Left); the possibility of building entire political legitimization and forms of very real state power on the threshold of the affections—fear, but also national pride—germinating from expulsion; and the vast material political economy that has to do with both the ways in which the Black other is governed and the ways in which they are made useful for the national economy.

These forms of extraction are key to the maintenance of the home/homeless bordering, because even when they do not directly concern housing policy or houselessness, they come to define how inhabitation is (un)made possible and for whom in Italy. The workings of this racial capitalist machine are of course related to wider European diagrams, clearly illustrated in the works of Nicholas De Genova and Martina Tazzioli, among others, which include the deliberate expulsive, militarized, and criminal management of the EU borders operated by agencies such as Frontex; the curbing of migration flows via migrants stopping and/or relocating in third countries such as Libya or Turkey; the shifting governance of border regimes; but also through the operations of agencies working within humanitarian frameworks that, as Maurice Stierl recalls, are enabling Europe "to cloak its maritime militarisations with a politics of life."[80] Here, as Dadusc and Mudu have it, "humanitarian interventions produce paternalistic (patriarchal) hierarchies that are the result of long-lasting colonial power relationships and racist ideologies: protection comes with dependency and domination, and control [of] access to resources and services."[81] All these operations, even ones seemingly there to save and to protect the expelled other (chapter 4), are a means to maintain a continuity of structures and intentions rooted in the colonial legacies, and neocolonial affairs, of the European continent. Two exemplary diagrams of extraction are operationalized, in today's Italy, through these processes.

The first is related to the provision of cheap labor to serve the national culinary needs. A whole system of liminal, yet crucial, economies hinges on the production of subjects that are made not to belong formally, in order to be forced to work illegally. Here I am referring to the so-called *agromafia* business, which Omizzolo defines as "a complex and carefully organized structure of contemporary capitalism, which is intertwined with the productive, transformative and commercial modalities of Italian food."[82] At the core of this is the practice of *caporalato*, a form of illegal recruitment of workers very common in the production of vegetables, and in particular in the picking of tomatoes, in the southern regions of Italy. Originally started by Italians, it is not uncommon nowadays to find *caporali* who have graduated from their original position of enslaved subjects who themselves become bosses of newly arrived migrants and asylum seekers. According to the late investigative journalist Alessandro Leogrande, in the Apulia region during peak season, there are around fifteen thousand such illegal workers.[83] Salaries—when given—vary from twenty to thirty euros a day; however, payment is often related to how many boxes of tomatoes one can fill, not how long one has to work to do so (Omizzolo reports three or four euros for a 375-kilo box).[84] Water, food, and transportation are charged to the worker, who very often lives in abandoned factories, self-made shacks, and tents for the entire working season.

Through this, Italy can maintain its standing as the second biggest producer of tomatoes in the world, and the Italian home can enjoy its whitened—heteronormative—pasta, seasoned with cheap *pomodoro* sauce.[85] The *caporalato* system is a productive expulsive-extractive diagram of power working through a double elision, through which it gets to replicate its structural violence. As the critical sociologist Gennaro Avallone argued, on the one hand, there is the disappearance of labor—tomatoes are produced and arrive in the Italian home without signs of the traumatic becoming inscribed in them. On the other hand, there is the social disappearance of the migrant, who is unaccounted for—never seen or heard, and whose request to belong is systematically rejected by the state. Through this double process of expulsion, migrant workers are (re)produced "as alien, extraneous, absent subjects, although present: present for production, absent for everything else. . . . They are there because they are useful, but only for this reason. Presences defined exclusively by their social position as male and female workers, by their ability to provide labour power in the relations of production."[86]

The second diagram of extraction is related to the *sistema di accoglienza*, the asylum seekers reception system. The rules are complex and ever-changing, but their operations are pivotal in the history I just sketched. It can be safely argued that the system is not there to receive, welcome, and process asylum seekers—the numbers of accepted asylum requests, cited above, are indicative in this sense—but to keep in line those who can serve a purpose, through the constant threat of imprisonment and repatriation. Since I return to this in chapter 4, here I only recall the basic structure of the Italian *accoglienza*. There are essentially four levels to this. The first reception is done through a number of hotspots (four, all in the south) and nine centers scattered across the peninsula. Once asylum seekers arrive, usually by boat, on Italian shores, they land in the hotspots, and then they are moved to one of the centers, where personal data is collected and processed. At that point, a person who requests asylum is moved to the second reception level, now called, after many reforms, Sistema di Accoglienza e Integrazione (SAI, System of Reception and Integration). In these places, the asylum seeker receives medical, material, and linguistic assistance, as well as help to find jobs in local contexts, often through agreements in place with local businesses. This is probably the only element in the whole system that can, in certain cases, provide meaningful help to the asylum seeker, given the kind of support available. However, spots in the SAIs are extremely limited. The government has therefore allowed the flourishing of a third level, the Centri di Accoglienza Straordinaria (CAS, Centers for Exceptional Reception), which, if originally designed to be temporary, are de facto the main tool of reception in place today in Italy. A CAS can be anything from a proper center—with dormitories, facilities, and integration services—to small private apartments, or worse.

As Avallone reports, "in 2014, there were 68,927 people housed in the reception system, of which 51.5% were in the CAS. In 2017, they rose to 186,681, of which 81% were in the CAS."[87] The problem here lies in the fact that, while SAIs are exclusively run by nonprofit entities, CAS can also be run by for-profit ones. This has generated a whole economy profiting from the financial support the state offers for each asylum seeker in the reception system. A CAS can decide how much to actually invest in the support of their clients and how much instead is for the CAS owner's own benefit. Stories emerging from these places once again express the racial capitalist extractions founding the Italian relationship with its Black others. An activist group based in Naples, called Ex-OPG Je So' Pazzo, has been investigating the conditions and the services provided by CAS in the city. It is worth quoting them at length, since their experience gives a glimpse of the tragedy of these places:

> The opening of a shelter and its management are . . . left to private initiatives and, in our experience, without adequate controls on the starting conditions (e.g., type of housing, staff qualifications) or the management of the center. . . . Since the CAS are opened where there are favorable conditions for profitability, all these services are often provided inadequately or not at all, trying to obtain a profit margin as high as possible at the expense of the "guests" of the structures. . . . Many managing bodies do not have any experience in this sector (famous are the cases, in the Campania region, of companies producing small electrical appliances converted, from one day to another, into cooperatives in charge of migrants' reception) and, in the wake of the emergency, taking advantage

of this exceptional situation, many entrepreneurial groups (managed or not by criminal organizations) have taken the opportunity to do business on the skin of migrants.[88]

Finally, for those who do not request asylum, or for those to whom refugee status is denied, there are the Centri di Permanenza e Rimpatrio (CPR, Permanence and Repatriation Centers, once called Identification and Expulsion Centers). In these centers—which are essentially jails that the asylum seeker cannot leave—individuals are detained for a maximum of ninety days within which a judge needs to decide their fate. Either the asylum request, or any other favorable solution, is accepted, or the individual is expelled from the country. Currently there are nine CPR across Italy, with roughly a thousand available places. As I describe in chapter 4, these are highly contested institutions, where the logic of detention is operationalized to work as the ultimate bordering practice for the Italian home, a home that, given past and present colonial histories, is now characterized not only by its pasta, mortgages, baptisms, and marriages, but also by the figure of the hanged Black person in a CPR, or that of the asylum seeker, riding around in circles on a bike—the cheapest and only form of transportation available to them. In the countryside where I was born, you immediately spot them because no one uses bikes there. In the flatlands of Puglia, you recognize them because they are the only ones around when the sun is right above your head. From north to south, no one knows their names. They have been refused citizenship, refused ground, defined as unwelcome, and yet kept close by, to feed and to justify homes where they will never belong but that need them to stand on their rotten foundations.

From Home to Homelessness

In this chapter, I have provided a sketch of the patriarchal and racial capitalist ritornellos making up the mainstream Italian home. Surely, one might say, not every Italian home is reproducing these operations. There are indeed many grassroots stances against them, as I have recalled in the history of the fight for housing justice in the country, and as I also recall in the following chapters and in part III. Yet a genealogy of home-related violence is structurally present, and it still gets reproduced in everyday practices, from advertising to national laws, from jokes to progressive discourse. This is particularly evident in the attitudes of the national Left—represented, in parliament, mostly by the Partito Democratico (Democratic Party)—and by its strong roots in the Catholic underbelly of the country. When tackling some of the big questions I've touched upon in this chapter around gender, racism, migration, and class, the paradigms of this Catholic-infused Left are, at best, those of compassion, inclusion, diversity, and calls to never fully specified and historicized human rights.

These, however, do not challenge the violent underlying structures of the country. Ida Danewid, in discussing the humanitarian frameworks of salvatory interventions in the Black Mediterranean, has said it right: "these discourses contribute to an ideological formation that disconnects connected histories and turns questions of responsibility, guilt, restitution, repentance, and structural reform into matters of empathy, generosity, and hospitality. The result is a colonial and patronising fantasy of the white man's burden based on the desire to protect and offer political resistance for endangered others, which ultimately does little to challenge established interpretations that see Europe as the bastion of democracy, liberty, and universal rights."[89] As much as these statements are valid for the migrant other, they are also true for the homeless one: both defined as the alterity of home to be protected; both structurally important to its cultural, political, and societal standing.

In this context, it is of little importance to define Italy as better or worse than other places on planet Earth. What matters, to me, is to show how the foundation of its home are diagrammed not around emancipatory and liberatory functionings but around foundationally unjust ones. On this basis, I ask, how can this home pretend to save its other? Why should the subject that is made to experience expulsion, in order to become a manageable value asset of the homely through extraction, be brought back home? The question is to transcend a separate reading of what is in and what is left out, and in showing what the constitution of these borderings entails. Certainly, there is material destitution at play—losing shelter, being continuously displaced, living in continuous precarious housing conditions, all with their traumatic psychological and emotional effects. But at the same time, there is the production of a persona that is rendered—bureaucratically, culturally, discursively—only through the prism of what it lacks, of its apparent being -*less*. The problem, here, is not just with the creation of such a subject—the poor, the asylum seeker, the homeless—but with what it is made to do. The latter carries an epistemic power, directly linked to the materiality underpinning it, which is proportionate to the power of those working with it.

What they do with it is the crux of the home/homelessness issue. On the one hand, the charitable and state institutions working with the *subjects made less* could disrupt the continuity between the home that has expelled them and the one that is supposed to take them back. That would mean directly tackling the ritornellos structuring home. It would mean, in the restoration of housing, to challenge the expulsive and extractive logics of patriarchy, national-ism, and racial capitalism—to cite just the processes unpacked in this chapter. Or, on the other hand, they could align with those same logics, reproducing their underlying violent processes and ultimately restoring the subject to the same violated home that originated the traumatic becoming in the first place. In the next two chapters, I want to illustrate how the latter option is de facto the mainstream modus operandi of interventions aimed at saving the so-defined homeless both in Italy and well beyond.

4

A LOCAL VIOLENCE

I still remember quite vividly the day my parents brought me to a train station to meet one of our relatives for what seemed to be, at least in my memory, the first time. I had to be five or six years old. I remember I did not understand why they were bringing me, all of a sudden, to meet a relative I had no recollection of. They were telling me that he had left his home when he was quite young and had been "traveling" since then. At the time I really had no idea what they meant by that. They only told me that he had "fought," *litigato*, with his dad (another man I had no real recollection of), and because of that fight, he left the house and never came back to it. That day at the station, I met a man carrying a rucksack and smiling at me; he seemed fun, and that satisfied my curiosity. A few years later, I understood that one of my parents, too, had to leave their household as early as possible, and that getting married at a very young age was the way of getting out. Throughout the years, more and more details of these stories came to the fore. Suffice to say here that for both my parent and relative, their home was a traumatic space, so much so that it pushed one to marry at a young age and the other to move from city to city, from station to station, for many years of his young adult life. That was, right at the core of my family history, the first encounter I had, as a young kid, with notions of home and homelessness. When, later in life, I began to look systematically into what makes people homeless, I started to encounter many similar stories, where violent households intersected with gambling, debt, or substance dependency, but also with migrant aspirations, work exploitation, economic destitution, financialized debt, and stubborn and unjust state bureaucracies, as well as blatant racism and other forms of systemic injustice.

The very different stories I have been encountering have something in common. It is because of violent processes crafted at home that one seemingly becomes its other—the homeless, the foreign, the one to be jailed and cared for. One might say that the processes pushing people in precarious housing and living conditions are matters of larger structural inequalities, reaching far beyond what we usually define as home. But this implies an unhelpful topographic understanding of life spaces and histories. Where is the boundary between a gendered society and a gendered household? Where is the threshold between an unjust mode of production and consumption, and the abode of the homely? How to draw a line between the becoming homeless of a queer individual, and their heteronormative household, sitting within a heteronormative society? How to distinguish between the processes racializing the foreigner, and their racialized experiences of securing shelter for the night? Compartmentalizing these experiences is about maintaining a sanitized, fictional idea of the homely, instead of embracing a transversal reading of inhabitation or dwelling (chapter 6).

Going with the latter means to acknowledge that, even when violence does not enter the household, the homely is not separated from the dispossessive diagrams structuring society, but matter of the same. The colonies of home are built on functionings not different from those found beyond its doorstep. As I have argued already in the previous chapters, this makes for a home defined by the potential for its impossibility. It makes for a home that brews within itself—in the reproduction of those functionings—the possibility for its own negation. And so it is in there that the potential for the creation of its other subject, the homeless, emerges too. Isn't it, after all, through the workings of the homely—both those going on within and those going on at the level of a society that needs to maintain a certain ideology of home (chapter 3)—that one of my parents, one of my close relatives, and the innumerable homeless of our times are created as subjects of expulsion and extraction? To explore this question means to investigate how the violent workings of home are made to work in homelessness management and praxis. For coherence of exposure and context, once again I stay close to Italian geography, specifically referring to ethnographic work that I have undertaken in Turin (this chapter). I will then expand on that, tracing how the connection between home and homelessness is maintained translocally too, at the level of cultural discourse and policy across place (chapter 5).

My analysis here is inspired by the illuminating critique of poverty management that has been carried to the fore by a number of scholars in the past decades. I am indebted to the work of Didier Fassin on humanitarian rationale; Nicholas De Genova on the conflicting biopolitics of the "autonomy of migration" at the EU borders; and Ananya Roy in unpacking the material interests and discursive truth founding the management of the urban poor, to name just a few.[1] The focus of the approach I am taking is twofold. First, it is to question how homelessness experts and their institutional settings are part—as Roy and her colleagues argue—"of the systems and processes that produce and reproduce poverty."[2] These systems work as bordering devices (chapter 1) or diagrams that, as Mudu and Dadusc put it, "discipline, de-politicise and commodify the lives and subjectivities of those who allegedly receive their care."[3] The problem here is not that the device does not understand the other, or that it does not share its suffering. The problem is around how the device works as a colonizing tool against the politics of life of its subjects. Unpacking such a working requires situating it in time and space. In Italy, this means to go back to the family/state/church triad that I discussed in chapter 3 and ask: In which ways are blueprints for actions and interventions on homelessness linked to the underlying foundations of those systems and processes? What are, to borrow from Sharma, the "stretched temporalities" cutting across these biopolitical formations?[4] Since, in the framework of this book, I place particular attention on the embodiment of housing precarity—its capacity to signal how lack is constructed, but also to point beyond it (chapter 6)—I seek a possible answer to this question in experiences of being managed and in their unfolding.

Such a method of enquiry requires one to stay, going back to Haraway, with the troubles of the embodied experience of housing precarity.[5] These troubles are a multiplicitous assemblage: partly expression of the effects of management—in the sense of being, again taking from Roy and her colleagues, "enlisted in the discourses and practices of development"—partly emergent from the foundations of home, but partly also crafting very localized and often unannounced counterresponses that do challenge the lessness they are made to inhabit.[6] And so my second focus here is to depart from the first, to prevent this text from becoming a specific analysis of service provisioning for the homeless in Turin (which I have noted elsewhere), or for chapter 5 to offer detailed global genealogies of homeless/poverty management (which others have done better than I). In the context of this book, staying close to the embodied experience of housing precarity means to show how the latter is connected—forming a whole political and affective economy—to home. The ethnographic methodology is therefore about using the experiential—and, taking from Stewart's *Ordinary Affects*, its affective registers—to get direct access to underlying structurations, linking homelessness management to the unjust doings of the homely.

Loving the Poor

At the risk of simplifying, one could say that, in Italy, the spectrum of initiatives for the homeless comprises charitable, managerial, and family-communitarian interventions underpinned by their own specific histories of racial dispossession and connivance with capitalist formations. At large, these are approaches common throughout the Western world.[7] In the charitable vein, faith-based models vary according to the geography and the religious tradition of reference, from community-based evangelical takes popular in the United States to the ones brought forward by faith-based NGOs underpinned by a logic of social interventionism in the UK, the institutionalized Roman Catholic approaches common in southern Europe, or the extensive role of charitable-oriented actions in the Islamic tradition in many parts of the world. As noted by scholars that have been writing about the so-called postsecular turn in Western cities, there is much to unite and to divide these faith-based approaches: goals and methodologies are often different, from more patronizing and disempowering takes to more progressive ones.[8] Still, most charitable or faith-based interventions in the broader Christian tradition—which is the category Italy falls into—have something in common. They pivot around the notions of agape and caritas emphasizing, respectively, a fraternal compassion toward the plight of the poor and its instrumentalization through concrete practices of care (indeed, in the Christian tradition agape typifies a supposedly unconditional love for the other, which then fuels love-oriented acts of caritas, or charity).[9] The services provided under this umbrella for the most part fall into the low-intensity or low-threshold category; that is, they are designed to provide basic support without complex entry requirements. These traditionally include the distribution of food packages, soup kitchens, night shelters and day hubs, although charitable institutes also operate more complex programs intersecting housing, recovery from substance abuse, and job reintegration. In contexts where a weak role of the state in social provision has been traditionally compensated by the organizational and economic power of churches, such as Italy, faith-based organizations play a considerable role in homeless service provision.

The role played by state agencies could be broadly defined as managerial, essentially because in this context homelessness is seen as an issue to be tackled, contained, addressed, removed, or solved—according to the social welfare and political tradition of the given context. The variety of approaches is considerable. Just within Europe, the ways in which welfare is structured varies wildly across the north, south, and east, with considerable difference within these blocks, too. The quality and quantity of services—from low threshold to social housing—is unavoidably affected by the investments, both economic and cultural, that each system of welfare, in any given territory, provides. This can vary within the same country, according to how power is distributed and who manages that power and related forms of conditionality, and often comprises services that are paid for with public money while being delivered (and often designed) by private entities, such as NGOs, with their own politics and agendas.[10] Moreover, access to those services is granted by, or includes, a direct relationship of the beneficiary with social workers, who are a key part of the public infrastructure around homelessness and can make a huge difference in how services are run and experienced by their clients.

Bearing in mind this complexity, state interventions in homeless provision follow defined orientations, at least in the West. The European Observatory on Homelessness (EOH) has identified four, according to their focus on housing and intensity of support.[11] In the first group, there are mostly emergency services, offering a low level of support and no real housing option: basic assistance is provided, interweaving with the interventions from faith-based and other private organizations. A common emergency provision is related to seasonal public shelters or to the establishment and management of special camps to provide for various populations that, at a given time, are rising to the forefront of public concern (as with the so-called migration crisis or the treatment of houseless individuals during the COVID-19 pandemic). A second group consists of medicalized interventions, where the focus is on the treatment of health problems and addictions of various kinds, without providing long-term housing. A common case is that of detox programs, which provide residential opportunity (if any) only for the duration of the intervention. Third, there are programs with a lower intensity of support, providing, however, rapid rehousing or interventions to preserve shelter. These are commonly defined, at least in Europe, as housing-led interventions: from shelters and temporary/transient accommodations (often shared with other individuals in the same program) to then more stable, individualized, housing solutions. Last, there are programs that match a high intensity of support with the provision of long-term ordinary housing. The most recent and recognizable example in this sense is the so-called Housing First approach, to which I return later. The ideal types of these programs unconditionally provide housing, with very few entry requirements, and sustain the individual by meeting their needs through comprehensive forms of case management.

Beyond these four kinds of public intervention, it is important to stress something that the EOH's model does not take fully into consideration. The ways in which the public interventions listed above are operationalized vary according to the political agenda of the given institutions. These interventions are underpinned by motivations spanning from socialist humanitarianism to policing, wildly varying across jurisdictions and geographies. At a bare minimum, each is characterized by forms of social control that are more or less explicit and evident.[12] In some cases, low-intensity services are used to control populations that are perceived as posing a threat to public safety. In others, they become agents of border control, being used as a way to track and denounce *sans papiers* (people without documents) accessing them. Moreover, public institutions can adopt apparently contradicting policies, offering, on the one hand, social programs and services to tackle homelessness while, on the other, using extreme violence and displacement as a means to advance urban neoliberal agendas and the related socioeconomic restructuring. The incredibly long list of incidents of revanchist policing operated by city administrations on both sides of the Atlantic ought not to be seen as something detached from the provision of services to those populations. This is a false distinction that has been reinforced by mainstream academic literature, which has tended to split between a focus either on service/policy or on revanchism/harassment. In reality, violent revanchism can sit alongside more humanitarian interventions in various ways, either by instrumentalizing them or by simply tolerating their presence as a helpful cushion that prevents social tension from escalating.[13] One can be scheming with the other, despite their apparent mutual disconnection.

Finally, a last group of interventions oriented at tackling homelessness sits at a level that is not often seen as one entrusted with interventions, programs, or policies: the family and the community. In many geographical and cultural contexts, as is the case in Italy, families and communities sit in between charitable and managerial responses, being invested with considerable expectations, at the societal level, to prevent, respond, and manage their members' homelessness or potential homelessness. Recalling their role here is about highlighting that, as much as the debate goes on around the best policy to be adopted from above, it is often in noninstitutional settings that maneuvering is used to respond to the challenges of home. Squatting, rallying, occupying, and articulating a single voice by means of collective organizing is only one of the ways through which communities of interest are managing homelessness (or its threat). Beyond these grassroots organized responses, there is a plane of intimate gestures and practices that often go unnoticed, captured neither by the rubric of resistance nor by the realm of policy or humanitarianism. For instance, what my parents did with that relative of ours, bringing him into our home, falls into this nuanced category. It goes without saying that, as for the charitable and managerial groupings, the family and communitarian response to homelessness can also be more or less reactionary, or more or less radical. The ways in which both family and community are assembled determine their departure from—or their adherence to—the lessness founding home.

The distinction between charitable, policy-managerial, and family-communitarian responses to homelessness is rather crude: these different modalities of intervention are often overlapping and nonexclusive, in more or less coherent or contrasting ways. Nonetheless, despite differences and possible nuances, most of these responses to homelessness have something in common: they never target other than the subject—individual or collective—they have defined as being in need. There is no attempt at going beyond that, because that would require asking deeper questions around the logics of a home that continuously, no matter how hard one tries to bring subjects back to it, breaks apart. In the following accounts, I show how, through mundane service provisioning, the services I have investigated in Turin follow this path, ending up not only aligning themselves to but factually reproducing the functions of expulsion and extraction underpinning home(lessness).

The accounts are for the most part taken from fieldwork I undertook in 2009 through 2012, with constant desk-based work I carried out in the following years to keep me up to date with the changes in the city's service provisioning. The latest narrative is instead very recent and comes from emerging investigations I am undertaking on service provision to migrants and asylum seekers. Despite dating back over ten years, these ethnographic explorations are still very relevant. First, even if some changes have taken place, the city system of help for its homeless has not radically altered, while the one provided by faith-based organizations (FBOs) has practically stayed the same.[14] In her excellent, more recent work on the homelessness industry in Turin, Daniela Leonardi reports many of the same approaches I have found. The system is still built around a staircase model, by which individuals are asked to approach the municipality office dealing with homelessness cases—the Servizio Adulti in Difficoltà (SAD)—and to use the city's homeless shelters before they are allowed to step up to more individualized (still temporary) housing solutions.[15] What's more, the public discourse around homelessness has not changed, and there is increased pressure on the services by the incoming influxes of migrants and asylum seekers. The poor, in Turin and elsewhere in the country, are marginalized, patronized, and racialized, and their management has increasingly become more normative and diagrammatic.

In what follows, I focus on two of the modalities of service provisioning specified above: first, on faith-based interventions, which speaks directly to the importance of the church in the triad structuring home illustrated in chapter 3; second, on the state, with a double focus on urban homeless management and on asylum seekers. As I've said, the context for these stories is Turin, the capital of Piedmont, a city home to some one million inhabitants. In the past, Turin was the capital of the Savoy region, then became the quintessential example of an industrial Italian city (Fiat was based here), and last it jumped on the bandwagon of cultural tourism with the 2006 Winter Olympics. Importantly, Turin is commonly considered the city of the "Social Saints" because of the high number of Catholic figures who have established institutions and initiatives to tackle poverty here, a tradition that started during the early modern era.[16] When we add the fact that Italy does not provide a clear and well-defined national strategy on homelessness, the space that FBOs occupy assumes full prominence. Most of my work in this sense was focused on two major institutions: the Small House of the Divine Providence, Cottolengo and the Company of the Daughters of Charity of Saint Vincent de Paul. Since I've expanded on my observations related to these two organizations elsewhere, here I mostly focus on a paradigmatic episode that occurred during my work with a third FBO, run by the Church of Saint Anthony of Padua, colloquially called Sant'Antonio by many of my homeless friends.[17] On the public institution side, I will instead give accounts related to some low-threshold services and bureaucratic entanglements provided by the city through its SAD office, as well as offering a first peek into the violent workings of Turin's center for repatriation (CPR), part of the broader national system of asylum management discussed in chapter 3.

Buttered Hands

The Church of Saint Anthony provided a number of low-intensity services, including a daily soup kitchen and a food bank. Both are among the most common services delivered by FBOs in Turin and more widely in Italy. The food bank allowed individuals in possession of a specific card to collect several items twice a month, including canned food, pasta, sugar, rice, and hygiene products. The church gave out these cards after a series of private consultations that explored the applicant's financial and family situation to assess their level of need. The whole process was framed around the notion of *la carità è benevola* (charity is benevolent), with visual and semantic references to caritas (charity) and *amore per il povero* (love for the poor) occurring frequently in the church's promotional material, volunteer speeches, and visual representations around the place (figure 4.1).

The room where the goods were given away was large, filled with rows of empty tables, each of which could accommodate six to eight people when the soup kitchen service was in full flow. At the far end of this space, a series of

FIG. 4.1. *La Carità: Or, How I Stopped Worrying and Learned to Love the Poor.* Photo by author.

FIG. 4.2. *Il burro per il povero* (Butter for the poor). Photo by author.

tables were positioned in a horseshoe shape, facing the main entrance. On each was a pile of boxes, containing the provisions to be given *ai poveri*, to the poor. That morning I was placed behind one of these tables and instructed to distribute butter, one pack per person. I positioned myself behind this improvised desk, the doors were opened, and the distribution immediately commenced, very quietly, very politely. Individuals approached with their bags and empty boxes and filled them with one product from each table. Volunteers extended their arms with a benevolent expression, the goods exchanged hands, and the recipients murmured a muffled *grazie* (thank you). Both volunteers and recipients kept their eyes down, avoiding direct contact with others. I imitated: handing out a pack of butter, smiling benevolently, and then handing out another (figure 4.2).

Then a middle-aged woman carrying two bags came up to my table and asked a very simple question: "Don't you have any other butter?"

The question surprised me. No one had asked anything like this before, to me or to other volunteers. I looked around, then at the box with the butter in it, and then again at the woman awaiting a response. Confused, I muttered, "No, I'm sorry. . . . That's all I have."

We remained there, suspended in the buttery atmosphere, just for a moment. A split second of immobility. I wanted to follow up by asking why she had asked that question, but she anticipated me: "I don't want this one. This one is expired."

I was puzzled. This was not something I was expecting. No one had told me the butter had expired. How could she possibly assume it was? I looked at the packages.

She looked at them, too.

Then our eyes met properly for the first time in the whole interaction. I was still confused. I did not know what to say. I had no idea if she was right or not, and I didn't have any other butter to distribute. And so, without knowing how to inhabit the tensioned politics emerging from our interaction (chapter 6), I took refuge in the safest reply at hand: "Do you still want one?"

She lowered her eyes from mine to the box on top of the desk. Again, a pause of a split second, enough for the crack and its opening to slowly close under the butter-love diagram.

"Yes. Give me one."

My benevolent expression, hand reaching in the box, right palm down, providing food; her left palm up, receiving caritas.

"Grazie."

"Prego."

I watched her walk away, while another client came toward me with his bag, "mirroring my heart": wide open.

A closer look at the packages that I was distributing revealed that the woman was right about the butter. Every single package had part of the wrapping foil removed, as you can see in figure 4.2. These scratches occurred where the expiration date had been printed, a date that had been removed because all of the butter was indeed past its "best before" date. Surprised by this realization, I surreptitiously took out my camera and snapped the photo in figure 4.2. I then walked up to the person who was coordinating the service and asked her why we were distributing expired butter. She replied that this was the norm, and that the butter was still perfectly safe to eat. I asked what I should do if someone asked whether other butter was available, to which she simply replied, "If they don't want it, then they won't take it."

The woman who came toward me and pointed at the butter represents the unnamed poor person of the Good Samaritan's parable, at least according to how the Roman Catholic Church (RCC) usually frames it.[18] In this charitable diagram, we can love and help her without inquiring about her personally: as a volunteer, I did not need to know anything about her to perform my assigned duty. Walking toward me, she was supposed to be a given quantity, a representative of the poor. And by standing there, in that FBO I was a given quantity, too: a stranger who is there to help my neighbor. Though there is undoubtedly more to the complex and nuanced theology of love fueling Christian charity, this encounter provides a clear example of the kind of mercy and compassion that is foundational for many FBOs working in the broader Christian tradition. Pope Benedict XVI was keen to remark on this in his first encyclical, in which he signaled a direction for the whole Roman Catholic Church. His 2005 paper was titled *Deus caritas est* (God is caritas), and it clearly signposts how caritas and agape are to be understood and practiced: "Following the example given in the parable of the Good Samaritan, Christian charity is first of all the simple response to immediate needs and specific situations: feeding the hungry, clothing the naked, caring for and healing the sick, visiting those in prison, etc. The Church's charitable organizations . . . ought to do everything in their power to provide the resources and above all the personnel needed for this work."[19]

The "hungry," the "naked," the "poor" woman coming toward me in Saint Anthony's church, is a given quantity in the diagram of Christian love. But this diagram is a reduction, and the woman I encountered is more than just a representative of the poor. Her becoming, like ours, is an articulation of matter that exceeds any attempt to categorize it in time and space. Her being poor (in that slice of time-space, in that context) is a biopolitical construction—that is, a way of molding her as a regularized, manageable, other.[20] She is assembled as such, in the affective entanglement with the church, in the counseling service where she got her card, in the performativity of her walking into that room, and in her relationships with me as a volunteer.[21] In other words, she was made as a particular breed of poor (the beaten, voiceless recipient of caritas) in the moment she entered Saint Anthony of Padua's food bank scheme.

Similar kinds of expulsive subjectification were common in all the FBOs I have spent time in. Take, for instance, the very common practice of counseling. In some cases—such as in the Saint Vincent de Paul organization I mentioned earlier, colloquially called Vincenziani institute—counseling sessions were done by lay volunteers without any specific qualifications. The role of the counselor was simply to provide a basic service: the approach was to listen to the homeless person for a few minutes and then give alms as a form of first aid. More interesting was the case of Cottolengo. Here the counseling, managed by a professional social worker, took place on two levels. First, an interview was necessary to obtain a renewable card that would allow the individual to access Cottolengo's basic services (such as their soup kitchen—the biggest in Turin, providing up to five hundred meals every day—and the distribution of clothes). Marco, a young man who started living rough just a few months before I met him, offered me an account that I had heard many times:

ME: What did they ask you?

MARCO: Well, you know. Usual stuff.

ME: What?

MARCO: Where I was coming from, how long I had been here . . . you know, these kinds of things.

ME: And what did you say to them?

MARCO: That I want the card for the soup kitchen!

ME: And did they give that to you?

MARCO: Not then. I've to go again, tomorrow. . . . Fuck them! I'm not going to tell them all my business. They can keep their card. I don't need that. I'm going to find food anyway.[22]

The counseling also included other services, such as specific consultations and financial help, which entailed consecutive in-depth interviews. According to the social worker running the counseling: "In 2009, I did 295 interviews. Of them, five individuals have decided to be helped by the Cottolengo and get on board with us." Asked how a person might "get on board" in this way, she answered, "They start to be monitored by us when there is interest on both sides."[23] Homeless people often complained about the kind of questions that they needed to answer in order to gain access to these personalized services. As Carlo, a middle-aged man living rough at the same time I met Marco, put it, "I can't understand them. They know everything about me. They know that nothing has changed. You can tell this! But they continue to ask me the same things. And for what?"[24]

In order to participate in Cottolengo's personalized services, individuals needed to demonstrate their willingness to follow a certain path, which would be literally designed after numerous interviews and meetings with the social worker. However, to fulfill the FBOs' counseling requirements, the homeless person would need to be patient, meek, and cooperative, not helped by any other institution, and ready to trust the Cottolengo as able to help them, albeit not immediately. Once again, they should be the "robbed man" ready to be helped by the Good Samaritan. The same dynamic also applied to the general interview necessary to gain—or renew—the Cottolengo service card. Just like Jesus, who does not tell us if the robbed man had anything to say about the help that he was receiving, the interview was designed not to give voice to homeless individuals but to offer the same standardized help to everyone (i.e., to every "neighbor"; see chapter 5).

However, this kind of love did not come unconditionally. As in the case of Marco and Carlo, anxiety and fear, but also boredom and frustration, were the most common feelings among the homeless people I encountered. As many homeless people told me, and as I found in the literature, counseling services are painful because individuals do not want to talk about their past without seeing a concrete opportunity of changing their situation.[25] The interviews are a source of stress, as they are asked the same questions every time without getting anything—or very little—in return. Liebow pointed out the same thing three decades ago, while talking about homeless women: "It is difficult to appreciate the intensity of feeling, the bone-deep resentment that many of the women felt at always having to answer questions, often very personal, and often the same ones, over and over again. But having to answer questions was part of the price they paid for being powerless."[26]

If, following Haraway, "naming a thing is the power of objectifying, of totalizing," the biopolitical constructions found at the threshold of the soup kitchen and the counseling room bring to the fore deeply lived and deeply felt consequences.[27] On the threshold of that love, a (re)subjectification takes place.[28] That operation is a bordering, the splintering of a subjective position, that is necessary for the service to operate, for it to produce its desired outcome. The encounter with agape and caritas is one that works only if a subject receiving love and a subject giving love are identified: the poor need to be constructed, morally and organizationally, for the entire love-serving diagram to endure. For that construction to happen, a border between who fits and who doesn't needs to be drawn. Bordering here is formed not only through explicit requirements and rulings, such as the ones needed to obtain the card at Cottolengo or the rules governing the distribution of food, one item per table. It is a matter of signs, gestures, speeches, acts, and, ultimately, material cultures that are, in a Foucauldian sense, a speech-to, a power-to: they are devices that enact bordering at the level of the unconscious, intervening in what Guattari calls a "chaosophy" of entities, a cartography of affective powers that constructs charitable and charity-seeking subjectivities.[29]

Devices involved in the diagramming of the poor subject include the speeches given by nuns before charity commences, the texts on flyers, the paintings on the walls, the organizational arrangements to distribute food and clothes, and all the values and norms transmitted through centuries of moralizing practice and doctrine, which become blueprints for action, setting the tone.[30] The butter, too, is among these devices. It is minor, but looking through it, one finds a passage point to address the paradigms within which it is made to operate. The butter is a way to read the lament of the poor as something more than bare discomfort; to put it into context as a form of resistance to the silencing (the expulsion, the bordering) of the woman's subjective experience of life. This is the role the butter is diagrammed to play: it forces the subject to deal with the politics of caritas, to become poor, to be ready for love, and, in doing so, it expels everything else from her that does not fit. And all of this is done charitably, through a gesture that mainstream reading would readily depict as care: after all, it's about feeding the hungry.

But how exactly does the butter expel, rather than care? Or, more accurately, how does the butter normatively care by expelling? It does so by inscribing in its assemblage the biopolitics within which it is made to operate. First, it is involved because it is butter, a staple foodstuff with substantial nutritional value. In its fundamental capacity to sustain life, the butter binds the subject to the church: one needs to go there to find it if one cannot afford it otherwise. Second, this is not just any kind of butter but an unbranded pack, simply marked as Prodotto CE, which means that it meets Conformité Européenne standards. This is because some of the products that are received as donations by food banks come from the European Union, meaning that this is, by definition, a product for the poor that marks its consumer as poor also, to itself and to others. Last, and fundamentally, the scratches on the packages are a clear signifier of what the institution thinks: the poor are destitute, and therefore, by definition, they have to accept any kind of help. They must take whatever is on offer. If they refuse, then they are either a con artist (see chapter 5) or *non se lo meritano* (they do not deserve help). The form of care that centers on this butter expels poor subjects who resist its diagrammatic definition, who refuse to comply with the role to which they are assigned.

Dismissing the butter as a minor case, a nuisance, would be a mistake. I have collected and discussed countless examples of this modus operandi, as have others.[31] What I want to highlight here is the capacity of the minor, the mundane detail, to offer a privileged access point to the molar, structured picture. Such things can be access points that reveal how gestures of care and related materialities splinter the subject at the door of the FBO. This is about reducing the multitudes of one into the individualized solitudes of the manageable many: "the poor" becomes a flattening category around which the specific form of biopower exerted by the service pivots. Extraction comes to the fore at this point, as the consequence of a primordial act of expulsion. The first extraction is of a moral kind. In the broad Christian tradition, the poor are to be loved because through this love, the person serving—the good neighbor—will be able to access Christ's love. The poor, in much of the writing promoting FBO services that I've encountered, are thereby characterized as a medium through which other subjects can reach eternal life and the eternal love of God. Why, to paraphrase Joseph Ratzinger, should Christian FBOs have to "do everything in their power" to love the poor? Jesus provides the answer: "Do this and you will live" (Luke 10:28).

The second extraction is of a monetary kind. The poor generate work and jobs, and this, of course, extends well beyond the remit of the Roman Catholic Church or even Christianity more broadly: it is a factor in the making of humanitarian nongovernmental interventions across the globe. Services are funded, people hired, particular programs promoted; on the other hand, donations are received, financial instruments and investment encouraged, and tax exemptions granted on estates and transactions. The poor, in all of this, are not only the beneficiaries of charity but the pivot around which a whole industry can flourish and be reproduced.

The third, final extraction has to do with the power and legitimacy conferred by the act of charity. This plays at the level of the individual volunteers and social workers, who construct their personal and professional identities around the making of the poor via expulsion, reduction, silencing, and management. This is no different from the way in which other experts, very much including academic writers, use them as a source of content and authority (chapter 2). The FBO extracts its moral and political legitimacy from the bodies it controls, by keeping at bay that which it cannot control within those bodies. In southern but also eastern European countries, as well as in places like the United States, Argentina, Brazil, and vast parts of the Muslim world, the power extracted through these charitable means fundamentally influences the civic arena, well beyond the remit of charitable institutions.

Bunk Beds

In late March 2010, Marco and I were walking toward the bus station at the end of a chilly day in Turin. I was accompanying him to a public park on the outskirts of the city, where a temporary shelter, made of converted shipping containers, had been set up to provide accommodation to rough sleepers during the winter season.[32] Approaching the park, I asked Marco how he was feeling about the fact that spring was coming, meaning that the temporary shelter would soon be closed. He looked at me with his wide-open eyes and answered, "It's about time that shit closed down!" "Why?" I asked. "You know why!" he rightly replied (I had, indeed, heard the story many times). He continued, "That place is not fit for humans. It's crowded. It smells, and it is cold. Perhaps for Romanians, Algerians—yeah, perhaps it's good for them. They are always there, making a fuss about everything . . . but not for people like me! It would be better if it closed down, and when it closes down those people should be locked in there!"[33]

Emergenza Freddo (Cold Emergency) was located in the middle of one of the biggest public parks in Turin, on the far western side of the city. The project started in 2003 and was advertised as "hosting homeless people during the night" during the cold season (usually from November to late March).[34] The camp consisted of fifteen containers, each of which could accommodate up to eight people in bunk beds (figure 4.3). It was open from 7:30 p.m. to 8:00 a.m. and offered a place to sleep, a shared bathroom, two showers, and free coffee (one cup in the evening and another in the morning). Two people, one from Military Civil Protection and another from the Red Cross, monitored the entrance of the camp, sleeping in a separate container located near the others.

Homeless people (almost entirely men) entered the camp without any document checks and could sleep there as long as there were free beds. Although formally forbidden, the consumption of alcohol and smoking were common practice in the units, and violent verbal and physical fights were the norm. The camp's assistants had to call the police to calm things down almost every night. Emergenza Freddo was definitely an exception compared to other public

FIG. 4.3. Sheltering the poor. Photo by author.

shelters of the city, where control was much tighter, and the codes of conduct were strictly implemented. The Red Cross guidelines for the activities of the camp stated, "Service staff must register the guests asking them their general information: Name—Surname—Nationality—Sex (it is not necessary to ask for any identity documents, as this area is recognized as a 'free zone' unlike the other dormitories of the city)."[35]

If, as Agamben states, "being outside and yet belonging . . . is the topological structure of the state of exception," Emergenza Freddo fits the bill, at least partially.[36] The camp was outside of the city's normal rules of service provision to the homeless but at the same time run by the city itself and established through the suspension of its norms. In the call for public finances to support the camp, it is possible to ascertain the reasons why such an exceptional space was created: "The project has among its objectives the assurance of a service that protects the physical integrity of vulnerable subjects, and the protection of the general interest of the whole community under the profile of security, health, public order and civilized living."[37] As the head of the camp working for the Red Cross admitted, "Listen to me. This is a thing that has been done to remove dangerous people from the streets. The mayor does not want them on the streets. They create problems, especially when they are drunk. Here, instead, they are left to their own devices and don't annoy anyone."[38]

Emergenza Freddo was created as an exception for a duplicitous reason: to offer a warm place during winter but with the agenda of controlling a population that was perceived as dangerous and deviant. Only those who could not enter the city's public shelters, either because they had no documents or because they were not enrolled in the city's social provisioning system, would sleep there. It was the last resort of the poorest, and this feeling was inscribed in the affective atmosphere of the place. As Marco told me, the first time he arrived there, he felt that he had reached "the bottom of society."[39] He couldn't stand the long queue to get in, or the forty-five minutes by bus to get there, or the idea of sleeping in such close proximity to complete strangers; he was terrified by the tiny space that was allocated to him; and he felt humiliated by the free coffee in a plastic cup offered every morning by a Red Cross volunteer. Moreover, the dark containers where he and his peers were sleeping were a constant, cold, subconscious reminder of their abnormality. These containers, originally designed for the transportation of goods, were now removing unwanted individuals from the streets of Turin, offering them a bed, but at a price: upon entry, Marco and his peers were accepting that they were the less-than-normal element within an already peripheral demographic (an intricacy, as explicit in the above quote from Marco, and as I've illustrated elsewhere, that triggered all sorts of racialized borderings within the homeless community).[40]

The assemblage of the Emergenza Freddo was a resubjectification exercise, expelling the desire to articulate an alternative life from its subjects, in order to cast them as deviant and therefore in need of isolation and confinement. As I've noted, recollecting the experiences of both Italian and migrant homeless men using the camp, the ultimate function of the Emergenza Freddo was to establish control over a seemingly uncontrollable subject. Established under the guise of protecting the "physical integrity of vulnerable subjects," the suspension of the norm within the camp was really used to isolate the alcoholics, the drug users, and those who were prone to fighting so that the city did not have to deal with them on its streets or in other public shelters. The less strong felt vulnerable there, and many preferred a cold night in one of the abandoned, unheated train cars of the Porta Nuova station (a refusal of institutionalized shelters is common among the homeless across many contexts, in both the United States and UK).[41] In this sense, places like Emergenza Freddo not only exercise a form of revanchist control but also act as a biopolitical machine, diagrammatically activated through the suspension of the norm. They expel the subjective demands of their users, in order to extract control and security for the many.[42]

An alternative way of operating, more seriously committed to harm reduction, working from a more radical proposition of taking care of the other in their otherness, could not be taken into consideration, because to do so would challenge the proposition of emergency intervention at its core. In using the recursive occurrence of a winter emergency as the established modus operandi to deal with the homeless, the public asserts powers of governance for the sole reason of protecting a certain kind of home (in the quite literal sense of removing potentially threatening individuals from its reach) by defining what deviates from it and then keeping it under control. The charities, practitioners, and local political figures who are usually quick to celebrate these interventions, picturing them as the best example of heartfelt humanitarianism, might be sincere in their affective responses. However, this does not detract from the role they play in reproducing and maintaining home on a plane where expulsion (silencing, reduction, control) and extraction (appropriation, celebration, capitalization) are the only games in town. What if Marco was allowed another choice, one where he did not need to be controlled; one in which there was enough space for multiple instantiations of being at home?

Bureaucratic Means

Via della Casa Comunale 1 is a fictional address created for administrative purposes by the city of Turin. In order to become fully eligible for the resources offered by the city (like shelters and social and medical assistance), homeless people applied to get their ID showing their residential status at this address, thereby declaring their homeless status. To obtain it, individuals needed to demonstrate to the city two fundamental things: that they did not legally reside anywhere and that they had no possessions. If the first point was quite easy to demonstrate, the second posed some issues. Daniele's story is representative of many I collected. Daniele was a middle-aged long-term homeless man, in the sense that he had benefited from the low-threshold services provided by the city for many years, moving in and out of friends' accommodations, public shelters, and abandoned train cars in Turin's main station. Like many of his peers, Daniele did not have many formal documents: no ID, no bank cards, no resident permits. However, he was still formally the owner of a car although no longer in possession of it. As a result, the procedure to obtain the Via della Casa Comunale 1 residency was taking more time than it should have.

He told me, "I got this car. . . . I can't even remember when [pause]. I don't have it anymore, of course! But their fucking PC still says that I'm the owner. But owner of what?! I don't have that car anymore."[43] The only solution for him was to cancel ownership of the car, but this would have cost around eighty euros and implied yet further paperwork: "How can I pay for this? I'm stuck. They won't pay for me. I don't have the money. I can't get the residence. And that's it. I do not understand this system [pause]. The best thing would be to go there [to the city offices] and say, 'Fuck you all.' Then to run away."[44]

The bureaucracy necessary to obtain fictional residence in Via della Casa Comunale 1 was an abstract machine of governmentality. This machine was territorializing the encounter between the city and homeless individuals under the spell of what is considered to be an efficient way of managing homelessness. In other words, it was creating a subjective position by expelling whatever did not fit within the bureaucratic framework, which, in turn, extracted a working, exclusionary, residency permit system. The creation of such a residency, allowing those at home to receive a normal ID, while those not at home to be clearly labeled as such, speaks directly to the ritornello of nationalization—with its charge of civic duties and functional economic roles—echoed in chapter 3. Not incidentally, the rules to obtain the ID, the formalities surrounding the encounters with the social worker, and the complexities of the whole system were constructing a very charged affective experience for the homeless who had to go through them. There was stress, leading the individual to a state of frustration and depression due to the troubles encountered in the process. But even when the residence was finally obtained, there was a further stigmatizing effect difficult—if not impossible—to counterbalance. Giuseppe—another rough-sleeper individual I met during my study—was claiming that to have written on his ID that he was residing at Via della Casa Comunale 1 was like wearing a sign advertising he was homeless. These are not simply side effects of the residency scheme, but fully fledged emotional and material grounds created by the lessness diagramming home/homelessness in Turin.

Another example in this sense was the so-called *uno su uno* (one-on-one) system, or "one plus one," as my homeless friends described it. If someone did not have a residence in Turin (either real or fictional), they were entitled to a bed in a public dormitory for no more than seven days. Afterward, they were placed on a waiting list for a new dormitory, and, while they waited, often for several weeks, they had three options: to sleep on the street (or in trains or other liminal spaces); to sleep at the Emergenza Freddo camp, but only during the winter; or to try the so-called one plus one, a day-by-day venture to get one of the two nonbookable places that every dormitory allocated per night. As Daniela Leonardi reports in her work on this system, "homeless people who need a place to sleep must come to the dormitory at opening times. At 8:30 p.m., an operator collects the names of those who request a place for that night; in service jargon this is called 'one on one.' The others, during the course of the evening, are sent to other dormitories in different areas of the city or are told that they will have to sleep outside."[45]

Silvano was a long-term rough sleeper whom I met at the beginning of my fieldwork. His description of the one-on-one system is emblematic (and was shared by all the homeless people I encountered). The first thing to notice is the emotional frustration of having to deal with such a system: "You have to stand in front of the dormitory at 4, 5 p.m., and start queuing. You stay there, and wait. You can't go later on. . . . You won't find any beds. The place is full of people that just stand in front of the dormitory all day long. There are even people that take the place for someone else . . . and then you have to fight. It's insane."[46] Then, there is the waste of time that such a system implies, a waste that influences the ways people spend their days: "If you go there at 4 p.m . . . do you know what this means? That you can't do anything else. You wake up, you go to the nuns [at a soup kitchen managed by the Vincenziani institute], then you hang around a bit and it's time for lunch. When you start to look for a job, it's already time to queue at the dormitory: what kind of life is this? Tell me. How am I supposed to deal with this? To get out of here?"[47] In the end, there is the stress of sleeping one night in one place without knowing what is going to happen the following night: "When you go out in the morning, you know that you have to start all over again, from the beginning. I can't leave my stuff anywhere. I can't settle. I've nothing with me. I can't think of anything else but where I'm gonna queue that afternoon. I can't go on like this. I have to get away, to find another way."[48]

Dealing with the one-on-one system affected homeless people emotionally on a daily basis: from feelings of success (having secured a place) to failure (the contrary). Moreover, the system forced the homeless to physically move around the city, continuously changing dormitories. This form of forced movement can arguably be conceived as a form of continuous displacement, as Catherine Robinson, Ananya Roy, Teresa Gowan, and other critical scholars have indeed done. By being forced to move across services and then to queue everywhere, the subject is made to perform the embodiment of their defined "home-less," which is the ground upon which the service can extract the possibility for its standing. Besides the obvious physical distress of this venture, there is once again an affective load associated with such movements, not least because the spaces of the dormitories for which one queues, as Desjarlais poignantly has put it, "could have moods and physiologies as much as people did."[49] For this reason, some of the individuals I encountered in Turin were deliberately refusing to engage with this system because they perceived it as denigrating. Ivano, another middle-aged individual sleeping rough long term at the time, helped to clarify the politics of embodied precarity inscribed by the system of help on its defined subjects. Once, describing the one-on-one, he told me, "No way am I going to queue there. You see? Everybody sees you. And you have to wait for so long. . . . I go to the Martini instead [one of the major public Turin hospitals]. I go there at 9:30 p.m. I go to the waiting room. They don't ask you anything. You just sit. And they've got RTL 102.5 playing [a popular Italian radio station]. . . . I sleep on the chair. . . . Wine helps. But the chairs are hard!"[50]

Central to Ivano's account of the one-on-one system is the queue, the assemblage where this policy took its most evident material form. The queue is an assemblage with a particular aesthetic, which is immediately understood by those passing by it and looking at it. Five to ten homeless individuals, drinking and smoking, sitting on a pavement or on the stairs leading to a dormitory signify only one thing: poverty, the thing expelled from home and managed, in its otherness, elsewhere. The relational powers enacted by the queue (of self-deprecation, stress, and avoidance) were not intentionally designed in the one-on-one approach. They were contingent and contextual effects brought about by the arrangements at play in the enactment of that policy, yet they were solidly structured around the violent ritornellos of the home/homelessness threshold they epistemically and materially defended: by particular discursive framings on homelessness and poverty ("the poor will wait under any condition, because they are lacking something they desperately need"); by the location of the queue (outside, on the pavement); by the proximity of individuals; by cigarettes, alcohol, and smells; by ten names on a list from which only two will be selected; by the fear, tensions, and competitiveness brought on by the act of waiting; and so on. The small one-on-one device, like the other seen in this chapter, brought to the fore a whole political and affective economy of home/homelessness, both being an effect of, and being a way to reproduce, its violent functions.

A final example, which speaks of the ways in which the normative management of the homeless other had effects beyond itself—and reproduced subjects in need to perform, in constant motion, their given antithesis of the homely—is related to sanitation. Here I am referring to practices of urinating, defecating, caring for the menstrual cycle, showering, washing, and healing one's own body. The main affordance for the rough sleepers I encountered was provided by the public bath managed by the city. Standing as a reminder of its industrial past, when many working-class houses did not have toilet facilities, Turin counts five public baths located outside the inner center of the city. In order to access these services for free, homeless people needed to obtain specific nominative access cards, allowing access to the bathrooms only once. Valerio, a young and lively individual sleeping rough short term at the time I met him, was very proud anytime he was able to obtain one of those cards. One day he explained that in order to obtain a card, he had to queue for hours in one of the charities distributing them (these were available also through public social workers); he had to partake in counseling sessions where private issues were discussed, and then he had to plead with the person distributing the cards in order to get more than the two granted to him. Not unlike what I have discussed above, in the FBO case, the affective impact of these encounters discouraged many people from even trying to get the cards, especially in the case of people living on the streets for a long time who preferred either to avoid the public bath or to obtain cards via bargains with peers. On the day I took the picture in figure 4.4, Valerio was proud of his brand-new card, both because he was now able to have a proper shower and because he was going to have the opportunity to wash his favorite pairs of trousers, which he did not want to throw away.

Moreover, Valerio was happy because, for at least a week, he did not have to look for new tickets. Time is central in the performance of home(lessness) all

FIG. 4.4. City of Turin's card granting a free shower.

the individuals I encountered had to endure. If one sleeps in a shelter, then has to commute to the other side of the city to eat in a soup kitchen, while looking for a job and going to counseling meetings and receiving other forms of help (like secondhand clothes), the day quickly passes by before it is already time to queue for the night shelter again (which, in Turin, was as early as 4 p.m. because of the queuing generated by the residency rules I have discussed). Valerio's relief is symptomatic of the struggle to access a public bath and maintain proper personal hygiene. The latter is the assemblage of a fragile and fragmented exoskeleton, very difficult to hold together. One could think of it as a sum of dots and strings scattered all over the city that individuals not only have to navigate but also have to coconstitute, in the making of an institutionalized cartographic subjectivity of weaving things together, of becoming clean while constantly being connected and disconnected with a frail sanitation net. Such an endeavor requires enormous mental and physical labor that is taken away from other priorities. In my doctoral study, I found out that what is really taken away is the desire for a different becoming, the willful power for a different kind of home. In order to learn, comply, and work with the system put in place to help them, subjects must become expressions of its requirements, timing, and topographies, an endeavor deeply rooted in the social and material infrastructure of the city and the idea of *home* for the city, including whom the city is home to.[51]

These are, of course, cartographies assembled at the intersection of other forms of power and are highly differentiated across the lines of gender, ableism, and race. It was usually easier for a homeless man to urinate in public spaces, while for women it was difficult to find appropriate spaces to do so. Turin—like most other cities—provides very few public spaces that are, at the same time, hidden and safe; a remote corner in a public park might be good for privacy but bad for personal security. As the female individuals I met in my line of work reported to me, activities like changing sanitary napkins during the menstrual cycle are incredibly difficult to undertake without proper protection and means. Besides finding the right spaces to change, women also had to find resources in order to buy those provisions (or get them for free), and they had to do so while being constantly exposed to environmental conditions that could both alter the regular menstrual cycle and facilitate the emergence of specific infections and diseases. In relation to the latter point, female rough sleepers in Turin found it particularly difficult to deal with sexually related issues due to the shame that was associated with them. As Carla, a long-term homeless woman, told me, sometimes it is just easier to wait for the problem to pass, or to try to find the money to buy the medicine (if and when available over the counter), rather than to enter a counseling room and confront the issue with a doctor, or a volunteer, who may be judgmental.[52] Even if, in Turin, the number of female rough sleepers is low due to the dedicated services that the city provides to them, sanitation for the ones on the street or who need to change housing frequently still entails a considerable amount of emotional and physical affordances, time, and financial means, which leads to results similar to those just mentioned.

Finally, homeless migrants and asylum seekers, who were often living outside the shelter system due to a lack of valid documentation and proof of identity, were forced to literally occupy the ruins of Turin's old and new industrial past to design their own sanitation. Besides shelters and public bathrooms, individuals took care of themselves in the most disparate spaces: public parks, fast-food toilets, train cars, and any other available bathroom that did not require payment (the number of which, like the number of publicly available toilets, has steadily decreased in recent years). In some cases, large, abandoned factories were occupied by asylum seekers or migrants looking for jobs in the city, and the ex–Olympic village was occupied for the same purpose, too.[53] In these spaces, keeping clean was a triangulation between old broken toilets, abandoned rooms, newspapers, rainwater collected with a plastic bottle, and little more. In other cases, communities occupied green spaces scattered across the fringes of industrial areas, such as those emerging in the northern part of Turin at the intersection of two of the city's major rivers—the Po and the Stura. The case, which I have investigated elsewhere, of the Roma communities that have lived for years alongside the Stura River, ranging from two hundred individuals in the early 2000s to more than four hundred in recent years, was the most evident.[54] There, people have not only dwelled in self-made shacks for lack of better opportunities but have also washed themselves, their kids, and their clothes and have cooked and fulfilled their metabolic needs either with the (polluted) water of the river or water taken from nearby public gardens or fountains.[55] All of this while the city was, to use Roy's term, "banishing" them as nonresidents, continuously evicting and demolishing shacks, and considering them worthy at most of living in city-authorized trailer camps: another example of the grounds upon which the line between a racialized and nationalist home and a racialist and nationalist homelessness was maintained and reproduced, as in what follows.

Iron Bars

To defend the boundaries of an exclusionary home means to constitute and control its negation, which goes beyond charitable and managerial endeavors. Sometimes, in a continuum with the racialized and nationalist underpinnings sketched in chapter 3, it means to physically tie up, to arrest, and to jail. As seen in chapter 3, the Italian asylum system is very much designed with these premises: the logic here is one of detention. In FBOs and state low-threshold provisioning, an intervention is set up by reducing a life to a workable device, from which to accrue forms of spiritual or political legitimacy, economic return, or the maintenance of economic circulations that serve the many. In detention, expulsion (as deprivation of personal freedom crafted in contrast to what is deemed to be free) and extraction (of a whole set of political-economic and cultural securities) are expressed through a multiplicity of forms and strategies. An exemplary expression of these is offered when detention is affirmed as the end point of justice, from which it becomes the starting point for a whole economy of racialized exploitation, as shown, for instance, in the US prison system.[56] However, another equally powerful expression takes place when detention is seen as a tool of border control, deployed through convoluted asylum systems and the violent patrolling of borders, which de facto become no-man's-lands activated for political gains.[57] Detention, in that case, diagrams a strategy of protecting the homely land via its colonial legacies and its contemporary neocolonial economic practice. The home is saved by projecting narratives of invasion, via producing subjects to be managed through their expendability.

Once again in Turin, one of the first encounters I had when moving back was with the story of Moussa Balde, a twenty-three-year-old Guinean man who migrated to Italy in 2017. His story is complex; however, its ending is tragically straightforward. On Sunday, May 23, 2021, Moussa took his life in Turin's CPR. He hanged himself in the cell where he had been locked up a few days earlier as the result of his arrest by local police in Ventimiglia, in the Liguria region. He was arrested after he was beaten up by a group of three fascists in the city streets, on May 9. The video of the brutal beating, which left Moussa nearly dead in the street, is available online.[58] The fascists got away free, but Moussa was detained because the police, while escorting him to the hospital, found out that his residency permit had expired. For this reason, after only ten days of hospital care, he was moved to the center for repatriation in Turin. Local activists were able to speak to some of the other inmates, and one of them confirmed that "despite showing clear signs of suffering caused by injuries to his body, Moussa was never examined by a doctor or member of the medical staff at the CPR." Activists also reported that the inmate told them "that after his transfer to solitary confinement, which took place without a clear reason, [the inmate] heard Moussa screaming and asking for a doctor's intervention without ever receiving a response."[59] Moussa took his life just a few days after his arrival in the CPR, a place designed to expel him from the country, but which ended up forcing him to take his own life. The CPR was part of the diagram Moussa was made to assemble after years spent trying to find a place to inhabit peacefully in Italy; after being entrapped in the perverse logic of the asylum procedures; then being beaten for the color of his skin; then jailed; then put in isolation; then denied medical care. In an interview recorded in 2018, not long after his arrival in the country, he stated his reason for making the perilous journey: "I have decided to come to Italy to escape the very difficult political situation in my country. . . . I would like to stay in Italy because in this country I have had a taste of how beautiful life can be." Moussa's dream for his own life, what he wanted to do in Italy, was "to study in order to find a good job and live well."[60]

But the state machines controlling the boundaries of the Italian home are not designed to give space to such a desire. Their purpose is precisely to shut it down, not simply because of an ephemeral or transitory political will, but because their foundations are much deeper, and speak to the much wider and shared racialized and nationalist Ur-fascism of which Eco was writing: an inner fascism, to echo Deleuze and Guattari, that is then reaffirmed in national political discourses—by the likes of politicians extracting their legitimacy from slogans such as #Primagliitaliani (Italians first)—but that is also practiced in the everyday maintenance of CPRs and other similar institutions.[61] Moussa's case is not an isolated one. According to a study from a prominent Italian coalition in defense of civic rights, from June 2019 to May 2021, at least six individuals lost their lives while being detained in one of the ten CPRs across the peninsula.[62] Staying closer to Turin, thanks to the impressive investigative work of the Association for Juridical Studies on Immigration (ASGI), we know that the conditions of life in Turin's CPRs defy imagination. In their recent report, ASGI tells stories of a man with broken legs to whom the police denied even a simple crutch, obliging him to constantly lie down; another who showed proof of a rare blood disease when admitted to the center, who would have to wait forty-nine days before receiving any medical care; or the case of a third young man, who self-declared as a minor (therefore someone who could not be detained in a CPR) but was not believed, and was kept in the center for ninety-five days without explanation before he eventually decided to cut himself on his right arm.[63]

Self-harm is one of the few ways detained individuals in the Italian CPR can make a—often ephemeral—stand. The only year, continues ASGI, for which we have data related to these practices is 2011. In the Turin CPR that year, there were "156 episodes of self-harm, 100 of which were due to ingestion of medicines or foreign bodies, 56 of which due to stab wounds." Material living conditions in the center are of course part of the problem. ASGI reports that "the living spaces reserved for the inmates include 50-square-meter modules, including bathrooms, where seven people live, eat and sleep." It then describes in full the conditions of life in such modules:

> Each bedroom has an en suite bathroom, which is accessed directly from the room itself. Between the bedroom and the bathroom there is no door, nor are there any dividing doors inside the bathroom to separate the two squat toilets from the rest of the room where there are two washbasins and a shower. In other words, a few meters separate the toilets from the nearest beds and there is no element of furniture, such as doors or at least curtains, to ensure a minimum of privacy to those who use the services. This state of affairs is unacceptable, unjustified and noncompliant in terms of security.[64]

The production of the legal and societal category of the refugee is still a device of power. It is still about segmenting a rich individual experience into a manageable category. But the underlying structures surrounding the notion, and material-legal framework, of the refugee don't speak of expulsion and ex-traction. Rather, they are inspired by a progressive understanding of the mul-tiple forms of violence characterizing life trajectories in the current global world. However, the potential emancipatory power of seeking and working through the refugee poses a direct threat to the entrenched power that the homely is built upon, for the many, in Italy today. And therefore, the "state of affairs" of the CPR room is "unacceptable, unjustified and noncompliant in terms of security," and yet, it is there, because what must be secured are not the subjects within its purview but the wider political and affective economy it institutionally and culturally serves.

In this context, where the harshest intensification of home(lessness) is con-structed through diagrammatic charitable love and state bureaucratic man-agement machines, including detention, notions of what is right, of security, and of justice fade away. What emerges, in tracing how the ritornellos of home/homelessness cut through these only apparently separate domains, is a land of violence and despair, where subjects are made expendable yet always kept close enough to continue the extraction of value from them. The justice offered to those seeking refuge is designed at home, in a place in which the decision has been made about the space and time that can be given to the other. And that cultural, societal, and political decision trickles down to the CPR in Turin, where, ASGI reports, "half of the validation hearings and 80% of the extension hearings do not exceed 5 minutes in duration, including the drafting of the judge's order. No more than 5 minutes means from 0 to 300 seconds in which the judge verifies the factual and legal framework, acquires the information from the foreigner, often slowed down by the filter of the interpreter, listens to the requests of the parties (which, in turn, may formulate preliminary re-quests) and takes a decision on the legitimacy of the decree of detention and of the presupposed decree of expulsion."[65] All that is needed for home to keep its standing is to allow its others to speak for three hundred seconds, be-fore they can be again safely restored to the perennial lessness they have been damned to.

Lessness Cutting Through

What I have tried to illustrate in this chapter and in the previous one is a structural continuum between the ways in which home and homelessness work, with reference to a specific geography: Italy. The grounding is needed because, if the point can be affirmed conceptually (as I have done in part I), its unfolding is situated in colonial, patriarchal, capitalist, and racist history (chapter 3) and in the systems of governance and the experiences emerging from them (this chapter). I have used the Italian case as illustrative of a methodology of inquiry—which is complemented in chapter 5—in order to prepare the ground for the illustration of its political value. This is a methodology that invites us to excavate the structural foundations of lessness—in their unfolding, or ritornellos—across home and its other. It serves to excavate how diagrams of expulsion and extraction work to maintain the fiction of home as a place of security, stability, and desirability, in opposition to insecure, unstable, and undesirable homelessness. Maintenance, here, is a productive endeavor. The role of charitable and public interventions in this scheme is not to challenge the violent foundation of mainstream modes of making home in the world, but to contribute to them by producing and then managing the other half of home, the homeless other who must be defined, delimited, and kept at bay.

In these two chapters, I have aimed to illustrate how this process of bordering, by working through the colonies of home (chapters 1, 2), does more than simply drawing a line in the sand. To be sustained and replicated through history, the construction of home needs to have a tested and reliable design at its core. It needs to mirror what it is there to protect, from the intimacy of beliefs about life and spirituality to the shared practices of governance implemented by cities, states, and supranational entities. If the interventions to create the fiction of home were not made of the same material as home, then they would have to be made out of an otherness that could not be defined and therefore could not be kept at bay. They would be made from a cut of difference, a singularity (to follow Jazeel), of which we cannot speak or hear.[66] Such a difference would be unintelligible and nonprogrammatic, and would therefore unavoidably challenge the stability of our safe harbor, of our home. Such a proposition would be impossible to silence, impossible to expel, impossible to use as a basis for extraction: it would be unmanageable, liberated.

Instead, both home and its other are designed (in the Escobarian sense of the world) to be managed and to be manageable within violent structures of power. One might say that focusing on low-threshold services and bare detention to illustrate this point is an easy win. Of course they are inadequate. Surely more progressive services would be better (and the elephant in the room here is Housing First, which I tackle in chapter 5). My aim in this chapter has not been to highlight the inadequacy of low-threshold services per se, but to reveal their structural foundation in expulsion and extraction. Comparing these services on the basis of superficial differences in appearance and outcome, or even on the grounds of the varying levels of gratification they provide to their users, is a partial game with partial results. What if the comparison is done at the level of their fundamental functioning? Are faith-driven and mainstream public approaches able to dismantle the diagrams lying at the heart of our current concept of home (chapter 1), at the core of its ritornellos (chapter 2), and at the nucleus of our understanding of the history and ideology of home in a specific geography, in this case Italy (chapter 3)? If not, then the only possible conclusion is that they are colluding with those functions. And collusion, at the tensioned margins of home, is a business proposition.

As with any business proposition, it would be naive to think about it as a one-way affair. The homeless people I have encountered in the past decade are the ones who taught me about the ways in which the self becomes splintered in the encounter with service provision. To a lesser or greater extent, in encountering FBOs or public emergency shelters, these people knew that they were undergoing a form of expulsion. They knew it from their bodily, daily encounter with interdiction and imposition as they became subjects of charity. For many of them, expulsion was a matrix that they played with and within: the more experience they accumulated on the street, the better they got at playing different personas. They got acquainted with the comings and goings between the different stages of poverty (a Goffmanian awareness that has been shown by countless anthropologists of homeless street life). The ability of any individual to perform that staging is always dependent on other kinds of intersections, for example those of gender, race, and class. However, to a greater or lesser degree, performing with and within the expulsion-extraction matrix is a simple rule of the game of street hustling.

Casting that play and its performative unfolding under the rubric of strategies and tactics of homeless survival—as is usually done in homelessness scholarship—is limiting. Yes, there are strategies and tactics involved. In Turin, my homeless friends knew every area of the city where free distribution of alms, clothes, shoes, and food were taking place, and they developed the appropriate mental maps to navigate that terrain, in a calculation that involved things such as the timing of buses, the schedule of service distribution, the average amount of traffic, and the chances of being caught without a ticket on public transport. In parallel with this, they had to secure the right connections at the biggest street market of the city, the Baloon, in order to sell the goods they had acquired, which also involved exercising some judgment on the current market for fashionable clothes so that they could choose the best pile from the FBO's tables. Yet focusing only on these abilities leads to a depoliticized narrative that centers on resilience and capabilities, which in turn leads to calls for programmatic agendas aimed at boosting individual capacities, as if it were somehow enough to get people through a narrative that would eventually see them leave the streets.

The reality is that resilience and capability-based approaches go hand in hand with expulsion; it's just that they don't provide enough deterritorialization of home/homelessness for this to be seen, and for the machinic makings of service provision to be challenged.[67] In the comings and goings at the border of charitable love, the subject of the butter case—with all her tactics and strategies—is unable to produce effects that are greater than those produced in her by the system in which she is subjectified. The butter, after all, was eventually accepted. What is more, the exchange of free clothes becomes a substitution for an alternative way of life out on the street, for a differential kind of being at home (chapter 6), which is still very much desired though it cannot be articulated. The strength is just not there, because it is sucked up in the machinic silencing, the fitting, the splitting, the expelling, and the extracting that are involved in receiving love or institutional care. This love and its care are never unconditional: in affecting and being affected, the subject is crisscrossed by lines of power that segment, intersect, and mold, like fragments on a vast gray plane, keeping it tight to it, tight to home. Loving and caring, here, are the condition through which a particular form and a particular content of care are abstracted and turned into sets of territorialized assemblages that relationally affect the subject through daily cumulative affective encounters. Before I turn to an alternative program for a home beyond the dichotomy with lessness, and its related grounding in a radically different form of care, I need to address a further element clouding the way: How is it that such violent material and affective political economy of home is maintained, and reproduced, translocally?

5

A GLOBAL CULTURE

This chapter expands on the previous one by showing how the logic of home(lessness) can be found translocally, and how it travels to (re)establish its power. Moving from a situated story to a global context is always dangerous. Things easily get out of hand; stories are flattened; the violence of writing from one of the world's epistemic and colonial centers becomes evident. But if approached with epistemic care, such a move is necessary to show how the ritornellos of home(lessness) reverberate through place and scale while, at the same time, grounding their recursive spinning within specific time and places. On the one hand, the ways in which home(lessness) takes place and situates its violence is a matter of local histories and dynamics. But also, and at the same time, those histories and dynamics are a matter of what Massey called translocal power geometries: of intersections of capital, cultural discourse, blueprints for action, policy, and more, which become situated through their power to connect and disconnect things, and through the (re)production of subjectivities, experiences, and modes of inhabitation across scales. In a sense, in this chapter I am not interested in narrating the global political economy of home(lessness), for which others are better equipped than I am.[1] Rather, I am interested in recalling some salient intersections among many global stories of lessness: an exemplification of the wider topologies of power one is dealing with when trying to think of a liberatory politics of home for our times.

Intersections of the home(lessness) diagrams throughout global topologies are many and varied. One that has gained much attention in recent years has to do with the financialization of housing—that is, the means through which estates have become key assets in the circulation and creation of financial monetary value. These means are varied and ever evolving. In recent years, these have included subprime mortgages and their derivative aggregates that were at the core of the 2008 crisis but also extensive practices of predatory equity, or even the direct involvement of financial institutions not only in extracting (and creating) value out of the exchange value of housing, but also in developing housing estates.[2] Central to these processes, as Raquel Rolnik recalls, is "the ideological and practical hegemony of a specific model of housing policy: one based on the promotion of home ownership through market purchase via credit loans—a model that spread around the world at the electronic speed of financial flows."[3] Crucially, Rolnik continues, "through the finance of private home purchase, global capital market expansion was based on private indebtedness, establishing an intimate link between individuals' biological lives and the global process of income extraction and speculation," a process that was not only facilitated by national authorities across geographies, but one in which "states actively deconstructed housing and urban policies and deregulated monetary and financial markets."[4] The dire consequences of this model in terms of a generalized crisis of affordability, massive displacement, renewed racialized dispossession, segregation, overcrowding, and all the emotional, psychological, and other painful physical consequences of these phenomena are well documented across the globe.

The financialization of housing is without a doubt one of the key violent ritornellos of home(lessness) of our age. But there are other processes, perhaps less evident and to which less attention has been dedicated, which are structurally maintaining and reproducing the violence of home and of its other in our global (urban) world. The *global* here—following geographers such as Massey, Amin, and Sheppard and building on my work with McFarlane—is not a territorial signifier, but a translocal formation of territories.[5] It is about how territories—of expulsion and extraction—are made, rather than a way to call a territory. Deploying such a processual view, I am here interested in staying closer to the conventional home/homelessness binary, by looking at those cultural and material devices that maintain and reinforce the affective and political economy of lessness across places, through space and history. Here, Arjun Appadurai's notion of "cultural facts" becomes handy to signal how the process of globalization, in its expression of linkages and productive ruptures across time and space, produces forms of power that maintain their edge of influence (their abstract power, to recall Deleuze and Guattari) beyond their immediate actuation. Contemporary (racial financialized) capitalism is a great example of this—through its production of dogmas and the ideologies Rolnik is referring to—but there are other, more subtle, diagrams at play, too.

Appadurai poses the following problem: "how can we compare social objects in a world where most such objects, whether nations, ideas, technologies, and economies, seem deeply interconnected?"[6] The proposed answer is to look at how cultural facts circulate across histories and regions, focusing on their longitudinal historical makings and their territorial assemblage. To do so, Appadurai proposes paying attention both to the circulation of cultural forms (what he calls "circulations of forms") and the speed, tempo, and shape that the forms of that circulation take. One thing is to look at the cultural fact of homelessness—of what that is and how it is formed, translocally; and another, complementary thing is to look at how that fact travels—through which means, and across space and time. Through this analysis, looking at cultural facts does not mean transcending their (global) political-economy structuring but accounting for it by looking at how the fact is forged and how it is allowed to travel, while at the same time maintaining a very clear focus on the point that, through these circulations, a culture is produced: a form is out there, as a diagram of power capable in itself of reproducing and maintaining those same forces and powers that have brought it into existence (and that have brought the means for its circulation into existence, too). To me, the binary home/homelessness is one of these cultural forms, a form that can be defined, as Appadurai has it, as "a family of phenomena, including styles, techniques, or genres, which can be inhabited by specific voices, contents, messages, and materials," which capitalism—together with the other ritornellos underpinning our expulsive and extractive ways of inhabiting this world—is able to axiomatize and work through.[7]

The homeless—in their binary opposition to home—are a cultural form of our time. As seen already, this does not mean to say that conditions of homelessness are a mere epistemological device, but that the materiality of life under precarious housing conditions has been colonized by and through powerful epistemic devices (chapter 2). The means through which the circulations of that form and the forms of that circulation are constructed and maintained globally are matters of specific political economies, but they are also, at the same time, matters of what these material forms are able to express at the "slightly more abstract level" of culture in their asynchronous durations.[8] The "abstract machine of homelessness," as I have called it elsewhere, is actively reproduced as a culture: one, to use the conceptual grammar advanced in this book, which is there to maintain the ritornellos of home(lessness) across time and space. If in chapter 3 I have focused on the underpinnings of a particular sense of home/ homelessness in Italy, and in chapter 4 I have illustrated how those are translated at the level of praxis oriented at managing that border, here I turn to how these makings are echoed at the level of their cultural abstraction at times of enhanced translocal interconnectedness.

In what follows, I trace how the cultural form of home(lessness) circulates, and how it is constructed in circulation, at three translocal intersections. The first has to do with global discourse, the second with global policy, and the third with global emergency. To unpack these, I focus on specific cases read through analytics that I have found helpful to maintain a focus on the bordering practices at play in each of these home(lessness) cultural facts. In the first case, with the help of theorists of cultural representation such as Stuart Hall, I trace the making and unmaking of online consensus on a major, viral story of homelessness. Starting from a specific case, the aim here is to showcase a method of inquiry to unravel and challenge the assumptions reproducing the home/ homelessness framework through the power of social media. In the second case, on the basis of my own engagement with it, and of critical scholarship, I focus on the quintessential global homelessness policy of our times: Housing First (HF). The goal here is to question the underpinnings of solutions that are sold as liberatory, and that partially are but lose their revolutionary power in avoiding direct engagement with the structures of home(lessness). Finally, for the third case, I refer briefly to collective work and reflections undertaken with my comrades in the *Radical Housing Journal* around the housing and homing dimensions of the emergency response to the first phase of the COVID-19 pandemic. The point of this third exploration becomes to link up global cultural discourses and assumptions regarding homelessness (evoked through the first case) with the power of policy interventions underpinned by spoken or unspoken translocal consensus (recalled in the second case) at times of global emergency. The requirement for rapid actions boosts and replicates the problematic foundations of home(lessness) further and decreases our collective critical capacity to question them. Through these journeys I adopt a form of what Tatiana Thieme has called "cross-pollination" across cases to show how expulsive and extractive logics are foundational to the home/homelessness story across geographies, making up for a global cultural fact—a ritornello—that can only be tackled from its interstitial assemblage.[9]

Exposing the Other (on Global Discourse)

Following Stuart Hall, we make sense of what we perceive through systems of representation.[10] These systems are tripartite: on one side, there are ideas/concepts; on the other, there are signs (language); and the two are brought together by our socialized self in order to signify (make sense of) a particular thing in the world. Through this process of codification—that is, through the arbitrary process of associating ideas and words with things—we understand, communicate, reproduce, and sustain cultural truths.[11] Exposure can therefore be understood as the initial gesture that brings something to our attention, and into a system of relations with us, our conceptions, and our language. It is that from which a representation (a signification) emerges. The key here is that, despite its arbitrariness, the association between ideas, words, and things is largely codified and follows established paths. For the most part, exposing something means to plug that thing into the dominant system of representation one is playing with. In our case, exposing homelessness means bringing it into the light of a given conception of otherness, which in turn is related to a mainstream idea of home. The homeless poor are exposed, in their otherness, in the light of established frameworks of home telling us that, by all means, home is home because there is something else that isn't. The homeless poor are not a social fact but the cultural interpretation of how we make sense of, and talk about, the experience of housing precarity. It is within a particular framework of reference—a particular system of representation—that the homeless poor become something one can render cognitively, epistemically, and politically.

The intensification of mediated connections brought to the fore by the information society means that today such a process of exposure is by default an affair of intersecting global topologies of meaning creation, meaning discussion, meaning disruption, and reproduction. The system of representation of home(lessness) is not different, but localized only in transcalar and topologically extended semiotics, assembled, among other things, through powerful cinematic representations, memes, and global social media Christmas appeals to stock the local food bank. Focusing our attention for a moment on the power of the cultural reproduction of home(lessness) does not mean to evaluate the merit of such narratives. My scope here is different: it is to show the performative logic at play in those representations, which I consider to be instrumental in the reproduction of the functions of lessness across geographies. The performative, here, works in using the home/homelessness dichotomy both as a point where discussions and representations are grounded (the system through which representation is made possible, and the other signified), and as a connector between those representations and their functional instrumentalization to institute forms of expulsion and extraction across time and space. As I hope the example given in this chapter shows, the exposure of home(lessness) in the contemporary information society offers multiple opportunities for instrumentalization, and all at the same time. That is to say, there is no one mastermind exposing and extracting, but a chorale, a collective subject that thrives in different ways on being part of the same system of representation.

This is equal to saying that the ideas of home and homelessness have become, in themselves, productive: they allow collectives to frame conversations around what is worth inhabiting and how and, on the basis of those framings, to reproduce the violent epistemic and material borderings of home(lessness). In the following passage, Hall speaks of the West as an idea that has agency over the ways in which we make sense of, and produce, the world. The idea of home and its fictional separation from its other works in similar ways. Once produced, the idea, underpinned by its colonies (chapters 1, 2), became "productive in its turn. It had real effects: it enabled people to know or speak of certain things in certain ways. It produced knowledge. It became both the organizing factor in a system of global power relations and the organizing concept or term in a whole way of thinking and speaking."[12]

Within the current dominant cultural paradigm of home, exposing the other of home often maintains the underlying conceptual and linguistic devices that have constituted that otherness in the first place. Here the problem is not just stigmatization—which is definitely part of the machine I am talking about—but more profoundly the reproduction of cultural systems of oppression. Cracking such systems is not as simple as changing the names of things, because a system of representation is a signifying machine built by language, ideas, and material references/conditions. When it comes to homelessness, therefore, it is not enough—as some progressive humanitarians advocate routinely—to challenge the nomenclatures of the other to alter its foundational otherness. Instead, we must look to demolish its cultural and economic functions—the expulsion and extraction that such representations enable—

which are the foundation upon which these concepts, words, and performative speeches have been forged.

But how to get there? How to get closer to the performative machinations of representing home(lessness)? For decades, critical thinkers have discussed the power of exposure in film, photography, and critical poverty studies, from a range of perspectives including feminism, queer studies, critical race scholarship, and the more general sociology of deviance, all of which have highlighted the recursive power of representation as instrumental to systems of oppression.[13] One compelling example is the work of Nicholas De Genova, who has convincingly shown how the spectacle of migrants at sea is used to produce an idea of their illegality as an objective fact rather than a construction of law, and to set a series of disciplinary expectations of instrumental and submissive behavior once they reach land.[14] Few, however, have connected the importance of exposure to the maintenance of homelessness in a broader sense, both as something experienced in real life and as something populated by many forms of industry and expertise.

Teresa Gowan has possibly provided the clearest insights into the workings of representation within home(lessness).[15] In her ethnographic work around homeless men in San Francisco, Gowan has discussed the work representation does in sustaining and (re)producing the experience of life in extreme, precarious housing conditions. She called her approach an "ethnographic discourse analysis," focused on "how competing discourses on poverty and homelessness affect poor people themselves, organizing and defining their existence and leading them to present themselves in archetypical terms upon the stage of the street."[16] Gowan expands on a longer tradition within American anthropology of taking the discourse of homelessness seriously, to avoid the differential treatment of discourse and practice, instead tending to treat "speech as action . . . but also to understand action as a kind of 'speech,' a vehicle of meaning in its own right."[17] Looking at the history of American homelessness and poverty management, Gowan shows how specific cultural discourses are deeply related to ways of approaching, understanding, and managing the poor. She identifies three important types of speech: a foundational moral "sin-talk," which is attached to strategies of exclusion and punishment but also redemption; a therapeutic framework of "sick-talk," associated with treatment; and a "systemic construction and system-talk" related to regulation and transformation at the social level.

Following Gowan's work, the methodological question becomes: What is the role of cultural representation in sustaining the expulsion and extraction of home(lessness)? Indeed, Gowan's "constructions of poverty" relate to moral, medicalized, and systemic understandings of homelessness that work as a blueprint for action for both homeless people themselves and service providers. In other words, constructing the "cultural fact" of poverty is about the ways in which sin-, sick-, and system-talk connect with idealized senses of belonging, nationhood, and personhood, ultimately reproducing their inner logics. Such semiotic, and yet very material work, assumes a profound significance at times of accelerated media reporting, hyperconnectivity, and ubiquitous commentary on social media. The power of this machine-of-machines, transversally cutting across geographies and subjects, cannot be underestimated. And yet, it is often taken for granted, as the unavoidable effect of the increased mediatization of lives under contemporary capitalism. In what follows, I aim to problematize such a reading, and follow Appadurai in positing questions around the making and unmaking of powerful global cultural facts. To do so, I conceive the production of the cultural fact of home/homelessness not simply as an effect of expulsion and extraction, but as being a specific affective capacity emerging from them.

The distinction is conceptually helpful to highlight how a cultural fact takes a life of its own: it is not just an expression, but a function that bears a capacity of instantiation, which serves the purpose of maintaining/reproducing the cultural/material project it ensues. In this sense, the global exposure of home/ homelessness works as a Deleuzian-Guattarian abstract machine: the system of representations and its circulation diagrams therefore actively codifies homelessness in a certain way to obtain a certain outcome.[18] Crucially, it is an immanent machine, not a metaphysical idea. Its diagramming works because it is connected to specific histories, their epistemic and material colonies, and concrete assemblages of practices, materialities, and becomings. What Deleuze means when he says that this machine "proceeds by primary non-localizable relations" and that "at every moment passes through every point" is precisely about this transversal localization of the machine, its anchorage in concrete stuff: enunciations, speech, and action, across planes and geographies.[19]

The ways in which meaning is diagrammed through history (the abstract machine) is a layered, powerful affair: "It is a machine that is almost blind and mute, even though it makes others see and speak."[20] When it comes to home(lessness), the abstract machine of exposing the homeless other extracts cultural understandings of alterity from the expulsive and extractive history of home-making, in order to sustain its reproduction. It provides a discursive-conceptual template that molds the way a situation is understood, and the repertoire of possible actions that this indicates. Again, this is not a matter of puppets governed by a master, but of layered cultural understandings that are able to do much of the work of comprehending the world for us. As Stuart Hall argues, conceptual maps and languages provide the *"codes which govern the relationship of translation between them."*[21] In other words, it is the codification of the relationship between our conceptual map of home/homelessness that frames our encounter with the homeless and our understanding of them as such.

THROUGH THE DIAGRAM

In the past few years, I have built up a database of hundreds of instances of homelessness exposure on the World Wide Web in order to trace their diagrammatic power. They range from news reports and feature films to charitable advertising and memes. One can find the president of the Federal Reserve Bank of Minneapolis, who spent a week as "a homeless person" and then told his tale to *Business Insider* as he prepared to run for governor of California in 2014; there's a report about a charitable experiment that turned homeless people into Wi-Fi hotspots, which led to a barrage of humanitarian criticism about loss of human rights, despite the fact that some of the homeless involved in the program liked it; there are hundreds of "uplifting" clips, pictures, and short stories on 9GAG, more often than not including dogs, or someone giving money to a rough sleeper and then filming how they spent it (and being surprised at the incredible outcome of the charade).[22] There are wonderful stories of homeless musicians and performers; homeless guides; a homeless man fishing using rocks; countless pointless individual stories in the UK *Guardian* that only amplify readings of the problem as a matter of personal failure; Pope Francis initiating a barbering scheme for the homeless in Saint Peter's in Rome, plus dozens of charitable Christmas appeals, which would deserve an entire book of their own.

One of my personal favorites involves Katrine, a French tourist in Times Square in New York. In 2014, she bought a massive pizza in one of Little Italy's corner shops, but she couldn't finish it. So she decided to approach someone who looked like a "hobo" to give it away. The two had a little chat, the *New York Post* reports, with Katrine apologizing to the recipient of her charity: "Je suis désolée, but the pizza is cold."[23] Then she left, and he took a bite. Later that day, newspapers all over the world reported the story, but with a twist. As the UK's *MailOnline* candidly put it, she gave "a homeless man her leftover pizza . . . only to realize it was RICHARD GERE playing a vagrant in his latest movie."[24] In looking at Gere's picture, one can understand why our French friend could confuse the multimillionaire actor with a grizzled rough sleeper.

In that moment, Gere was shooting a scene in which he had to scavenge food from a public bin, and he had a distinctly shady look: unshaven, with a gray wool cap, and a large beige waterproof jacket over baggy pants. He was fitting the paradigm. Indeed, all of the students and colleagues to whom I have shown the same picture mistook Gere for a homeless man. In doing so, they were making sense of this particular representation through a particular abstract (yet very immanent) diagram that dictates what a homeless man should look like. That understanding—that system of representation—as said in the introduction to this chapter, does not need specification at an individual level precisely because its powerful framing is deeply ingrained, arising from a whole history of paradigmatic forms and meanings. That is the same diagram that guided Katrine's actions too, showing how the discourse around homelessness is more than what one can hear.

When, however, a different diagram is provided, the whole story changes. When Katrine read the newspaper, she realized the gap between her perception and her encounter. "It's unimaginable that something like this could happen," she told the *New York Post*. But she added a whole new layer of affective response, which couldn't have come to the fore in the original abstract machine: "I think he's very handsome, even at his age. . . . 'Pretty Woman' was not my favorite movie, but I really loved 'Chicago.'"[25] The same thing happens with my undergraduates: once they are told that the man is Gere, they can see only him. There is no homelessness at play after that moment, because the diagram changes to one focused on jet-setting, art, moralistic tales about the importance of representing poverty accurately, and the skills of doing so (the story becomes a way of praising Gere's realistic acting, because he was able to fool us, escaping the Gere-machine). What this little story tells us is not that we can misunderstand something if we are not given appropriate information, but that we make sense of the world only through highly diagrammed systems of representation that guide both our thinking and our actions, in a circular formation, or ritornello. The consequence is that the exposure of the homeless is never neutral, never unconditional, not just because it solidifies stereotypical readings, but because it fundamentally forecloses the possibility of imagining the otherness of home as a true alterity—that is, in a way that isn't defined against the fiction of home and the paradigmatic representation attached to it. These dominant diagrams refuse to allow homelessness to signify another, very different way of becoming in the world: it is either Gere or the homeless, nothing in between.

To understand what is lost, we need to dig deeper. The Gere story is just one of many more thousands circulating ceaselessly, framing encounters with poverty on an everyday basis. Pop culture and social media offer an apparently infinite number of case studies in this sense. Each and every one of them could be analyzed discursively and visually, to deconstruct the way that they work to reinforce or to challenge the abstract diagram. But deconstruction wouldn't be enough to understand and fight what Ash Amin calls "the framings" of the other.[26] To appreciate how exposure is not only a power-from, but also a power-to, it is key to analyze the ways that those images, texts, and collages are received and made sense of. To do so is to trace how their systems of representation are diagrammatically constructed by the constitutive relationship between their parts: the representation, its understanding, its misunderstanding, its reproduction, its solidification, and its circulations. Traditionally this has been hard to do since our collective exposure to these things played out at the level of individual reactions and affairs. Until recently, we hardly left any permanent traces of our immediate affective responses and modes of understanding. The likes of Mark Zuckerberg, however, have changed all of that. Now it is relatively easy to unpack the power of exposure, precisely because the many are involved in its structuring of the system of representations founding ideas of home. The following case, I believe, is paradigmatic in this sense. The spectacle that emerges from it exemplifies how a very diffused racialized, capitalist, and charitable diagram of home/homelessness gets reproduced as a global cultural fact.

WELCOME TO THE SPECTACLE OF THE POOR

On the night of November 14, 2012, an officer of the New York Police Department (NYPD) encountered a homeless person while on duty around Times Square. He was sitting on the ground, barefoot, and the officer was so moved by his plight that he bought him a pair of boots from a nearby shop. Jennifer Foster, a tourist from Arizona, witnessed the scene and took a photo of it on her mobile phone (figure 5.1). A few days later, on November 20, she sent the photo to the NYPD via email, "thinking of it as a sort of compliment card."[27] The NYPD contacted her and asked her permission to report the event on its official Facebook fan page, and she agreed. The story was published on November 27, and by evening, the New York Times reported, "the post had been viewed 1.6 million times, and had attracted nearly 275,000 'likes' and more than 16,000 comments."[28] When I first read this story (reported in an Italian newspaper on December 3, 2012), the numbers had increased further: the post had received 609,687 likes and more than 47,800 comments, and it had been shared (on other Facebook pages) by almost 220,000 people. Further, it had achieved

FIG. 5.1. The first picture of DePrimo and Mr. Hillman, published on the NYPD's Facebook page.

global reach, with newspapers from Mexico City to Rome and from Sydney to Toronto reporting the story. It had gone viral.[29]

When the photo was originally posted, the identity of the officer was still unknown, but he was eventually identified as Larry DePrimo, age twenty-five. The NYPD posted again on November 30 with a photo of him and a quote from an interview he had given the day before: "I didn't think anything of it."[30] Besides Facebook, the story was widely shared on other social media, including Reddit and Twitter. Donald J. Trump's response was fairly representative:

"NYPD Officer Larry DePrimo has made the entire city proud with his generous act of kindness [link] NYC loves the NYPD."[31] However, by December 2, 2012, the *New York Times*, and subsequently many other newspapers and online blogs, also identified the homeless man as Jeffrey Hillman. They added another detail: Mr. Hillman was barefoot again, and "the $100 pair of boots that Officer DePrimo had bought for him at a Skechers store on 14th November were nowhere to be seen."[32]

This story clearly exemplifies exposure: an event is grabbed from the magma of everyday life, captured in images and writing, shared, reappropriated, and given meanings. But what are the meanings that this exposure brings to the fore, and what are its consequences? As is so often the case, the story begins with a small gesture of care (think of those charitable Christmas initiatives). A contested and debated notion, *care* can be generally defined as the "proactive interest of one person in the wellbeing of another" (the officer noticing the homeless person) and the "articulation of that interest (or affective stance) in practical ways" (the purchase of the boots).[33] This is a very conventional articulation of caring for the poor, as we have seen in chapter 4, and fighting home(lessness) requires a radically different take on the matter (chapter 7). Nonetheless, this unidirectional act of care is the pivot upon which the diagram of this, and many similar stories, unfolds. DePrimo's act of caring was provisional and fluid, but exposure translates it into something that encompasses and embraces the original act (by means of a photo, a social network, media releases, and the rationales underpinning people's comments). It thereby feeds right back into the wider sociocultural matrix that structures our understanding of (racialized) homeless people like Jeffrey Hillman.

The exposure of the original space of care through online and print media is anything but neutral. It is indicative of personal engagement/disengagement, of a set of attitudes toward care and the poor, and of new framings that feed into our collective cognitive mapping and wordings.[34] In order to exemplify the performative power at work in these processes, I have looked at the online debate around this story, focusing my attention on the Facebook comments published from November 27, 2012, to January 10, 2013 (a period that covers the rise, expansion, and decline of public attention to the story). Using scraping software, I downloaded 44,753 comments out of 48,284 (private comments couldn't be downloaded). The text file was anonymized and exported to CAQ-DAS (Computer Assisted Qualitative Data Analysis Software), which I used to analyze it.[35] From the analysis of these comments and of related media releases, I identified three specific spaces of exposure, which are shaped by (power-from) and contribute to (power-to) particular understandings of care and the poor.

The first space exposes care by capturing it, and it is represented by Jennifer Foster's act of taking the photo and its appropriation by the NYPD's communications team. The second space exposes care by making it viral, bringing Foster's photo into a vortex of online sharing, liking, and commentary. Finally, the third space consists of the follow-up stories, which reveal elements missing from the original depiction.

CAPTURING

Foster's photograph capturing DePrimo's act of care on her mobile phone is the first instance of exposure (figure 5.1). In so doing, she translated the officer's action from a momentary act of care into a perpetual translation in its representation.[36] The account that Foster gives of her gesture, reported on the NYPD Facebook page, helps to clarify the rationale behind it:

> Right when I was about to approach, one of your officers came up behind him. The officer said, "I have these size 12 boots for you, they are all-weather. Let's put them on and take care of you." The officer squatted down on the ground and proceeded to put socks and the new boots on this man. The officer expected NOTHING in return and did not know I was watching. I have been in law enforcement for 17 years. I was never so impressed in my life. I did not get the officer's name. It is important, I think, for all of us to remember the real reason we are in this line of work. The reminder this officer gave to our profession in his presentation of human kindness has not been lost on myself or any of the Arizona law enforcement officials with whom this story has been shared.[37]

The picture that Foster took could have remained on her mobile phone; it could have been shared among her friends. However, she decided to send it to the NYPD because she had been "in law enforcement for 17 years," and DePrimo's gesture represented, to her, a morally inflected reminder why she and others were "in this line of work." Sending the picture to the NYPD was, therefore, a political statement about how law enforcement ought to operate, via an exemplary case that Foster deemed worthy of applause. The political charge of this space was greatly amplified by the NYPD's decision to post the photo on its Facebook page. It is important to highlight that these two translations are both charged with power: they have an underlying rationale, an affective grounding, and a mundane affective power, the relevance of which becomes evident when we look at the spaces that subsequently emerged.[38]

Facebook users turned the photo and the story into a viral phenomenon in a matter of hours. A close reading of the comments posted in the first phase of this response shows a set of defined discursive repertoires, which I have reported in table 5.1. Religious themes, the goodness of the officer, and the wholesomeness of the story, as well as a good wealth of emulative stances, are the positive viewpoints characterizing this space.

These comments show forms of expulsion and extraction at play and illustrate their deep connection with the foundational logics of home(lessness). The first offers collective reassurance about the form of state power that is there "to protect and to serve" our home: the police.[39] Their institutional power secures the border between home and homelessness by enacting active or passive expulsions of all kinds—from the economic to the legislative and judicial realms—both in the context of DePrimo's story and well beyond. Across geographies, the police maintain the bordering between home and homelessness, allowing for variegated economies of extraction to continue, including, to be clear, not only private property but also the intimate value of prizing a secure home in a society otherwise represented as a jungle (it is dangerous out there). Police's bordering practices are often performed violently, on the street and in the institutions designed to keep the border in place, such as tribunals, jails, and other forms of incarceration and constraint. This violence is often racialized, something that is becoming increasingly visible across all media, thanks to the ability people now have to share footage. These representations are sufficiently powerful that they are leading even those who are disinclined to be critical of state power to become suspicious of the ways in which the police protect and serve, especially when it comes to the poor, the Black, and the homeless.[40]

The power of DePrimo's story is to stand out, in this context, as a novel surprise: his act of care seems good precisely because collective cognitive mapping associates the couplet "police officer—homeless man" with negative stories. The following comments vividly highlight this tension (emphasis added):[41]

> Why is this such a big deal. . . . Why are there no pictures of other volunteers that serve the homeless every day. Where is there [sic] notoriety and recognition. This is ridiculous, *if he was not in a police uniform this would have absolutely no coverage.*

> Despite of [sic] NYPD Stupidity, this is something very rare to see. Very little officers even act kind hearted and very few will even give boots to a homeless man like him.

TABLE 5.1 The good police officer: Most common comments in the first phase of the story going viral

Topic	Example 1	Example 2	Example 3	Example 4	Example 5
Reference to God or religion	In the Holy Bible a Good Samaritan helped a poor man, This officer has done the same Luke 10:33 He will be blessed in doing so.	Talk about seeing God in surprising places! This officer saw God in a dirty homeless man most of us would cross to the other side of the street to avoid. God bless them both and shame on the rest of us!	Officer DePrimo, thank you for helping this homeless man. He was really JESUS, You have no idea the BLESS- ING that is coming to you. God Bless U my brother.	the true love, Jesus preached this kind of love: luke 4:25–37. God bless this Officer	Angels are everywhere and in disguise. God bless this officer, and all NYPD.
On DePrimo	So beautiful! What an amazing officer! God bless the NYPD <3	Officer DePrimo is a hero in my eyes, he is the epitome of what human- ity with heart and soul should represent. Officer DePrimo I salute you <3	What a nice gesture done by this officer, hard to find these days! :)	Larry DePrimo, words can not describe the generosity that comes from your heart. Your a true inspiration. Thank you.	Officer Lawrence DePrimo is a wonder- fully kind man. Great good deed What a hero!!
On the story	One of the greatest stories of kindness I have heard in a long time. Thank you kind officer.	I loved this story—it made me cry!	That is such an amazing story. That just goes to prove that people still have a heart; and this Officer went Above and Beyond for one home- less person!	I was very moved when I read the story of Law- rence Deprimo reach- ing out to the homeless man. Humanity starts with an act of kindness. Thank you.	I absolutely LOVE this story! It restores my faith in humanity.

Reporting own experiences or wishing to emulate	I would have done the same thing and so would my mom	If that was me saw him with no sock or no shoes, I do the same way that the police man did.	Great work man, I drive a NYPD cruiser on London streets and see many homeless people I was pull over to give them coffee.	I have given clothes to the homeless in my community many times.	I gave a homeless man in Harlem a warm meal In January and it does feel good! Doesn't have to cost much to help people in need!
Emulation will bring change	let's all go out and do a random act of kindness tonight, today, this week, this month, imagine the power of each of us doing just 1 random act of kindness per day, wk or month . . .	Well what are YOU waiting for ! I do it how about you, let's all make a difference . If you want to make even more of a stand, try what I did once .. Bring a homeless person out to lunch, inside a restaurant.	True Hero!!! Such a huge heart. Now if EVERYONE who sees this could do at least one kind thing for a homeless person, wouldnt that just be awesome.	Officer DePrimo is an inspiration and my hero. There are 312 million of us in this country—we could END HOMELESSNESS in five minutes if we wanted to.	Wonderful!! Now if ALL people stepped up to the plate and helped the homeless THAT in itself would be wonderful!! Step up to the plate people! :-)

Source: Author's collection of comments from Facebook.

Note: This phase includes comments from two periods, November 27–28 and November 29–December 1. In order to preserve their original form, comments have not been edited to correct grammar, spelling, or punctuation.

Giving shoes to a homeless person? I've done this. It's not a big deal. It's not a newsworthy story. It's common decency. Why, then, is such a big deal being made about this? Would people be this excited if the shoes came from a student? How about a nurse or a teacher? Fireman? Business person? Et cetera? I doubt it. *It's because it's a cop and police have a well-earned reputation as being less kind than, not more kind than, people who aren't cops.*

DePrimo's act to protect a homeless person's space of survival is framed by a dominant narrative that expects him to seize and control (another comment reads, "*And tomorrow the officer goes back to enforcing the system that keeps this man homeless*"). Through this lens, one could read the exposure of DePrimo's act as an important, worthwhile deframing. After all, it's surely a good thing if the (white) police start to care for the (Black) homeless instead of beating and choking them to death.

But such a reading is reductive. It treats care and its exposure superficially and in isolation, without connecting it to the underlying logic that the story contributes to maintaining. In celebrating the uncanny vision of a white police officer clothing a Black homeless man, the NYPD is legitimizing its position as the organizer and manager of a border that serves to protect the fictional— and definitely very racialized—distinction between home (what is lawful) and homelessness (the unlawful other). By definition, this is the NYPD's job: according to its own official statement, its mission is to "maintain order" and to "protect the lives and property of our fellow citizens and impartially enforce the law." The NYPD's act of exposing DePrimo's act of care is diagrammed within that framework: it is not about questioning what kind of order, and what kind of law, needs to be maintained. It is, on the contrary, a strategic move to avoid that kind of questioning. A story that centers on care provides the NYPD's clientele with a more palatable version of control than the usual servings of brutality and racial profiling so common in the contemporary American city.

In exposing the seemingly good relationship between DePrimo and Jeffrey Hillman, the NYPD is attempting to rewrite—consciously or unconsciously is of little importance here—the cognitive map through which we understand their role in the world. Crucially, it does so by building upon a second, even more powerful framework: the cultural repertoires of humanitarianism and love, as contextualized in a highly individualistic, conservative, and classist Western world. The evidence for this second, shared cognitive map lies in the astonishingly high number of Facebook comments responding to the original picture in terms of "God," "charity," "love," and other religious themes. As in other

Western contexts (see the Italian case in chapters 3 and 4), a useful abstract machine to unpack these processes is the figure of the "Good Samaritan" of Luke's Gospel (see table 5.1). This well-known and powerful tale illustrates how a man (*sic*) is supposed to love other human beings, including his enemy. The Good Samaritan is a diagram built around the two basic tenets of Christian-infused social interventionism, the agape and caritas that came up also in the previous chapter. Arguably, the parable has become virtually synonymous with Christian attitudes toward the less privileged, exemplifying an act of generosity that people of different cultural and religious backgrounds consider admirable. Given the prominence of references to this tale in the case above, and in much of the charitable and NGO humanitarian advertising around the homeless, it is worth briefly recalling the content of this story.

In the parable, a Samaritan—who represents the archetypal stranger or enemy—offers his help to a man lying in the street who has been beaten and robbed (see Luke 10:30–37 for the full text).[42] The message carried by this tale is that we should love our neighbor, not only in terms of our emotional attitude but also in terms of concrete practices of care: "he went to him and bandaged his wounds"; "he put the man on his own donkey"; "he took out two denarii and gave them to the innkeeper"; and so on. DePrimo's case shares many features with this parable (and even with its pictorial depiction; see figure 5.2): the dispossessed man (Mr. Hillman) is given material support (the boots) by a potentially dangerous stranger (DePrimo), who does not ask anything in return. But there is more than simple comparability.

In the parable, the relationship between the Samaritan and the robbed man is one-directional: it is the Samaritan who loves the robbed man; it is he who cares, and it is he who defines the tempo of the encounter. At no point in the parable is the robbed man given a voice. We do not know—since Jesus is silent on these points—if he appreciates what the Samaritan did, or what he thinks about the whole affair; and we can only assume his emotional response. Similarly, in DePrimo's case, the homeless person is given neither a name nor a voice. We hear him talking only through two speeches reported by the officer. In the first, we hear the homeless person saying, "I never had a pair of shoes," and in the second, when asked by DePrimo if he would also like a coffee, we hear, "No, officer, you've done enough. . . . I love the police. God bless you."[43] We don't know what he thinks of the boots, what use he is going to make of them, and we cannot know much about the affective encounter between the two. Why hadn't he owned a pair of shoes before? Why did he not want a hot coffee on a cold night? We cannot answer these questions because they have never been asked.

The two stories are diagrammed around the same paradigm of care, one based on unbalanced, vertical power relations, where one actor is dependent on a more powerful other and where the basis of that dependency cannot be discussed or challenged.[44] Since no proper account of the robbed/homeless man is given, the idea that we have of the encounter is derived not from the encounter itself, but from its framing. The audience can only perceive DePrimo's actions as "just," "good," and "awesome" because its affective response has already been diagrammed by powerful cultural and moral blueprints. The latter are reinforced by minor but important details, including the visual representation of the scene (a powerful man bending toward the powerless) and the fact that the picture was posted on the official NYPD page, where only exemplary acts are portrayed. For the many, DePrimo became good by definition (it is unavoidably signified as such), much as the Samaritan is (the Good Samaritan). The officer was also honored by the NYPD with "a special set of cufflinks."[45]

FIG. 5.2. Jan Wijnants, *Parable of the Good Samaritan* (detail), 1670, State Hermitage Museum, St. Petersburg. Photo by Vladimir Terebenin. Compare Wijnants's representation of the Good Samaritan with DePrimo's picture reported in figure 5.1. The two Samaritans bend toward a man, providing material help—a specific take on "care for the poor."

The narrative surrounding DePrimo's photo involves such strongly in-grained ideas that represent a powerful, if mostly unconscious, relational dia-gram involving their interpreters. I found very few comments openly criticizing or questioning what DePrimo did. It offers reassurance about the increasingly powerful position of the police, while expounding the value of caritas, lending it broad appeal. It is an easy tale to follow, one that does not require much en-gagement from the listener, and so it is light enough to travel fast—in the Ap-padurian sense, to circulate with its form—across the online world. The story does not ask us to question, to evaluate, or to see the homeless man as anything but a stereotypical recipient of an equally stereotypical form of care.

UNRAVELING

On December 2, the *New York Times* published an article reporting that Mr. Hillman was grateful for what DePrimo did, and that he also appreciated "everyone that got onto this thing. . . . It meant a lot to me."[46] However, the article also highlighted the fact that, at the time of the interview, Mr. Hill-man was once again barefoot. Moreover, other interventions started to ques-tion whether he was actually homeless. In particular, an article in the *New York Daily News* read, "The barefoot homeless man who received new shoes from a kind-hearted NYPD cop isn't actually homeless—and has a sad history of refus-ing help from loved ones and the government."[47]

Confronted for the first time at close range with "the barefoot homeless" who might not be homeless after all, the massive online audience suddenly became confused. The circulation of forms of this particular story took a twist in the form of its circulation, shifting the systems of representation deployed in its global decoding. Why was the homeless man barefoot again? Interrogated on this specific point, Mr. Hillman replied, "Those shoes are hidden. They are worth a lot of money. . . . I could lose my life."[48] Moreover, he added, "I was put on YouTube, I was put on everything without permission. What do I get? . . . This went around the world, and I want a piece of the pie."[49]

These two statements give us, for the first time, the opportunity to recon-sider the encounter between DePrimo and Mr. Hillman. Hillman is grateful for the donation, but at the same time he feels that the gift may have put his life at risk (ironically enough, he risks being beaten and dispossessed). Moreover, although he appreciates DePrimo's actions and the media attention, he also feels that he did not gain much out of it. His identity was revealed, without his permission, and he apparently did not like this very much (besides the photo published on Facebook, the *New York Daily News* article posted pictures of him as a young man, essentially reconstructing—and thus exposing—his life history). Commentators on Facebook started to question his actions and statements, and for the most part, they did not seem to like them. Comments on the topic read: "Soon after, the bum sold the boots. . . . He claims he's 'hidden' them . . . suuure buddy" or "I see the homeless man now wants a piece of the pie that his image is creating, what a dick." There is more in this vein (table 5.2).

Although this third space is still characterized by comments that praise DePrimo's act and refer to religious themes, their relative importance diminishes. The few comments blessing the homeless person disappear, and there is a surge in the number of people inquiring about his homeless status and the destiny of the boots DePrimo had bought. The latter, in particular, cease being a medium for delivery of care and come to symbolize a particular kind of life (and a set of personal failings): "The guy is still on the streets barefoot. Where are the shoes? Delivered for a bottle of Schnapps??" As soon as a voice is given to the poor man, the whole Good Samaritan framing of the incident is on the verge of falling to pieces.

Mr. Hillman's voice cuts through the diagram, but it is not, in Deleuzian terms, a line of flight: it does not allow us to challenge the framing. The latter is too strong. Instead of questioning the intrinsic shortcomings of the good cop–Good Samaritan fairy tale and questioning the fiction of home those framings are there to protect, the mood turns reactionary. DePrimo's story provides something so Disneyesque it cannot be questioned: his individual act reassures the audience that everything is good and possible, that ultimately the separation of home and homelessness can be dealt with, provided good love and good care are enacted. Commentators unconsciously held onto that fiction and virulently attacked Mr. Hillman in order to remove him from a narrative in which he no longer fit, from a story that they wanted to preserve in spite of his voice (table 5.2). Following a path that many critical scholars of deviance have highlighted, Mr. Hillman's removal takes place through his recharacterization. He is no longer the dispossessed and deserving poor, but one of the many ungrateful, undeserving, feckless rough sleepers. His refusal to wear the boots makes him responsible for his plight and, therefore, undeserving of Officer DePrimo's care.

THE TRANSLOCAL POWER OF THE CULTURAL
REPRESENTATION OF HOME(LESSNESS)

The story of Larry DePrimo and Jeffrey Hillman could be dissected further, underlining the structural racialized violence that made that encounter possible in the first place. My aim here has been, more modestly, to focus on the

TABLE 5.2 The bad homeless man: Common comments on Mr. Hillman's subsequent reaction to DePrimo's "act of care"

Topic	Example 1	Example 2	Example 3	Example 4	Example 5
Ungratefulness of homeless man	I just read a story that the homeless man wants money for the pic being disclosed without permission . . . How ungrateful!	are you kidding me, the update on this guy is ridiculous! . . . this man has chosen to be homeless & do whatever it is he's doing to put him there. sorry, but i will totally think twice before i give them anything.	Seems this guy is very ungrateful now and wants his piece of the pie because his picture was posted online without his permission. Should be arrested for loitering now.	What a great officer to help, now this homeless man "Wants a piece of the pie" for the photo, what a loser, he should just be grateful for the boots but he wants a handout, what a loser	It was on the news today that unfortunately this man isn't homeless, he lives in an apt in Brooklyn or the Bronx? So sad to hear this amazing and good deed went to someone selfish
Homeless is a fraud	Turns out the man is not homeless and won't wear the boots because they are worth a lot of money to him! Geez!	HE ISN'T HOMELESS!!! FRAUD!!! FRAUD!!!	For those who don't know, this man is not homeless, it's a choice.	He's Not Homeless!!!!	this man is NOT homeless at all. for the last 3 years he has been pooling this but i have seen him dressed better then most. His hustle will always be this.
Like the story "despite"	I heard the homeless guy was a "scammer." It was all over the news. Still, that was very nice of that Officer.	Listen if its in your heart to help people like this homeless man or anyone else for that matter, it doesn't matter what he does after you did ur deed. As long as you did what you felt was right.	No matter what happened to the boots once officer DePrimo gave them to the gentleman, it doent matter. We are supposed to help those that cannot help themselves.	It isn't even about the boots. It is about a police officer that showed the world how to be like Jesus. Thank you so much officer for . . . telling us by your act of kindness that Jesus still lives in the heart of man.	Even with all the new details that have come out concerning the homeless man, your compassionate heart for action is what makes you a hero!

(Continued)

TABLE 5.2 (Continued)

Topic	Example 1	Example 2	Example 3	Example 4	Example 5
Linking "barefoot again" news	The homeless guy is bare foot again!! http://news.yahoo.com/blogs/lookout/nypd-homeless-man-boots-tillman-134758145.html	"Those shoes are hidden," Jeffrey Hillman, the 54-year-old homeless man, told the New York Times. "They are worth a lot of money," http://news.yahoo.com/blogs/lookout	http://thestir.cafemom.com/in_the_news/147491/homeless_man_barefoot_again_after?utm_medium=sm&utm_source=facebook&utm_content=thestir_fanpage	OLD NEWS. . . . and the latest was NY TIMES caught up to homeless man, who was barefoot again.	http://news.yahoo.com/blogs/lookout/homeless-man-boots-nypd-apartment-155517489.html
Getting more viral	Respect fm Russia! Policeman is a good man. Let God bless him!	This news was published along with picture in Pakistan's newspaper (DAWN) today "... we appreciate this act of kindness for Allah is kind to human being.	A good samaritan in our time! Bless you! Greetings from Norway	Hi I'm from Sydney Australia I can't belive what this police officer he is so kind not like the up your self cops in Sydney good on you officer your number 1	im from Ukraine, its a good policeman, good man with big heart . . . .

Source: Elaboration of the author on Facebook public data

Note: This phase includes comments from one period, December 2–10. In this period comments on "God" and on the "DePrimo" act were still largely present. In order to preserve their original form, comments have not been edited to correct grammar, spelling, or punctuation.

"viralization" of that story, in order to illustrate how certain kinds of representation tap right into entrenched repertoires that diagram our understanding of home(lessness), reproducing a dichotomous division between home and its other, across geographies. The value of such an exercise in deconstruction lies in a simple predicament: if home is founded upon the expulsion of the other in order to allow a whole plethora of extractions, then every exposure that does not attack this premise serves to maintain its diagrammatic logic. When the lights of the spectacle turned away from the NYPD story, readers and commentators walked away with two key messages reinforced: the police can be good, and the (Black) poor are usually undeserving. A hierarchical, racialized, normative, and conservative understanding of the roles of each was reinforced, one that aligns strongly with—and ends up reinforcing both semantically and culturally—the logic of the home/homelessness binary as it is lived and felt by the dispossessed individuals involved (such as in the cases presented in chapter 3 and 4, but also as illustrated by Mr. Hillman's complaint about the representation game).

A radically different story would have questioned the NYPD's appropriation of Hillman's poverty and DePrimo's decision to buy boots for someone who never asked for them. It might also have accepted Hillman's choice not to wear the boots and to do whatever he pleased with the gift. It would almost certainly not have led to an audience commenting en masse and appropriating a problematic biblical narrative to do so. The premise of such an alternative story would be a radically different understanding of the relationship between DePrimo, Hillman, the media, and the Facebook users. One has to challenge the role that each and every one of these characters plays in order to instantiate a genuinely liberatory system of representation around home(lessness). This would give rise, in turn, to more emancipatory abstract machines of alterity and poverty, making tactical use of alternative representations crafted from the interstices of home(lessness) life, such as those forms of creative activism that Sarah Elwood and Victoria Lawson refer to as "disruptive poverty politics."[50] These would be forms of representation where the long-standing histories of racialized dispossession (expulsion) and accumulation (extraction) founding our current conceptions of home and homelessness are discussed, ridiculed, and countered. Cultural representation is the bread and butter of those connections, since they provide a basic mainstream grammar—a shared system of representation—to make sense of, and recharge, normative ideals of being at home.

To complement the illustration of the critical method offered by this book—for an analysis of home and homelessness as home(lessness)—I will now expand on these translocal connections looking at a different kind of cultural discourse: a second exemplificatory intersection, which, in a sense, is even more powerful than bare representation. I am referring here to the realm of international policy debate and policy transfer, a form of discursive power that carries with itself strong actionable diagrams. The policy discourse is not, in fact, just about representing the other of home but about organizing, shaping, instituting, and, ultimately, ordering and managing both expectations and populations related to it. It goes without saying that international policy discourse is central to the reproduction of many forms of lessness of our times: spanning from the maintenance of state borders to the control of people's movements across those borders, from national to international agencies of state and capital power, from the preservation of neoliberal modes of extraction to the governance of climate change—policy discourse and policy transfer are central to all of those—and the list could go on. But when it comes to the nexus this book is focused on, in recent years two intersections of international policy discourse have arisen above all others in terms of their power to mobilize people and institutions translocally. The first is the so-called Housing First approach, one that is of particular interest to me not only because it provides a good case to exemplify how the bordering home/homelessness is maintained globally, but precisely because from the outset this is an approach that, at least nominally, seems precisely crafted to challenge that same border. It is, as its creators stated, sold as a way to end homelessness. The second has been the global management of the COVID-19 pandemic, with its mantras of "staying home to save lives," repeated across geographies with a resonance and intensity rarely seen before.

Ending Homelessness (On Global Policy)

At some point in 2014, I was approached by the Italian federation of organizations working for homeless people (fio.PSD), a branch of the European-wide FEANTSA.[51] At the time, fio.PSD was launching a pilot to test a policy called Housing First across Italy. Since I have recalled the intrinsic limits of that experiment elsewhere, I won't go into detail here.[52] I remember, however, one of the first summer schools that they organized around this project, which took place in the beautiful town of Ragusa, a UNESCO World Heritage site in Sicily. The event gathered together more than fifty organizations working with homeless people in Italy, some of them very big (such as CARITAS), others much smaller. Together, they represented a good spectrum of the sector's

Catholic charities, public partnerships, and secular providers *per i senza tetto d'Italia* (Italy's homeless). The idea was to run a series of workshops and lectures offered by the so-called Comitato Scientifico, the scientific committee comprising a dozen experts, including myself. We came from several disciplinary fields, including sociology, community psychology, anthropology, and statistics, and some very prominent names were involved. I believe I was included not only because of my academic work but also for the prestige brought to the table by my institutional affiliation at the time, the University of Cambridge.

Housing First (HF) was conceived in New York in 1992 by Sam Tsemberis, a community psychologist who ran an organization called Pathways to Housing.[53] Though the organization's name might seem to imply a route to a home, Tsemberis's main intention was to challenge conventional ways of dealing with homelessness. The Pathways model of HF was targeted at chronically homeless people, those defined by the US Department of Housing and Urban Development (HUD) as long-term street dwellers, who, always according to the HUD definition, often have severe mental illness or addiction-related issues. Crucially, if traditional operations argued that a chronically homeless person either had to go through preparatory stages to be ready for a home (the staircase model) or had to be continuously, and compulsorily, taken care of (the continuum of care), Pathways' HF reversed these propositions. Chronically homeless people did not have to be prepared in order to attain housing: the latter is to be offered permanently, as the precondition for any other intervention, accompanied with sustained forms of optional support. Brought down to its basic ethos, HF follows a harm-reduction principle: housing is provided even if the individual does not stop consuming addictive substances, and the support offered by the program (multidisciplinary teams of care workers, psychologists, and doctors) can be refused by the client.

Pathways to Housing began by using an economic argument to promote HF in the United States. It is financially costlier to maintain a homeless individual on the street (due to the expense associated with night shelters, emergency hospital rooms, etc.) than to offer them a permanent housing solution (even in the private market, where most HF units were located in New York). On that basis, HF was promoted by the George W. Bush administration (through the head of the Interagency Council on Homelessness, ICH, Philip Mangano) and then by the Obamas (especially Michelle Obama) as "the way to end homelessness." Tsemberis was quick to mobilize scholars to validate the results of his approach, with studies often focusing on the high rates of housing retention and the reduction of local, state, and federal costs associated with it. Dozens of papers were produced presenting and analyzing these results, with some even developing rigid fidelity scales to assess it (for instance, the thirty-eight-item quantitative assessment of program adherence offered by Gilmer and colleagues).[54]

Mangano and the ICH played a crucial role in the promotion of HF in the United States, calling on local authorities to establish ten-year action plans based on the approach.[55] The political appropriation of HF thus filtered down to federal and local levels, triggering a process of policy contagion from one context to another. This is policy boosterism in action: a chain of assessments indicate a particular way of doing things to ensure best practice and benchmark status.[56] From these shores, HF quite rapidly became a textbook example of "urban policy mobilities."[57] On the basis of a strong cultural legitimization—often generated within a center of economic, cultural, and political power—a means for Appadurai's "forms of circulations" is generated, and a circulation of forms enacted. Housing First became constructed as a Foucauldian truth: a type of knowledge wielding the power to mobilize interests, setting processes in motion and changing the state of affairs of things. Once that truth was established by experts—such as the researchers and politicians involved in the legitimization of the approach—the policy moved forward via reports, conferences, encounters, forums, emails, and websites. As McCann argues, "These mobilities facilitate the production of a particular form of relational knowledge in and through which policy actors understand themselves and their cities' policies to be tied up in wider circuits of knowledge—regional, national, and global networks of teaching and learning, emulation, and transfer."[58]

But there is more to it than that. Conventionally, these movements are understood as transfers: policy A, devised in context X, is judged best practice and rationally implemented in contexts Y and Z by experts in the field, in the (positivist) assumption that any divergence from A is an unacceptable divergence from the reference benchmark.[59] However, the real world is often different and less linear. As the case of HF demonstrates, in the transition from an operation conducted by a group of individuals based in New York to a good practice model ripe for export to every corner of the world, HF did not remain the same as it was, but changed. It was assembled into the contexts it encountered, inevitably turning into something else. In this sense, policies are always mobilized, not simply transferred: policy A, devised in context X, is subject to a set of discordant appraisals at various levels, which renegotiate its premises and purposes at the discursive level; it is implemented in different contexts, such as Y and Z, by a wide range of social players who will be constantly renegotiating its application in the light of the dynamics prevailing in their context. The policy changes in its contextual implementation and during its innocuous (only in appearance) travels. As Peck and Theodore recall, "mobile policies rarely travel as complete 'packages,' they move in bits and pieces—as selective discourses, inchoate ideas, and synthesized models—and they therefore arrive not as replicas but as policies already-in-transformation."[60]

When mobilized, a policy is demobilized and remobilized. In other words, it is assembled, disassembled, and reassembled according to the elements (both discursive and material) that it encounters. In this process, a global cultural policy form is produced, one that brings with itself its own foundational assumptions and structural violence. When it came to the creation of such a form in the case here analyzed, once legitimization was accrued in the United States, HF was actively promoted internationally, as a good to be exported and sold off, with Pathways to Housing undertaking ad hoc consultancy work (for agencies, policy makers, and organizations) in the United States, Canada, and all over Europe (including with fio.PSD in Italy). A number of HF experts gained prominence, consulting with governments, agencies, and local charities. For a while, I was part of the circus too, consulting in Italy and with the Welsh government. I produced a policy review for one of the major homelessness charities in the UK (Shelter), contributed to the definition of the approach at the institutional level in Wales, and took part in celebrating the success of Housing First in Finland with the main provider of the program there (Y-Saatyo).

My main aim through these engagements was to get a better sense of how policy and scholarship collude to produce very powerful assemblages—of knowledge, and therefore of power—which are then capable of diagramming the world, in an epistemic and material sense, as illustrated in the previous section. I was also motivated to play devil's advocate with the policy makers and practitioners I encountered. I did not do so because I believe HF is fundamentally wrong; I believe it is a great improvement on any conditional model of sheltering, because it allows its clients to extract something substantive from the system. For a while, I was even convinced that a fundamental attack on home(lessness) could be founded on the practical goal of rapidly rehousing as many people as possible. However, as time went on, my ideas shifted and became more critical. By the time I was in Ragusa, meeting committed practitioners under the beautiful Sicilian sun, I had become suspicious of the enthusiasm for importing a policy that originated elsewhere and translating it to another multifaceted context, where resources and institutional frameworks were completely different than the originating one. Concerns among long-term practitioners in Italy that HF was little more than a reinvention of the wheel were widespread and motivated.

As I have argued with my colleagues Stefanizzi and Gaboardi, HF in Italy was rapidly sold as a best practice at the national-political level (emulating what happened in the US with HUD), but it was much more complex to manage on a practical level.[61] Even if the organizations involved in the experimentation with HF in Italy were deeply interested in, and motivated toward, finding new ways of challenging homelessness, at the same time, participants were frustrated by the difficulties of applying HF—and in particular the Pathways HF approach they had been exposed to—in the Italian context(s): some complained about the inappropriateness of the original model, while others requested greater guidance and presence in its everyday implementation. Practitioners were preoccupied by the rigid remit of the original program (the chronically homeless as defined by HUD in the US was not representative of the homeless population of the peninsula), by the need to find houses on the private market (a key component of the Pathways HF approach, which sat uncomfortably with the greater availability of social housing and charitable homes in the Italian case), as well as by the lack of resources available to sustain the distinctive harm-reduction approach of HF, through forms of intensive case management that most organizations involved in the Italian experiment could not afford.

I grew more concerned when I heard echoes of the questions raised by Italian practitioners in those expressed by their Welsh counterparts during a workshop I did in Cardiff for the leading Welsh homeless providers, back in 2016 (similar concerns were common in other contexts too, as scholars have reported).[62] Confronted with the scientific proof and the international validation of HF coming from international policy makers, as well as with scholars and local politicians pressing for this new revolutionary approach to be taken into consideration, practitioners were puzzled. Their doubts were not so much about the program itself but around revealing practicalities:

- Who is paying for this?
- How can we find housing?
- How can we define the target population?
- How can we break the silos of public services?
- How can we deal with legacy schemes that need to be transformed or decommissioned?

At first glance, I thought that these questions and other similar doubts represented the fundamental uneasiness of a sector confronted with a push toward change. Indeed, for some of these questions, the literature does provide some answers: HF is sufficiently flexible that it can be implemented using scattered or communal housing, with onsite support or service brokerage, or with or without state support, and so on.[63] Yet these answers don't tackle the more fundamental issues raised by these questions. And here comes the second, deeper level of criticism that can be directed at HF.

The problem is not simply related to policy boosterism and to the passive adaptation of policy frames and practice. Rather, within the lines, the questions raised by committed Italian and Welsh practitioners about HF signaled underlying uneasiness around key foundational matters of the homeless issue: the worry around finding permanent housing was pointing at the intrinsic failure of housing markets; the struggle to define who the program should be addressed to was signaling an increased uneasiness with predefined targets, incapable of mirroring traumatic individual experiences and grasping local contingencies. The perceived resistance toward radical change by some practitioners had less to do with individual inertia and unwillingness to change accustomed practices, and more to do with the deep realization of how much the homelessness industry is structurally layered, segmented, and bounded in its intersections with other similarly specialized fields of intervention, and with the broader functioning of the neoliberal society it's plugged into. Even though it was never stated explicitly, the novelty of HF, its invitation to rethink current practices, was leading the practitioners I have encountered to question some of the structural problems with the mainstream home/homelessness binary. But those questions, crucially, had almost immediately outrun the scope of HF: the experts summoned to these workshops had no space to deal with these broader matters, because HF (like any other policy carved out from a segmented and bounded approach to homelessness) is not designed to question the fundamental basis of the violence and traumatic experiences it claims to address.

In HF, a subject is reduced to a client who needs to be housed. What is expelled in this procedure is that which exceeds the perceived needs that are to be addressed, the problem that is to be solved. The extractions obtained from the operation range from enhanced social prestige and status for scholars and providers to electoral capital and more efficient forms of social control for the political sponsors. Where HF is decisively different from more conventional approaches is that in this system the client of the program extracts major value, too: they gain the benefit of a stable abode, with all that means in terms of personal security. These are undeniable positives, and they distinguish HF from many of the available interventions that fell under the broad umbrella of homelessness policy. Yet, as much as this is incrementally better than a conventional staircase or charitable model, which give only limited benefits to their clients, HF still remains an intervention solidly grounded within a wider system of oppression and value extraction. When and how does HF challenge the capitalist, patriarchal, anthropocentric, and racist underpinnings of mainstream modalities of inhabiting the world? Is HF really about ending homelessness, or is it about sheltering individuals without challenging the foundational parameters that render all grounded in the possibility of being made less? In other words, is it enough to house all the homeless people of the world in order to end homelessness? If you believe, as I do, that there is no end to homelessness unless we collectively transcend the colonies of home, then HF becomes just the most progressive version of a very reactionary way of doing things.

The point is not to find fault with, and then provide incremental adjustments to, HF (as is common practice in the scholarly debate, particularly when scholars are asked to validate its implementation by policy makers).[64] To question the validity of HF, one does not need a fidelity scale but must question what HF does: what kind of home it contributes to reproducing. Along these lines, scholars such as Löfstrand and Juhilia have argued that HF was born as an alternative to the linear residential treatment approach, but nonetheless shares commonalities with it. In particular, they show that the Tsemberis model tends to lead to professionals negotiating clients' choices with them, something that in turn leads to forms of neoliberal consumer dependence. For these authors, HF can be considered just another instance of the "larger discursive formation called advanced liberalism."[65] Baker and Evans also criticize HF for its neoliberal ethos, arguing that it advances "(i) a discursive and material emphasis on individual pathologies (i.e. mental illness, addiction and physical impairment) over structural causes of homelessness, (ii) the premising of intervention based on the fiscal savings thought to result from addressing a 'high cost' sub-group of the homeless population, and (iii) the realisation of 'clean and safe' streets by removing a small but highly visible type of homeless person and their behaviours from public view."[66] In New York, after all, HF targeted a small group of homeless people, which led to the diversion of resources and attention from other groups, such as families and low-skilled workers.[67] One of its unintended consequences was that these groups then started to fill the city's dormitories, as a result of structural cuts to housing and other welfare funding. Paradoxically, HF did not end homelessness but contributed to relocating it to a new set of social groups.

These critiques are important because they implicitly invite us to look beyond the given status quo around policy interventions, which define a problem, provide a solution, and segment a population through which to circulate a truth. Radical critiques of HF aim to question the kind of system HF emerges from and reinforces, and to interrogate its broader vision of the social realm, especially when it reaches the level of a global cultural fact. A fundamental quote in this sense is provided by Kim Hopper, when he reminds us that "no targeted program suffices to rewrite cultural scripts or to undo structures of discrimination centuries in the making."[68] This line must be taken very seriously. One thing is to advocate the end of homelessness within current frames, which might end up reproducing the foundation of homelessness in itself. Another thing is to refuse adjustments to a corrupt system and to question the continuum where both home and homelessness are founded on the same violent expulsive and extractive principles. Through this lens, we must question whether any intervention in the field of homelessness, including HF, can break through existing conditions, or whether it will reproduce the given. Though HF has its merits in challenging punitive aspects of previous approaches, it still solves homelessness by breaking it down to a set of defined segments, as if the problem of "the other of home" can really be solved by isolating it from the entrenched (homely) violence structuring it.

Some might counter that HF could be the starting point to challenge the deeper functioning of home. I agree that housing—the securing of a permanent and unconditional abode—must be the unconditional ground of the struggle for a liberatory way of homing the world. However, it can't be the only founding principle, simply because there is more to homing than just housing (a point homelessness scholarship and policy recognize in theory, but fall short of implementing in practice). As controversial as it might sound to some, housing, the technical fix, does not need to come first, but should be subordinated to the ideological and material praxis of redoing homing. This is not merely a normative assertion on my part but an insight drawn from what is already happening: within the rubric of socially progressive and globally marketable approaches to solving homelessness as a problem lies a clear ideology of social segmentation and policing, one offering individualized solutions to an individually framed problem, therefore renouncing the ambition to deal with housing and homing systemically, looking at the underlying violence of home/homelessness. In other words, already within HF, housing does not come first but is part, and a function, of a precise homing ideology, structuring what housing is then allowed to do for people: a cage within lessness, rather than a liberation from it.

In the global cultural fact of HF, in its translation across space and time, these ideological foundations are not paid attention to. Such erasure is strategic. One needs to ask: when HF is promoted and sold by practitioners, policy makers, and scholars, what kind of socioeconomic vision, and what kind of cultural fact, are bundled up with it? Advocates of the policy would say they are selling a world without homelessness. But in immanent terms, they are really selling a horizon of what housing and inhabitation can be with clear socio-material consequences: one in which a minority of worse-off individuals experiencing extreme forms of housing deprivation are moved out of sight, while the fundamental problem of home(lessness), the precarity and dispossession of the many, is untouched. The cultural global formations emerging in the channeling of these propositions throughout national programs, local law, and the investment of resources are one of the major obstacles to the liberation of home.

Virological Austerity (On Global Emergency)

To conclude this chapter, I want to briefly recall the ways in which nation-states and international agencies have dealt with the intersection of the COVID-19 pandemic and housing. Especially in the first and second wave of lockdowns, the international consensus around what home can do for people at the time of the emergency mirrored, very clearly, two of the tenets illustrated in the previous sections. First, there was a clear othering of the other of home: people without shelter had to be confined, kept at bay, secured, in order to extract security for the many. Second, there was a global consensus around what has to be protected in times of emergency: lives, surely, but in their capacity to fulfill a role within the larger housing-homing financialized diagram of current modes of inhabiting the world. The segmentation operated by this latter point during the COVID-19 pandemic is similar, in nature, to the logic operating at the heart of HF: one proactively reproducing a specific ideological take on housing and homing, reinforcing, rather than challenging, the expulsive and extractive functioning of what in this book I have called home(lessness).

The pandemic has caused much suffering, pain, and death, both during its peaks and in the unfolding of its provided fix, as vaccine distribution globally has clearly followed long-formed lines of economic injustice. Memories of impotence and tragic life losses are still vivid across geographies. In March 2020, during the first wave of the pandemic, the province of Bergamo in northern Italy rose to prominence worldwide for its number of cases and the meltdown of the—rather solid—national health care system in the region.[69] When much of the world was still relatively safe, the situation in Bergamo was genuinely dramatic. As friends living in the province reported to me at the time, people in intensive care were dying alone, suffering incredible pain, and were then buried without any funeral service. There was no time, no space, and no organizational capacity left to provide for those in need. During the total lock-down, individuals spent their days at home with their relatives, hoping that none of them would cough too hard and that their mobile phones wouldn't ring to announce someone they knew had entered the Giovanni Papa XXIII hospital—one of the best equipped and efficient in the region, which back then was at the point of complete meltdown.[70] Similar stories had already been reported from Wuhan and other Chinese provinces just a few weeks earlier, where the virus brought the most populous country in the world to advance unprecedented measures of containment and control. Soon after, these experiences became common worldwide, with an out-of-control number of cases in the United States, Brazil, and Iran, to mention just a few.

Notwithstanding national and regional differences, in this context, a global cultural fact emerged very clearly: home surged as the undisputed epicenter where individuals and collectives retreated to protect their intimate lives. It is at home where people were told to secure their biological beings, for their own sake and for the sake of others. It is there where we had to individual-ize the risks posed by the pandemic, sharing and managing them with our kids, partners, relatives. #StaySafeStayHome, or the equivalent Italian version #iorestoacasa, was the call to arms of millions of people invoking and celebrat-ing homely seclusion, social distancing, and self-isolation. In times like these, the form of the home as the most immediate socio-material body beyond our intimate selves becomes more apparent than ever before. Notably, the 2008 global financial meltdown posed a similar question: for the first time since 2000 on a large scale in the West, housing clearly became the terrain of con-testation. At that point in time, and in subsequent years too, the detrimental effects of the ways in which financialization had colonized the estate realm became clear, felt and lived from Detroit to Dublin, São Paulo to Barcelona. However, the intersection of COVID-19 and housing was of a different nature, posed different challenges, and highlighted very clearly what home was within the rubric of contemporary global home(lessness).

And rightly so: I was part of the choir at the outbreak of the pandemic, which included housing practitioners, activists, and charities, raising its voice to demand protection for the precariously housed and houseless. Petitions, manifestos, pledges, and online campaigns across geographies posed a simple, yet fundamental, question: how can the houseless stay home if they don't have a home to stay in? Leilani Farha, UN special rapporteur on the right to adequate housing at that time, signed a COVID-19 Guidance Note called "Protection for Those Living in Homelessness." The document clearly states why the homeless were vulnerable to the worst and most violent effects of the pandemic: "In the face of this pandemic, a lack of access to adequate housing is a potential death sentence for people living in homelessness and puts the broader population at continued risk. . . . Homelessness, including during a crisis, and irrespective of nationality or legal status, is a prima facie violation of human rights. . . . In this context, States must address the housing needs of homeless people on an urgent and priority basis to ensure their equal protection against the virus and the protection of the broader population."[71]

Leaving aside the human rights framework, the rapporteur's document provides a good summary of key action points, which were also promoted by countless other activists across the world. Far from being a great equalizer, COVID-19 carried consequences that were directly proportional to a person's socioeconomic and racial conditions. The virus not only intersected with human bodies; it interlaced with housing and labor, as well as with unequal personal and collective histories. For these reasons, activists urged the emergency response to the virus, its biopolitical management, to take into account more than the threat of infection. The response had to consider, among other things:[72]

- the immediate provision of shelter "to all homeless people living 'rough' or on the streets. This might require procuring hotel or motel rooms, or repurposing buildings such as army barracks, or unused hospitals";
- the role of governments in taking "measures that might result in people becoming homeless, such as evictions";
- safe accommodation for those fleeing violent households;
- the provision to the homeless of health care, testing facilities, hygiene infrastructure, and food banks, following health recommendations from the World Health Organization; and
- a safe place to stay for those testing positive for COVID-19, the avoidance of criminalization and punishment for those who cannot conform with containment measures, and the cessation of eviction proceedings, including the dismantling of encampments of homeless people.

Governments across the world responded to the initial phases of the crisis by meeting at least some of these demands. Though most focused on the first and second points, their reaction has frequently encompassed measures that many would have considered unthinkable not too long ago. Across the global north, several countries imposed temporary bans on eviction, suspended mortgage repayments, and offered resheltering initiatives for the homeless.

In the UK, where I was living at the time, councils and local charities were instructed to rehouse homeless individuals rapidly, in privately owned hotels or unused council-owned properties. Similar measures were adopted in the United States. In these and other countries, such as Argentina, Australia, Belgium, Brazil, Canada, France, Germany, Hungary, Senegal, South Africa, and Spain (to name just a few), governments introduced short or long bans on eviction. Some forms of protection for those in rent and mortgage arrears were introduced too, both via formal legislation (for instance in Italy) or more informally (in Romania, for instance, where private landlords and tenants struck informal agreements to lower rent, or postpone payments). Colleagues at the Anti-eviction Mapping Project captured much of this experience on a very informative global map. Alongside these top-down initiatives, this map also records actions taken from below, especially rent strikes.[73]

However, critical readers of housing and homing matters started to look into the cracks in these operations quite soon. Our editorial collective at the *Radical Housing Journal* was among the first, already in April 2020, to question the timeliness, extent, and novelty of these emergency measures in light of the structural foundations and dynamics they were built upon. At the very least, the renewed global cultural concept of defending the home demanded caution:

> Who, and what, are these measures really protecting? Who is really being saved by emergency programs advanced by those same institutions that have allowed for financialized, precarious dwelling to become the norm across the spectrum? It seems to us that the key role played by these programs is to maintain the basic infrastructure that allows for the exchange value of housing to be a pivotal axis of capitalist circulations. If everyone were to be evicted, if no one could pay their mortgage, and if the unhoused were allowed to legally occupy vacant property, what would the authorities, the state, and global capital do?[74]

At the core of this and other similar analyses, there was an attempt to go beyond the short-term benefits that some of these measures bring to the fore, in order to look at their makings and long-term effects. Such an operation is a challenging one, because it requires understanding the duplicitous nature of these programs. On the one hand, they do offer relief and immediate, albeit very selective, benefits to their users. On the other, they also serve the purpose of maintaining a system of monetary circulation and extraction that pivots around the exchange value of housing. After all, the COVID-19 crisis wouldn't be the first time in the history of capitalism that the state was forced to intervene to sustain capitalism. Indeed, when it comes to housing, 2008 witnessed a massive bailout delivered to the very financial institutions who were responsible for creating the recessionary crisis in the first place, with their management of mortgage derivatives.

The emergency sheltering and housing-protection initiatives promoted by governments as they responded to COVID-19 were ultimately designed not to break but to maintain the expulsive and extractive functional dynamics of home(lessness). On the one hand, complex life histories and socioeconomic conditions were strategically expelled and reduced, within the logic of emergency, to a series of faceless and therefore manageable icons: the home(less) to be housed; the poor family to be protected from eviction; the rightful homeowner to be assisted with debt repayments. On the other hand, besides voices amplified by vocal community activists, there has not been much policy interest in the longer-term picture beyond the immediate state of emergency. The future of the homeless person, or the struggling household, lies beyond the horizon of these programs, which are designed to preserve the status quo, allowing the circulatory extraction of value to continue. At the time of writing, it is difficult to say what this post-COVID extraction might look like. But it is clear that it is likely to involve stringent enforcement of mortgage debt repayment, greater controls on tenants (to be enabled by the invasive use of digital technologies), and the intensification of those lines of segregation that have confined the (often racialized) urban poor in overcrowded and poorly maintained dwellings, forcing them to bear the deadliest consequences of this crisis.

It should be clear, at this point, that the duplicitous nature of emergency programs is not limited to COVID-related housing interventions but is key to any other emergency and low-threshold programs for the home(less) (chapter 4) and to most progressive interventions such as HF. Just as loving the poor, in the context of FBOs, is about expelling subjects and recasting them within a particular and extractive diagram of faith and charity, the emergency functions as the platform for a similar extraction within the context of an apparently more public or universal state- or city-led approach. In this sense, COVID-19 has just amplified logics and modi operandi that were already in action within the cultural paradigm—and the affective and political economy—of lessness. The crisis and its disastrous management are not new, but only (re)newed. As my colleagues and I wrote to the *Radical Housing Journal* right in the midst of the first wave of the pandemic: "Institutions that don't directly oppose the structural conditions reproducing housing inequalities are, with their 'emergency quarantine politics,' simply allowing for the renewal of housing injustice."[75]

Transcending the Other

My aim with this chapter has been to further illustrate a methodology of inquiry around the impossible possibility of home. If the problem with the latter becomes apparent in looking within the structural violence linking the makings of home and of its supposed other locally (chapters 3 and 4), moving trans-locally shows how much deeper and how much further-reaching the unjust makings of home(lessness) are. The question of how lessness is ingrained and translated in global cultural formations is key to understanding its power, as one derived not only from specific (financialized) political economies but from epistemological and material cultural forms assembled through social media exchange, policy travel, and consensus on what home turns out to mean and to be in a global emergency.

I have argued that, at a time of increased interconnectivity, the act of exposing the poor is a powerful means through which home(lessness) gets coded into home/homelessness; it diagrams ideas and language in a certain way to sustain a precise representation of the world, enabling the (re)production of expulsive and extractive practices. No single retweet, no single line of comment, no single resharing is neutral within the systems of representation through which the colonies of home get reproduced. As with any form of affect, this is a power-from and a power-to, which means that it is not a simple device that can be plugged into and unplugged from a social realm. In sin-, sick-, and system-talk around home(lessness), exposure works as a means to make sense of things via producing new things, always in a way that does not break from but conforms with established narratives and their power relationships. Exposure works by cutting through the visible and the intelligible without announcing its presence. We can't see how the machine works because it is not announced and is nonlocalizable. Yet, if one is aware of the baseline foundations of this affective power, it is possible to trace its working, to map its diagrammatic tempo and circulatory power. It is immanently present in the assemblage of home/homelessness, and the number of cases one could examine to illustrate this is potentially unlimited.

In this context, excavating how the ideological construction of home gets circulated, and reactivated in global discourses and in their policy implementation, is not a call to put epistemology before material conditions but an invitation to take their coconstitutive nature seriously. As Housing First and the global response to the COVID-19 pandemic show, challenging the uneven foundations of home involves more than granting housing for all. A renewed ideological foundation needs to come to the fore, in order to imagine, and then assemble, homing anew. The outcome would be a liberatory take on inhabitation that does not require a policy to work, one that fights against normative tendencies and allows nonnormative dwelling propositions to emerge and endure. The point of such an approach would not be to renounce the ontological security that HF grants to its clients but to devise a different form of homing for a different kind of personal and collective security. In this sense, this chapter offers more than a critique in the negative, providing the foundation for the affirmative questions tackled in part III. What kind of affirmation, what kind of politics, what kind of praxis would work to cut through lessness?

Faced with the situated and the translocal powers of home(lessness)—with their entrenched molarity—in part III of this book, I will look for minor pathways, beyond institutional channels and current policy making and radically closer to the interstices where housing precarity is lived and felt. Liberation, here, is an affair of those interstices, not for those interstices: it is not about saving them, but about engaging in forms of accompliceship to affirm another kind of home within the cracks of the lessness plateau (chapter 7). Can we house without expelling and extracting? Can we get away from industries—of knowledge and political (re)production—that work to the detriment of those who have been defined as in need, and thus reproduce the conditions that make them homeless at a cultural, economic, and social level? Can we house otherness without having to save it, in ways that can radically alter what it means to house and to home the world? In other words, can housing be taken into consideration as a gateway for liberatory forms of inhabitation, centered on the affirmative power to change and emancipate life histories, rather than being treated as a technological solution to construct, contain, and police its supposed other?

Part III

6

THE MICROPOLITICS OF HOUSING PRECARITY

So how to think beyond home(lessness)? How to encompass our current home and imagine one that does not require a negation to stand? And what to do, in the here and the now, to fight the harshest intensification of the lessness diagram? The choice that I make at this point is to avoid jumping straight to a definition of what this liberated kind of home should look like. I want to insist on the need to find a renewed—and necessarily collective—way of thinking about that question. I want to stay with the methodological and epistemological issue, rather than jumping to the meta-answer. Yes, we need an anticapitalist, nonpatriarchal, antiracist, more-than-anthropocentric way of inhabiting the world: but what kind of role can homelessness and home play in that struggle? How to forget about the urge to solve homelessness within current frames and bring the problem back home, so as to crack both—and their inner violences—

wide open? And finally: Where to start? Can we find, within the situatedness of home(lessness), traces of liberatory edges of becoming already pointing beyond current conditions?

After years of ethnographic and activist work with communities and individuals facing precarious housing and homing conditions, the answer to this question lies for me squarely within the experience of housing precarity. The reason to choose such a starting point is political rather than analytical. It has to do with the locus of the colonizing power of home, which, as I have discussed, manifests in how bodies are made to work through its expulsive and extractive functionings. It is in the everyday experience of dispossession that proprietorship unfolds; where financialization is reproduced; where patriarchy lands its marks. And it is always there, at that level, where the subject of that experience is expelled, put in place, and extracted to and from, so that the violent ontological security of mainstream homing can endure. Starting from experience means to stay close to the colonizing power of home(lessness), both to understand how everyday colonies of home work and to retrieve related struggles in a situated, immanent way. This is about choosing a vantage point, charged with peculiar political significance, to intercept the ritornello of home(lessness) and to start working through its structural power from the embodiments of its effects.

The peculiarity of the political significance of housing precarity lies in its going largely unnoticed. What is conceived as political, when it comes to homelessness, homing, and housing, is usually the struggle to attain an end goal. That can range from self-determination and intersectional liberation to local and global policy: all forms of struggle that I am going to link up to in this last part of the book. But here, to start this discussion on the liberatory politics beyond lessness, I don't aim to define the political as that which is declared, but as that which is embodied and sometimes not announced; sometimes only muddled; sometimes silenced under layers of humanitarian colonizing epistemologies that have reduced desperation and need to matters of survival and, therefore, through those rubrics, to matters of resilience and presumed apolitical action. My goal is to question how the intersections making up the everyday experience of housing precarity might offer insights to reapproach the homing and the homeless political. The guiding question would be: What goes on beyond our habitual way of looking at the political in struggles that have to do with housing precarity?

As already indicated, the gist is that there is more at stake in housing precarity than the humanitarianisms of housing rights seem to suggest; more than traditional political-economy approaches are willing to register; more than celebratory accounts of the resilience of the homeless indicate; and more than the homelessness industries mentioned in previous chapters are prepared to accept. That more is a conatus, a politics of life, of being and becoming in the world, sometimes in ways that are deemed incompatible with normative ideas of home or that inhabit places that are conventionally defined as uninhabitable.[1] These modalities of life are alive, kicking, and sometimes contesting home(lessness) from its embodied makings. From within the cracks of housing precarity emerge ways of being and becoming that indicate other possible paths, "still possible worlds," as strange as those might seem from the standpoint of the white middle-class Westernized cultural doxas through which many of us—and certainly myself—operate professionally.[2]

The displacement advocated for in these pages is feminist and decolonial: feminist because it is grounded in a subjective and embodied take on precarity, and decolonial because it is situated, because it destructures apparent neutral understandings of homing, and it refuses to define a politics of liberation and instead looks through precarious propositions as a potential opening to a differential way of thinking about resistance, struggles, and, ultimately, inhabitation.[3] From the ground of use value (what housing does for people), the radicality of resistance against housing precarity is not defined in advance but is instead traced as it emerges from weird places, uninhabitable homes, and multiple violent histories. This is a form of understanding and embodying dwelling that is able to challenge our compromised habitus of home at its root, from the ground of its everyday propositional unfolding. To get there, one has to learn how to radically hear from, how to work through minor intersections that we have forgotten about or have left to the colonizing power of nonliberatory agencies. In what follows, I propose a radical housing epistemology that follows this path. The term *radical* here means two things: first, a focus on housing as political struggle—that is, as a lived and felt concern far beyond its reduction to a matter of policy; second, an invitation to consider that struggle through an intersectional and embodied viewpoint, complementary to that used by those focused only on the exchange value of housing.

Housing as a Gateway

For radical housing justice activists worldwide, the housing struggle is rarely seen solely in terms of exchange value—that is, it does not focus exclusively on the market cost of housing provision; nor is it suggested that the institution of public control over that market will solve all of its problems. Instead, activists tend to focus on the ways in which housing struggles are framed, lived, and embodied as a fight to affirm a different way of being in the world. This requires an expanded understanding of the use value of housing, and calls for a broader view of what home can do for people.[4] The Spanish Plataforma de Afectados por la Hipoteca (PAH) (with its call for grassroots solidarity); the US-based Anti-eviction Mapping Project (with its focus on the ways in which race entangles with capitalist urban development); the *pobladores* urban poor alliance in Chile (cutting across old and new class struggles); the work of activists in Ecatepec, Mexico City (with their incremental urbanism and makeshift infrastructures); and autonomous groups in eastern Europe (with their decolonial takes on the transition to capitalism) have something in common: they are united, in their many differences, by their effort to use housing as a gateway to challenge the unequal structural functioning of their homes and the way that it is grounded in forms of violence, including patriarchy, racism, class exploitation, and, of course, deprivation of shelter (chapter 2).

The generative power of many of these grassroots movements has been brought under academic scrutiny by a new generation of scholars whose work has gained momentum in the global north following the 2008 crisis. They are attentive to practices such as direct housing action, grassroots organizing, and squatting.[5] As I indicated earlier, some of this scholarship contends that housing precarity and housing struggles are both a product and a producer of the urban political.[6] Displacement and related forms of direct action and organizing therefore not only are the effects of uneven urban development but have the capacity to configure alternative modes of being and living in the city.[7] This is what Vasudevan calls the "make+shift" city: the construction of new forms of urbanity from the ground of radical action.[8] His line of thinking draws on a longer tradition, which includes anarchist approaches to housing developed in the UK and United States during the 1970s, as well as the work coming out of housing movements across the urban global south in the 1980s and '90s.[9]

For the most part, the current wave of critical housing scholarship, especially in its European unfolding, pivots around the Marxist-inflected tradition of critical urban studies developed from the 1970s onward on both sides of the Atlantic.[10] However, notwithstanding the fundamental importance of a traditional political economy framework in understanding contemporary uneven urban development, this approach has its limitations (for a notable discussion in this sense, see the works of Gibson-Graham, among others). First, in focusing on exchange value within capitalism, it tends to neglect other intersectional injustices making up the mainstream idea and practice of home/homelessness. Second, and consequentially, it tends to register the counterpolitics of housing precarity only when its emergence (in theory and practice) orients specifically to anticapitalist politics and uses their recognized languages. Actions and struggles that are grounded in a broader reenvisioning of home(lessness), but that fail to translate immediately into a familiar conceptual framework of capitalist exploitation, can be dismissed as irrelevant; or, worse, can be automatically treated as subproducts of the dominant script. These are arguably old debates in the field of urban studies, and certainly more progressive housing scholars are not unaware of the issues involved.[11] There are now some thought-provoking attempts to unite openly anticapitalist housing scholarship with a broader intersectional politics: examples include the volume edited by Mudu and Chattopadhyay, which successfully (re)approaches contemporary housing and migration struggles as coconstitutive of new political terrains, as well as numerous critical contributions that are infused with attention to feminist methodologies, political ecology, and autonomist housing politics (to which I will return in chapter 7).[12]

Yet in the mainstream radical left of the West, there is still a tendency to single out certain forms of housing struggle as political while neglecting others. The problem is essentially epistemological: it centers on what is made to count as politics and resistance in our reading of these processes.[13] Why is it that the efforts of millions of urbanites to assemble decent life conditions in slums across the urban south are read, for the most part, as the effect of large-scale economic restructuring as it is entangled in urbanization and as a matter of endurance and resilience in the face of overcrowding and environmental threats?[14] Why are the efforts of millions of women fighting to live within their homes relegated to the rubric of empowerment and capabilities, or registered only within the remit of feminist debates, rather than being seen as part of a fight to liberate housing from its patriarchal, masculine, violent ethos? Why is it that homeless people in our cities are still framed as the residual force of the *Lumpenproletariat*, bored products of neoliberal entrepreneurialism or grateful bodies used to celebrate supposedly loving acts of care, instead of being seen, in their everyday embodied struggles and occupation of public space, as a primary example of resistance against housing precarity? Or why, in an otherwise excellent volume around squatting in Europe, are we told that "immigrants, ethnic minorities such as the Roma, [and homeless] people" who are living in squats throughout the continent cannot be taken into consideration in the analysis, since their reason for action, their desperation, "has little to do with what is usually called 'political squatting'"?[15] Why can't they be seen as equally political in their rejection of life in confined Roma camps as a technique for controlling their racialized otherness, and in their occupation of the squat as a new terrain of affirmation?[16]

What all these examples have in common is a tendency to impose radical frameworks developed in the West on the lived experience of housing struggle as it unfolds on the ground. If there is a common political foundation to the ways in which these slum dwellers, homeless people, beaten women, and racialized bodies are struggling for housing in order to advance a more liberatory politics of home, this is not registered by such an approach. If there is a politics of emancipation in there, within the cracks of those precarious housing struggles, it is not allowed to emerge but remains silenced by the theoretical/political canon. The problem is one of perspective. As AbdouMaliq Simone recognizes, "if we only pay attention to the rollout of contemporary spatial products as exemplars of urban neoliberalism, we might miss opportunities to see something else taking place, vulnerable and provisional though it may be."[17] Out there, in the extended margins that cut through—and beyond—cities across the world, everyday housing struggles take a more complex and nuanced form than that which is registered in narratives of the creative-destructive force of contemporary capitalism.[18] Though these offer one helpful lens on the problem, they should not be allowed to obscure other accounts.[19] Taking desperation seriously is important if we are to appreciate the ways in which home/homelessness is contested in its everyday articulation. As communities I have encountered have taught me: desperation is political.

To get closer to these politics means to read housing and its precarious assemblage and experience as a gateway to broader concerns. Such a move requires a decentering of the dominant paradigm through which we come to understand the politics of housing precarity. I offer three epistemological suggestions in this sense, centered, respectively, around the effort of decolonizing, tracing, and working with the politics of housing precarity. I explore the first two in this chapter, and unpack the third in chapter 7. Before moving on, I want to take a short detour to establish that considering every form of inhabitation as political is not a novelty nor a particularly radical proposition but lies deep, if often forgotten, in established grammars of thinking about dwelling and being in the world. The problem is what one decides to do with the political charge of inhabitation: it can be liberated or used to constantly recharge ritornellos of despair.

Inhabiting Is Always Political

Inhabiting can be understood as our way of being and becoming in the world. I use it interchangeably with the word *dwelling* because I understand both as indicating the processual makings of life through space and time.[20] As McFarlane reminds us, these makings of life are not a given but are learned in a fragmented, yet historically and geographically specific, and also creative way.[21] Dwelling in the world cannot be conceived in isolation from the structural, historical, economic, and cultural environment that constitutes it, yet it is also a matter of embodied experiences and endurances that constantly reproduce what earthly habitation is and means. In this context, housing becomes more than a simple container for disparate forms of dwelling but is understood as part of the process of dwelling itself. If this might appear obvious at first sight, in reality housing is often seen as something of its own, separated from its wider ontological and political implications around how—and which kind of— inhabitation is made possible on this planet. As the anarchist architect Turner pointed out four decades ago, the question to be asked is not around what housing is, or just around how many houses we need, but must be around "the performance of housing, i.e. what it does *for* people."[22]

But inhabitation cannot be taken at face value. As a notion, it can be used in extremely conservative ways, including those that dictate a given form of housing.[23] To avoid this, we need what I would call a tensioned understanding of dwelling, one that is able to hold together its complex and contested unfolding without reducing it to a predetermined paradigm. Such a reading must involve an understanding of both stability and change, habitus and difference. In terms of stability, dwelling is about endurance, about our way of constructing a locus of being and meaning in the world. At this level, it is about the everyday social reproduction of resolved, unconscious, and sometimes—as Olga Lafazani reminds us—only apparently insignificant modalities of being at home (see chapter 1).[24] In terms of change, it is about the ways that locus shifts as it reproduces itself, so that it is always becoming and mutating. Advancing a tensioned reading of inhabitation means taking both aspects together, without imposing a moral aspect on either: change cannot be treated as inherently more progressive than stability; instead, we need to be attentive to stillness as well as movement. This enables us to develop an intersectional reading of the way that power relations reinforce habitus or enable differential articulations. This is a reading of dwelling that invites a closer engagement with its lived and felt unfolding, whether unconscious or expressive. Advancing a situated and intersectional reading of dwelling is about getting closer to its assemblage, to its micropolitical life.

To illustrate this point critically, I choose to get uncomfortably close to Heidegger, a problematic thinker that, with his insistence on attachments and belongings, couldn't be further away from the genealogies of thought I am most comfortable working with. Yet he is perhaps the philosopher (in the Western tradition) who has accrued the most prominence for thinking explicitly on dwelling. For Heidegger, dwelling is about a habitual and creative way of inhabiting the world, as something more than the mere building of dwelling. He proposes the idea of "building as dwelling" to capture this productive form of inhabitation that finds and holds our place in the world, while actively caring about it: "the basic character of dwelling is to spare, to preserve. . . . Dwelling itself is always about staying with things. Dwelling, as preserving, keeps the fourfold in that with which mortals stay: in things."[25] But what does Heidegger mean when he says that dwelling is about "staying with things"? The crux of the Heideggerian concept of dwelling is on preserving, holding, and gathering. This is about grounding a habitual form of care with and within the elements of what he calls the fourfold: the sky, earth, divinity, and mortals. For Heidegger, that holding together of, and caring for, the fourfold is the quintessential feature of his normative conception of how "man" should inhabit the world. It is about being concerned with the conservation of a habitual (*gewohnte*), harmonious equilibrium.

What is genuinely interesting about Heidegger's viewpoint is the invitation to look within dwelling (its creative process) and to understand it as unavoidably situated—that is, interlinked with the environment. However, his argument can be taken in both progressive and violently regressive ways. A compelling example of the former is Vanesa Castán Broto's reading, where she stresses how our being-in-the-world is, ontologically speaking, "a unitary phenomenon": there is no other way to understand our being than to "examine how the world itself becomes a constitutive feature of Dasein. . . . Being-in is not a property that Dasein chooses to have or not to have; Being-in is always there already because humans are always already adopting a disposition towards the World."[26] Being-in means taking care of what is constitutive of us, contextually and immanently: in relation to Castán Broto's main concern, urban energy transition means to advocate for the centrality of localized practices and dispositions to build sustainable energy futures that cannot be reduced to a centralized, technocratic solution.

Castán Broto's reading is an important and progressive way to mobilize Heidegger's thought. But the Heideggerian understanding of dwelling, with its stress on the habitus of holding the ground, can also be articulated in a more conservative way. As the compromised history of the philosopher himself shows, one can dwell in ways that are repressive or oppressive. For instance, Iris Marion Young, following Luce Irigaray, argues that Heidegger "seems to privilege building as the world-founding of an active subject, and . . . this privileging is male-biased."[27] But there is a further and more profound kind of oppression in his writings, which helps me to discuss the inherently political essence of inhabitation.

The Heideggerian project was founded on the urge to counter what he saw as threatening technological developments via a more harmonious, rural form of living that would enable a poetic form of dwelling (one that was careful about the world that it was a part of). For him, it is the German countryside, its values and its norms, and the German people (because of their connection with the genesis of the European tradition and the relationship of the German language to ancient Greek) which are to be at the forefront of this spiritual and material mission. By qualifying his building-as-dwelling in such a way, Heidegger is not simply illustrating a point but is also outlining a direction (the rediscovery and preservation of an idealized set of values) that resonated with the racial and national-supremacist views of the cultural context in which he lived. The apparent neutral—and potentially progressive—ideas that building is always also dwelling, and that the two are always also thinking, are made to work in order to propose a specific kind of exclusive, reactionary being-in-the-world.

My point here is simple: such a tensioned sense of direction is not the outcome of dwelling—the end of a process, or the moment where we have clarity on what is built—but is instead the main feature of how things get built, of how habitation unfolds in practice. Sometimes, as in the case of Heidegger, in order to see such sense of direction one needs to excavate the ideological foundation of a proposition. As I said, Heidegger is not only proposing a way to understand the inextricable relationship between dwelling, building, and thinking; he is also providing a resolution, in the form of a reactionary tempo, a folding of becoming into being. If I refuse and fight the latter, like Castán Broto, I nonetheless see value in the former invitation: becoming into the world, inhabiting it, needs to be seen as something being always and unavoidably concerned with the disposition it constantly (re)brings to the fore. The resolution of the struggle between building our way into the world and being into it is not a matter of strategic resolve or a problem to be fixed but, more simply, a feature (a fundamental baseline) of inhabitation. To an extent, this is also what Marxism, especially in its Gramscian reading, has taught us: being-in-the-world is not just about the material conditions of the assemblage; it is also about its project, its ideology, its thinking. Crucially, though—and in direct opposition to conventional Marxist notions of what counts as politics—a tensioned reading of inhabitation reveals multiple senses of directions, multiple projects, and multiple embodiments of the "political." The latter needs to be brought back from the grand narrative to a more prosaic level: the political is always there, in the conscious and unconscious concern around resolutions and dispositions unfolding in the process of becoming-into-the-world.

One might argue that if everything is political, then nothing is. But such a rebuttal is superficial. On the one hand, it is precisely the colonization of what can be defined as "political" that has limited our collective capacity to register prosaic forms of affirmations, lateral moves, and only partial deterritorialization that, even if they might not comply to the given radical script, are nonetheless charged with power. Being political is bound up with being-in-the-world, even if its operations are largely unconscious. Think of the hundreds of computations our bodies constantly engage with behind the scenes in order to maintain a sense of direction—the capacity to sustain our metabolic life. Those are not announced forms of politics, and yet they are matters of concerned engagement, through constant adjustment, vis-à-vis the political ecologies, extractions, phenotypical renderings, and more, of contemporary capitalism. It is not just that the political is embodied but also that the embodiment of the ecologies and topologies making and unmaking life is in itself a political process: a process of resolutions, negotiations, calculations, arrangements across diverging—struggling—senses of directions.

On the other hand, saying that the political is an immanent feature of habitation does not mean that every sense of direction it takes is the same. The Heideggerian *gewohnte* will not liberate home. If "the political" is the concern around resolutions and dispositions, then the way in which things get constantly resolved and disposed of matters: it creates cartographies, subjects, and becomings (chapters 1 and 2). The connotation of the latter is what counts, not its apparent language. So, the liberation of home and homing might be announced, or it might be instead about muddling the supposedly apolitical language of desperation: in order to register its power-to, one needs to go deeper than what is known, and farther than what is proposed as resolution. It follows that, for what is of concern in this book, if one takes the affirmation "inhabiting is always political" seriously, as the starting point of the analysis around matters of home, homing, housing, and homelessness, then each one of these cannot just be reduced to a problem of policy. That would be equal to reduce life to the end point; a subject to its segments; the political to a scripted declaration. Rather, matters of housing, homing, home, and homelessness need to be read always, at any point of the topologies of relations going on between their experiences and their substratum (chapter 1), as cartographies of tensioned resolutions, populated by contesting dispositions, and charged with affections and power with their own sense of direction.

Reapproaching the housing question as a quintessential question of inhabitation means not only paying attention to the ways dwelling unfolds through and with the world but also investigating the orientation its becoming takes. The political, in this reading of housing struggles, is an inevitable, even mundane, feature of dwelling. From there, liberatory forms of dwelling are registered, in their immanent praxis, before they are silenced by the dogmatic canons preserving both our oppressive idea of home and the preestablished idea of emancipation. This is both about enabling one to hear those insurgent propositions and about working with the orientations—the propositional politics, as I've called it elsewhere—they set out.[28] I now turn to the two epistemological moves, on decolonizing and tracing, which are needed to get closer to the "housing political" lingering in the most precarious and violent manifestations of home(lessness).

Decolonizing the Politics of Housing Precarity

I was sitting with Paolo on a stone bench, right in front of the Duomo in Turin. Sunny day, clear sky, sometime around April 2010. The location of our meeting was a peculiar one. In front of us, there was the Duomo: a fifteenth-century Renaissance cathedral. Inside, in a chapel designed by Guarino Guarini, is the Sacra Sindone, a piece of cloth that many believe to be the shroud of Jesus of Nazareth. Two hundred meters to our left was the Porta Palatina, a red Roman gate that used to provide access to the old city. Back then, it was called the Julia Augusta Taurinorum. And just in front of the Duomo, on our right, the pièce de résistance: a brilliant chunk of brutalist architecture, an H-shaped, concrete-molded, gray-orange block colloquially called Il Palazzaccio. Right in the middle of this triangle, carelessly smoking on the edge of Turin's historic schizophrenia, Paolo and I sat on our stone bench.

We had just bought two beers and two slices of pizza, because in Turin that's what you eat when you are out and about, walking and chatting, exploring the city and the self. We munched, smoked, and talked. Paolo was telling me about the Comunità di San Patrignano, a rehab community for drug users in Emilia Romagna. He spent some time there in the early 2000s. He told me how hard it was, how people criticized the community's methods, but, he said, it had helped him. Recalling this experience led him to tell me how, in the early 1980s, to seed the market, drug dealers had made opiates freely available in Turin, a marketing experiment designed to develop customer loyalty at a physical level. His body liked it, and he got hooked. To support his new habit, he then started to smuggle cocaine for tourists when he was working for the travel company Alpitur in a Kenyan village. This was the late 1980s, when you could bring anything you liked in your luggage. But then the story, like any story, went beyond this. There was, for instance, this whole affair of trying to get by in Turin, a city where he could sometimes afford to pay for shelter, but sometimes not.

Distributing flyers played a big role, he told me. Leafleting advertisements for a supermarket chain, for a pizza joint, for a new furniture shop that had just opened at the edge of town. Above him, a chain of commissioning and percentages, a boss who received the leaflets from another boss, who got them from the company. And Paolo was extracting too. He had three employees, whom he described as *più fottuti di me* (more fucked up than me). They worked a little, pretending mostly, and then threw most of the leaflets in bins scattered along the banks of the Dora River. Others they pushed through *i portoni dei palazzi di Torino*, those huge wooden doors opening onto a tiny piss-reeking courtyard, with dark stairs, chunky stone steps, and cast-iron railings climbing to the upper floors in the silence life makes when it is regimented by days that are all the same.

Life was also the same for Paolo, and its cast was raw. The showers in the homeless day hub on Via Sacchi, shared with dozens of others. The nights without heating in the *soffitta* he managed to rent: a stuffy, dark attic room for which he needed no documents, no proof, only ready cash and enough physical and mental balance to make it up the steep stairs, without looking back too much, or down the well either. The cheap alcohol he drank: a trade-off for heroin. The lack of meaningful encounters. He once told me, "It seems as if the only people I meet are people like me, *e non abbiamo niente da dirci* (we have nothing to say to each other). His body, shaking. Frail. Cold. The lack of any real opportunity to make any kind of real money in Turin, a city designed for others. He could not stand the stares of passersby, when he was acting as an impromptu valet near the main train station, showing drivers to free parking spots for spare change. Especially those of women. Paolo was still a good-looking man, but hollowed out by his years of drugs and his exposure to urban concrete. *Un berrettino*, a baseball hat, hid his eyes from their eyes.

The painful conversations with his mother. The fights. Someone accusing him of stealing a bag at the Via Sacchi center. His landlord throwing him out for three nights, because he hadn't paid the rent. The argument with one of his junkies, when he threw away all the leaflets without even pretending, and the big boss found out, and no one got paid. For arguments with himself. For not drinking less. For not answering that phone call. For not sleeping. For not speaking. For having bet his last ten euros.

The struggle to find energy, especially to face the city's social worker. To convince him that no, he did not have the forty euros necessary to apply for the new ID. Yes, he went to the public job center. Yes, and the dozen private ones. And yes, he did call about jobs he found online. Every day. And yes, he went to the shelter and behaved. And yes, actually, right now, right after that meeting, he was going to the day hub in Via Sacchi. Yes, he would stay put, stay calm, wait in the queue for a shower, without a fuss. Yes, he'd have a discussion and help to fill in yet another questionnaire, also without complaining. And yes, then he'd go to queue again, well-behaved, clean-shaven, for Nun Teresa's sandwiches at the Vincenziani soup kitchen. And just before getting his hands on the charitable fruit juice and panini, he knew he would feel his body craving for more, *una scimmia sulla schiena urla impazzita e batte sulla sua testa, sul cappellino*, for his past love, brown queen, frail veins, *dolci sogni*, sweet dreams, as he put it.

Paolo used to say that he was like *una foglia d'autunno*, an autumn leaf holding on to the branch by a thread, day after day, hour after hour. He was writing a book about this feeling and the life that had caused it. It was going to be called *Il rumore dell'erba che cresce* (The sound of growing grass). It was about his journey through addiction, and then out of it, in the becoming he was going through, when I met him. He was typing it on his Alcatel mobile phone by addressing SMS messages to himself. Later on, I got him a secondhand laptop. "I fear that I will lower my guard," he wrote, "sometime, eventually, but I don't have to. *Lo sai perché?* I fear jail. I have been there. In there, people like me are separated from the main group . . . and they are treated like shit, like the last of the last. I don't want to go back in there."

But to get a better job, to access more services, he needed an identity card. And for that, as I mentioned, he needed forty euros. To get it, he was going to have to deal with a word he hated: *compromesso*, compromise. How to get that money, without cutting even more corners? Paolo did not want to take the free ID provided by the city, the one with the fake homeless residence as his address (chapter 4). He wanted the real one, with the address of his attic space that he fought so hard to hold on to. He did not want to collect free clothes from Nun Teresa, or to queue at 6 a.m. to get breakfast from the service she ran, or to beg at the train station, or to walk from church to church to get five euros from the priests, or to spend an entire day on a bench, a charged nothingness—no sound not a breath same grey all sides earth sky—in his mind. Paolo had all sorts of life plans and hopes-in-the-making to keep him busy. He wanted to tend to them.

He wanted to populate life to its full extent, instead of inhabiting a chain of endless lessness and compromising.

Soon after I left Turin, he followed suit. He found a place in a small village, population 2,500, outside of the big city. He lived in a shed at the end of town, on land belonging to a local surveyor, for whom he started to do some cleaning and gardening. He wrote to me that he wasn't paid for this, *il geometra non mi paga*, but the book was coming along, and the village was less cold, less harsh, *più tranquillo* (calmer) than the city. He sent me chapters and collages he had started to make on his PC. He opened a Facebook account, made a YouTube video, delivering a peaceful message, in search of a voice, a narrative that moved at his tempo. And then there was the rapprochement with his mother. And a woman he was now seeing, whom he liked. His life was more serene. He could think about his passion for football and dogs. He would download pictures of puppies from the web, then put glasses on them using Windows Paint, adding some flowers, the symbol of Cagliari Calcio (his favorite football team), and the word *peace*. He was taking care of his own dwelling in his own becoming.

We chatted through Messenger. He had now moved to a coastal town. There, he had found a new woman. He was not moving in with her, but things were going well. "I'm still a leaf," he said, "but spring is here: *sono sempre una foglia. . . . Ma la primavera è alle porte.*" Paolo the heroin addict, the drunk, the homeless, the peer educator, the giver and taker, the informant and friend, the sunburned hustler. The Moretti-nicotine-and-pizza Paolo. His story may have been that of a city that had no space for the precariat, but his way of articulating it was all his own (figure 6.1).

There are two potential ways to approach Paolo. The first is the Foucauldian "speaking-to." It listens to the other, using this as a way of making a connection, but in a way that is politically preemptive. This is the listening that happens in most counseling sessions, confessional rooms, and semistructured interviews. The political—that which is of concern—is not to be defined by what the speaker says or does, because they have already been expelled, reduced to a predetermined paradigm that they then need to fit. In hearing and encouraging them to share their plight, job, home, addictions, and past experiences in this way, one is speaking-to them, defining what kind of subject one needs them to be, and extracting from it. Speaking-to is a way of expelling the other to keep them at a distance, yet under close control. It is a way to keep the other at home, with the pretension of bringing them back into it. It reduces Paolo to a series of already-segmented categories: the homeless, the addict, the client of a service, the patient with a sick liver, the subject of poverty

FIG. 6.1. One of Paolo's collages, taken from his draft book *Il rumore dell'erba che cresce*.

research, a source of labor to be exploited. It helps to reproduce those industries that deal professionally with the homeless, and it reproduces the home/homeless divide, materially and epistemologically. Without the creation and management of the latter, there would be no instantiation of the former as we know it.

A radical "hearing-from" would not be concerned with understanding or saving Paolo, but with the recognition of the impossibility of his containment, and would therefore refuse the colonization of his possible becomings through charity, professionalism, and knowledge production. Hearing from Paolo would mean to displace the colonies of home, to move toward their decolonization. On the edge of that refusal, to paraphrase Gloria Anzaldúa, something might open: a crack in the usual bordering through which Paolo is governed, which is the same bordering structuring the violence of current home, as seen in part II.[29] From there, something we currently don't know how to deal with (and are perhaps even afraid of) might come through: a queer, precarious story, telling us about an alternative type of doing, being, and becoming at home. In this sense—and this is why I am bringing Paolo in at this point in the book—decolonizing home needs to start from the decolonization of housing precarity, of its experience, and of its politics. What if Paolo does not need to be saved? What if Paolo does not want to be brought back home?

In this framework, not saving Paolo does not mean to refuse social interventions, but to radically change their scope: from being designed by one population for another to becoming a matter of concern for all; from being about fixing housing to becoming concerned with the inherent tensioned troubles of inhabitation; from being addressed to a subject purposely defined as lacking to affirming a beyond, a movement encompassing the colonies and functions upon which that same lack is reproduced for the many. Hearing from Paolo would mean to dispose of the idea that precarity—and dwelling precarity in particular—is a condition outside the norm, to embrace instead the view that it's the normal function (and politics) of our current mode of inhabiting the world. As seen in chapter 1, this is different than Butler's quests to find a common humanitarian ground around precariousness. The focus is not around a shared sense of being human, but around immanent material and epistemic conditions that are grounded in transversal violent logics, albeit experienced at very different degrees of intensity. Those conditions are not making us human, but are diagramming our dwelling in the world in dispossessive and unjust ways. Decolonizing the politics of precarity is a first step toward a situated fight against those conditions, centered at the intersection of housing and its struggles. It is about the double move of stopping the conception of the different intensifications of lessness as matters of separate camps—precarious, nonprecarious; homelessness, home—and about recentering the focus on what precarious experiences can do.

The focus on the body—as also shown in the work of feminist scholars of "homelessness" such as the late Josie Jolley or in the accounts provided by Lindsey McCarthy—is key to working toward the decolonization of the politics of precarity.[30] It is Paolo's experiences of life across the lessness of Turin—his embodiment—that signal the surface where precarity and its politics of inhabitation are made and unmade. Crucially, this embodiment—the assemblage of Paolo through the wider mechanosphere and ritornellos of his home(lessness)—is alive and is political because, following Sarah Ahmed, it is affective: it produces new bodies and new conditions.[31] It is not important to hear a radical enunciation in Paolo's collages, or in his efforts to keep Turin's homelessness services at bay, because it is enough to register these lateral moves as an affirmation of a desire to live beyond what inhabitation has made available to him. In this sense, it is the performative, affective, and material assemblage of precarity that connects with, and speaks of, politics. It is there, in the micropolitics of precarious performance, that possible homing futures are disclosed or foreclosed.

Tracing the Politics of Housing Precarity

In a recent contribution, Saidiya Hartman tells the story of Esther Brown, a young Black woman living in Harlem at the time of World War I, who "hated to work, the conditions of work as much as the very idea of work."[32] Like other Black women and men, Esther resists the disciplinary pressures of everyday life by strolling in the open. In a beautiful piece of writing, Hartman tells us that the ways in which bodies move is about more than simple coming and going: in her strolling, Esther constructs a different modality of being, in Harlem and in the world. She dwells in a way that contests the dominant habitus, the demand that her body stay still, work, get out of the way of white people. The "wandering and drifting" of Esther and her peers is not just about survival but instead represents how "she engaged the world and how she perceived it."[33] That engagement—without organization, without declared politics, without recognition—is political in its precarious embodiment and in its embodiment of precarity. It is a "revolution in a minor key," a form of resistance that "was driven not by uplift or the struggle for recognition or citizenship, but by the vision of a world that would guarantee to every human being free access to earth and full enjoyment of the necessities of life, according to individual desires, tastes, and inclinations."[34]

The body of Esther Brown was not supposed to move in the way it moved. By walking, she traces a counterpolitical ritornello, a refrain against expulsion and extraction, which cuts through habitual racialized segregation and displacement in the US city.[35] Eventually, she is captured and thrown into the criminal justice system, in an attempt to institutionalize her freedom, to recapture her within (habitual) modes of erasure and concealment, in a matrix that connects prison to the ghetto and the plantation.[36] But Esther and her peers refuse to stay either still or silent. They make so much noise and so much anger in prison that their chant reverberates in the memories of those who heard it.

Yet, as Hartman points out, within the frameworks of both the wider society and the academy, both Esther's rebellion and, more fundamentally, Harlem's everyday "choreography of the possible" have been silenced, segmented, enclosed by the canons of political and scholarly discourse.[37] They go unheard: "The potentiality of their lives has remained unthought because no one could imagine young black women as social visionaries, radical thinkers, and innovators in the world in which these acts took place."[38]

The story of Esther tells us that precarity is never a finished project; it is a condition that is always in the making. It is instantiated at the level of the body, where it leaves its racialized marks, but also where it can be challenged and appropriated. The body is a surface where the premakings of precarity in the past relate to its present-day urban forms, its lived and felt contemporary makings. In the encounter between what Ash Amin has called "the debris of the past" and present-day life, the body works as a hinge.[39] In so doing, it can at times assemble a counterpolitics "in a minor key" to oppose the precarious framings it is made to fit. This reading does not conceive the body as a site of relegation or as in need of salvation. Following hooks, it becomes the site of constitutive labor, the locus where histories and multitudes of everyday life intersect to produce tensioned formations; some are tame, but some, taking from Ahmed, are willfully resistant.[40]

Analytically speaking, registering the politics of embodied housing precarity means tracing the mechanisms of discipline and control that form part of the assemblage of precarious inhabitation, as well as affirming that the governmentalities of home(lessness) are rarely totalizing: while they produce manageable subjects, a segmented body is always more of what it is made to do and of what it is inscribed into. The proposition is that by following Esther wherever she goes, at her own tempo, we can trace an alternative tune: one that channels individual preoccupations into collective reverberations. But how to do this without essentializing and romanticizing experience? How to trace and signal what goes beyond inhabitation—the propositional politics of housing precarity— without losing track of the situated ritornellos that link experience to the inner structurations of home and back again? What is needed to grasp the ways that the political is produced in, and reflected by, precarious urban lives?

Analytically, one can excavate the politics of housing precarity by deploying a processual and nuanced approach to the pre-, in-, un-, and remakings of the embodiment of precarity itself. There are four main questions driving this approach:

- How does the historical context intersect with the present (premakings)?
- How is the subject affected (inmakings)?
- What can a body do (unmakings)?
- How is governance reasserted (remakings)?

As I have illustrated elsewhere, once careful attention is devoted to these intersecting processes, the politics of embodied precarity emerges at the nexus of historical contingency and present (re)articulation.[41] This approach recognizes that collective politics exists before the subject, but also views these same collective politics as a supple series of embodied relations that can be revealed by paying attention to individual and collective experiences. As Simone has argued, within the assemblage of these experiences, a pragmatics without any relation to morality or any normative dimension can take hold: "constellations are torn apart and recomposed without relying on some clear sense of what should have taken place or what must take place."[42] The politics of housing precarity is one of these constellations, grounded in its own historical making, while at the same time being inherently an operator of emerging futures.

In Esther's case, the politics of precarity is made of four intersecting processes, which cannot be reduced to each other: the racialized and neoliberal premakings of precarity; the discursive and material displacement of its inmaking; as well as its bodily unmakings and remakings, which must be considered together. It is not about giving prominence to one or another, but about unpacking their spatiotemporal becoming: in showing how modes of inhabitation are dependent on violent histories, yet sometimes contested in their experiential unfolding (forms of inhabitation, as Simone would put it, "within and beyond capture").[43] As Hartman shows, the importance of tracing and narrating the politics of these experiences lies in its capacity to speak truth to the normative power of policy and scholarship too. But there is more. Excavating such a politics is about finding grounds for action, as defined by the ones actively embodying their own struggle, for their own kind of habitation. So if the starting point, which we have seen with Paolo, is purely epistemological in how it speaks of how we can decolonize imaginaries around precarious dwelling, the second is squarely methodological, in how it asks on what to focus and on the questions that need to be asked, questions that are not about understanding experience, or saving it, but about tracing its own propositional politics of and for life. This leads to the third set of points, which are of political praxis, and that I explore in chapter 7.

Conclusion

Paolo passed away in September 2015. His last post on Facebook was a shot of a sunset taken from the room of the hospital where he spent his last days. The text read simply, "Buonanotte :-)." I don't know in what kind of energetic new *agencement* of life he now lies. But I do know that every inch of his dwelling in the world was a struggle, a tensioned becoming, between the powerful intersections he had to navigate and his own sense of direction. His course was hindered, not assisted, by an entire industry aimed at helping him. The institutions with which he interfaced completely disregarded his own way of assembling his own habitation, instead treating him as a case to be managed, an individual to be brought back home. A radical approach to housing would refuse this kind of expulsion and instead treat Paolo's everyday life, and those of millions of others, very differently. It would understand housing as political beyond questions of policy and exchange value, right within its suffering and orientation. It would work to hear the proposition arising from unusual forms of inhabitation, without the urge to fix them—to control them.

As Sousa Santos puts it, "the diversity of world experience is inexhaustible and therefore cannot be accounted for by any single general theory"; consequently, this chapter has sketched not a rigid theoretical framework but an epistemology that allows us to access different ways of looking at and making sense of housing precarity, its struggle, and its inner political proposition.[44] Coherent with the minor ethos cutting through these pages, this epistemology is, to follow the feminist geographer Cindi Katz, about finding a way "of working inside out, of fugitive moves and emergent practices interstitial with 'major' productions of knowledge."[45] Ultimately, this is very close to the project of fighting against the queer othering that is foundational to home/homelessness and instead allowing alterity to speak in its own tongue. It's about crafting concepts, decolonizing their meaning, and working through situated practices. What emerges is an epistemology that invites us:

- to consider inhabitation as inherently political;
- to enable a reading of the most intensified experiences of home(lessness), not only as sites of relegation but as sites performing their own politics of inhabitation; and
- to work with and through those minor, often not announced, propositions moved by a situated approach to, and understanding of, their becoming.

Before moving forward, I want to note three important characteristics of this epistemology, which are particularly relevant for those who are building, dwelling, and thinking from a privileged epistemic site within the academy. First, hearing from the margins of home(lessness) is first and foremost a political endeavor, not a research exercise. This is not about obtaining more ethnographic nuances of Paolo's life; that would be another scholarly extraction. Ethnography can be extremely exploitative, as its history shows. Housing and homelessness scholarship are filled with troubling examples in this sense.[46] Hearing from is therefore an act of epistemological liberation not geared at gathering data but oriented at producing a form of knowledge that can be appropriated, reworked, and operationalized by the collective of which one is part.[47] This may not be the kind of knowledge that is recognized within institutional frameworks oriented toward impact, however. Yet it is the only knowledge a liberatory politics of home can love in ethical terms. As Freire says, interests within it must be aligned to shared goals: "as an act of freedom, it must not serve as a pretext for manipulation."[48]

Second, even if the epistemology of radical housing is about a political stance, it offers concrete pathways for a differential way of doing research around home/homelessness, too. At its core, it invites us to center experiences of housing precarity without speaking over the multiple desires emerging from, and produced by, their struggles. There are no management strategies, policy recommendations, or even explanations here, but an attunement to hear out grammars and countergrammars of dispossession. The experience of housing precarity—as one of the harshest intensifications of the lessness diagram—becomes the ground from which to trace the violence of an entire economic/cultural/social model while simultaneously registering affirmations emerging at the level of lived life. To me, such affirmations—as articulated through speech, gesture, walk, trajectory, place, food, poetry, and art—are an assemblage of the ways one inhabits the world. The composite assemblage of these affirmations suggests a liberatory focus on housing's use value, through which different kinds of dwellings are signaled. I expand on this point in chapter 7 and the conclusion.

Third, the epistemological angle proposed in these pages is designed to intersect cognate kinds of thinking. Although I intended this book to focus mostly on the canonical otherness of home, the approach outlined here cuts across all the colonies of home that I laid out in chapters 1 and 2. It is to look at the propositions emerging from the tensioned cracks of housing racial capitalism, from the heteronormatization and unecological patrolling of its borderings. It is, increasingly, about (re)approaching the migration question and the violent ways in which it is managed: from boats left afloat in the Black Mediterranean to offshoring of detention centers in Australia, but also to the segmentation of asylum seekers into a population that has nothing to do with conventionally defined homelessness, in order to reduce and control their chance of becoming collective struggling subjects.[49] "Being radical" here means intersecting with multiple terrains of struggle populated by many, in a multitude of ways, each with its own tempo and quotidian politics, yet united in their attempt at moving beyond current modes of planetary inhabitation. In getting closer to the places where the struggle for a new kind of home is lived and felt, one can hear a collective refusal to fit in, grounded in suffering and in a differential productive desire for life. By hearing from it, one can work with it to occupy, to make do, to assemble, to partake. This is an invitation to rethink housing from the contested multiplicity of its use value, from what housing does for people and what people do with housing. Chapter 7 explores three operations that will make these insights more concrete.

7

DEINSTITUTE, REINSTITUTE, INSTITUTE

The time to dare more, to transcend the remit of policy, and to cut across the entrapment of home/homelessness is here. We live at a moment of increased politicization around matters of housing and inhabitation, intersecting other powerful mobilizations around climate concerns and against racial and patriarchal violence. At this juncture, how can one define interventions that invite, rather than prescribe; that open, rather than silence; that enable, rather than control; that liberate, rather than expel and extract? This book has been an effort to tackle this question, staying close to the making and unmaking of what I have called the "impossible possibility of home." The core idea is that to solve the housing issue one needs to go deep down into the expulsive and extractive diagramming operating throughout the homing question. I have taken an approach mostly inspired by processual, ontological thinking and by a vision of the political grounded in autonomy and affirmative action. In this chapter, building on the micropolitical groundings laid out in chapter 6, I am going to offer some propositions on how collectives and communities fighting for housing justice can bring the question back home, to move toward a liberatory assemblage of inhabitation. What I am going to say is inspired by radical grassroots organizing, but it is also indebted to specific traditions of liberatory thinking that have emerged throughout the book. When it comes, specifically, to the issue of home, there are in particular three traditions of thought to which I often return in my thinking. The first is presented by queer thinkers and doers. The second is a composite of theories and praxis arising from feminist Black organizing and related community action. The third is advanced by recent attempts at nurturing a terrain of organizing in and outside of academia around the question of housing justice. The ways in which these traditions tackle the question of liberating home speaks and informs the critique advanced in this book. I will briefly recall their positions, to then unpack the complementary proposition that I am advancing.

Ideas and praxis of queering home are perhaps those that resonate the most with the ultimate horizon of this book. Queering home—and therefore, here, queering home(lessness)—means to engage in explorations of the never-finished project of constructing a place in the world that is open, multiple, and autonomous, in both its theorization and its praxis. It means to go back to the question asked by Anne-Marie Fortier in chapter 2: "Is it possible to conceive of being 'at home' in a way that already encounters/engenders queerness, but without deploying an original narrative of 'home'?"[1] According to Bryant, this queering of home requires a twofold movement: "On the one hand . . . [it means] deconstructing home ideology as a set of particular, heteronormative social constructs that disallow wider conceptual possibilities for spaces and sexualities. On the other hand, queering the home means guaranteeing that queers have access to real-world spaces of shelter and comfort."[2] Using the grammar advanced in this book, this means both to decolonize home(lessness) and to fight for the constitution of real-world spaces of affirmation and becoming. The deinstituting, reinstituting, and instituting propositions advanced later in the chapter offer a possibility of how to go about such a (revolutionary) program of work.

Here, I don't engage in the broadening of the queering lens to detract from the specificity of Bryant's argument, which is that the home/homelessness dichotomy contains heteronormative assumptions that need to be decolonized on their own specific terms at the level of cisnormative framings, heteronormative gender praxis, and sexualized normativity. These, as a nonbinary man myself, are concerns central to my heart and politics. Yet, *queering* speaks of a wider political affection and program, very much in the same vein of how housing can speak of more than sheltering. Queering home, even though grounded in the specificity of its struggle, provides for a wider and rounder challenge to inhabitation. Earlier in the book, I followed Natalie Oswin in approaching this as a locus where the fight against heteronormativity could be paradigmatic for a whole series of other intersectionalities, with their different forms of expulsion and extraction.[3] Although I ultimately write from a different, albeit cognate, conceptual tradition, I am inspired and I share the sense of direction imposed by the affection and praxis of queering, a praxis affirming that liberating home passes both through its epistemological decolonization and through the interstitial work needed to construct immanent spaces of radical political care, across the multiple forms of expulsion and extraction that make us matters of less.

A number of queer thinkers remind us that work requires experimenting with liberatory designs and the delicacy of pan-ecological intimacies, remaining true to their unfolding and registering the "edgework" that arises in their makings.[4] From there, one can imagine homes that are queer for all of us, in their radical opening, or what Gorman-Murray calls "porosity."[5] Working in that direction means to stay in the fold, to inhabit the tensioned space of an otherwise form of caring for inhabitation (see the section "Reinstituting, in Caring" below), as it cuts across conventions and thresholds of what Sarah Elwood refers to as the inescapable doings of "oppression" and "liberation."[6] Although I am not expanding further on these—and I stay instead closer to the conceptual and political tradition I have decided to write from—I am recalling these queer invitations to signal connections that complement, expand, and intersect with the broader epistemological exercise sketched in these pages precisely because, as I've said, this book is just a proposition, not a dogmatic operation. At the bare minimum, going beyond home(lessness) requires a queering of home in theory and practice, which is related to an anticapitalist and antiracist program and a critique of anthropocentric modes of dwelling. So commutations, as hard as they are, are not just desirable, but necessary.

A second group of scholarship—which is currently inviting for a radical rethinking of notions of care and housing justice practice—emerges from the Black radical tradition at the intersection of feminist and community organizing.[7] As I have already shown throughout the book, such traditions are central to excavate the housing political beyond the pastiche of institutional politics, both in theorizing the body as the prime site of affirmation and in showing, longitudinally so, how entrenched structures and praxes of racial violence (re)constitute terrains and subjects of dispossession. If in urban studies there is a long tradition looking at how racial injustice not only permeates but also structures, planning regimes and everyday urban lives for communities of color across the globe, it is only recently that a renewed attention has been dedicated to the specific role of the housing assemblage in the production of racialized functions and experiences of inhabitation. Research here is being done by academics and activists across the Atlantic and beyond, on the role housing policy takes in reproducing what Ananya Roy has labeled "racial banishment," which includes direct repression and displacement through gentrification, as shown in the work of Brandi T. Summers on Washington, DC, but also through the withdrawal of the state from its commitment to public housing, as powerfully illustrated by Akira Drake Rodriguez in the case of Atlanta.[8] Along similar lines, there is an increasing amount of work unreveling the means through which the financialization of housing is crucial in the (re)production of contemporary racialized geographies. As Desiree Fields and Elora Raymond effectively put it, "financial violence is racial violence."[9]

Contributions attentive to the intersection of racial capitalism and embodied practices through questions of housing and homing are also providing a renewed focus to matters and practice of the counterpolitical. If contemporary housing markets and policy are of racial capitalism, what kind of escape is possible and for whom? What kind of nondispossessive elsewhere can be prefigured, in the here and the now? As we have seen in the previous chapter, how can one step out of these violent formations, if even the act of walking away is always already partly captured by racialized forms of finance and planning, by the ways phenotypes have been diagrammed culturally and socially, by the law? Inhabiting such impossibility is about staying at home in racial capitalism, and that "staying" necessarily transcends resilience: to paraphrase Donna Haraway, it is about staying with the freight of the trouble one has been given while at the same curating a way of getting beyond it.[10] In this dispossessive plateau the question, to follow AbdouMaliq Simone, becomes how to grasp forms of the counterpolitical that are effected "within and beyond capture."[11] For Simone, these forms have a spatial component, a gathering of and in space that he calls "the surrounds": a modality of urban inhabitation done by residents at the tail end of dispossession to carve out a chance to inhabit what has been made uninhabitable. This is both being "beyond" and a being "in," because, as I've sketched earlier, conditions to fully get out, and to be fully cared for, seem to be out of the question. The surrounds are not immune from capture. But when space is striated, when the material and affective relations making up the urban become fragmented and conflicting, a transversal milieu of dwelling otherwise, a terrain of and for struggle, can also emerge. Housing, in being turned into a means of extraction through brutal force and trauma, produces renewed forms of embodied politics that sometimes are dispersed and recaptured but at points are mapped onto new collective subjects.[12]

The constitutions of those individual and affective stances are an emergence from the plane of possibilities that can come together as a form of infrastructural support for more of the same. A "threshold," following Tadiar, constitutes both the everyday liminality of vitality for racialized poor communities in-place, and a significance to (re)understand the urban/housing political at large.[13] This is clear, for instance, in a recent contribution by Summers and Fields, where a performance of the intimate elaborates, as a knitting, a fragile yet strong infrastructure of support, for many Black residents in Oakland to fight the violence of racialized financialized housing.[14] Or, similarly, in the accounts of Jessi Quizar, where a grounded approach excavates forms of Black spatial imagination and resistance against, and within, the dispossessive logic of Detroit housing market. The provided counterlogic here is one where relationality and well-being are centered from below, by members of racialized communities, to reapproach the land question in Detroit anew by affirming emancipatory "place-claiming" praxis.[15] These are just two examples of an emerging and inspiring housing justice scholarship centering the embodiment of the racialized everyday as a site where the tension of being within and beyond capture becomes apparent and assembles as a threshold where the "radicality" of struggles consists in the propositional (in a material, affective, and relational sense) habitation of the stolen ground.

Finally, a third group of interventions that is providing much material to work with in order to imagine, and create, a liberated kind of home has been emerging in the aftermath of the 2008 global financial crisis and its effects on housing. Critical writers, both within and outside academia, are paying increasing attention to practices such as direct housing action, grassroots organizing, and squatting, transcending the remit of scholarship interested in reading housing just as a matter of policy and, instead, exploring how housing precarity and housing struggles are both a product and a producer of the urban political (introduction).[16] Displacement and related forms of direct action and organizing are therefore not only seen as the effects of uneven urban development but are registered in their capacity to configure alternative modes of being and living in the city.[17] One key aspect, which speaks directly to explorations on a new horizon for the homely political, is the attention paid, in theorizing housing justice, to grassroots direct action as the key means to change the status quo. These efforts increasingly include critical reflections on the role and positionality of scholars and activists within housing struggles. In the wake of the Occupy and Podemos movements, there has been a resurgence of reflections on activist-researcher network approaches across disciplines, which has taken various institutional and noninstitutional forms. An example of which I am particularly proud is the collective effort at the *Radical Housing Journal*, through which we connect scholars and activists across geographies, producing radical housing knowledge that was simply not available—in such an open-source fashion, and on such a scale—before.[18]

One illuminating example of this kind of renewed activist-oriented scholarship has been brought to the fore by Ananya Roy and Raquel Rolnik, both in their individual work and in their joint interventions. The open-source *Methodologies for Housing Justice Guide,* which they edited together with Terra Graziani and Hilary Malson, offers a good example of the renewed, politically driven yet scholarly sound, attention to housing struggles that I am evoking. Roy and Rolnik ask, "What does an orientation towards housing justice entail for methods of research and methodologies of social action?"[19] For them, the answer lies in a number of intersecting focuses. First, there is a focus on "structural mechanisms of dispossession and displacement . . . specifically the financialization of land and housing and the criminalization of poverty."[20] Second, there is the attempt at reading these processes translocally and embracing a comparative research approach to housing justice, while, third, centering the importance of "technologies of research and representation in struggles for housing justice," such as data sets, archives, and maps.[21] Last but not least, they also stress the importance of looking beyond dispossession and of tracing, and giving room in the theorization of housing justice to, "strategies and imaginaries of emplacement."[22] This guide and other collective works are providing a clear set of tools to reapproach the housing question as both a matter of violent structures and as a locus of affirmative forms of emplacement, where the latter are not celebrated to discard the former but are traced to avoid their silencing by the binaries of policy or humanitarian thinking.[23]

This book is aligned with the epistemic and material task of queering our current understanding and praxis of home, of (re)centering meaning and doings of "care" from the ground of action, and it also espouses the insistence of Roy and Rolnik when they say "that housing justice is not a gift handed by governments to communities but rather is forged through insurgency, resistance, and conflict."[24] Inspired by these cognate efforts, my intention here has been to add a specific epistemological angle to these concerns—that is, a specific demand on how we come to know what we know (and therefore to do what we do) about home. The epistemology of home(lessness) advanced in these pages brings the question of the other of home straight into the homely, proposing to read the two as a matter of the same possible-impossible way through which inhabitation is structured for the many. Ultimately, exploring home(lessness) means questioning how one comes to know and to inhabit the less: a question that can offer insights to cognate lines of thinking such as the ones sketched above.

A crucial part of the approach here proposed is the preoccupation with embodiments and the immanent experience of precarious dwelling (chapter 6). Because that embodiment—in its being variously situated—is the minimum common denominator uniting concerned humans who, through their struggle for a proper place not simply to live in but to fulfill life through, are tackling the profound structures constantly reproducing the many as matter of less. Keywords for this common denominator are not to be found in the current lexicons of the political. The talk is of desperation, trauma, fear, sense of loss, and violence. Yet these are more than words, more than utterances of discontent, more than problems to be fixed (as they are diagrammed through the kind of speaking-to I mentioned in chapter 6). These are instead fully-fledged grammars—generative structures—that have the capacity, as Audre Lorde rendered in her writing, to germinate in affirmative action. At the threshold of that love, individuals and collectives define, on an everyday basis, the praxis of the global fight for just housing and its sense of direction. The book centers these practices as politics because what they have to say is of concern for everyone, beyond the usual calls for provisioning and grand plans. They move the horizon, in asking for infrastructures to sustain collective solidarities; in demanding harm reduction instead of institutionalization; in asserting the right to be vagrant and free; in advocating radical care as a method; in promoting makeshift autonomous arrangements and locally based provisioning; in fostering intersectional housing agendas; and in demanding dwellers' control for dwellers' futures.

These efforts tell us that to end home(lessness), we need an emancipatory ideology and praxis of inhabitation. In what follows, I lay out three propositions in this sense, which emerge from the anti-institutional, autonomous, and affect-oriented ethos that has underpinned much of my thinking throughout the book. These are invitations to expand and become accomplices of radical forms of caring for and through inhabitation, to listen to grammars of precarity and record their propositions, to work toward a liberatory politics of home. The first is based around programs to come together in order to *deinstitute* current diagrams of power, the second around the need to *reinstitute* the basic means to rework power, and the third around the collective organizing to *institute* differential forms of power.[25] If for current homelessness practitioners and policy makers—but also students versed in the canons of sociologies of home—these moves will appear as something transcending what they are demanded to think and do, the displacement required from radical thinkers and autonomous grassroots organizers is of a different kind. The invitation for them is to reconsider how, programmatically, it might be possible to enhance the demand and fight for unconditional shelter with the reenvisioning of what a shelter can do, in terms of affording people liberation in homing the world. The question is not only around what kind of inhabitation we are fighting for but around what is required to make that question the ritornello of every step taken in any given fight; for it to be a constant reminder that emancipation from lessness cannot be about incremental provisioning but must institute its own form of radical care for itself, at the interstices where it operates. Ultimately, deinstituting, reinstituting, and instituting are about what Achille Mbembe has called "a giant rupture, the result of radical imagination," which I propose here to understand as an assemblage of situated, minor efforts: ongoing oriented revolutionary affections, more than a revolutionary program.[26]

Deinstituting, in Striking

In developing a liberatory politics of home, we must confront the question of what to do with the secular and sacred industries that currently deal with the harshest intensifications of home(lessness). If we start with the premise that many of these approaches are not fundamentally altering the expulsive and extractive functions of the home/homelessness binary but are instead reproducing them, then the only possible way forward is to dismantle these services and think anew. By restricting our political horizon to the status quo of these services, we are silencing alternative becomings. Indeed, the need for fundamental change is felt by many service providers themselves, which helps to explain the initial wave of enthusiasm for the alternative strategy offered by Housing First.[27] However, as I argued in chapter 5, while superior to many existing solutions, Housing First's offer remains grounded in an individualizing, pathologizing, market-oriented framework that does not challenge mainstream ideologies and practices of home(lessness). We need to ask for more and dare more. Humanitarians will claim that, in dismantling current industries of homelessness, we will cause untold harm to their clients. Yet such an outcome is not a given. A programmatic reform based on a radical care approach (see the section "Reinstituting, in Caring" below) will do all but harm to its clients. It would, instead, *listen-from* their struggle for inhabitation and register its sense of direction, which, most likely, will point straight beyond the shelter, the peripheral and disconnected housing block, the shared dorm without lockers, the temporary hotel room, the camp, the jail, the death from withdrawal, the cudgels, and the control.

But how can such a listening-from happen? How can desire be let free to circulate, and who has to respond to its call? Throughout the book, I have offered some interconnected suggestions. The main tension here lies between what should be done by the state (and the market), and what should instead be done out of its remit. I believe the state could do a lot. It could teach the violence of current modes of inhabiting the world in its schools; it could stop the financialization of dwellings, nationalizing banks, and prohibiting the accumulation of private property in a few hands; it could defund its police; it could close its jails; it could reappropriate its markets; it could reduce working hours and allow people to explore their creative nature in time and space; it could realize its place in the world is only temporary, and there are wider and more important ecologies to be nurtured; it could, eventually, cease to exist. Yet none or little of this is going to happen. Looking at what is in front of me—the state I live in, the European Union I am part of, the West where I belong—I have lost most of my hope in any form of radical top-down provisioning and change. As I have argued in chapter 6, a close link to the grassroots, and especially to the mundanity of radical housing suffering and struggle, needs to be privileged: there, propositions about the kinds of homes communities wish to fight for are already articulated and could be sustained to form semiautonomous spaces, or spheres, beyond lessness. To further unpack this tension, let me give an example.

One thing that surely needs to be done to end home(lessness) is the permanent closure of homeless shelters and of any other machine of ordering the other through management. This does not mean to invest in prevention, while maintaining the paradigm of the shelter, but to factually disinvest in the latter. It means to fragment a system where caring for *l'autre*—in a merry orgy of charitable humanitarian entrepreneurialism—is not a side product, a recuperation from annihilation, but the acceleration of a logic of dispossession and colonization.[28] Such a disinvestment has nothing to do with revanchist cuts to service provisions but must go hand in hand with substantive investment providing the basis for more profound forms of radical care to flourish. There are two possible scenarios here, one led by the state, the other by the grassroots. In the first, the state would provide public housing instead of temporary shelters, but with a much broader interpretation of what *public housing* means. Progressive scholars would say one option could be to move in the direction traced by Finland, where homeless shelters are being progressively closed and replaced by permanent housing under the umbrella of Housing First. In this first scenario, the kind of defunding I am talking about goes in the same direction but with a fundamental twist. The provision of permanent housing should not limit itself with the provision of mononuclear units aligned within the individualizing—and ultimately neoliberal—logic of Housing First but should be oriented at enabling not only the inhabitation of housing but also its wider, intersectional design. This would be a large-scale program, like the Finnish example, but one opening up the design of the type of housing that is offered for discussion, so that its inhabitants could feel at home in a whole variety of different ways. Crucially—to go back to chapter 1—*design* here does not just mean to enable a discussion around the size and shape of rooms and the availability of bus stops and green spaces. In this context, *design* means to embrace the pluriversal nature of housing as that assemblage where a number of domains intersect and come to the fore. Enabling housing design would mean therefore to forefront the multifaceted nature of the use value of any given shelter as a place that can be shaped in order to transcend, by design, the lived and felt violence experienced by those doing the dwelling.

If done properly, such a discussion would eventually lead to a conversation around what the client of the service desires beyond what is currently given to them. In such a context, someone escaping a violent household would hardly request just sheltering; a burned-out person, soaked in debt and dependence, would hardly need just a box to sleep in or an intensive case manager to care for their addiction; an individual seeking refuge from war would most certainly want more than four walls to sleep within. The latter are a fundamental starting point for all these individuals, the same way food, clothing, and access to adequate health provisioning are. But to transcend home(lessness), to crack through the ceiling of a home that, respectively, violates/enslaves/jails its subjects, those bare material arrangements won't be enough to chart a new terrain, a new plateau, a genuine liberation. And so, a state program to enable a liberatory housing design would essentially be about the provisioning of the infrastructural arrangements to start and to care for such a conversation, and the delivery of its own plan, for its own salvation. This is more than the recognition that "housing" might provide for an infrastructure of care.[29] This is a process that, if done well, could well challenge itself: it would question the whole program, its providers, and the relationship between a top-down provisioning and conflicting envisioning of homing, and of how to become new subjects through it. However, these challenges shouldn't bring the program to a halt, but transform it into a tensioned zone to be inhabited with propositions, attentive to the power dynamics unfolding in the conversation, and eventually leading to different radical housing solutions for different kinds of homes for different people. In such a context, to follow Colin Ward, the state should be no more and no less than the facilitator for multiple plans to emerge, not the one doing the planning.[30]

I can already hear the voices of those who disagree, speaking the language of impossibility. Some would say that this argument is utopian, particularly at a time when the number of people who are homeless is increasing due to an intensification of dispossessive practices. "How can we defund shelters," they ask, "when there are so many people on the streets?" This bureaucratic mind-set promotes the idea that inhabitation cannot be changed. This is because it works within institutions—the state, the church, the charities, the academy—that are designed to maintain the logic of home(lessness) in place, not to dismantle it (chapters 1, 3, 4, 5). Ultimately, this is the reason why, when it comes to breaking home(lessness), the institutional path seems like a dead end. Fundamentally, we are trained not to believe in the kind of democratic practice that sees democracy as a struggle waged by ordinary people. To follow Mark Purcell, rather than taking a "journey down a path towards more democracy, autonomy, and activity," we seek reassurance from top-down institutional structures, the same reproducing the home(lessness) we all live in.[31] And so the choice is either for the shelter to stay on or to admire the Finnish Housing First as the benchmark of optimal change, although it ultimately does not challenge the expulsive and extractive logic of the milieu it is built upon.

The best option, when it comes to the state, seems to be infiltrating and co-opting its resources to support other kind of maneuverings that have more concrete propositions to offer when it comes to an alternative to the homeless shelter. What needs to be done is to deinstitutionalize service provisions both from within, through defectors, and from the multiplication of outside countercolonizing experiences and the praxis of sheltering, feeding, playing, dreaming, and living. As Vallerand has it, this kind of defunding should be oriented at the assemblage of a collective home: "not one where different groups exist within separate spheres, but one where space is understood and used as a collective sphere where they interact in full relationality."[32] Fortunately, our cities offer many inspiring practices in this sense. I am thinking here of the grassroots praxis of squatting, where people occupy and maintain autonomous homes in a range of buildings, sometimes illegally, sometimes using rental property, sometimes in buildings offered by municipal authorities. The liberatory kind of home I have been arguing for in this book is already being made experimentally in these spaces, and there is scope to expand their remit (chapter 6, and below). These are places that tackle housing precarity in its material emergence, but they do not confine it there. Notwithstanding the different kinds of political and so-called nonpolitical squatting, at a bare minimum in these spaces there is the attempt to shelter precarious individuals, but on a different basis than institutional services.

I am not referring to wide and profound political differences with established states and charitable provisions, which are undoubtedly there. I am referring, instead, to a more prosaic ground of everyday practices, a ground that speaks directly to the place where the most intense facets of precarious housing conditions are lived and felt. I am talking about the ways in which food is cooked and distributed, outside of a paternalist economy of charity. I am referring to the culture of mutual assistance that rejects patronizing or overly bureaucratic and medicalized attitudes toward the other. I am referencing the simple nurturing of individual desires into forms of creative play and endeavors, through the cinematic, theatrical, and sports-oriented activities enacted in many autonomous establishments. As much as the encounter with the abstract machine of homelessness—made of its agape, its punch cards, its documentations—can push the subject into diagrams of pure lessness, an everyday praxis of radical care can deeply change the poetics of one's own life. If I expand on the latter in the next two sections, here I want to evoke what such current autonomous grounds can offer to deinstitute current machinic provisioning.

If shelters are not going to be meaningfully defunded by the state, through the grassroots, we can take away their clients and bring them into old and new forms of occupations founded on otherwise forms of caring. This must be seen as an act of radical deinstitutionalization and opening. Does this mean grassroots organizers will have to run their own low-threshold soup kitchens and dormitories (when and if they are not already doing so), within their current occupied spaces? Not necessarily. In doing so, the risk of falling back into a posture of provisioning for an "other" who is never fully at home could still be in place. I believe, instead, that the fight should be brought into current spaces of state and charitable assistance. A possibility in this sense would be that of taking place, occupying state shelters, and probing liberatory takeovers of soup kitchens and clothing distributions taking place within the holy walls of a Catholic oratory. But another option—not less daring and disruptive—could be that of igniting the fire of striking into the ranks of the homeless, of the houseless asylum seekers, of the inhabitants of the camp, and of those who are housed but dependent on charitable affordances. Striking—as the affirmatory action to seek independence, rather than just the posture of being against—could provide for a first step to establish a common ground of action:

a deinstitution of the current, upon which praxis of reinstitution and institution could come to the fore.

There are of course important unions of the homeless (such as the National Union of the Homeless, in the United States), but these are examples of grassroots and NGOs that do not necessarily use striking as a strategy for political change. Indeed, one can find only very few and scattered examples of organized striking by the so-defined homeless, and these are—for the most part—emergency responses to immediate threats of eviction from provisional camps or occupied buildings.[33] Here, however, I am arguing for something different. If the state fails to deinstitutionalize the means through which it keeps the other of home at bay, that same other can and should organize to interrupt their work in the maintenance of home. What if that other refuses to be counted, refuses to receive patronizing help, stops complying, ceases to do the rounds of all the shelters, and starts, instead, to articulate its own proposition and desire for inhabitation? Such a provocative question does not mean to elude the obvious issue at hand—that is, that shelter and other immediate material and affective things have to be provided. Striking, if seen as a practice to reach deinstitution of current harmful provisioning, is not the simple refusal of help but the appropriation of what is given and its rewiring, its repurposing, its reassembling for the good of those doing it. As will become clearer later on, this grassroots approach to deinstitution requires—and goes hand in hand with—the work to reinstitute to people the ability to care for collective struggles, and the clear institution of an autonomous, yet shared, sense of direction for that collectivity.

There are many historically empowering examples of what forms of collectively organized striking can do. To illustrate my point further, I take inspiration from the emancipatory struggles of feminists in Latin America, in the powerful narration and praxis of Veronica Gago. In that context, striking is not just the refusal of a defined subject position. It is not about workers stepping out of the factory, because there is not a unifying group to start with and not a clearly defined enemy to work against. Rather, to strike becomes a generative endeavor, a form of radical pedagogy, or, as Gago beautifully puts it, "a new form of practical cartography."[34] It means to chart a new terrain where one can situate oneself as a subject of power against the given dispossession; and to use that new ground both to disrupt old structures (provisions of services in this case) and to chart a new "organizational horizon" (the reinstitution and institution of which I will speak in a moment). Even if "there is no clear or identifiable boss, no one with whom to enter into immediate negotiations, and no clearly defined working hours during which to strike," I agree with Gago when she says that such an impossibility "immediately becomes its strength: it forces those experiences to resignify and broaden what is suspended when the strike must accommodate those realities, widening the social field in which the strike is inscribed and where it produces effects."[35]

In home(lessness), spaces and subjects are (re)produced, some at home, others outside, and yet both are part of the same expulsive and extractive substratum (re)producing violent ritornellos of inhabitation for the many. To strike from the far side of this system of power would be to interrupt the continuity of its (re)production, and that, of course, could take many shapes and forms. On the cusp of COVID-19, rent and mortgage strikes were an example of this and the suspension, granted by many governments in the West, of rent and loan payment was arguably a way to preempt the devastating blow that a serious massive refusal to pay would have meant for the workings of the global financial housing market.[36] In staying closer to the deinstitution effort, striking would mean first and foremost organizing the ability to collectively stand against the normalization of a subject position as recipient of extant care. It would mean to institute, in the words of Gago, "an act of disobedience to the constant expropriation of our vital energies, plundered by exhausting routines," which in the case of the other of home are days filled with meaningless and violent bureaucracies and the pain of having, emotionally and psychically, to constantly perform, to comply, to receive the promised assistance, to fill in.[37]

The state will not intervene to deinstitute the diagrams keeping the other of home at bay, yet conveniently close and manageable. A similar immobility will be found in the faith-based realm and within a wide range of humanitarians involved in practices of salvation or who are working within rights-based frameworks that never really question what is just and for whom. This is because all these actors are an expression of a specific ideology of inhabiting the planet that needs, at its core, to work with the impossible possibilities offered by its negation. But such a lessness can be fought against and, very specifically for the point of departure that I have chosen, it can be hit at the core workings of its boundary-making processes. Defections from inside normative services are welcome and needed, but even if they don't come, the grassroots could organize the clients of those services under a different paradigm, one in which striking against the given subjectivity is not just the negation of a subject position but the announcement of a movement—a getting beyond a whole machinery of social, economic, political, and affective control. Paraphrasing Gago, "from the conjunction between impossibility and desire, a radical imaginary emerges about the multiple forms" of the strike for a liberatory kind of home, a strike that can take its doers "to unsuspected places, prying it open in order to include vital experiences, and reinventing it based on bodies that are disobedient to what is recognized as labor," or to what is recognized as home.[38]

Reinstituting, in Caring

Deinstituting the industry caring for the currently defined homeless and re-claiming precarity and its suffering as the key terrain of the housing political needs to be accompanied by concrete effort to reinstitute what has been stolen, what has been robbed, what has been expelled in order to allow for extraction to take place. The question therefore becomes how to overcome a racialized mode of production and consumption, which has axiomatized and captured all other domains of life. There are many who are working in this direction, though on different paths, including those fighting against racist justice systems, those drawing attention to radical antiracist ecology, those championing a more-than-monetary postcapitalist politics, and those advocating a renewed politics of recognition and redistribution.[39]

When it comes to housing and its markets, a crucial fight is around the restitution of land stolen in the past through settler-colonial processes (but also in the present, for example, the Israeli state), and to reinstitute the grounds stolen through the coloniality of capital.[40] Public land has been systematically handed over to private hands, across the globe, through devious political and private interests.[41] The problem is not only around what has been dispossessed but also on how restitution schemes can, as Fay and James contend, "produce unintended consequences . . . [and] replicate segregated patterns of land use."[42] As I have been able to investigate in my own work in Romania, frameworks of restitution can be used as a means to forcibly construct housing markets where the public control of lands and housing was the norm (a dynamic very common in the whole postsocialist area). In these cases, the language of reparation and rights becomes a double-edged sword to (racially) displace communities of the urban poor and allow capital to gain space it did not have before.[43]

In this context, communities across the world fight to seize their land back and struggle against the wrongdoing of capitalist-driven restitution processes. As beautifully illustrated by Keisha-Khan Perry in her work on Brazil—but also as I have been able to witness in my own work with Roma communities in Romania—fighting to get back what is rightfully one's own is a matter of getting deep down into structures of racialized, but also patriarchal and capitalist, injustice.[44] In fighting settler colonialism, land grabs, and privatizations, what communities ask to recover is not just land upon which they can bestow a form of concessionary dignity but land through which they can instantiate their autonomous and affirmative habitation. I expand on this critical juncture in the next section, but here I want to stay close to the problem of reinstitution and, again, take a lateral step. What else needs to be reinstituted, beyond land? To end the coloniality of home, it is necessary to win settler-colonial structures, past and present, that materially and violently have expelled, raped, and seized both bodies and earths. But to really end the power of these violent processes at home (chapter 2), there is the need for more. I am not referring to a different kind of fight, but I am seeking to learn from the fact that progressive fights for land restitution are, as I have just said, intersectional and prefigurative in nature. They are radical, as much fighting for housing can be, because they question the inner functioning of inhabitation (chapter 6).

Fighting for reparative land and housing justice is crucial to affirm a liberated kind of home. But for that fight to be successful, there is a further component to be repaired and to be repossessed, because it has been violated and stolen by the colonies of home—that is, the collective capacity to radically care for inhabitation, the ability to genuinely envision housing as a gateway for emancipatory struggles. The provision of housing and land can be a gateway to radical change, but it is not as such by default. For that to happen, the diagram of housing justice needs to contain already in itself the capacity to redesign the violent functions of our current home. That justice will need to fight to gain the stolen land, the occupation and possession of the stolen house, and at the same time, it will need to care for the kind of inhabitation it aims to activate, to foster its assemblage, to curate the sense of direction it aims to coconstitute with its subjects. To my mind, that justice cannot be fully attained with reparations from above. Even in those contexts in which a historically meaningful restoration is provided by the state, the envisioning of a careful futurity for what has been reinstituted must be built by the ones fighting for it, because it concerns their own design for their own liberation.

But what does caring even mean within the framework of our home and its lessness? What does caring mean, within the most intense experiences of home(lessness), where subjectivities are produced and reproduced, circulated and sustained, allowing much that suffices for extractive practices to go on, from the embodied to the financial, from the digital to the charitable, and back again? How to think and to talk about care in spaces in which the legal frameworks allowing lives to be confined so that several forms of extraction can go on are accepted, evoked, and embraced by the many as the solution to lingering fears and a fluctuating sense of doom? As I have illustrated throughout the book, and as central also to the question of deinstitution, the problem with the boundary making of home/homelessness is one in which care and caring—as a diagram of power operated toward the other of home—plays a huge role. This is what Clare Hemmings has called the "cannibalisation of the other masquerading as care."[45] Loving the poor—as a machinery of social control. Protecting the other from the other—as a justification for a whole racialized industry of incarceration, containment, and border control. Treating the sick—as a way to define a domain of knowledge based on the definition of someone else's fundamental inadequacy-to-be. Recuperating the damned—as the moral caging of those addictions deemed in need of control. Care has been reduced to a practical solution rather than being enacted as a daring proposition.

However, as argued in chapter 6, precarious dwelling experiences can indicate radical gateways toward multiple liberatory home(s). That is what I have called the micropolitics of housing precarity: the emergence (from sites of the colonized uninhabitable) of propositions for their own inhabitation. Part of that struggle is about deinstituting what entraps the other of home, and part is about instituting a form of autonomy for what has been deinstituted. But in between, there is the material struggle to reinstitute what has been stolen and that includes both the materiality of reparative justice and the immediate concern of reappropriating a capacity to care, to curate, and to construct a sense of shared direction, a sense of what home might be. If the latter is emergent and already there (chapter 6), its standing is not a given. It must be reinstituted, because it has been dispossessed to make home stand.

To appreciate what this reinstitution is about, the question must be around what care and treatment can do, not around what they are and how they work.[46] The latter is a preoccupation of those holding onto extant praxes of power, which ultimately colonize, steal, expel, and extract. The former gets closer to a liberatory affordance one gives to oneself: what can this do for us? What this book learns from progressive fights for land restoration and reparatory justice is that in fighting for reinstitution, in its wider prefigurative sense, one needs to leave what one knows of care aside and embrace a more demanding and affirmatory take on care and caring, even, and especially so, when one is not directly affected by dispossession and is instead moved by the desire to intervene and to save the other of home. Demanding more from care means to stop questioning its absolute value and to demand clarity about its purpose and sense of direction. As Samantha Thompson argues, "care is intimately embedded within housing, not only, as usually understood, through the doings of reproductive labour but also through the relationship that goes on in defending housing from dispossessive practice."[47] What follows is that reinstituting, in caring, means to ask questions on what curating a collectivity implies and for whom, and around where that curation is going.

Here I am arguing for a notion of radical care, a term that I take and expand from Hobart and Kneese to indicate the effort to ground the fight against lessness and to curate the emergence of a beyond.[48] The *radical* in this context is not the simple alternative to being homeless, nor is it just restoration of a possession, but it is framed as that which is working toward another proposition through restoration. The importance of bringing this understanding of care when talking of reinstituting lies in its crucial significance to enable the emergence of alternative functionings to expulsion and extraction. If land is gained and simply brought back home, the result won't be different than barely housing all the homeless of the world. Both endeavors are crucial but will be recaptured. In the making of both, a curation of a collective proposition on inhabitation needs to be brought to the fore, at the level of theory and practice. It needs to be waved into the fight. As I illustrate with the third move, on instituting in affirmation, this requires principles of autonomy and solidarity. But before getting there, there is the need to reacquire the capacity to radically care for the possibility of a breakthrough. On the threshold of deinstitution, fighting for reinstitution provides the ground for a renewed caring to come forward and to spring to life.

There are two key elements defining a recentering of care in this way. First, radical caring takes place on the side. It is not mainstream, and it does not want to be. It is, as AbdouMaliq Simone would have it, "a lateral move," a way of staying, unavoidably so, *within* and *beyond* capture because one needs to stay low to survive against the entrenchments of the types of care that shore up the home/homelessness boundary.[49] "Caring otherwise," as I have called it elsewhere, following Cubellis and Lester, or "radical care," as Hobart and Kneese put it, is a strategy of affirmative survival, which requires an "audacity to produce, apply, and effect" because it is situated within "dark histories and futures."[50] In this sense, "radical care can present an otherwise, even if it cannot completely disengage from structural inequalities and normative assumptions regarding social reproduction, gender, race, class, sexuality, and citizenship."[51] This means to say that in the praxis of fighting for reinstitution, radical care—notwithstanding the violent foundations it has to live in—finds its space to craft plans that are undisclosed, unannounced, and not performed to those who do not belong. It shows a face to the institution that it is fighting, and it works with it as long as it is able to open for itself a passage, to paraphrase Harney and Moten, and then take what it can take.[52] But crucially, the affective and material capacity enabling a collective to stay low and sneak in needs to be curated and maintained. Radical care is the curation of an affective consciousness in the minor key, reassuring its bodies that one is not alone in the fight, and that there is a plan even if it must be kept under wraps, to prevent it from being stolen.

The second aspect, following thinkers like Grosz and Haraway, is that the morality of this kind of caring is constructed and negotiated in situ, in relation both to a historically specific material and cultural lineage, and to a process that is at stake in the present. What is good or what is bad about a particular form of collective concern cannot be defined transcending the event. Radical care emerges as an assemblage around a particular concern at a given moment.[53] In this definition, *care* comes to mean something close to the maintenance of a collective struggle (see below), something that rejects detachment and distance from its object of care because it can only be declined as a subject of its own caring, one refusing to engage with institutional forms of judgment, amelioration, and solutions from afar. This embodied positioning does not take a normative configuration. It is guided by its principles, but the latter are situated, not universal. This is why such a form of care can exert violence against its oppressor, if it decides that is its path. It can burn and it can occupy: reinstituting, in caring, means that the definition of what needs to be reinstituted and what it means to be cared for are of those struggling for their own inhabitation. There is no need to constitute an "other" for this form of care—and its related envisioning of home—to stand. At that point, a fragile, ephemeral, and subterranean form of collectivity might be able to foster and sustain into life its own micropolitical desire for a liberatory kind of homing, the affirmation to which I now turn.

Instituting, in Affirmation

Deinstituting and reinstituting need to be conceived as ongoing revolutionary struggles, not as end goals. The latter will provide the false perception of having solved the matter, or even just the perception that the matter is solvable. It will mean again to say that we can be at home, while before we were not. This maintains the possibility of falling back into that before, its lack, its lessness. Yet, conceptually speaking, it is hard to think of pure affirmation. This is partially because we have been educated in the binaries and colonies of home, because of our innate finitude as humans (however, the latter, in a panecological perspective, can be rethought). Language does not help either. Even in the writing itself, "pure affirmation" seems to signal an end point, an arrival, an attainable result—a solution.[54] To crack through this impasse—which is at the core of the home/homelessness formulation (chapters 1, 2)—one has to conceive of the revolutionary work to get beyond lessness as a processual platform in constant expansion, a being as becoming.[55] Such a perpetual revolutionary move is, to bring back the framework deployed in chapter 1, not the object of desire, but desire itself: an affirmation that does not require an external boundary to be defined, because its definition consists constantly in caring for itself, by itself. It is precisely by avoiding a universal value set attached to the definition of what *liberated* looks like, and by insisting that *liberated* is the process and not the end goal, that one can step out of a binary reading of the possible and can conceive the space beyond lessness as that which constantly expands beyond itself, beyond what it holds and what it has achieved, not just beyond its entrapments and negation.

In thinking this way, one is not losing ground or sense of direction. As illustrated in chapter 6, this whole reasoning must be situated within the experience of housing precarity or, better said, within the proposition indicated by that experience for its own liberation. It is that sense of direction that indicates the expansion to follow, the process to institute. Crucially, there won't be just one path. A liberated home can only be multiple. It is the liberation of the desire for homing: a variegated emergence, a ritornello for the many, a design of multiple designs. Deinstituting the industries scheming to maintain the impossible possibility of home and reinstituting the (material and affective) means of power to those that have been dispossessed are quintessential steps in this sense.[56] *Instituting* is what expands on deinstitution and reinstitution, to constitute the new ground for action. For going beyond the violence of mainstream inhabitation is a creative act: it is about providing the grounds upon which collectives can self-define, self-liberate, and otherwise care about their inhabitation of the planet.

In this sense, a liberatory politics of home comprises the fight against home(lessness) and its violence, but it is not defined by its relationship to it. The negation, the refusal—the deinstitution—is just the minimum common denominator to move forward. The definition of a political praxis and of its horizon are in the latter, in the moving, in how and where the conventional other of home wants to move. This is why the reinstitution of the capacity to think and the concrete institution of a ground of radical care are quintessential to sketch the liberatory effort around the housing political within the framework here proposed. It is only providing for such a ground that the possibility of a liberatory home becomes possible. It is not just in the fight against home(lessness) that the latter will end but in the affirmative gesture of instituting a new plateau, of forging the means to leave lessness altogether, if just staying on the cracks of the given, that something radically new can emerge.

The effort to constantly renew such a ground is what will make for a politics of home to become, and reaffirm itself, as liberatory for its subjects.

But can such a politics begin at times in which unconditional sheltering is not granted to all? It can, because this is a politics of sneaking in and carving out spaces of affirmative endurance, which is already what most communities faced with the harshest intensities of lessness are doing. This is not the UN-HABITAT call to shelter all as the salvatory end goal. And it is not even the call for the public ownership of the fundamental means to produce and control housing. Although I genuinely hope, and struggle, for housing to be publicly granted to everyone on planet Earth and brought out of local and translocal financialized market control, here I am arguing something else. The politics I am evoking sits on the side of that struggle, contributing to it but also having its own standing. Instituting the ground for a liberatory home is not just about securing housing for all but about using the use value of housing to challenge the profound violence of homing at large, and build, dwell, and think anew through that praxis. Faced with the immediacy of the trauma of houselessness, such a politics will be concerned with securing shelter, but as the point of departure, the minimum organizational gesture. Its affirmative ethos will have to point beyond that. It will have to build on the struggle to avoid institutionalization (deinstitution) and the effort to empower through care (reinstitution), to work on the constitution of a collective dwelling proposition from—led by—its subjects.

Instituting is about constructing the milieu—economic, discursive, affective, and infrastructural—for the inhabitants of lessness to get beyond inhabitation. Constituting such a ground for renewed homing action will have to be a situated, geographically and historically specific enterprise. Yet I would like to indicate at least two principles that could provide some initial framing, since they speak directly of alternative functionings to expulsion and extraction, and could therefore provide for a very different tempo of inhabitation.

The first is autonomy. If expulsion is about defining, dividing, and then controlling what is made of the other, autonomy is the explicit beyond of such a practice. It encircles something, as in expulsion, but, crucially, its encircling is not projecting outside; autonomy does not speak to something that does not belong to itself. In expulsion, the bearer of power segments, creates, and controls the other for its own return. In autonomy, the bearer of power carves out a space for itself, in relation to itself. It goes without saying that such a form of autonomy has nothing to do with autarchy: epistemic and material relations cutting through and beyond what is rendered autonomous are always there.

And yet autonomous pronunciation marks a terrain; it speaks a language; it seeks a way to center its concerns while maintaining those peripherals, giving rise to its proposition and program. In autonomy, the power comes from the emancipation of those expressing it, not from the expulsion of another. This also means that autonomy is not the simple negation of expulsion but an altogether different function. To provide an alternative to expulsion would mean to reassert the rights of the other as such; or to include the other in a redundant majority. Autonomy stands on its grounds and speaks only of those.

This principle can be found in many liberatory struggles across the world. In my thinking of it, I am indebted to the notions of *autogestión* and *autonomia*. The first comes from a long tradition of *autogestión*, a set of theories and practices brought forward by southern European and Latin American workers and anarchist thinkers to construct a noncapitalist way of collectively organizing both labor and the distribution of its products. As Vieta explains, "*Autogestión*, or self-management, alludes to a processual movement of self-creation, self-conception, and self-definition."[57] It represents a way of establishing collective work practices that push back "against ideologies and practices of hierarchical control and coercion."[58] The second term, *autonomia*, resonates with *autogestión* and was one of the keywords of the Italian extraparliamentarian Left during the 1960s and '70s, and one that is explicitly part of a "minor" working of politics.[59] *L'autonomia operaia*, and *l'autonomia* more generally, involved a diverse set of social actors who grounded their actions in *operaismo*, a grassroots recentering of the struggle of the working class as the privileged site of inquiry and action. They distinguished themselves from the Italian Communist Party and all other forms of centralized politics. *L'autonomia* was a form of insurgency against hierarchical, centralized decision making, and fundamentally antiauthoritarian in tenor. It advocated a position outside of both institutional politics and the institutionalized Left, while maintaining an openness and fluidity that allowed intersectional relationships to develop.[60] The goal was to unfold multiple streams of autonomous, affirmative action. As Toni Negri put it, "It is only by recognising myself as other, only by insisting on the fact of my different-ness as a radical totality that I have the possibility and the hope of a renewal."[61]

Despite their differences and different histories, *autogestión* and *autonomia* play an alternative tune to the ritornello of home(lessness). In bringing the two together, I conceive autonomy as that which keeps expulsive tendencies at bay. If the latter try to define life in opposition, and in control of, a purposely defined other of home, the former is concerned with the modalities of its own governance and maintenance, therefore thinking, dwelling, and building its own kind of home. The relevance of autonomy to institute the grounds for a counterpolitics to home(lessness) is duplicitous. First, autonomous politics, in centering practices of mutual aid and solidarity, fights the central tenets of the expulsive and extractive functions of home(lessness): it is not about individual appropriations or plans, but about individuals joining together for a collective good, the latter grounded in negotiations and sharing rather than imposed from above.[62] Such a dis-alignment is, to follow Paulo Freire, a "radical posture," a move on the side that requires precisely what the *autonomia operaia* tried to do with itself and for itself: an affirmative solidarity "requiring that one enter into the situation of those with whom one is solidary," therefore refusing the detachment artificially pronounced in expulsion.[63] Through its stress in—extremely tiring and uneasy for sure—collective laboring and autonomous praxis, it provided a challenge to expulsions by attacking its underlying authoritarianism and imbalanced power dynamics.

Second, in instantiating self-determination and organizing as the driving principles of any unit of action, autonomous politics is not reducible to one dogmatic expression but uses concrete praxis to prefigure the worlds that it would like to inhabit. In the context of homelessness, notions of prefiguration have been widely developed on the anarchist squatting scene. Squatters have embraced the idea that inhabitation should be defined by the ones doing it, as a form of what Vasudevan calls "make+shifts": something assembled from within as a lived politics rather than imposed by an external party or policy.[64] But self-determination and prefiguration extend well beyond the—sometimes limiting (chapter 6)—canons of politicized Western squatting practice. As Ward and Turner concede, autonomist praxis occurs in everyday practices of dwelling across the globe: in forms of mundane dwelling and getting-by, which capitalist and normative forces can tame but cannot entirely control. It is within the cracks of these makings that a ground for liberation can be instituted because these are the spaces that could have been appropriated by the repressive canons of home/homelessness, yet they constantly stay within and beyond capture.[65] It is of little importance if their precarious propositions are not recognized by the scholar or the activist of autonomy, because the political they enact is embodied in ways that fit uncomfortably with given paradigms (chapter 6). If we are serious about instituting a ground for a space beyond home(lessness) to emerge, what counts is not the declaration of prefigurative politics, but its autonomous and self-determining embodiment and sense of direction.

At that juncture, a second principle of instituting liberation comes to the fore: becoming an accomplice, or accompliceship. The notion, as Ana Vilenica reminds us, has been developed in anarchist thinking and in the Black Lives Matter movement, as a way to fight rights-based forms of alliance that pivot on "patronizing relations between those who assist toward those who need assistance."[66] Accompliceship uses epistemic and material privilege more radically, collectively, and profoundly. As also reported by Vilenica, Indigenous Action Media explains this quite well: "Whereas ally politics suggest that in shifting one's role from actor to ally, one can diminish one's culpability, a liberating or anarchist approach presumes each person retains their own agency while also accounting for and responding to others' desires, revealing how our survival/ liberation is fundamentally linked with the survival/liberation of others. This fosters interdependence while compelling each person to take responsibility for their own choices, with no boss or guidance counsellor to blame for their decisions."[67]

Bringing the notion of accompliceship to the fore means to center the problem of how to work, in practice, outside the colonizing frameworks of home and its deputies of salvation (chapters 1, 2). What accompliceship requires is not a nominal negation of privilege. Indeed, thinking through home(lessness) means to center the notion that, in the current modalities of dwelling in the world, the many are a matter of the same affective and political economy, not that all experience that economy the same way. In this sense, to work together in the dismantling of lessness means to institute a ground where autonomy is lived and felt by all as a shared, albeit variously experienced, sense of direction. Individual preferences and standing, in such a politics, are there. Yet these are not defined through extraction from somebody else but are affirmed on the refusal of extraction. Individuals get their freedom on how to inhabit the world only through their collective becoming accomplices of such a refusal. On such a standing lies the basis for a function other than extraction because it is about recognizing that "our survival/liberation is fundamentally linked with"—not extracted from—"the survival/liberation of others."

In accompliceship, we are asked to care for the endurance of the collective struggle to institute the grounds where the liberatory politics of home can be experimented with, articulated, and inhabited through. What matters is not what the collective is, but how it becomes—that is, how it decides to constitute and share its political space. It is important to state very clearly that here I am not talking about the end form, or outcome, of what can germinate from such a space. In some cases, it will be about shared dwellings, shared facilities, centralized resources. In others, it will be about scattered mononuclear houses, or about something I cannot imagine from my end. What I am interested in stressing is that a liberatory politics of home is not about the end form but the ongoing institution of its grounds through functions that chart a terrain beyond expulsion and extraction. Accompliceship, therefore, does not necessarily mean shared bathrooms. It means to care for the endurance of the collective struggle to be autonomous and have the minimum allowance to institute one's own affordance to think, build, and dwell in a liberated home.

Such endurance is hard and conflicting: it needs to be cultivated, in ways that sometimes require enormous energy and effort, as all radical housing justice activists know. It needs a form of what Hawthorne has called "transgressive solidarity," to cut through the numerous segmenting ritornellos of lessness, including specific processes of racialization of the other of home, to "imagine political possibilities beyond the nation-state and its practices of exclusion." These forms of solidarities "cultivate relationships of care based on shared histories of struggles rather than on blood, birthplace, or legal status."[68] Much of this is already taking place in the interstices of home(lessness). Forms of this radical care are present in declared political collectives but also within many so-called nonpolitical squatting arrangements. I am thinking of the occupied buildings in the extended peripheries of many European capitals, where communities of migrants and locals are concerned with the shared inhabitation of uninhabitable spaces and stand on those grounds as the only way to institute their presence in the world. But examples of this have also been present beyond squatting, in the makings of horizontally diffused movements such as the Plataforma de Afectados por la Hipoteca (PAH) in Spain.[69] One key element of that struggle was the successful mobilization of millions of Spaniards, across races and classes, in direct housing actions to prevent thousands of evictions from taking place across Spain.[70] As research that is attentive to the everyday makeshift nature of the movement shows, PAH was largely about the construction and maintenance—the caring—of a collectively lived and felt (embodied) struggle.[71] Importantly, and in direct contradiction to conventionally more radical Marxist readings, the endurance of that collective struggle encompassed the end of the movement, precisely because people actively care about it beyond themselves. As Melissa García-Lamarca has argued, "the experience of the PAH shows that what Rancière sees as rare and intermittent moments of disruption can be sustained in some fashion through collective advising assemblies, as solidarity and equality-based practices where mutual aid and pedagogy occur on a continuous basis."[72]

The interplay of autonomy and accompliceship speaks the language of the radically poetic: it becomes a question of allowing the unfolding of caring to become apparent, before one forecloses the situation with a normalizing moral judgement on it, which often morphs into a classification of otherness, followed by value extraction. Working through principles of autonomy and accomplice-ship is not about evaluating effects but about following affections: under-standing how something becomes of concern, and what care makes possible. Following Isabelle Stengers's cosmopolitical proposal, the task for the radical thinker and activist of home(lessness) is to allow a situation to unfold rather than prejudging it. In this sense, working to institute a ground for liberation "makes the decision as difficult as possible, precludes any shortcut or simplifi-cation, any differentiation a priori between that which counts and that which does not."[73] Ultimately, what unites humans fighting for housing justice across the globe is not a well-theorized, conscious alliance grounded in their subordi-nate position within the cogs of the neoliberalizing capitalist machine. Before such an alliance is even possible, before its enunciation can become a possibil-ity, there is a mundane collective insurgence assembled from the embodied experience of very marginal spaces: a resistance to a historicized, racialized, and financialized habitus, and a collective commitment to go beyond current forms of inhabitation as the only possible chance to stay meaningfully alive.

Coda

A liberatory politics of home is a politics of the multiple, a politics of the process, a revolution without ending point but with a clear sense of direction, against and at the same time beyond lessness. I have illustrated it as a tripar-tite matter of deinstitution, reinstitution, and institution, processes that come with their own strategies of striking, caring, and affirming. In this view, a liber-ated home is not a place, nor a thing. A liberated home is about deinstituting, in striking, its negation; about reinstituting, in caring, the capacity of fighting the violence of its past; and, fundamentally, about instituting, in the ongoing effort to affirm its own struggle to be and to become, the multiple forms of inhabitation required for its collective life to endure.

Although they intersect wider concerns, these are processes and strate-gies that I have discussed as staying close to the boundary making of home/homelessness, a boundary that, I believe, has great potential to offer a gateway to wider radical change. Even without getting too far, tackling the home/homelessness question not through policy, but through the kind of instituting sketched above, can bring to the fore three very immediate outcomes. At a bare minimum, it will provide for safe autonomy for those involved, which is by and large what radical housing groups and squatters have been doing for decades, globally. But if accompanied with deinstitution and reinstitution, it will offer two additional benefits. First, by centering the desire for inhabitation of the dispossessed, it will morph housing demands and propositions, generating an unconventional culture of the housing political, with its own material and affective strategies and registries. Through such an ongoing struggle, a new grammar on how to read the interrelations of financialization, patriarchy, racism, institutionalization, and more, will come to the fore. In contexts in which grounds of radical affirmative care through housing have been already instituted, much of this is already happening. However, in pushing further and in expanding such grounds, a new collective public culture of liberatory homing might start to emerge in a more pronounced and vivid way. That culture might not speak the given language of anticapitalism, but in forefronting the need for its autonomy and its collective care, it will be about refuting the expulsion and extraction structuring the latter.

The second benefit of going minor, of refusing the distinction between home and homelessness, of looking suspiciously at policy, of refuting homelessness scholarship and cognate charitable and managerial interventions, concerns the perils of reproducing new forms of homely violence. For we know of the current functionings of home, of their expulsive and extractive workings at the level of gender, race, ableism, and ecologies, but we don't really know if—notwithstanding the affirmation of the beyond—we will eventually see the emergence of new injustice in liberating homes. As one might argue, it is not granted that a liberatory politics of home will not end up producing its annihilation and, from there, will fall back into binaries and related segmentations. What if the new functionings going beyond expulsion and extraction don't get to chart a new terrain? What if all remains fragile, provisional, scattered, and constantly questionable? What if liberation will never really come, will never really be attained, will never craft a new home?

In embracing the processual view discussed in this book, these questions are not a matter of *if*, but a matter of certainty. Indeed, it is not granted that autonomy and accompliceship will be enough to institute new functions and new grounds for homing. It is not granted that such a ground will be stable, and it is, indeed, sure that liberation will never, ever just come. But these are not disempowering narratives. A deep, collective acknowledgment of the ongoing nature of the struggle to get beyond lessness can be the ultimate liberatory gesture. In such a view, no formation can be considered entirely safe, not for all. No arrangement, and no design, can accommodate once and for all. In such a view, to follow hooks, home genuinely becomes an open-ended process, a "place which enables and promotes varied and *everchanging* perspectives, a place where one discovers *new ways* of seeing reality, *frontiers of difference*."[74] Liberating home means to constantly get it beyond itself, to push for its change, to experiment with new ways, to explore the frontiers of its love—always grounding this search in the institution of its self-affirmation, not around the impossible possibility offered by the colonies of domination. Such a homely place, to be coherent with its definition, can only be an ongoing revolution; a home that is always in constitution, beyond its negations, beyond the incapacitations that will emerge along the way; a liberatory homing praxis leading to a variety of forms, a multiplicity of housing use values, united by guiding principles pointing beyond expulsion and extraction. From my limited vantage point, I have mentioned three: the refusal to control so-defined home-less others; the need to center a differential way of caring about our capacity to constantly be redoing home; and the practice of constituting, in autonomy and accompliceship, affirmative ways of working through the unjust, violent grounds of the lessness that the many currently inhabit.

CONCLUSION. Beyond Inhabitation

Would it be enough to house all the homeless in the world to end homeless-ness? A resounding *yes* is the answer from many programs, most notably Housing First. For them, #endinghomelessness through rapid rehousing interventions is the way to go. In this book, I have taken a different stance. I have questioned the opposition of home and homelessness and have argued that something much deeper is necessary for liberation. I have repositioned the question of homelessness around an interrogation of ideas of the normal, which is an in-vitation to approach homelessness as part of home. This does not mean to say that life without shelter is the same as life with shelter. Nor does it mean to deprive houseless people of a standpoint from which to articulate their own liberatory politics. There are excruciating differences in being or not being sheltered, and I take the politics deriving from these as a fundamental element of the discussion. Stating that home and what we currently define as homelessness are not apart means to say that those conditions are not opposed—one the solution/negation to the other—but are conniving: part of the same affective and political economy, which I have called home(lessness).

The fiction of home/homelessness is the ground upon which the lives of the many are made expendable. Across the world, it is the site of precarity, as well as trauma, policing, imbalanced power dynamics, and violence. As a diagram, it enables processes of expulsion, which create a normal that is opposed to conditions of otherness. The strategic importance of the fiction of home lies in the way that it categorizes: it makes certain people feel less and count less. And this is in order to extract a whole range of different types of value. Both functions, expulsion and extraction, are at the same time material and epistemological, and work as a transversal ritornello across anthropocentric, racial capitalist, and heteronormative logics, deployed within histories and everyday practices of homing in popular culture, but also throughout the industries devised to care for or to understand the other of home both locally and globally (chapters 3–5).

The starting point for this book is that the binary between home and homelessness is used to generate a complex diagram of expulsion and extraction structuring mainstream modes of dwelling across the West, and possibly beyond. It follows that housing all the homeless cannot possibly end homelessness. Aspects of this argument are not new. Queer and feminist readings of home have long traced its violent makings and argued for more progressive home-making practices.[1] The most radical takes on the "fight for the right to housing" (especially those infused with autonomous principles) are not just about the reduction of housing to its exchange value, but about appropriating its use value to tackle wider inequalities.[2] Critical approaches to migration, bordering, and detention have enriched our understanding of becoming in and through institutionalized spaces.[3] On top of these, we are at a time of intense mobilization around housing issues, which more often than not morph directly into a wider critique of systemic forms of dispossession. Communities worldwide are fighting against gentrification, foreclosures, and evictions, and for rent control, investment in social housing, and fair housing policy and allocation of resources. Some add to this a battle for reparations against the types of financial theft operated by banks, landlords, and landowners. The extent and strength of this global housing mobilization has energized many and has undoubtedly brought concrete changes and victories. Groups have not only stopped evictions; they have constructed affective atmospheres of solidarity over the longer term, well beyond the instantiation of direct action. In this context, as I have argued, it is not uncommon for organizers to see housing as a strategic passage point to broader change, partially because the ontological security granted by a permanent abode allows us to fight for more, but also because housing questions are clearly linked to wider issues around inhabitation, the economy, patriarchy, racism, and ecology, to name just a few. Yet activists and campaigners working with this expanded understanding of the housing struggle are a minority if one considers the broader spectrum of the housing political. And this is, of course, one of the major problems when one wishes to tackle the question of how to work with an epistemology, like the one outlined here, which centers the experience of housing precarity affirmatively, as a locus toward autonomous radical change. For this reason, throughout the book, I proposed to look at home(lessness) as something more than a problem to be fixed. I have argued that the housing political is wider than any policy can possibly deal with. It requires a transversal approach, one to break with the status quo and to envision a renewed politics of home.

Humanitarian pragmatists would say this is too much. They would argue that while we await deeper change, many unsheltered individuals continue to populate our streets, and many, albeit housed, face challenges to their ontological security on a daily basis. They would say that securing housing for the many is already difficult enough, and that a wider and deeper approach is too ambitious. They would add that it is perhaps a different fight, one that could be approached synchronously with campaigns aimed at securing shelter for the many. But to me, this ignores the way in which this approach to the homelessness question is inextricably tied into harmful social, cultural, and economic relations. It cannot be detached from the intrinsic injustices of home/homelessness; indeed, it needs to be tackled as something that reproduces the same violent logic. Otherwise, we are simply maintaining the fiction that supports an unequal status quo, and the epistemic privilege of those administering it. Instead of struggling for an incremental adjustment to an unjust system, we should be fighting for a radical alternation of that system. Securing housing for all is still a crucial goal, but it must be strategically linked up to an approach that is sensitive to a differential kind of inhabitation, or dwelling, of and for the world.

> And therefore in this book I have argued that in order to end homelessness, we must liberate home.
> A liberated home is a home that does not require an alterity to stand.
> It is a place of affirmation, not one of negation.
> It is a home that cannot be made expendable because its core functions are not about expulsion and extraction.

It is a home beyond anthropocentrism.

Beyond racial capitalism.

Beyond patriarchy and heteronormativity.

Beyond making subjects of and for lessness.

Does such a home need new groundings, then?

And who defines them?

Can we seriously think of changing inhabitation within the diagrams of
lessness, which seems to have channeled our collective eight billion
lives already?

To tackle these questions, in this book I have slowly tried to move away
from a politics of negation to a politics of affirmation. Although I grounded
part of the discussion within the geography of Italy, my intention with this volume has been to disrupt modes of thinking around home and homelessness at
large. Refuting the idea of providing a theory that can cut across locales, I have
squarely situated my proposition at the epistemological level, conscious that
the ways an epistemology is acted upon, and morphed throughout, are entirely
situated acts that encompass the scope of this volume. I have embraced a decolonial approach, inviting one to seek alternatives to how questions are posed;
yet, what is to be said about the liberatory homing grammars that emerge is
not for me to determine.[4] Instead, the book has been pointing at those tensioned spaces where such a grammar is already used, experimented with, and
in dire need of noncolonizing hearing-from. In the most intense manifestation
of home(lessness), lateral moves and unannounced struggles are already moving beyond inhabitation. What they have to say takes the form of fragile forms
of propositional politics, which are easily silenced within the rubric of salvation and resilience. But in real—actual and virtual—terms, every inhabitation
is political, because it is always about dealing with the practical and ideological
foundations of its becoming. So, when one fights what life has given one, and
does so by pointing beyond that given, such a struggle might have something
interesting to say about the kind of renewed groundings one wants, the kind of
desire for inhabitation one might have.

By staying close to the other of home, I have chosen the nexus of housing
as a key intersection to excavate these propositional forms of dwelling. It is not
that desperation and trauma arising from housing precarity are all liberatory,
but it is that in them there is more than a cry to be saved and being brought
back home. This echoes and builds upon the concerns of many grassroots radical housing activists worldwide. As Raquel Rolnik once told me in conversation for the *Radical Housing Journal*:

When we struggle to stay put, we are not just struggling for the right to housing as part of our struggle for human rights, as in the liberal thinking. No. We are also struggling to keep parts of the planet out of the playground of global financial capital. We are seizing part of the planet to provide ground for us to live on. We are fighting to retain at least part of it for life—for the production and reproduction of life. That's how I see the connections. I think it is very important to demonstrate how much one can, through housing, be more exploited, more marginalized, more stigmatized, and more oppressed, and also how one can, through struggles around housing, do the reverse.[5]

My argument is that "reverse" is put in place, more often than not, also by those that are not framing their struggle for housing in the canons of activist political language. In there, there is a much more diffused resentment against expulsion and extraction, and a variety of reverse affirmations of the housing political. By refusing institutionalization, by staying on the side, by wandering and maddening, by caring for collective infrastructures and affective capacities, by occupying uninhabitable spaces, or simply by staying put, there are hints, senses of direction, echoes of other ritornellos of home that emerge from these mundane acts. I have therefore offered ways to hear from these ephemeral chants, focusing on the necessary work of decolonizing, tracing, and working with the politics of housing precarity. The latter point is, to me, very much about going beyond policy and focusing on the ways in which many grassroots organizers are already deinstituting current modes of control and fighting for the reinstitution of means of control, while at the same time instituting praxis that does not require control in order to think, radically care, and build home.

In advancing these moves, I have offered three kinds of answers to three specific questions. First, there is the problem of what to fight for. Rethinking home(lessness) to fight for a liberatory politics of home knows nothing of incremental adjustments. The approach I have proposed offers a fundamental challenge to conventional frameworks of intervention, refuting policy recommendations or prescriptions to add to a conventional research strategy, offering instead a radical pedagogical attempt to work through and with the tensioned politics of the interstices where home and homelessness are already reconfigured and challenged. Second, there is the problem of where to start, which is about the double epistemological-methodological move toward seeing the political from within and working from there. In such a view, the political is never exhausted in its enunciation: it is not simply something that is proclaimed but, to follow both AbdouMaliq Simone and Elizabeth Grosz, it is a way of inhabiting the supposedly uninhabitable, a mode of dwelling in the world that offers liberatory propositions but does not have a unitary orientation.[6] Last, the book offers a contribution to the problem of how to work together, or who needs to care and how to get the job done. The book has chosen its camp. It is around centering the experience of housing precarity as political, in its capacity to propose its own salvation, and it is about believing that autonomous organizing is the best equipped to trace and work with that politics. Liberation requires forms of what I have called caring otherwise, a caring for collective struggles that many community organizers know how to practice.

And yet, I don't want to close this book by pointing exclusively to collective praxis. In the previous chapters, I have been particularly concerned with the positions that can be taken within the current homelessness industry, but also within grassroots organizing, which needs to expand its definitions of the housing political to recenter desperation and to accommodate multiple forms of a liberatory politics of home. I have stressed the need for housing students, scholars, and practitioners to reapproach the ritornellos of home holistically and to question how one inhabits the tensioned politics of home(lessness) within our institutional settings dealing with it. Given my privileged role within one of these industries, the academy, I believe that part of the work required to liberate home can find its spaces within classrooms, teaching curricula and the making of discourse, and praxis of inhabitation. I conclude by recalling three moves in this sense, which have been, more or less explicitly, presented in the book.

The first is a call to dismantle the industry of homelessness scholarship. Following a number of available critiques, across the book I have recalled how homelessness scholarship reproduces the expulsive and extractive functions of home(lessness) at the level of ideas and practice. Fighting this means to work toward a postcategorical scholarship, one that does not other its subjects, or force them into taxonomies, or speak for them, or think that it can save them. Would such a scholarship be the end of knowledge? Or would it be a liberating form of knowledge, intersecting with the excellent literatures we already have on the construction of alterity? I would argue the latter, but only if the knowledge produced is thoroughly decolonized from the kind of assumptions that uphold the violent binary thinking that currently dominates the field, reducing the experience of life to something manageable and knowable. We need to work from a different place: "To create such a distance is the precondition for the fulfilment of the most crucial theoretical task of our time: that the unthinkable be thought, that the unexpected be assumed as an integral part of the theoretical work."[7]

Homelessness scholarship, with its medicalized and/or policy-driven forms of expertise, its categorization, its modeling, its policy commentaries and recommendations, is precluding the possibility for radical home(lessness) thinking to emerge. This is why, in chapter 2, I described it as degenerative. To fight back, one needs to speak an intersectional language and convince others of the need to step away from the canons of current debates. Those who are tied to the conventional epistemology won't refute such a proposition; in fact, they will probably invite their proponents to speak, encouraging their critical voice. We should not mistake this for a readiness to decolonize. On the contrary, it is common for a few high-profile critical challenges to be allowed to take place because this makes the status quo look robust, which means that it doesn't have to change. It's like reshuffling Beckett's sentences: everything changes but nothing changes. Refusal is the precondition for an affirmative reconstruction. We need to reject, as Sandra Harding has written, "the dominant conceptual frameworks of [our] disciplines and institutions."[8]

Such a move is not an abandonment but a reappraisal. Abolition, after all, following Fred Moten, "is also about presence. It's about being present in a different way. . . . That means, doing shit differently right now."[9] There are examples, in this sense, of scholarship linking in nonextractive ways with current liberatory housing struggles. We now have collectives for differential knowledge production at the threshold of housing scholarship and activism—such as the *Radical Housing Journal*—and also entire methodological frameworks to reapproach the housing political anew, such as the one brought to the fore by Ananya Roy, Raquel Rolnik, and their colleagues. Joining these spaces is a place to start. But in the everyday of scholarly work, ridicule can also be a useful tactic to diminish the authority of mainstream debates and publications, calling them out in teaching, in discussion, and perhaps especially in reading groups that involve those who have experienced home(lessness) in its harshest forms, and who have invested in the grassroots work of organizing around and through suffering. This could move us closer to the day in which the science of the other is debunked as part of the problem.

A related, second call is around the efforts that are needed to change our culture of home(lessness) exposure. I have touched upon this in chapter 5: the exposure of homelessness is problematic beyond its reaffirmation of stereotypical notions. It constantly reactivates what Stuart Hall calls a "system of representation," a way of understanding and intervening in the world, which serves to provide the epistemic justification for the expulsion and extraction at the core of housing injustice. To put this another way, there is a direct link between the ways in which we represent and make sense of home and the way we intervene to suppress its supposed alterity in order to maintain the fiction of the home/homeless binary. Conservative moralities, medicalized epistemologies, and institutional framings of home(lessness) (or, as Gowan puts it, "sin-talk," "sick-talk," and "system-talk") are solidified and reiterated through the mainstream cultural presentation of home and homelessness.[10] After all, always borrowing from Stuart Hall, "our statements, however factual, have an ideological dimension": they work to diagram relations of power.[11]

A simple individual task: contest and affirm a differential cultural viewpoint on Twitter, on Facebook, on TikTok, Instagram, or 9GAG, by using the power of these platforms to affirm a more progressive understanding of the interplay between homelessness and home. Make noise at the movies. Be honest when your pal asks you to comment on the short film they're directing or story they're writing on the subject, when your colleagues and friends donate money to a charity that keeps on reproducing binaries between us and them, or when nine out of ten of the undergraduate students you are supervising propose to undertake semistructured interviews with homeless people or service providers. We must contest how home(lessness) is flattened into the home/homeless binary so prominently and powerfully in films, advertising, and mundane tweets, and insist on a fuller, rounder picture of inhabitation. I am wary of protocols, so I won't provide one, but a guiding question that could be used when confronted with the cultural representation of home(lessness) is:

> How is this reproducing expulsion (the segmentation, reduction to, and therefore production of, the other) and extraction (the variegated assemblages extrapolating societal, cultural, and economic value from expulsion)?

In interrogating cultural representations of home/homelessness, our role is to engage in questioning, confrontationally so, rather than offering answers, though always with an awareness of the greater picture of precarious life that I have presented in these pages. These efforts lead to the final proposition that has cut throughout the pages of this volume, one that can go along with a liberation of scholarship and public discourse: the incessant challenging of public and charitable industries of homelessness—that is, the secular and sacred interventions that currently manage the experience of housing precarity for the many.

If we start with the premise that many of these approaches are not fundamentally altering the expulsive and extractive functions of the home/homelessness binary but are instead reproducing them, then the only possible way forward is to abolish these services and think anew. If this is done irresponsibly, such a move will cause untold harm to the current clients of these services. The good news is that to work in the direction of pushing institutionalization back, we don't have to start from scratch. The liberatory kind of home I have been arguing for in this book is already being made experimentally in autonomous spaces, squats, and community organizations across the globe. On a daily basis, new autonomous dwellings are springing up at the intersection of migration, long-term homelessness, and new precarity caused by the intensification of an affordability crisis. These are bringing to the fore collective responses that have their own embodied housing politics: they shelter but on a different basis. The reason why I haven't centered these experiences at the core of this book is because, ultimately, I have been more interested in taking a step back—in providing a reading of home and homelessness that, in questioning the two as a matter of the same, might enable many to find their own way of occupying, their own way of envisioning, and their own collective ways of going beyond inhabitation. The practical invitation is to excavate how the everyday borderings of home(lessness) are sustained and reproduced—at the level of monetary economies, but also socially, culturally, epistemically—and to stay close to the experiences these borders produce. I wrote this book to remind myself that staying awake, at the border of home(lessness), requires a joyful, propositional, and positive anger. I say *anger* because the diagrams of home have appropriated our bodies, and we all need to be frightened by that. But then, on that threshold of fear, one can morph into many, beyond what is deemed conventionally political, and many can push from the most disparate sites until the walls of what we think is home are flattened and a thousand emancipatory homes are sustained into existence.

PREFACE

1 I use the term *bisexual* strictly in a nonbinary sense, and I recognize myself in the definition provided by Robyn Ochs: "I call myself bisexual because I acknowledge that I have in myself the potential to be attracted—romantically and/or sexually—to people of more than one gender, not necessarily at the same time, not necessarily in the same way, and not necessarily to the same degree." "I Call Myself Bisexual Because . . . ," Robyn Ochs's website, posted October 9, 2020, https://robynochs.com /2020/10/09/i-call-myself-bisexual-because.

INTRODUCTION

1 "Lessness" is composed of 120 sentences in total, but the second half of the story is a rearrangement of the first 60 sentences.
2 Drew and Haahr, "Lessness."
3 Beckett, "Lessness."
4 Beckett, "Lessness," 14–15.
5 See Mads Haahr and Elizabeth Drew, "Possible Lessnesses," accessed December 23, 2022, https://www.random.org/lessness.
6 Here I am referring to the 1958 novel by Giuseppe Tomasi di Lampedusa.
7 Subject-of, rather than "subjected to," precisely because the power of recurrence comes from the whole arrangement of things—not from a center.
8 A nexus that, nonincidentally, was also central in the opera by Beckett. Who better to depict homelessness than Estragon and Vladimir, men who have to sleep in a ditch, waking up waiting for a better future that never arrives?
9 I see Samuel Beckett's story as a pointer to envisioning this: art, after all, is to be used to reveal and contest the nonapparent faces of being. I am not tied to this story in any particular way. I am using it as an illustration of two otherwise rather abstract points: first, the sheer power of lack, absence, desperation, loss, and other similar affections, as something diagramming a whole politics of life; second, the

need to conceive what lies beyond that politics as something true in itself, affirmative of its own liberatory power that knows nothing of the colonies of lack.

10 Deleuze, "Bergson, 1859–1941."

11 UN-HABITAT, "Forced Evictions."

12 Kothari, "The Global Crisis of Displacement and Evictions"; Harvey, *The Condition of Postmodernity*; Rolnik, *Urban Warfare*; Lees, Shin, and López-Morales, *Planetary Gentrification*.

13 Osborne, "For Still Possible Cities," 2.

14 Desjarlais, *Shelter Blues*.

15 Robinson, *Beside One's Self*.

16 One superficial resemblance that might fall in this category can be found in research showing how one can be homeless at home. However, notwithstanding the importance of these contributions in challenging normative ideas of home and homelessness, I haven't encountered any that attempt to rework the ontological foundations of these notions and their functions, as this book does.

17 Somerville, "Homelessness and the Meaning of Home"; Somerville, "Understanding Homelessness." Ultimately, Somerville's understanding of home and homelessness flattens a binary reading only nominally, as shown by a critical reading by Lindsey McCarthy on the *unheimlich* of homelessness.

18 McCarthy, "(Re)Conceptualising the Boundaries."

19 Veness, "Neither Homed nor Homeless"; Ruddick, *Young and Homeless in Hollywood*; Blunt and Dowling, *Home*; Brickell, "'Mapping' and 'Doing.'" These are different contributions, but united by their effort in showing how homely belongings can be found within what Veness has called "un-homes" or Ruddick has understood as "heterotopias" of homelessness.

20 Veness, "Neither Homed nor Homeless," 337.

21 Desjarlais, *Shelter Blues*; Lyon-Callo, *Inequality, Poverty, and Neoliberal Governance*; Gowan, *Hobos, Hustlers and Back-Sliders*; Roy, "Dis/Possessive Collectivism"; Rolnik, *Urban Warfare*; Robinson, *Beside One's Self*; Simone, "The Uninhabitable?"; Hopper, *Reckoning with Homelessness*; Basaglia, *L'istituzione Negata*; Kotef, *The Colonizing Self*; Butler and Athanasiou, *Dispossession*.

22 Amin, *Land of Strangers*; Mezzadra and Neilson, *Border as Method*.

23 What is meant by "Italy" and "Turin" is, without question, highly contested. This is not the case of current topographical and/or nationalistic contestation, but a simpler reference to what Doreen Massey would call the complicated topologies making up any place, or the even more (because explicitly vitalist) "mechanospheres" of the urban (see Massey, *For Space*; and Amin and Thrift, *Arts of the Political*).

24 For details, see chapter 3.

25 Katz, "Towards Minor Theory."

26 Deleuze and Guattari, *Kafka*, 18.

27 Hardt and Negri, *Empire*; Nash, *Black Feminism Reimagined*.

28 Deleuze and Guattari, "What Is a Minor Literature?" 17–18.

29 Katz, "Revisiting Minor Theory."

30 This is at least how Deleuze sees the notion of "concept" but also, albeit coming from a different tradition, how feminists like Nash see the relevance of thinking relationally and politically about intersecting struggles.

31 Deleuze and Guattari, through their notion of "abstract machines" (essentially, another way of calling for diagrams), were very clear on stressing both the historic and situated nature of the latter and their capacity to "abstract" (or "extract," as Guattari for once more clearly has it) events from history.

32 Amin and Lancione, *Grammars of the Urban Ground*; Boano, *Progetto minore*; Katz, "Towards Minor Theory"; Deleuze and Guattari, "What Is a Minor Literature?"

33 Simone and Pieterse, *New Urban Worlds*.

34 Simone, "The Uninhabitable?," 145.

35 Deleuze and Guattari, *A Thousand Plateaus*, 219.

36 Duneier, *Sidewalk*.

37 Madden and Marcuse, *In Defense of Housing*, 197.

38 Ward, *When We Build Again*, 120.

39 Watts and Fitzpatrick, "Capabilities, Value Pluralism and Homelessness," is an example of the problematic teleologies of homelessness this book aims to transcend.

1. THE SUBJECT AT HOME

1 Miller, *Home Possessions*.

2 De Boeck, "'Divining' the City."

3 Blunt and Dowling, *Home*, 277.

4 This is true both for the most political aspects of home, as I illustrate later in the chapter, but also for its most mundane affairs. In this latter sense, home becomes in the everyday, through ideas of what counts as comfortable, and its instantiations through concrete objects and dispositions. The work of cultural anthropologists such as Miller (*Home Possessions*) or Rybczynski (*Home*) on the ways in which homely belongings are assembled and made sense of culturally provides important insights in this sense.

5 Brickell, "'Mapping' and 'Doing' Critical Geographies of Home."

6 Massey, "A Place Called Home?," 13.

7 Escobar, *Designs for the Pluriverse*, 133.

8 Escobar, *Designs for the Pluriverse*, 110.

9 Hill Collins, "It's All in the Family," 64.

10 Baker, "Shelter in Place."

11 Blunt and Varley, "Introduction."

12 Mezzadra and Neilson, *Border as Method*.

13 Mezzadra and Neilson, *Border as Method*, 22.

14 Mezzadra and Neilson, *Border as Method*, 31.

15 Mezzadra and Neilson, *Border as Method*, 32.

16 Mezzadra and Neilson, *Border as Method*, 32.

17 Mezzadra and Neilson, *Border as Method*, 32.

18 Amin and Lancione, *Grammars of the Urban Ground*. For inspiring earlier contributions, see also Roy, "'The Shadow of Her Wings'"; Oswin, "An Other Geography."

19 Mezzadra and Neilson, *Border as Method*, 33.

20 Deleuze and Guattari, *Anti-Oedipus*.

21 Anzaldúa, *Borderlands/La Frontera*.

22 hooks, "Choosing the Margins as a Space of Radical Openness."

23 To clarify, I do not intend for these functions to be dissociated from material structures and matter. Rather, they are the expression of those, an expression that assumes an operational tempo, which I later define more clearly as ritornellos of expulsion and extraction.

24 Madden and Marcuse, *In Defense of Housing*, 197.

25 Butler and Athanasiou, *Dispossession*.

26 Analytically, this means that the subject can be identified but not individualized. The subject is not something but a recollection, a collectivity, a moment: "humans constitute a machine as soon as this nature is communicated by recurrence to the ensemble of which they form a part under specific conditions." Deleuze and Guattari, "Balance-Sheet for 'Desiring-Machines,'" 91.

27 Amin and Thrift, *Arts of the Political*, 50. See also Lazzarato, *Signs and Machines*.

28 Butler and Athanasiou, *Dispossession*, 69–70.

29 O'Sullivan, *On the Production of Subjectivity*, 2.

30 Honig, *Antigone, Interrupted*.

31 Danewid, "White Innocence in the Black Mediterranean."

32 Danewid, "White Innocence in the Black Mediterranean," 1683.

33 Guattari, *Chaosophy*, 43.

34 Williams, *Gilles Deleuze's Difference and Repetition*; Buchanan, *Deleuze and Guattari's Anti-Oedipus*.

35 Grosz, "A Thousand Tiny Sexes."

36 Buchanan, *Deleuze and Guattari's Anti-Oedipus*; Deleuze and Guattari, *Anti-Oedipus*. Their argument offers a profound critique of the way in which a violent and phallocentric diagram of control colonizes the virtual terrains of our psyches, intersecting with our desires in a way that can lead us to seek our own repression (they call this "microfascism").

37 Deleuze, *Pure Immanence*; Anderson, *Encountering Affect*.

38 I am referring to my writings on homelessness and marginality that explicitly embrace a Deleuzian-Guattarian framework. For instance, Lancione, "Pathways to the Machinic Subject"; Lancione, "The City and 'the Homeless'"; Lancione, "Homeless People and the City of Abstract Machines."

39 Foucault, *Space, Knowledge and Power*; Deleuze, *Foucault*.

40 Deleuze and Guattari, *Anti-Oedipus*, 36.

41 Hardt and Negri, *Empire*.

42 Colebrook, "The Space of Man," 196.

43 Spivak, "Can the Subaltern Speak?"

44 McElroy, "Digital Nomads and Settler Desires."

45 It is important to center Guattari's endeavor to operationalize their micropolitical thinking in his antipsychiatry practice at La Borde clinic and in his encounters with the autonomist movement in 1977 Italy. See Berardi, *Félix Guattari*.

46 I call the home, and homely security, a fiction because it hinges on the possibility of its annihilation. I use *fiction* very much like Butler does in her works, a term to "suggest

a certain form of idealization that is historically effective." In this sense, saying that home is a fiction does not mean to deny its status. It is not to say that home is, continuing with Butler, "a 'lie' or an 'illusion'; it is a materialized form of an ideal that acquires historical efficacy" (out, obviously, of specific material histories). Butler and Athanasiou, *Dispossession*, 97–98.

2. EXPULSION AND EXTRACTION

1 Said, *Culture and Imperialism.*
2 Grosfoguel, "The Epistemic Decolonial Turn," 221.
3 Gago, *Feminist International.*
4 Kotef, *The Colonizing Self.*
5 Kotef, *The Colonizing Self*, 74.
6 I am referring to the liberal idea of the "original position," developed by John Rawls in his *A Theory of Justice.*
7 Wynter, "Unsettling the Coloniality."
8 Guattari, *The Machinic Unconscious.*
9 Foucault, *Abnormal.*
10 Willse, *The Value of Homelessness.*
11 Heynen, Kaika, and Swyngedouw, *In the Nature of Cities.*
12 Pile and Thrift, *Mapping the Subject.*
13 Anzaldúa, *Light in the Dark (Luz en lo oscuro)*; Escobar, *Designs for the Pluriverse*; Maturana and Varela, *Autopoiesis and Cognition*; Guattari, *The Machinic Unconscious*; Haraway, *Simians, Cyborgs, and Women*, 67.
14 Kaika, "Interrogating the Geographies of the Familiar," 272.
15 Kaika, "Interrogating the Geographies of the Familiar," 266.
16 Castán Broto, *Urban Energy Landscapes*; Edwards and Bulkeley, "Urban Political Ecologies of Housing"; Wood and Young, "A Political Ecology of Home"; Apostolopoulou, *Nature Swapped and Nature Lost*; Gandy, "Cyborg Urbanization"; Gandy, *Natura Urbana*; Silver and Marvin, "Powering Sub-Saharan Africa's Urban Revolution."
17 Escobar, *Designs for the Pluriverse*, 10–11.
18 The "double colonial and environmental divide of modernity," Ferdinand, *Une écologie décoloniale*, 22, my translation.
19 I came to Ferdinand's book after I had essentially finished writing my text. Albeit we are interested in nominally different "fractures" (to use his term), namely, home/ homelessness and environment/colony, our way of thinking through these borders seems, to me, rather close. In navigating these borders, the challenge is to keep relational thinking constantly activated. As Ferdinand himself contends, referring to the fracture he is interested in, "la véritable difficulté à les *penser ensemble* et à tenir en retour une double critique" (*Une écologie décoloniale*, 22, emphasis in the original), which translates into "the real difficulty of putting them together and holding a double critique in return" (my translation).
20 Lancione and Simone, "Dwelling in Liminalities."
21 "Outre le génocide des peuples indigènes et les destructions d'écosystèmes, cet habiter colonial a transformé les terres en puzzles d'usines et de plantations qui caractérisent

cette ère géologique, le *Plantationocene*, entrainant des pertes de relations matricielles a la Terre: *des matricides*. Le recours à la traite négrière transatlantique et à l'esclavage colonial, cantonnant des êtres humains et non humains dans la cale du monde, des 'Nègres,' permet aussi de qualifier cette ère géologique de *Négrocène*. Depuis ces histoires, les catastrophes telles que les cyclones réguliers qui ravagent les côtes américaines ne font que répéter ces fractures de l'habiter colonial et prolonger l'asservissement des domines, faisant de la tempête écologique un véritable *cyclone colonial*." (Ferdinand, *Une écologie décoloniale*, 44, emphasis in the original.)

22 Shabazz, *Spatializing Blackness*; Gibbons, *City of Segregation*; Hunter and Robinson, *Chocolate Cities*; Davis, *If They Come in the Morning*; Gilmore, *Golden Gulag*.

23 As Wilhelm-Solomon notes in his "Dispossession as Depotentiation," looking at the case of dispossessed communities living in informal occupations in the inner core of Johannesburg, this is a process that at the same time reproduces racialized others and diminishes capacity of resistance and collective organizing (what he refers to as "depotentiation"). For a similar yet differently theorized case of the implication of dispossession for organized resistance, see Ferreri's "Painted Bullet Holes," focusing on the Heygate estate in London.

24 Brar and Sharma, "What Is This 'Black' in Black Studies?"; Hawthorne, "Black Matters Are Spatial Matters"; Lancione, "Inhabiting Dispossession in the Postsocialist City"; Picker, *Racial Cities*. See also Powell and Lever, "Europe's Perennial 'Outsiders.'"

25 Nast, "Mapping the 'Unconscious,'" 222.

26 Deleuze and Guattari, *Anti-Oedipus*, 53.

27 Nast, "Queer Patriarchies, Queer Racisms, International," 877.

28 Nast, "Mapping the 'Unconscious,'" 220, 227, 232.

29 Nast, "Mapping the 'Unconscious,'" 244.

30 Hayden, *Grand Domestic Revolution*; Blunt and Dowling, *Home*, 27.

31 Elias and Rai, "Feminist Everyday Political Economy," 219.

32 Elias and Rai, "Feminist Everyday Political Economy," 202.

33 Butler, *Gender Trouble*.

34 *Voluntary* here means "no questions asked." There are a few more countries in which it is possible to obtain a nonbinary type of formal identification for intersex people.

35 Taylor and Richardson, "Queering Home Corner," 165.

36 Gorman-Murray, "Queer Politics at Home."

37 Oswin, "The Modern Model Family," 257.

38 McKeithen, "Queer Ecologies of Home," 133.

39 Matthews, Poyner, and Kjellgren, "Lesbian, Gay, Bisexual, Transgender and Queer Experiences."

40 Fortier, "'Coming Home,'" 405.

41 Nichols, *Theft Is Property!*

42 Cedric J. Robinson, *Black Marxism*, 14.

43 Kotef, *The Colonizing Self*, 9.

44 Anderson, *Encountering Affect*.

45 Glynn, *Where the Other Half Lives*, 40.

46 Harvey, *The Urbanization of the Capital*.

47 Rolnik, *Urban Warfare*.

48 Chelcea, "The 'Housing Question'"; Tsenkova and Polanska, "Between State and Market"; Popovici, "Residences, Restitutions and Resistance."

49 Rolnik, *Urban Warfare*, 3.

50 Rolnik, *Urban Warfare*, 27.

51 Gibson-Graham, *The End of Capitalism*.

52 Hardt and Negri, "Empire, Twenty Years On," 19; Nash, *Black Feminism Reimagined*.

53 Byrd et al., "Predatory Value," 7.

54 Byrd et al., "Predatory Value," 3.

55 Byrd et al., "Predatory Value," 3.

56 Byrd et al., "Predatory Value," 7, emphasis added.

57 Best and Ramírez, "Urban Specters," 1051–52.

58 Fassin, *Humanitarian Reason*.

59 Pleace, "Researching Homelessness in Europe."

60 Tarde, *Essais et mélanges sociologiques*.

61 Anderson, *The Hobo*.

62 Busch-Geertsema, Culhane, and Fitzpatrick, "Developing a Global Framework," table 1.

63 Elwood, Lawson, and Sheppard, "Geographical Relational Poverty Studies"; Roy, *Poverty Capital*; Bhan, *In the Public's Interest*.

64 Tadiar, "Life-Times of Disposability," 42.

65 Lancione and McFarlane, *Global Urbanism*; Amin and Lancione, *Grammars of the Urban Ground*.

66 Dadusc and Mudu, "Care without Control"; Stierl, "A Fleet of Mediterranean Border Humanitarians"; De Genova, *Borders of "Europe"*; Vradis, Painter, and Papoutsi, *New Borders*.

3. ITALIAN RITORNELLOS

1 Meo, *Vite in bilico*; Leonardi, "Modelli di accoglienza"; Santinello and Gaboardi, "Presentazione del numero"; Filandri and Olagnero, "Housing Inequality and Social Class in Europe"; Grazioli, *Housing, Urban Commons and the Right to the City*; Storto, *La casa abbandonata*; Gainsforth, *Airbnb città merce*; Boccagni, *Migration and the Search for Home*; Avallone, *Il sistema di accoglienza in Italia*; Mudu and Chattopadhyay, *Migration, Squatting and Radical Autonomy*.

2 Some good exceptions include Esposito and Chiodelli, "Beyond Proper Political Squatting"; Tulumello, "The 'Souths' of the 'Wests'"; Grazioli, *Housing, Urban Commons and the Right to the City*; Annunziata, "Staying Put!"

3 To date, the country still has among the highest numbers of NATO and US personnel and bases in Europe.

4 At that point, which coincided with the geopolitical shifts in the aftermath of the fall of the Berlin Wall, Italy stayed solidly related to the US and its NATO allies, but the pace of internal change accelerated.

5   For a critique in this sense, see Tulumello, "The 'Souths' of the 'Wests.'"

6   García-Lamarca and Kaika, "'Mortgaged Lives.'"

7   Filandri and Paulì, "La finanziarizzazione del bene casa."

8   Agenzia delle Entrate, *Rapporto Mutui*.

9   Sgambato, "Il mutuo 'copre' il 65% del valore della casa."

10 For a discussion related to the Italian context, see Dagnes, "Finanza e vita quotidiana."

11 Baldini, *La casa degli Italiani*.

12 Analysts say that "investments in renovations conveyed by tax incentives increased from 9.4 billion in 2008 to 28.1 billion in 2017, nearly +200%." Di Giacinto, "Il settore delle costruzioni."

13 This is evident in the case of the so-called *palazzinari* in Rome.

14 Despite its timing, the measure was thought of before the unfolding of the COVID-19-induced economic downturn.

15 In order to access these generous benefits, individuals have to go through complex procedures, which can be better managed by construction companies and big real estate agencies. The end users tend therefore to sell their tax credits to the companies, which take a substantive cut but offer back a discount on the final work and the reassurance of a hassle-free experience. Delays have been very common due to the tendency on the part of the construction companies to take on more projects than they can handle in order to gain as much as possible from the 110 percent superbonus scheme. For an analysis, in Italian, see Latour, "Superbonus"; and Cimmrusti, "Frodi sugli sconti."

16 Baldini, *La casa degli Italiani*, 73.

17 ISTAT, "La povertà in Italia."

18 Da Rold, "Altro che Airbnb."

19 Interestingly, ISTAT also reports that "looking at citizenship, 70.7% of poor families with foreigners live in a rented house, while only 15.6% have a house of their own, compared to 32.2% and 55.7%, respectively, of families in poverty with only Italians." ISTAT, "La povertà in Italia."

20 Unione Inquilini, "Sfratti anno 2018."

21 The law is number 43 of February 28, 1949, named "Provvedimenti per incrementare l'occupazione operaia, agevolando la costruzione di case per lavoratori" (measures to increase blue-collar employment by facilitating the construction of workers' housing).

22 GESCAL stands for "Gestione Case per i Lavoratori" (housing management for workers).

23 The mobilization is recalled in the—now very hard to find—beautiful volume by Daolio, *Le lotte per la casa in Italia*.

24 Storto, *La casa abbandonata*, my translation.

25 Quirico, "Lotta Continua and the Italian Housing Movement."

26 De Lucia, preface to *La casa abbandonata*, my translation.

27 Three major *condoni edilizi*, by Craxi in 1985 and Berlusconi in 1994 and 2003, and an administrative one in 2021 by the big coalition of the Five Star Movement, Lega Nord, Forza Italia, the center-left Partito Democratico, and other parties.

28 Law 431/1998 instituted a national fund to support low-income tenants, but its reach has been small, and subsequent reforms have limited its capacity to make a real difference at a national scale.

29 According to ISTAT, "If in 2015 people between 0 and 14 years of age represent 13.8% of the population, in 2065 (according to the central scenario) they will stand at 12.7%. The population aged 65 and over, on the other hand, will grow from 21.7% to 32.6% between 2015 and 2065. The population aged 85 and over, again, which in 2015 represents 3.2% of the population, is expected to stand at 10.0% in 2065. Finally, the working-age population (aged 15–64) will contract from 64.6% in 2015 to 54.7% in 2065." My translation from ISTAT, "Popolazione e famiglie." On migration, see ISTAT, "Bilancio demografico" and ISTAT, "Gli stranieri residenti." The above numbers include only legally registered migrants and therefore do not account for illegal presences, upon which I expand later in the chapter.

30 Madden and Marcuse, *In Defense of Housing*.

31 Eco, *Il fascismo eterno*.

32 "Una serie di caratteristiche tra cui il machismo, il culto della tradizione, l'appello alle classi medie frustrate, la paura della differenza, disprezzo per i deboli." Eco, *Il fascismo eterno*, my translation.

33 Nast, "Queer Patriarchies, Queer Racisms, International," 875.

34 For a discussion on this point in the Italian case, see Pasquinelli, *La vertigine dell'ordine*; Grilli, "Case, cibo e famiglia."

35 Francis, *Amoris laetitia*.

36 Novelli, "Matrimonio e famiglia nel magistero dei pontefici del '900," 132.

37 Brugger, *The Indissolubility of Marriage and the Council of Trent*.

38 Novelli, "Matrimonio e famiglia nel magistero dei pontefici del '900."

39 Saraceno, *Mutamenti della famiglia e politiche sociali in Italia*, 12.

40 Betta, "La morale familiare," 1.

41 Despite Italy formally being among the winners of World War I, the sentiment in the country at the time was one of loss. Nationalist sentiments—fueled by figures such as the Poet of the Nation, Gabriele D'Annunzio—led many youth to believe in the violent and imperialist rethoric at the basis of the Fascist regime.

42 Loffredo was one of Mussolini's favorite intellectuals. In the book condensing his views—*Family Politics* (1938)—Loffredo writes,

> The family can lead to the overcoming of the current system, inspired by liberal individualism, in which each citizen counts as an individual, and the family has no direct relevance. And so the family demographic policy, if it does not stop in the middle of its journey, must lead to the overcoming of the conception of the state formed by individuals and to the attainment of a conception which, even if it will not have to be that of the state made up of family nuclei, is an intermediate conception, which matches the latter in many points, and which in the others is inspired by it (p. 432). Cited in Brienza, "Ferdinando Loffredo."

43 Betta, "La morale familiare," 15.

44 Betta, "La morale familiare," 26.

45 Romeo, "L'editto fascista."

46 In this case, an honor killing is perpetrated by the husband against a supposedly adulterous wife.

47 Cofini, "2021, un anno di femminicidi."

48 ISTAT, "Violenza sulle donne."

49 Pullella, "Gay Marriage a Threat to Humanity's Future."

50 When the son of comedian Beppe Grillo, who runs the movement, was accused by a young woman of having gang-raped her, Grillo said, "These are 19-year-old boys who are having fun, who are in their underwear and jumping around with their dicks like this because they are four assholes not four rapists." Le Iene, "Beppe Grillo."

51 Apostolic exhortations are official documents written by the pope addressing key themes for the church. Of less importance than an encyclical, they are nonetheless important to understanding the direction the church takes on specific issues. They are usually released after a synod of bishops. The synod is an official gathering of bishops held to offer support to the pope on specific matters. The two Synods on the Family gathered around 250 bishops from all over the world in a series of meetings and discussions around the role and sacrality of families in the Catholic Church.

52 The exhortation states, "Because of forms of conditioning and mitigating factors, it is possible that in an objective situation of sin—which may not be subjectively culpable, or fully such—a person can be living in God's grace, can love and can also grow in the life of grace and charity, while receiving the Church's help to this end. Discernment must help to find possible ways of responding to God and growing in the midst of limits." To this, the pope adds the controversial footnote, number 351: "In certain cases, this can include the help of the sacraments. Hence, I want to remind priests that the confessional must not be a torture chamber, but rather an encounter with the Lord's mercy. I would also point out that the Eucharist is not a prize for the perfect, but a powerful medicine and nourishment for the weak." Francis (pope), *Amoris laetitia*, 236–37.

53 Including a document signed by four bishops, called "Dubia," where they expressed serious doubts and questioned Pope Francis's framing of the "irregular situations" and denied the need to reform the current rules.

54 Francis, *Amoris laetitia*, 32.

55 Francis, *Amoris laetitia*, 45–46, my emphasis.

56 In 2016, the highest Italian court allowed a case of stepchild adoption by a same-sex couple, but there is still no national law on the matter.

57 Cottone, "Ddl Zan contro omofobia affossato al Senato."

58 If you really want to watch this, go to around 1 minute: "Ddl Zan affossato dal Senato, il centrodestra esulta per la tagliola a voto segreto," Fanpage.It, posted October 27, 2021, YouTube video, https://www.youtube.com/watch?v=nRAdj52OmsQ.

59 With an average TV share of 27 percent across eleven seasons.

60 Nast, "Queer Patriarchies, Queer Racisms, International," 877.

61 Here I am not interested in providing a fine genealogy of the nation-state, for which historians have already done the work. In simple terms, I just aim to evoke the crude fact that, in order for something called Italy to exist and for someone called Italian to be recognized, there must equally be something that Italy isn't and someone identified as not Italian. The relation of negation of the nation-state with its other is a productive expulsion, through which the extraction of the national home becomes possible. This basis is the same one that informs the military and colonial action through which the state fulfills its nationalizing mission.

62 Gramsci, "Alcuni temi sulla questione meridionale."

63 Conelli, "Razza, colonialità, nazione," 152; Verdicchio, "The Preclusion of Postcolonial Discourse."

64 Hawthorne, "*L'Italia meticcia?*," 186.

65 Del Boca, *Italiani, brava gente?*; Randazzo, *L'Africa del Duce*; Cresti, *Non desiderare la terra d'altri*; Salerno, *Genocidio in Libia*.

66 Libya became an Italian settler-colonial state in 1911, but for a long time Italians only controlled major cities. The "reconquering" was the campaign launched by Mussolini to take control of the entire country, including the arid eastern lands of Cyrenaica.

67 Cresti, *Non desiderare la terra d'altri*, 99–100.

68 Caminiti, "L'impero del 'Piccolo Italiano,'" 112.

69 Poidimani, "Ius sanguinis," 223.

70 Poidimani, "Ius sanguinis," 223. In the original: "Loffredo fornì al regime un progetto complessivo sulla famiglia in funzione della 'patria' e della 'razza' proprio mentre era in atto l'attacco finale di Mussolini contro le organizzazioni femminili che avevano tentato di mediare tra femminismo e fascismo."

71 Deplano, "Within and Outside the Nation," 395.

72 Deplano, "Within and Outside the Nation," 405.

73 Deplano, "Within and Outside the Nation," 405.

74 Hawthorne, "*L'Italia meticcia?*," 176.

75 Colucci, *Storia dell'immigrazione straniera in Italia*.

76 Colucci, *Storia dell'immigrazione straniera in Italia*, 169.

77 Colucci, *Storia dell'immigrazione straniera in Italia*, 171.

78 Hawthorne, "In Search of Black Italia," 162.

79 Hawthorne, "*L'Italia meticcia?*," 186.

80 Stierl, "A Fleet of Mediterranean Border Humanitarians," 708; De Genova, *Borders of "Europe"*; Aru, "Abandonment, Agency, Control"; Tazzioli, *The Making of Migration*.

81 Dadusc and Mudu, "Care without Control," 10.

82 Omizzolo, *Sotto padrone*, 21.

83 Leogrande, *Uomini e caporali*.

84 Omizzolo, *Sotto padrone*.

85 By *heteronormative*, I am referring to the comment made in 2013 by the CEO of Barilla, the Italian multinational pasta manufacturer: "Our advertisement won't

include homosexuals because we like the traditional family. If gays don't agree, they can always eat another brand of pasta. Everyone is free to do what they want as long as they don't bother others." My translation. Rosa, "Barilla."

86 Avallone, *Sfruttamento e resistenze*, 9; Peano, "Turbulences in the Encampment."

87 Avallone, *Il sistema di accoglienza in Italia*.

88 Ex-OPG Je So' Pazzo, "Controllo popolare e sistema di accoglienza," 45.

89 Danewid, "White Innocence in the Black Mediterranean," 1676.

4. A LOCAL VIOLENCE

1 Fassin, *Humanitarian Reason*; De Genova, *Borders of "Europe"*; Roy, *Poverty Capital*.

2 Roy et al., *Encountering Poverty*, 13.

3 Dadusc and Mudu, "Care without Control," 6.

4 Sharma, *In the Meantime*.

5 Haraway, *Staying with the Trouble*.

6 Roy et al., *Encountering Poverty*, 44

7 Bhambra and Holmwood, "Colonialism, Postcolonialism and the Liberal Welfare State."

8 Cloke, May, and Johnsen, *Swept Up Lives?*

9 Cloke, May, and Johnsen, *Swept Up Lives?*; Cloke, Thomas, and Williams, "Faith in Action." For a critique of FBOs and homelessness, see Lancione, "'Entanglements of Faith.'"

10 A key issue here is also that of welfare conditionality or how the state, through the provisioning of welfare services, is not only able to control access to services but also actively reproduces subjects *of* service. For an insightful account in the case of the UK, see Flint, "Encounters with the Centaur State."

11 European Observatory on Homelessness, *Homelessness Services in Europe*.

12 Johnsen, Cloke, and May, "Transitory Spaces of Care."

13 DeVerteuil, *Resilience in the Post-welfare Inner City*.

14 Some of the city services I discuss, such as the one-plus-one system or the Pellerina emergency camp, have been reformed. The camp, for instance, is no longer in the park but is still running in the same emergency fashion. Ultimately, the underlying logic described in the chapter has remained in place.

15 Leonardi, "Modelli di accoglienza," 98. Leonardi reports how stepping up to more individualized services is, in reality, very difficult. As she writes in her doctoral work (my translation): "In 2018, the number of places available in the Case di Prima Accoglienza Overnight were 288 throughout the year, and increased to 505 during the period of the so-called Cold Emergency. The places in the first-level facilities—Marsigli for men and Sidoli for women—are 31 and 14 respectively, remaining unchanged throughout the year. These numerical data show that the number of places in basic reception, in the dormitories, increases in an emergency perspective during the winter months; the additional beds are in precarious structures; not all those who enroll in the dormitories are accepted, and, among those accepted, only a small percentage can access first-level structures. The numerical disparity

between accommodations in dormitories and first-level facilities is significant." See also Porcellana, *Dal bisogno al desiderio*.

16 Cavallo, *Charity and Power in Early Modern Italy*.

17 Lancione, "Entanglements of Faith"; Lancione, "Assemblages of Care."

18 Arguably, as my friend Kiera Chapman reminds me, the Good Samaritan parable is not only about charitable love but also about immanent sectarian violence. Indeed, the Jews hated the Samaritans, yet it is the Samaritan who acts in a morally superior way to help the beaten and injured Jew. The radicality of this point is, however, diluted by two facts: first, it is not the reverse of sectarian violence that is evoked in the parable but the praxis of RCC-oriented FBOs (see the papal encyclical I describe in the text); second, even this progressive element contains a very reactionary truth: the other is still silent, reduced to flat, manageable, lovable, alterity.

19 Benedict XVI, "Encyclical Letter *Deus Caritas Est*."

20 Foucault, *Power*.

21 Anderson, *Encountering Affect*; Stewart, *Ordinary Affects*.

22 Marco (pseudonym), semistructured interview, December 2009, audio recorded and transcribed by the author.

23 Social worker, semistructured interview, February 2010, audio recorded and transcribed by the author.

24 Carlo, semistructured interview, March 2010, audio recorded and transcribed by the author.

25 Allahyari, *Visions of Charity*.

26 Liebow, *Tell Them Who I Am*, 137.

27 Haraway, *Simians, Cyborgs, and Women*, 78.

28 Guattari, "Subjectivities."

29 Guattari, *Soft Subversion*.

30 Allahyari, *Visions of Charity*.

31 Desjarlais, *Shelter Blues*; Allahyari, *Visions of Charity*; Robinson, *Beside One's Self*; Lancione, "Entanglements of Faith."

32 From Tokyo to Moscow, Vancouver to Sydney, LA to Turin: there is virtually no major city across the world that has not at least some kind of organization that sets up tents, shipping containers, or repurposed public housing to rapidly rehouse the homeless population in variously defined emergency situations. These situations range from the eventful arrival of the winter season to the problems posed by influxes of asylum seekers and economic migrants, events that are defined as emergencies in strategic terms, to avoid tackling their structural causes. Lately, implementation of such measures has become frequent, as city administrations have tried to cope with the 2020 Coronavirus pandemic by establishing large-scale emergency resheltering initiatives for the precariously housed and houseless. What we have witnessed during this latest crisis is the expansion and reproduction of practices and logics that were well established before the advent of COVID-19.

33 Marco, semistructured interview, January 2010, audio recorded and transcribed by the author.

34 Città di Torino, "Nuovi criteri per la presa."

35 Croce Rossa Italiana, "Emergenza Freddo Stagione 2008–2009."

36 Agamben, *State of Exception*, 35.

37 Città di Torino, "Accesso competenze e servizi."

38 Anonymous worker, semistructured interview, February 2010, audio recorded and transcribed by the author.

39 Marco, semistructured interview, January 2010, audio recorded and transcribed by the author.

40 Lancione, "Racialised Dissatisfaction."

41 McMordie, "Avoidance Strategies."

42 Evans, "Exploring the (Bio)Political Dimensions of Voluntarism"; Willse, *The Value of Homelessness*; Lyon-Callo, "Homelessness or the Violence of Poverty."

43 Daniele (pseudonym), semistructured interview, April 2010, audio recorded and transcribed by the author.

44 Daniele, semistructured interview, April 2010, audio recorded and transcribed by the author.

45 Leonardi, "Modelli di accoglienza," 97.

46 Silvano (pseudonym), semistructured interview, October 2009, audio recorded and transcribed by the author.

47 Silvano, semistructured interview, October 2009, audio recorded and transcribed by the author.

48 Silvano, semistructured interview, October 2009, audio recorded and transcribed by the author.

49 Desjarlais, *Shelter Blues*, 58.

50 Ivano (pseudonym), semistructured interview, February 2010, audio recorded and transcribed by the author.

51 Snow and Anderson, *Down on Their Luck*.

52 Liebow, *Tell Them Who I Am*.

53 Bolzoni, Gargiulo, and Manocchi, "The Social Consequences of the Denied Access."

54 Lancione, "Giustizia sociale, spazio e città."

55 Rosa, "Marginality as Resource?"

56 Gilmore, *Golden Gulag*.

57 An example of which are the notorious agreements of asylum offshore processing and control between Europe and Turkey, the UK and Rwanda, or between Australia and Papua New Guinea.

58 "Ventimiglia, il video del migrante aggredito e picchiato dopo un tentato furto," Corriere della Serra, posted May 10, 2021, YouTube video, https://www.youtube.com /watch?v=rztxymff7F8. The video portraits extreme acts of violence, which some will find disturbing or triggering. Viewer discretion is advised.

59 La Talpa e L'Orologio, "Aggiornamento dal CPR di Torino in Rivolta," Facebook post, May 24, 2021, https://www.facebook.com/latalpa.elorologio/posts /3993066990787975.

60 "Così si raccontava Moussa Balde, il 23enne morto suicida nel CPR di Torino," Redazione Il Nazionale, posted May 26, 2021, YouTube video, https://www.youtube .com/watch?v=LrxORKMlyzA.

61 One of the favorite slogans of Matteo Salvini, former minister of the interior: "Prima gli italiani, il loro diritto al lavoro, alla sicurezza e alla felicità," Facebook post, May 27, 2018, https://www.facebook.com/salviniofficial/photos/prima-gli-italiani-il-loro-diritto-al -lavoro-alla-sicurezza-e-alla-felicit%C3%A0abbia/10155797353938155/.

62 CILD, *Buchi neri.*

63 ASGI, "Libro Nero del CPR di Torino."

64 ASGI, "Libro Nero del CPR di Torino."

65 ASGI, "Libro Nero del CPR di Torino." The extension hearing is the judicial process an individual seeking asylum has to go through as their only chance to make their case heard and see their application for refugee status accepted.

66 Jazeel, "Singularity."

67 Deleuze and Guattari, *A Thousand Plateaus*; Lancione, "Homeless People and the City."

5. A GLOBAL CULTURE

1 An excellent example in this sense includes Rolnik's *Urban Warfare*, where the author is able to show how, translocally, housing struggles have become a key matter for many around the world.

2 Silver, *From Homes to Assets*; Aalbers, "The Revanchist Renewal of Yesterday's City"; Di Feliciantonio and Aalbers, "The Prehistories of Neoliberal Housing Policies"; Fields, "Contesting the Financialization of Urban Space."

3 Rolnik, *Urban Warfare*, 3–4.

4 Rolnik, *Urban Warfare*, 27–28.

5 Massey, "Power-Geometry and a Progressive Sense of Place"; Amin, "Placing Globalization"; Sheppard, Leitner, and Maringanti, "Provincializing Global Urbanism"; Lancione and McFarlane, *Global Urbanism.*

6 Appadurai, *The Future as Cultural Fact*, 65.

7 Appadurai, *The Future as Cultural Fact*, 66.

8 Appadurai, *The Future as Cultural Fact*, 66.

9 Thieme, "Beyond Repair."

10 Hall, "The Work of Representation."

11 hooks, *Outlaw Culture.*

12 Hall, "The West and the Rest," 187.

13 Ferguson et al., *Out There.*

14 De Genova, "Spectacles of Migrant 'Illegality.'"

15 Gowan, *Hobos, Hustlers and Back-Sliders.*

16 Gowan, *Hobos, Hustlers and Back-Sliders*, 103.

17 Gowan, *Hobos, Hustlers and Back-Sliders*, 50.

18 The concept of abstract machines can help us to grasp how the content/expression couplet of any given assemblage is, according to Deleuze and Guattari, articulated in terms of their vertical axis (Massumi, *A User's Guide to Capitalism and Schizophrenia*, 152). In Guattari's own terms, "when we speak of abstract machines, by 'abstract' we can also understand 'extract' in the sense of extracting" (Guattari, *Chaosmosis*, 35), and that which is extracted is just one of the infinite forms that an assemblage can take. This is a way for Deleuze and Guattari to historicize the making of

assemblages—for them, abstract machines are abstracted from history. For instance: Galileo is an abstract machine, diagramming for us the ways in which we conceive the relationship between the heart and the Sun, but also other things too (like religious censorship). In this sense, abstract machines do not come from nowhere but are assemblages themselves, with a certain stability and power. They are capable, in a Deleuzian sense, of affecting the form (content/expression) of other assemblages in the making. They are, therefore, not abstract in a metaphysical sense, but an "'immanent cause,' which explains the mutually supportive interaction between the forms of content and expression in any given assemblage" (Patton, *Deleuze and the Political*, 57). In this sense, abstract machines are "always singular keys that open or close an assemblage" (Deleuze and Guattari, *A Thousand Plateaus*, 368). They close it, because they tend to territorialize the assemblages in a certain way; but they can open it too, reframing that assemblage in different ways. In his work on Foucault, Deleuze is quite explicit about what an abstract machine is: "The diagram or abstract machine is the map of relations between forces, a map of destiny, or intensity, which proceeds by primary non-localizable relations and at every moment passes through every point" (Deleuze, *Foucault*, 36). It is a diagrammatic cause, a relational power without a clear design, form, or function. And it is capable of organizing things.

19 Referring to the notion of an abstract machine, by speaking of the representation of home(lessness), one provides a way to appreciate the pervasiveness and affective power of the system of representation we are dealing with. This is not simply a matter of reshuffling *signifié* and *signifiant*, but of dealing with an ingrained, historicized, and powerful way of coding and decoding meaning and sense. One can think with the abstract machine of home(lessness), much as one can think with the West, but, to stay close to Stuart Hall, this entails more than the deconstruction or relabeling of things.

20 Deleuze, *Foucault*, 34.

21 Hall, "The Work of Representation," 21, emphasis in the original.

22 A story that went viral (it came to my attention through an Italian newspaper): Wile, "A California Gubernatorial Candidate Spent a Week." This *Wired* piece offers some grounds, and further links, on the Wi-Fi hotspot story (which also went viral): Carmody, "The Damning Backstory behind 'Homeless Hotspots.'"

23 Looking at the picture of Gere might give a sense of why my students, when confronted with this story, never identify the actor but instead see a homeless man: Isabel Vincent and Natalie O'Neill, "The Tourist Who Gave 'Hobo' Gere Pizza," *New York Post*, April 27, 2014, https://nypost.com/2014/04/27/french-do-gooder-stunned -gere-was-homeless-man-she-helped/.

24 Kirk Maltais, "Tourist Gives Homeless Man Food, Later Finding Out It Was Richard Gere," *Daily Mail*, April 27, 2014, https://www.dailymail.co.uk/news/article -2614301/Tourist-NY-gives-homeless-man-leftover-pizza-later-finds-recipient -famous-actor-Richard-Gere.html.

25 Isabel Vincent and Natalie O'Neill, "The Tourist Who Gave 'Hobo' Gere Pizza," *New York Post*, February 27, 2014, https://nypost.com/2014/04/27/french-do-gooder -stunned-gere-was-homeless-man-she-helped/.

26   Amin, *Land of Strangers*.

27   J. David Goodman, "Photo of Officer Giving Boots to Barefoot Man Warms Hearts Online," *New York Times*, November 29, 2012, http://www.nytimes.com/2012/11/29 /nyregion/photo-of-officer-giving-boots-to-barefoot-man-warms-hearts-online .html.

28   Goodman, "Photo of Officer Giving Boots to Barefoot Man." The story can still be found on the NYPD's Facebook page: NYPD, "Jennifer Foster of Florence, AZ," Facebook post, November 27, 2012, https://www.facebook.com/nypd/photos/a .274991665910956/388162557927199/.

29   Supporters advocated for Officer DePrimo to become *Time* magazine's Person of the Year. An ad hoc Facebook fan page was created for this purpose.

30   This is still available online: NYPD, "I didn't think anything of it," Facebook post, November 29, 2012, https://www.facebook.com/NYPD/photos/a.267916766618446 /388820624528059/.

31   Donald J. Trump, Twitter, November 30, 2012, 3:00 p.m., https://twitter.com /realDonaldTrump/status/274603852836245505.

32   Marc Santora and Alex Vadukul, "Homeless Man Is Grateful for Officer's Gift of Boots. But He Again Is Barefoot," *New York Times*, December 3, 2012, http://www.nytimes.com /2012/12/03/nyregion/barefoot-homeless-man-says-hes-grateful-for-boots.html.

33   Cubellis, "Gestures of Care and Recognition"; Mol, *The Logic of Care*; Lester and Cubellis, *Traces of Care*; Conradson, "Geographies of Care," 508.

34   hooks, *Outlaw Culture*.

35   For the full method, see Lancione, "The Spectacle of the Poor."

36   Callon, "Some Elements of a Sociology of Translation."

37   NYPD, original post on DePrimo story, "Jennifer Foster of Florence, AZ was visiting Times Square with her husband Nov. 14 when they saw a shoeless man asking for change," Facebook, November 27, 2012, https:// www.facebook.com/photo.php?fbid =388162557927199.

38   Stewart, *Ordinary Affects*.

39   The motto of many police departments across the United States.

40   Davis and Kelley, *The Meaning of Freedom*.

41   Comments on the original story published by the NYPD on its Facebook page ("Jennifer Foster of Florence, AZ was visiting Times Square . . ."), Facebook, November 27, 2012, https:// www.facebook.com/photo.php?fbid=388162557927199.

42   The Samaritan is a "foreigner" since the Jews, at the time of the parable, were enemies of the Samaritans. An online version of the parable is available at Luke 10:25–37, Bible Gateway, accessed January 5, 2023, http://www.biblegateway.com /passage/?search=Luke+10%3A25–37&version=NIV.

43   Andrea Peyser, "Officer's Inspiring Kindness Is NYC at Its Finest," *New York Post*, November 30, 2012, http://nypost.com/2012/11/30/officers-inspiring-kindness-is-nyc -at-its-finest/.

44   Fine and Glendinning, "Dependence, Independence or Inter-dependence?"; Elwood, Lawson, and Sheppard, "Geographical Relational Poverty Studies."

45 Anthony M. Destefano, "Larry DePrimo Honored by NYPD," *Newsday*, November 29, 2012, http://www.newsday.com/news/nation/larry-deprimo-honored-by-nypd-1.4276919.

46 Santora and Vadukul, "Homeless Man Is Grateful."

47 Stephen Rex Brown, "Barefoot Homeless Man Immortalized in Photo Isn't Actually Homeless," *New York Daily News*, December 3, 2012, http://www.nydailynews.com/new-york/homeless-shoe-guy-history-rejecting-article-1.1212779.

48 Santora and Vadukul, "Homeless Man Is Grateful."

49 Santora and Vadukul, "Homeless Man Is Grateful."

50 Elwood and Lawson, "The Arts of Poverty Politics."

51 FEANTSA is the European Federation of National Organisations Working with the Homeless, https://www.feantsa.org/en.

52 Lancione, Stefanizzi, and Gaboardi, "Passive Adaptation or Active Engagement?"

53 Tsemberis, *Housing First*, 20.

54 Gilmer et al., "Development and Validation."

55 Klodawsky, "Home Spaces and Rights to the City."

56 McCann, "Policy Boosterism, Policy Mobilities, and the Extrospective City."

57 Temenos and McCann, "Geographies of Policy Mobilities."

58 McCann, "Expertise, Truth, and Urban Policy Mobilities," 6.

59 Peck, "Geographies of Policy."

60 Peck and Theodore, "Mobilizing Policy," 170.

61 Looking at the first phases of the Italian experiment around HF, it is possible to argue that fio.PSD's experiment was designed to transfer into Italy the established, internationally accepted and successful version of HF. This is evident looking at the international experts who were involved in the program, as well as the importance given to the scientific evaluation of the experiment, which was framed around measurement scales adopted internationally in research on HF, translated and minimally adapted to the national context. Gilmer et al., "Development and Validation." A fidelity scale molded around the one designed by Pathways HF was also requested by fio.PSD, and later devised by the scientific committee, in order to understand the progress of each organization involved in the experiment. This latter point, in particular, demonstrates the will to use what are considered to be appropriate (because they are internationally recognized) measurements to justify the approach adopted in Italy in the eyes of political observers, both domestic and international—heedful of the role played by good practices. In line with these practices and in connection with the model's political appropriation, fio.PSD's advocacy work has made it possible to include HF as one of the Guidelines for Countering Severe Adult Marginalisation in Italy, as promoted by the Labour and Welfare Policies Ministry in 2015. This accreditation is in line with the aspiration to win endorsement at the institutional level for the HF project, not unlike what happened in the United States in the triangulations between the ICH, Philip Mangano, and Pathways to Housing. This time, however, the accreditation was not based on the national result, but purely on the publicized international success of the policy (the validation by the Italian Labour and Welfare Policies Ministry preceded most of the analysis of the implementation of HF in the country).

62 Tsai and Rosenheck raise concerns about the exportability of the model and its usability in contexts that are different from that in which it was initially developed. See Tsai and Rosenheck, "Considering Alternatives to the Housing First Model."

63 Pleace, "Housing First."

64 See, for instance, Pleace, "The Action Plan for Preventing Homelessness in Finland."

65 Löfstrand and Juhila, "The Discourse of Consumer Choice."

66 Baker and Evans, "Housing First and the Changing Terrains," 32.

67 Baker and Evans, "Housing First and the Changing Terrains."

68 Hopper, "Commentary," 461.

69 Angela Giuffrida and Lorenzo Tondo, "'A Generation Has Died': Italian Province Struggles to Bury Its Coronavirus Dead," *Guardian*, March 19, 2020, https://www.theguardian.com/world/2020/mar/19/generation-has-died-italian-province-struggles-bury-coronavirus-dead.

70 See Marcus Walker and Mark Maremont, "Lessons from Italy's Hospital Meltdown: Every Day You Lose, the Contagion Gets Worse," *Wall Street Journal*, March 17, 2020, https://www.wsj.com/articles/every-day-you-lose-the-contagion-gets-worse-lessons-from-italys-hospital-meltdown-11584455470.

71 Farha, "COVID-19 Guidance Note."

72 Taken and adjusted from Farha, "COVID-19 Guidance Note."

73 Available at Anti-eviction Mapping Project, https://www.antievictionmap.com/.

74 RHJ Editorial Collective, "COVID-19 and Housing Struggles."

75 RHJ Editorial Collective, "COVID-19 and Housing Struggles," 12.

6. THE MICROPOLITICS OF HOUSING PRECARITY

1 Simone, "The Uninhabitable?"

2 Osborne, "For Still Possible Cities," 8.

3 Haraway, "Situated Knowledges"; Brickell, "Geopolitics of Home"; Butler, "Bodies in Alliance and the Politics of the Street"; Grosfoguel, "The Epistemic Decolonial Turn"; Mignolo, "Epistemic Disobedience and the Decolonial Option"; Sousa Santos, *Epistemologies of the South*.

4 Glynn, *Where the Other Half Lives*.

5 Lees, Annunziata, and Rivas-Alonso, "Resisting Planetary Gentrification."

6 Lancione, "Revitalising the Uncanny"; Vasudevan, "The Autonomous City"; Vasudevan, *Metropolitan Preoccupations*.

7 Brickell, Fernández Arrigoitia, and Vasudevan, *Geographies of Forced Eviction*.

8 Vasudevan, "The Makeshift City."

9 Turner, *Housing by People*; Ward, *Housing*; Hardoy and Satterthwaite, *Squatter Citizen*.

10 Brenner and Theodore, "Neoliberalism and the Urban Condition."

11 Katz, "Towards Minor Theory"; Massey, "Power-Geometry and a Progressive Sense of Place"; Oswin, "Planetary Urbanization"; Brickell, Fernández Arrigoitia, and Vasudevan, *Geographies of Forced Eviction*.

12 Mudu and Chattopadhyay, *Migration, Squatting and Radical Autonomy*; Huron, *Carving Out the Commons*; McElroy and Werth, "Deracinated Dispossessions"; Polanska and

Piotrowski, "The Transformative Power of Cooperation"; Dadusc, "The Micropolitics of Border Struggles."

13 Sousa Santos, *Epistemologies of the South*.

14 Or why, when these urbanites are approached in terms of housing struggles, is the scholarship that emerges filed under development studies (or studies of urban informality) rather than as part of a translocal and transversal effort for a different kind of planetary inhabitation?

15 Squatting Europe Kollective, *The Squatters' Movement in Europe*.

16 Again, when this is done, contributions do not fall within the remit of mainstream housing scholarship; for excellent examples in this sense, see the works of scholars such as Maestri, "Are They Nomads, Travellers or Roma?"; Grazioli, "From Citizens to *Citadins?*"

17 Simone, *Always Something Else*, 43.

18 Brenner and Schmid, "Towards a New Epistemology of the Urban?"

19 Oswin, "Planetary Urbanization."

20 Recently Camillo Boano and Giovanna Astolfo expanded on the difference between inhabitation and my own take on dwelling (Boano and Astolfo, "Inhabitation as More-Than-Dwelling"). Their contribution is important to think through these themes, but ultimately, I don't see a major difference between what they are arguing and the kind of revisioning of dwelling I am proposing in this text. Therefore, I use the two terms interchangeably.

21 McFarlane, *Fragments of the City*; McFarlane, *Learning the City*.

22 Turner, *Housing by People*, 61, emphasis in original.

23 As some housing scholarship clearly shows, e.g., King, *Private Dwelling*. A more interesting, nuanced and counterpolitical reading is that offered by Handel, who reconceptualizes the nexus of house/home through dwelling (Handel, "What's in a Home?"). I find his contribution intriguing and generative but, ultimately, too narrowly focused on the need to explain the human and nonhuman elements in the house/homing processes. For me, it falls short of a liberatory epistemology of inhabitation, which is what interests me in this chapter. However, Handel's work remains an important reflection in the right direction: one aimed at reimagining the use value of housing in a fuller, deeper sense.

24 Lafazani, "The Significance of the Insignificant."

25 Heidegger, "Building Dwelling Thinking."

26 Castán Broto, *Urban Energy Landscapes*, 58.

27 Young, *On Female Body Experience*, 124.

28 Lancione, "Weird Exoskeletons."

29 Anzaldúa, *Light in the Dark (Luz en lo oscuro)*.

30 Jolley, "Embodying Plurality"; McCarthy, "(Re)Conceptualising the Boundaries between Home and Homelessness."

31 Ahmed, *Willful Subjects*.

32 Hartman, "The Anarchy of Colored Girls," 468; Hartman, *Wayward Lives, Beautiful Experiments*.

33 Hartman, "The Anarchy of Colored Girls," 468.

34   Hartman, "The Anarchy of Colored Girls," 471.

35   Roy, "Racial Banishment"; Gibbons, *City of Segregation*; Shabazz, *Spatializing Blackness*.

36   Hartman, *Wayward Lives, Beautiful Experiments*.

37   Hartman, "The Anarchy of Colored Girls," 468.

38   Hartman, "The Anarchy of Colored Girls," 470–71.

39   Amin, *Land of Strangers*.

40   Ahmed, *Willful Subjects*.

41   Lancione, "The Politics of Embodied Precarity."

42   Simone, "The Urban Poor and Their Ambivalent Exceptionalities," 17.

43   Simone, *The Surrounds*.

44   Sousa Santos, *Epistemologies of the South*, 76.

45   Katz, "Revisiting Minor Theory," 598.

46   For example, Desmond's acclaimed work on evictions in the United States has been criticized for its use of problematic qualitative and quantitative data, and its undermining of a politics of life and liberation that underpins housing precarity (Desmond, *Evicted*). Aiello's counterreading deploys a sensibility that takes precarious dwelling on its own terms, thereby staying close to its liberatory politics (Aiello et al., "Eviction Lab Misses the Mark").

47   Lancione, "Caring for the Endurance of a Collective Struggle."

48   Freire, *Pedagogy of the Oppressed*, 63.

49   Mudu and Chattopadhyay, *Migration, Squatting and Radical Autonomy*; Dadusc and Mudu, "Care without Control"; Grazioli, "From Citizens to *Citadins*?"

7. DEINSTITUTE, REINSTITUTE, INSTITUTE

1   Fortier, "'Coming Home,'" 405.

2   Bryant, "The Meaning of Queer Home," 263.

3   Oswin, "The Modern Model Family at Home."

4   Vallerand, "Home Is the Place We All Share"; McKeithen, "Queer Ecologies of Home"; Matthews, Poyner, and Kjellgren, "Lesbian, Gay, Bisexual, Transgender and Queer Experiences."

5   Gorman-Murray, "Queer Politics at Home."

6   Elwood, "Lesbian Living Spaces."

7   For an insightful conceptualization of the intersection between feminism, racialized women labor, and community activism, see Banks, "Black Women in the United States."

8   Roy, "Racial Banishment"; Rodriguez, *Diverging Space for Deviants*; Summers, "Reclaiming the Chocolate City."

9   Fields and Raymond, "Racialized Geographies."

10   Haraway, *Staying with the Trouble*.

11   Simone, *The Surrounds*.

12   For a recent and rich description of what such a process might entail, see García-Lamarca, *Non-performing Loans*.

13   Tadiar, *Thresholds*.

14 Summers and Field, "Speculative Urban Worldmaking." For another interesting contribution on Black and Indigenous resistance in Oakland, see Ramírez, "Take the Houses Back."

15 Quizar, "A Logic of Care."

16 Burgum, *Occupying London*; Lees, Annunziata, and Rivas-Alonso, "Resisting Planetary Gentrification"; Madden and Marcuse, *In Defense of Housing*; Squatting Europe Kollective, *The Squatters' Movement in Europe*.

17 Brickell, Fernández Arrigoitia, and Vasudevan, *Geographies of Forced Eviction*.

18 Yet not all of this scholarship and networking is at the same level of quality and awareness, and not all is genuinely tackling the housing question as a gateway for deeper change. There are examples of problematic assumptions made, especially on the side of scholarship, between the realm of the academy and that of activism.

19 Roy et al., *Methodologies for Housing Justice Guide*, 15.

20 Roy et al., *Methodologies for Housing Justice Guide*, 15.

21 Roy et al., *Methodologies for Housing Justice Guide*, 15.

22 Roy et al., *Methodologies for Housing Justice Guide*, 16.

23 In this sense, see also Roy and Malson, *Housing Justice in Unequal Cities*.

24 Roy et al., *Methodologies for Housing Justice Guide*, 14.

25 These emerge from my experience in investigating stories of housing precarity in Italy and Romania through longitudinal ethnographic work, and across a number of other geographies through the encounters afforded in the makings of the *Radical Housing Journal*. The line I am navigating here is once again between epistemology and methodology, but how these proposed moves are put in place is squarely a situated affair, varying according to the ways in which expulsion and extraction are made to work in the ground of action, which encompasses local space and stories, as well as the circulations of their form and the forms of their circulations (chapters 4 and 5 in this volume).

26 Mbembe, "The Universal Right to Breathe."

27 See chapter 3; see also Willse, *The Value of Homelessness*.

28 Bellacasa, *Matters of Care*; Roy et al., *Encountering Poverty*; Fassin, *Humanitarian Reason*.

29 Power and Mee, "Housing: An Infrastructure of Care."

30 Ward, *When We Build Again*.

31 Purcell, *The Down-Deep Delight of Democracy*.

32 Vallerand, "Home Is the Place We All Share," 68.

33 As in the case, for instance, of the recent displacement of houseless individuals in Echo Park, Los Angeles. See, for a clear and informative account, After Echo Park Lake Research Collective, *(Dis)Placement*.

34 Gago, *Feminist International*, 11.

35 Gago, *Feminist International*, 29.

36 RHJ Editorial Collective, "COVID-19 and Housing Struggles."

37 Gago, *Feminist International*, 27.

38 Gago, *Feminist International*, 210.

39 Davis, *Are Prisons Obsolete?*; Ferdinand, *Une écologie décoloniale*; Gibson-Graham, *The End of Capitalism*; Fraser, *Fortunes of Feminism*.

40 Yiftachel, *Ethnocracy*; Kotef, *The Colonizing Self.*

41 For the accuracy of the method of inquiry and clarity of argument, see Christophers, *The New Enclosure.*

42 Fay and James, *The Rights and Wrongs of Land Restitution*, 1.

43 See Lancione, "The Politics of Embodied Precarity"; Lancione, "Inhabiting Dispossession in the Post-socialist City." See also my documentary on restitutions processes and related displacement in Bucharest, Michele Lancione, dir., *A început ploaia / It Started Raining*, A Community Productions, 2017, https://www.ainceputploaia.com/. For a historical analysis of the Romanian context and restitutions, see also Chelcea, "Marginal Groups in Central Places"; Vincze, "The Ideology of Economic Liberalism"; Popovici, "Residences, Restitutions and Resistance."

44 Perry, *Black Women against the Land Grab.*

45 Hemmings, "Affective Solidarity," quoted in Danewid, "White Innocence in the Black Mediterranean."

46 Lester and Cubellis, *Traces of Care.*

47 Thompson, "Caring Housing Futures," 6.

48 Hobart and Kneese, "Radical Care."

49 Simone, *Improvised Lives*; Simone, *The Surrounds.*

50 Lancione, "Underground Inscriptions"; Hobart and Kneese, "Radical Care," 3.

51 Hobart and Kneese, "Radical Care," 3.

52 Harney and Moten, *The Undercommons.*

53 Grosz, *Time Travels.*

54 Incidentally, it seems also to suggest a sort of metaphysical affirmation. Coherently with the material and affective analysis deployed in the book, it is important to stress that the affirmation is also grounded in situated material and affective processes, and would not exist otherwise.

55 This obviously is connected to the framework exposed in chapter 1. For my own take and the limitations of this vitalist and processual understanding of being, see that chapter.

56 This is not only because, in deinstituting and reinstituting, things and people are actually liberated, but fundamentally because deinstituting and reinstituting are about fighting the core functionings of home(lessness), directly attacking its expulsive and extractive logics—anthropocentric, patriarchal, heteronormative, racist, and capitalist.

57 Vieta, "The Stream of Self-Determination and Autogestión," 783.

58 Vieta, "The Stream of Self-Determination and Autogestión," 782.

59 Deleuze and Guattari, *Kafka.*

60 Wright, "Mapping Pathways within Italian Autonomist Marxism"; Lotringer and Marazzi, *Autonomia.*

61 Negri, "Domination and Sabotage," 63.

62 Mudu, "At the Intersection of Anarchists and Autonomists."

63 Freire, *Pedagogy of the Oppressed*, 23.

64 Vasudevan, "The Makeshift City."

65 Ward, *When We Build Again*; Turner, *Housing by People*; Simone, *The Surrounds.*

66 Vilenica, "Becoming an Accomplice in Housing Struggles," 210.

67 Indigenous Action Media, "Accomplices Not Allies," 6.

68   Hawthorne, "*L'Italia meticcia?*," 173.

69   Platform for People Affected by Mortgages, a grassroots housing group that emerged in the wake of the 2008 crisis in Spain. It helped to stop thousands of evictions affecting Spaniards at all levels by adopting direct housing actions but also by providing grassroots-led and horizontally structured group support to its members (at its peak, it had more than 150 active groups across the country). One of the spokespeople of La PAH, Ada Colau, was elected mayor of Barcelona in 2015.

70   Martinez, "Bitter Wins or a Long-Distance Race?"

71   Building on the work of Gibson-Graham, Di Feliciantonio has shown how La PAH was able to articulate a politics of language, subjectivity, and collective action, which built a new sense of the possible, using affective atmospheres in a way that went beyond (and challenged) the canons of anticapitalist policy (Di Feliciantonio, "Social Movements and Alternative Housing Models").

72   García-Lamarca, "Creating Political Subjects," 432.

73   Stengers, "The Cosmopolitical Proposal," 1003.

74   hooks, "Choosing the Margins as a Space of Radical Openness," 20, emphasis added.

CONCLUSION

1   Fortier, "'Coming Home'"; Gorman-Murray, "Queer Politics at Home"; Oswin, "The Modern Model Family at Home."

2   Roy et al., *Methodologies for Housing Justice Guide*.

3   Hartman, *Wayward Lives, Beautiful Experiments*; Basaglia, *L'istituzione negata*; De Genova, *Borders of "Europe."*

4   Sousa Santos, *Epistemologies of the South*.

5   Rolnik and Lancione, "Building Territories to Protect Life," 143.

6   Simone, *Improvised Lives*; Grosz, *Time Travels*.

7   Sousa Santos, *Epistemologies of the South*, 73.

8   Harding, *Sciences from Below*, 133.

9   Fred Moten, "Fred Moten & Stefano Harney—the University: Last Words," FUC, posted July 9, 2020, YouTube video, https://www.youtube.com/watch?v=zqWMejD_XU8. The quote is taken around minute 38 of this powerful seminar, organized as part of the FYUP graduate-led series at the University of California, Irvine.

10   Gowan, *Hobos, Hustlers and Back-Sliders*.

11   Hall, "The Work of Representation," 203.

Aalbers, Manuel B. "The Revanchist Renewal of Yesterday's City of Tomorrow." *Antipode* 43, no. 5 (2011): 1696–724. https://doi.org/10.1111/j.1467-8330.2010.00817.x.

After Echo Park Lake Research Collective. *(Dis)Placement: The Fight for Housing and Community after Echo Park Lake*. Los Angeles: UCLA Luskin Institute on Inequality and Democracy, 2022.

Agamben, Giorgio. *State of Exception*. Chicago: University of Chicago Press, 2005.

Agenzia Entrate. *Rapporto Mutui Ipotecari 2021*. Rome: Agenzia delle Entrate, Divisione Servizi, 2021. https://www.agenziaentrate.gov.it/portale/documents/20143/263042 /RMI2021_202191021.pdf/73bda63b-ab72-b9a6-6665-7e40e690e602.

Ahmed, Sara. *Strange Encounters: Embodied Others in Post-coloniality*. London: Routledge, 2000.

Ahmed, Sara. *Willful Subjects*. Durham, NC: Duke University Press, 2014.

Aiello, Daniela, Lisa Bates, Terra Graziani, Christopher Herring, Manissa Maharawal, Erin McElroy, Pamela Phan, and Gretchen Purser. "Eviction Lab Misses the Mark." *Shelterforce*, August 2018. https://shelterforce.org/2018/08/22/eviction-lab-misses-the -mark/.

Allahyari, Rebecca Anne. *Visions of Charity: Volunteer Workers and Moral Community*. Berkeley: University of California Press, 2000.

Amin, Ash. *Land of Strangers*. Cambridge: Polity, 2012.

Amin, Ash. "Placing Globalization." *Theory, Culture and Society* 14, no. 2 (1997): 123–37. https://doi.org/10.1177/026327697014002011.

Amin, Ash, and Michele Lancione, eds. *Grammars of the Urban Ground*. Durham, NC: Duke University Press, 2022.

Amin, Ash, and Nigel Thrift. *Arts of the Political: New Openings for the Left*. Durham, NC: Duke University Press, 2013.

Anderson, Ben. *Encountering Affect: Capacities, Apparatuses, Conditions*. Farnham, UK: Ashgate, 2014.

Anderson, Nels. *The Hobo: The Sociology of the Homeless Man*. Chicago: University of Chicago Press, 1923.

Annunziata, Sandra. "Staying Put! Un manuale anti-gentrification per le città dell'Europa del Sud." Rome: Eticity, 2020.

Anzaldúa, Gloria E. *Borderlands/La Frontera: The New Mestiza*. San Francisco: Aunt Lute, 1987.

Anzaldúa, Gloria E. *Light in the Dark (Luz en lo oscuro): Rewriting Identity, Spirituality, Reality*. Edited by Annalouise Keating. Durham, NC: Duke University Press, 2015.

Apostolopoulou, Elia. *Nature Swapped and Nature Lost: Biodiversity Offsetting, Urbanization and Social Justice*. London: Palgrave Macmillan, 2020.

Appadurai, Arjun. *The Future as Cultural Fact: Essays on the Global Condition*. London: Verso, 2013.

Aru, Silvia. "Abandonment, Agency, Control." *Antipode* 53, no. 6 (November 2021): 1619–38.

ASGI. "Libro nero del CPR di Torino: testimonianze di ordinaria ferocia." Turin: ASGI, 2021. https://www.asgi.it/asilo-e-protezione-internazionale/libro-nero-del-cpr-di -torino-testimonianze-di-ordinaria-ferocia/.

Avallone, Gennaro. *Il sistema di accoglienza in Italia: Esperienze, resistenze, segregazione*. Naples-Salerno: Orthodes Editrice, 2018.

Avallone, Gennaro. *Sfruttamento e resistenze: Migrazioni e agricoltura in Europa, Italia, Piana del Sele*. Verona: Ombre Corte, 2017.

Baker, Catherine. "Shelter in Place: The Feminist and Queer Insecurities of 'Home.'" *Disorder of Things* (blog), March 30, 2020. https://thedisorderofthings.com/2020/03/30 /shelter-in-place-the-feminist-and-queer-insecurities-of-home/.

Baker, Tom, and Joshua Evans. "Housing First and the Changing Terrains of Homeless Governance." *Geography Compass* 10, no. 1 (2016): 25–41.

Baldini, Massimo. *La casa degli Italiani*. Bologna: Il Mulino, 2010.

Banks, Nina. "Black Women in the United States and Unpaid Collective Work: Theorizing the Community as a Site of Production." *Review of Black Political Economy* 47, no. 4 (2020): 343–62. https://doi.org/10.1177/0034644620962811.

Basaglia, Franco, ed. *L'istituzione negata: Rapporto da un ospedale psichiatrico*. Turin: Giulio Einaudi Editore, 1968.

Beckett, Samuel. "Lessness." London: Calder and Boyars, 1970.

Bellacasa, María Puig de la. *Matters of Care: Speculative Ethics in More Than Human Worlds*. Minneapolis: University of Minnesota Press, 2017.

Benedict XVI (pope). "Encyclical Letter *Deus Caritas Est*." Vatican City: Roman Catholic Church, 2006.

Berardi, Franco. *Félix Guattari: Thought, Friendship, and Visionary Cartography*. London: Palgrave Macmillan, 2008.

Best, Asha, and Margaret M. Ramírez. "Urban Specters." *Environment and Planning D: Society and Space* 39, no. 6 (2021): 1043–54. https://doi.org/10.1177/0263775821103286.

Betta, Emmanuel. "La morale familiare." In *Cristiani d'Italia*, edited by Alberto Melloni. Rome: Treccani, 2011. https://www.treccani.it/enciclopedia/la-morale-familiare _%28Cristiani-d%27Italia%29/.

Bhambra, Gurminder K., and John Holmwood. "Colonialism, Postcolonialism and the Liberal Welfare State." *New Political Economy* 23, no. 5 (September 3, 2018): 574–87. https://doi.org/10.1080/13563467.2017.1417369.

Bhan, Gautam. *In the Public's Interest: Evictions, Citizenship, and Inequality in Contemporary Delhi*. Geographies of Justice and Social Transformation 30. Athens: University of Georgia Press, 2016.

Blunt, Alison, and Robyn Dowling. *Home*. Abingdon, UK: Routledge, 2006.

Blunt, Alison, and Ann Varley. "Introduction: Geographies of Home." *Cultural Geographies* 11, no. 1 (2004): 3–6. https://doi.org/10.1191/1474474004eu289xx.

Boano, Camillo. *Progetto minore: Alla ricerca della minorità nel progetto urbanistico ed architettonico*. Milan: Lettera Ventidue, 2020.

Boano, Camillo, and Giovanna Astolfo. "Inhabitation as More-Than-Dwelling: Notes for a Renewed Grammar." *International Journal of Housing Policy*, June 10, 2020, 1–23. https://doi.org/10.1080/19491247.2020.1759486.

Boccagni, Paolo. *Migration and the Search for Home: Mapping Domestic Space in Migrants' Everyday Lives*. London: Palgrave Macmillan, 2017.

Bolzoni, Magda, Enrico Gargiulo, and Michele Manocchi. "The Social Consequences of the Denied Access to Housing for Refugees in Urban Settings: The Case of Turin, Italy." *International Journal of Housing Policy* (August 2015): 400–417. https://doi.org/10.1080/14616718.2015.1053337.

Brar, Dhanveer Singh, and Ashwani Sharma. "What Is This 'Black' in Black Studies? From Black British Cultural Studies to Black Critical Thought in UK Arts and Higher Education." *New Formations*, no. 99 (December 1, 2019): 88–109. https://doi.org/10.3898/NewF:99.05.2019.

Brenner, Neil, and Christian Schmid. "Towards a New Epistemology of the Urban?" *City* 19, no. 2–3 (2015): 151–82. https://doi.org/10.1080/13604813.2015.1014712.

Brenner, Neil, and Nik Theodore. "Neoliberalism and the Urban Condition." *City* 9, no. 1 (2005): 101–7. https://doi.org/10.1080/13604810500092106.

Brickell, Katherine. "Geopolitics of Home." *Geography Compass* 6, no. 10 (2012): 575–88. https://doi.org/10.1111/j.1749-8198.2012.00511.x.

Brickell, Katherine. "'Mapping' and 'Doing' Critical Geographies of Home." *Progress in Human Geography* 36, no. 2 (2012): 225–44. https://doi.org/10.1177/0309132511418708.

Brickell, Katherine, Melissa Fernández Arrigoitia, and Alexander Vasudevan, eds. *Geographies of Forced Eviction: Dispossession, Violence, Resistance*. London: Palgrave Macmillan, 2017.

Brienza, Giuseppe. "Ferdinando Loffredo." *Ricognizioni*, April 16, 2010. https://www.ricognizioni.it/ferdinando-loffredo/.

Brugger, E. Christian. *The Indissolubility of Marriage and the Council of Trent*. Washington, DC: Catholic University of America Press, 2017. https://muse.jhu.edu/book/52109.

Bryant, Jason. "The Meaning of Queer Home: Between Metaphor and Material." *Home Cultures* 12, no. 3 (September 2, 2015): 261–89. https://doi.org/10.1080/17406315.2015.1084754.

Buchanan, Ian. *Deleuze and Guattari's Anti-Oedipus*. London: Continuum, 2008.

Burgum, Samuel. *Occupying London: Post-crash Resistance and the Limits of Possibility*. London: Routledge, 2018.

Busch-Geertsema, Volker, Dennis Culhane, and Suzanne Fitzpatrick. "Developing a Global Framework for Conceptualising and Measuring Homelessness." *Habitat International* 55 (July 2016): 124–32. https://doi.org/10.1016/j.habitatint.2016.03.004.

Butler, Judith. "Bodies in Alliance and the Politics of the Street." *Occupy and Assemble*, October 2011, 1–15.

Butler, Judith. *Gender Trouble: Feminism and the Subversion of Identity*. London: Routledge, 1999.

Butler, Judith, and Athena Athanasiou. *Dispossession: The Performative in the Political*. Cambridge: Polity, 2013.

Byrd, Jodi A., Alyosha Goldstein, Jodi Melamed, and Chandan Reddy. "Predatory Value." *Social Text* 36, no. 2 (June 1, 2018): 1–18. https://doi.org/10.1215/01642472-362325.

Callon, Michel. "Some Elements of a Sociology of Translation: Domestication of the Scallops and the Fishermen of St Brieuc Bay." In *Power, Action and Belief: A New Sociology of Knowledge*, edited by J. Law, 196–223. London: Routledge and Kegan Paul, 1986.

Caminiti, Luciana. "L'impero del 'Piccolo Italiano': Formazione e informazione attraverso le copertine dei quaderni scolastici." In *Quel che resta dell'impero: La cultura coloniale degli Italiani*, edited by Valeria Deplano and Alessandro Pes, 107–28. Milan: Mimesis, 2014.

Carmody, Tim. "The Damning Backstory behind 'Homeless Hotspots' at SXSW." *Wired*, March 12, 2012. https://www.wired.com/2012/03/the-damning-backstory-behind -homeless-hotspots-at-sxswi/.

Castán Broto, Vanesa. *Urban Energy Landscapes*. Cambridge: Cambridge University Press, 2019. https://doi.org/10.1017/9781108297868.

Cavallo, Sandra. *Charity and Power in Early Modern Italy*. Cambridge: Cambridge University Press, 1995.

Chelcea, Liviu. "The 'Housing Question' and the State-Socialist Answer: City, Class and State Remaking in 1950s Bucharest." *International Journal of Urban and Regional Research* 36, no. 2 (2012): 281–96. https://doi.org/10.1111/j.1468-2427.2011.01049.x.

Chelcea, Liviu. "Marginal Groups in Central Places: Gentrification, Property Rights and Post-socialist Primitive Accumulation (Bucharest, Romania)." In *Social Changes and Social Sustainability in Historical Urban Centres: The Case of Central Europe*, edited by György Enyedi and Zoltán Kovács, 127–46. Pecs: Centre for Regional Studies of Hungarian Academy of Science, 2006. http://books.google.com/books?id=NxLbPAAACAAJ.

Christophers, Brett. *The New Enclosure: The Appropriation of Public Land in Neoliberal Britain*. London: Verso, 2018.

CILD. "Buchi neri. La detenzione senza reato nei Centri di Permanenza per i Rimpatri (CPR)." Rome: Coalizione Italiana Libertà e Diritti Civili, 2021. https://cild.eu/wp -content/uploads/2021/10/ReportCPR_Web.pdf.

Cimmarusti, Ivan. "Frodi sugli sconti fiscali per l'edilizia: Coinvolti professionisti e società." *NT + Fisco*, 2022. https://ntplusfisco.ilsole24ore.com/art/frodi-sconti-fiscali-l -edilizia-coinvolti-professionisti-e-societa-AEf4N55.

Città di Torino. "Accesso competenze e servizi: Vademecum per gli operatori dei servizi sociali territoriali." Turin: Ufficio Adulti in Difficoltà della Città di Torino, 2009.

Città di Torino. "Nuovi criteri per la presa in carico dei cittadini senza dimora con residenza rittizia in v. della casa comunale che afferiscono ai servizi sociali circoscrizionali ed al servizio adulti in difficoltà." Turin: Ufficio Adulti in Difficoltà della Città di Torino, 2009.

Cloke, Paul, Jon May, and Sarah Johnsen. *Swept Up Lives? Re-envisioning the Homeless City.* Oxford: Blackwell, 2010.

Cloke, Paul, Sam Thomas, and Andrew Williams. "Faith in Action: Faith-Based Organizations, Welfare and Politics in the Contemporary City." In *Working Faith: Faith-Based Communities Involved in Justice*, edited by Paul Cloke, Justin Beaumont, and Andrew Williams. Milton Keynes, UK: Paternoster, 2013.

Cofini, Fabiana. "2021, un anno di femmincidi. In aumento in Italia la violenza di genere." *RaiNews*, December 12, 2021. https://www.rainews.it/photogallery/2021/12/2021—primato-negativo-per-la-violenza-sulle-donne-in-Italia-aumento-dei-femmincidi -1d3fa33c-a616-4c45-a72e-f17f10ac4ade.html.

Colebrook, Claire. "The Space of Man: On the Specificity of Affect in Deleuze and Guattari." In *Deleuze and Space*, edited by I. Buchanan and G. Lambert, 189–206. Edinburgh: Edinburgh University Press, 2005.

Colucci, Michele. *Storia dell'immigrazione straniera in Italia: Dal 1945 ai nostri giorni.* Rome: Carocci, 2020.

Conelli, Carmine. "Razza, colonialità, nazione: Il progetto coloniale Italiano tra mezzogiorno e Africa." In *Quel che resta dell'impero: La cultura coloniale degli Italiani*, edited by Valeria Deplano and Alessandro Pes, 150–67. Milan: Mimesis, 2014.

Conradson, David. "Geographies of Care: Spaces, Practices, Experiences." *Social and Cultural Geography* 4, no. 4 (December 2003): 451–54. https://doi.org/10.1080 /1464936032000137894.

Cottone, Nicoletta. "Ddl Zan contro omofobia affossato al Senato con 154 voti contro 131: Sì alla tagliola, stop all'esame." *Il Sole 24 Ore*, October 25, 2021. https://www .ilsole24ore.com/art/ddl-zan-27-ottobre-prova-voto-aula-AEoTuIs.

Cresti, Federico. *Non desiderare la terra d'altri: La colonizzazione Italiana in Libia.* Rome: Carocci, 2011.

Croce Rossa Italiana. "Emergenza freddo stagione 2008–2009, vademecum." Turin: Croce Rossa Italiana, Comitato Provinciale di Torino, 2008.

Cubellis, Lauren. "Gestures of Care and Recognition: An Introduction." *Cultural Anthropology* 35, no. 1 (February 12, 2020). https://doi.org/10.14506/ca35.1.01.

Cubellis, Lauren, and Rebecca Lester. "Care at the Nexus of Power and Praxis: Anthropological Engagements with Caring Otherwise." Wenner-Gren Workshop. Saint Louis, 2018.

Dadusc, Deanna. "The Micropolitics of Border Struggles: Migrants' Squats and Inhabitance as Alternatives to Citizenship." *Citizenship Studies* 23, no. 6 (August 18, 2019): 593–607. https://doi.org/10.1080/13621025.2019.1634377.

Dadusc, Deanna, and Pierpaolo Mudu. "Care without Control: The Humanitarian Industrial Complex and the Criminalisation of Solidarity." *Geopolitics* 27, no. 4 (2020): 1205–30. https://doi.org/10.1080/14650045.2020.1749839.

Dagnes, Joselle. "Finanza e vita quotidiana: La finanziarizzazione delle famiglie italiane." *Quaderni di Sociologia*, no. 76 (April 1, 2018): 35–56. https://doi.org/10.4000/qds.1873.

Danewid, Ida. "White Innocence in the Black Mediterranean: Hospitality and the Erasure of History." *Third World Quarterly* 38, no. 7 (July 3, 2017): 1674–89. https://doi.org /10.1080/01436597.2017.1331123.

Daolio, Andreina, ed. *Le lotte per la casa in Italia*. Milan: Feltrinelli, 1974.

Da Rold, Cristina. "Altro che Airbnb: Gli italiani abitano in case sovraffollate e malsane." *Il Sole 24 Ore*, July 15, 2018. https://www.infodata.ilsole24ore.com/2018/07/15/altro -airbnb-gli-italiani-abitano-case-sovraffollate-malsane/.

Davis, Angela Y. *Are Prisons Obsolete?* New York: Seven Stories, 2003.

Davis, Angela Y. *If They Come in the Morning . . . Voices of Resistance*. New York: Verso, 2016.

Davis, Angela Y., and Robin D. G. Kelley. *The Meaning of Freedom*. San Francisco: City Lights, 2012.

De Boeck, Filip. "'Divining' the City: Rhythm, Amalgamation and Knotting as Forms of 'Urbanity.'" *Social Dynamics* 41, no. 1 (2015): 47–58. https://doi.org/10.1080/02533952.2015 .1032508.

De Genova, Nicholas. *The Borders of "Europe": Autonomy of Migration, Tactics of Bordering*. Durham, NC: Duke University Press, 2017.

De Genova, Nicholas. "Spectacles of Migrant 'Illegality': The Scene of Exclusion, the Obscene of Inclusion." *Ethnic and Racial Studies* 36, no. 7 (July 2013): 1180–98. https://doi .org/10.1080/01419870.2013.783710.

Del Boca, Angelo. *Italiani, brava gente?* Rome: Neri Pozza, 2005.

Deleuze, Gilles. "Bergson, 1859-1941." In *Desert Islands and Other Texts, 1953-1974*, edited by D. Lapoujade. Los Angeles: Semiotext(e), 2004.

Deleuze, Gilles. *Foucault*. Minneapolis: University of Minnesota Press, 1988.

Deleuze, Gilles. *Pure Immanence*. New York: Zone, 2001.

Deleuze, Gilles, and Félix Guattari. *Anti-Oedipus: Capitalism and Schizophrenia*. New York: Penguin, 1977.

Deleuze, Gilles, and Félix Guattari. "Balance-Sheet for 'Desiring-Machines.'" In *Chaosophy: Texts and Interviews, 1972-1977*, edited by S. Lotringer, 90–115. Los Angeles: Semiotext(e), 2009.

Deleuze, Gilles, and Félix Guattari. *Kafka: Toward a Minor Literature*. Minneapolis: University of Minnesota Press, 1986.

Deleuze, Gilles, and Félix Guattari. *A Thousand Plateaus*. New York: Continuum, 1987.

Deleuze, Gilles, and Félix Guattari. "What Is a Minor Literature?" *Essays Literary Criticism* 11, no. 3 (1983): 13–33.

De Lucia, Vezio. Preface to *La casa abbandonata: Il racconto delle politiche abitative dal piano decennale ai programmi per le periferie*, by Giancarlo Storto, 5–10. Rome: Officina Edizioni, 2018.

Deplano, Valeria. "Within and Outside the Nation: Former Colonial Subjects in Post-war Italy." *Modern Italy* 23, no. 4 (November 2018): 395–410. https://doi.org/10.1017/mit.2018.27.

Desjarlais, Robert. *Shelter Blues: Sanity and Selfhood among the Homeless*. Philadelphia: University of Pennsylvania Press, 1997.

Desmond, Matthew. *Evicted: Poverty and Profit in the American City*. New York: Crown, 2016.

DeVerteuil, Geoffrey. *Resilience in the Post-welfare Inner City: Voluntary Sector Geographies in London, Los Angeles and Sydney*. Bristol, UK: Policy, 2015.

Di Feliciantonio, Cesare. "Social Movements and Alternative Housing Models: Practicing the 'Politics of Possibilities' in Spain." *Housing, Theory and Society* 34, no. 1 (January 2, 2017): 38–56. https://doi.org/10.1080/14036096.2016.1220421.

Di Feliciantonio, Cesare, and Manuel B. Aalbers. "The Prehistories of Neoliberal Housing Policies in Italy and Spain and Their Reification in Times of Crisis." *Housing Policy Debate* 28, no. 1 (January 2, 2018): 135–51. https://doi.org/10.1080/10511482.2016.1276468.

Di Giacinto, Moreno. "Il settore delle costruzioni in Italia." Italia in dati, 2019. https://italiaindati.com/edilizia-e-costruzioni-in-italia/.

Drew, Elizabeth, and Mads Haahr. "Lessness: Randomness, Consciousness and Meaning." Paper presented at the Fourth International CAiiA-STAR Research Conference, "Consciousness Reframed," Perth, Australia, August 1–4, 2002. https://www.random.org/lessness/paper/.

Duneier, Mitchell. *Sidewalk*. New York: Farrar, Straus and Giroux, 1999.

Eco, Umberto. *Il fascismo eterno*. Milan: La nave di Teseo, 2019.

Edwards, Gareth A. S., and Harriet Bulkeley. "Urban Political Ecologies of Housing and Climate Change: The 'Coolest Block' Contest in Philadelphia." *Urban Studies* 54, no. 5 (April 2017): 1126–41. https://doi.org/10.1177/0042098015617907.

Elias, Juanita, and Shirin M. Rai. "Feminist Everyday Political Economy: Space, Time, and Violence." *Review of International Studies* 45, no. 2 (April 2019): 201–20. https://doi.org/10.1017/S0260210518000323.

Elwood, Sarah. "Lesbian Living Spaces: Multiple Meanings of Home." *Journal of Lesbian Studies* 4, no. 1 (May 26, 2000): 11–27. https://doi.org/10.1300/J155v04n01_02.

Elwood, Sarah, and Victoria Lawson. "The Arts of Poverty Politics: Real Change." *Social and Cultural Geography* 21, no. 5 (June 12, 2020): 579–601. https://doi.org/10.1080/14649365.2018.1509111.

Elwood, Sarah, Victoria Lawson, and Eric Sheppard. "Geographical Relational Poverty Studies." *Progress in Human Geography* 41, no. 6 (2016). https://doi.org/10.1177/0309132516659706.

Escobar, Arturo. *Designs for the Pluriverse: Radical Interdependence, Autonomy, and the Making of Words*. Durham, NC: Duke University Press, 2018.

Esposito, Emiliano, and Francesco Chiodelli. "Beyond Proper Political Squatting: Exploring Individualistic Need-Based Occupations in a Public Housing Neighbourhood in Naples." *Housing Studies*, July 9, 2021, 1–22. https://doi.org/10.1080/02673037.2021.1946017.

European Observatory on Homelessness. *Homelessness Services in Europe*. Brussels: FEANTSA, 2018. https://www.feantsaresearch.org/public/user/Observatory/Feantsa-Studies_08_v02%5B1%5D.pdf.

Evans, Joshua. "Exploring the (Bio)Political Dimensions of Voluntarism and Care in the City: The Case of a 'Low Barrier' Emergency Shelter." *Health and Place* 17, no. 1 (January 2011): 24–32. https://doi.org/10.1016/j.healthplace.2010.05.001.

Ex-OPG Je So' Pazzo. "Controllo popolare e sistema di accoglienza in Campania." In *Il sistema di accoglienza in Italia: Esperienze, resistenze, segregazione*, edited by Gennaro Avallone. Naples-Salerno: Orthodes Editrice, 2018.

Farha, Leilani. "COVID-19 Guidance Note Protection for Those Living in Homelessness." Geneva: OHCHR, 2020. https://www.ohchr.org/Documents/Issues/Housing/SR_housing_COVID-19_guidance_homeless.pdf.

Fassin, Didier. *Humanitarian Reason: A Moral History of the Present*. Oakland: University of California Press, 2011.

Fay, Derick, and Deborah James, eds. *The Rights and Wrongs of Land Restitution: "Restoring What Was Ours."* Abingdon, UK: Routledge-Cavendish, 2009.

Ferdinand, Malcom. *Une écologie décoloniale: Penser l'écologie depuis le monde caribéen.* Paris: Éditions du Seuil, 2019.

Ferguson, Russel, Martha Gever, Trinh T. Minh-ha, and C. West, eds. *Out There: Marginalization and Contemporary Culture.* New York: New Museum of Contemporary Art, 1990.

Ferreri, Mara. "Painted Bullet Holes and Broken Promises: Understanding and Challenging Municipal Dispossession in London's Public Housing 'Decanting.'" *International Journal of Urban and Regional Research* 44, no. 6 (2020): 1007–22. https://doi.org/10.1111/1468-2427.12952.

Fields, Desiree. "Contesting the Financialization of Urban Space: Community Organizations and the Struggle to Preserve Affordable Rental Housing in New York City." *Journal of Urban Affairs* 37, no. 2 (2015): 144–65. https://doi.org/10.1111/juaf.12098.

Fields, Desiree, and Elora Raymond. "Racialized Geographies of Housing Financialization." *Progress in Human Geography* 45, no. 6 (2021): 1625–45. https://doi.org/10.1177/03091325211009299.

Filandri, Marianna, and Manuela Olagnero. "Housing Inequality and Social Class in Europe." *Housing Studies* 29, no. 7 (2014): 977–93. https://doi.org/10.1080/02673037.2014.925096.

Filandri, Marianna, and Gabriella Paulì. "La finnziarizzazione del bene casa: Accesso al credito e disuguaglianze sociali." *Quaderni di Sociologia*, no. 76 (2018): 81–105. https://doi.org/10.4000/qds.1862.

Fine, Michael, and Caroline Glendinning. "Dependence, Independence or Interdependence? Revisiting the Concepts of 'Care' and 'Dependency.'" *Ageing and Society* 25, no. 4 (2005): 601–21. https://doi.org/10.1017/S0144686X05003600.

Flint, John. "Encounters with the Centaur State: Advanced Urban Marginality and the Practices and Ethics of Welfare Sanctions Regimes." *Urban Studies* 56, no. 1 (2019): 249–65. https://doi.org/10.1177/0042098017750070.

Fortier, Anne-Marie. "'Coming Home': Queer Migrations and Multiple Evocations of Home." *European Journal of Cultural Studies* 4, no. 4 (2001): 405–24. https://doi.org/10.1177/136754940100400403.

Foucault, Michel. *Abnormal: Lectures at the Collège de France, 1974–1975.* London: Verso, 2016.

Foucault, Michel. *Power: Essential Works of Foucault, 1954–1984*, vol. 3. Edited by J. Faubion. London: Penguin, 2000.

Foucault, Michel. *Space, Knowledge and Power.* Edited by J. D. Faubion. London: Penguin, 2000.

Francis (pope). *Amoris laetitia.* Vatican City: Roman Catholic Church, 2016. https://www.vatican.va/content/dam/francesco/pdf/apost_exhortations/documents/papa-francesco_esortazione-ap_20160319_amoris-laetitia_en.pdf.

Fraser, Nancy. *Fortunes of Feminism: From State-Managed Capitalism to Neoliberal Crisis.* Radical Thinkers. New York: Verso, 2020.

Freire, Paulo. *Pedagogy of the Oppressed.* London: Penguin Random House, 1970.

Gago, Veronica. *Feminist International: How to Change Everything.* New York: Verso, 2020.

Gainsforth, Sarah. *Airbnb città merce: Storie di resistenza alla gentrificazione digitale.* Rome: Derive Approdi, 2018.

Gandy, Matthew. "Cyborg Urbanization: Complexity and Monstrosity in the Contemporary City." *International Journal of Urban and Regional Research* 29, no. 1 (2005): 26–49.

Gandy, Matthew. *Natura Urbana: Ecological Constellations in Urban Space*. Cambridge, MA: MIT Press, 2022.

García-Lamarca, Melissa. "Creating Political Subjects: Collective Knowledge and Action to Enact Housing Rights in Spain." *Community Development Journal* 52, no. 3 (July 2017): 421–35.

García-Lamarca, Melissa. *Non-performing Loans, Non-performing People: Life and Struggle with Mortgage Debt in Spain*. Athens: University of Georgia Press, 2022.

García-Lamarca, Melissa, and Maria Kaika. "'Mortgaged Lives': The Biopolitics of Debt and Housing Financialisation." *Transactions of the Institute of British Geographers* 41, no. 3 (2016): 313–27. https://doi.org/10.1111/tran.12126.

Gibbons, Andrea. *City of Segregation: 100 Years of Struggle for Housing in Los Angeles*. London: Verso, 2018.

Gibson-Graham, J. K. *The End of Capitalism (As We Knew It): A Feminist Critique of Political Economy*. New ed. Minneapolis: University of Minnesota Press, 1996. https://www.jstor.org/stable/10.5749/j.cttts7zc.

Gilmer, Todd P., Ana Stefancic, Marisa Sklar, and Sam Tsemberis. "Development and Validation of a Housing First Fidelity Survey." *Psychiatric Services* 64, no. 9 (2013): 911–14.

Gilmore, Ruth Wilson. *Golden Gulag*. Berkeley: University of California Press, 2007. http://www.jstor.org/stable/10.1525/j.ctt5hjht8.

Glynn, Sarah, ed. *Where the Other Half Lives: Lower Income Housing in a Neoliberal World*. London: Pluto, 2009.

Gorman-Murray, Andrew. "Queer Politics at Home: Gay Men's Management of the Public/Private Boundary." *New Zealand Geographer* 68, no. 2 (August 2012): 111–20. https://doi.org/10.1111/j.1745-939.2012.01225.x.

Gowan, Teresa. *Hobos, Hustlers and Back-Sliders: Homeless in San Francisco*. Minneapolis: University of Minnesota Press, 2010.

Gramsci, Antonio. "Alcuni temi sulla questione meridionale." Turin: Fondazione Antonio Gramsci, 1935. http://bd.fondazionegramsci.org/bookreader/libri/questione_meridionale_124749.html.

Grazioli, Margherita. "From Citizens to *Citadins*? Rethinking Right to the City Inside Housing Squats in Rome, Italy." *Citizenship Studies* 21, no. 4 (May 19, 2017): 393–408. https://doi.org/10.1080/13621025.2017.1307607.

Grazioli, Margherita. *Housing, Urban Commons and the Right to the City in Post-crisis Rome: Metropoliz, the Squatted Città Meticcia*. Cham: Palgrave Macmillan, 2021.

Grilli, Simonetta. "Case, cibo e famiglia: Pratiche dell'abitare e della relazionalità parentale." *Lares* 80, no. 3 (2014): 469–90.

Grosfoguel, Ramón. "The Epistemic Decolonial Turn: Beyond Political-Economy Paradigms." *Cultural Studies* 21, no. 2–3 (March 2007): 211–23. https://doi.org/10.1080/09502380601162514.

Grosz, Elizabeth "A Thousand Tiny Sexes: Feminism and Rhizomatics." *Topoi* 12, no. 2 (1993): 167–79.

Grosz, Elizabeth. *Time Travels: Feminism, Nature, Power*. Durham, NC: Duke University Press, 2005.

Guattari, Félix *Chaosmosis: An Ethico-Aesthetic Paradigm*. Indianapolis: Indiana University Press, 1995.

Guattari, Félix. *Chaosophy: Texts and Interviews, 1972–1977*. Edited by S. Lotringer. Los Angeles: Semiotext(e), 2009.

Guattari, Félix. *The Machinic Unconscious: Essays in Schizoanalysis*. London: Semiotext(e), 2010.

Guattari, Félix. *Soft Subversion*. Los Angeles: Semiotext(e), 2009.

Guattari, Félix. "Subjectivities: For the Better and for the Worse." In *The Guattari Reader*, edited by G. Genosko. Oxford: Blackwell, 1996.

Hall, Stuart. "The West and the Rest: Discourse and Power." In *Formations of Modernity*, edited by Stuart Hall and B. Gieben, 275–331. London: Polity, 1992.

Hall, Stuart. "The Work of Representation." In *Representation: Cultural Representations and Signifying Practices*, edited by Stuart Hall, 15–71. London: Sage, 1997.

Handel, Ariel. "What's in a Home? Toward a Critical Theory of Housing/Dwelling." *Environment and Planning C: Politics and Space* 37, no. 6 (September 2019): 1045–62. https://doi.org/10.1177/2399654418819104.

Haraway, Donna. J. *Simians, Cyborgs, and Women: The Reinvention of Nature*. London: Free Association, 1991.

Haraway, Donna. "Situated Knowledges: The Science Question in Feminism and the Privilege of Partial Perspective." *Feminist Studies* 14, no. 3 (1988): 575–99. https://doi.org/10.2307/3178066.

Haraway, Donna. *Staying with the Trouble*. Durham, NC: Duke University Press, 2016.

Harding, Sandra. *Sciences from Below: Feminisms, Postcolonialities, and Modernities*. Durham, NC: Duke University Press, 2008.

Hardoy, Jorge, and David Satterthwaite. *Squatter Citizen: Life in the Urban Third World*. London: Routledge, 1989.

Hardt, Michael, and Antonio Negri. *Empire*. Cambridge, MA: Harvard University Press, 2000.

Hardt, Michael, and Antonio Negri. "Empire, Twenty Years On." *New Left Review*, no. 120 (November–December 2019).

Harney, Stefano, and Fred Moten. *The Undercommons: Fugitive Planning and Black Study*. New York: Minor Composition, 2013.

Hartman, Saidiya. "The Anarchy of Colored Girls Assembled in a Riotous Manner." *South Atlantic Quarterly* 117, no. 3 (July 2018): 465–90. https://doi.org/10.1215/00382876-6942093.

Hartman, Saidiya. *Wayward Lives, Beautiful Experiments: Intimate Histories of Social Upheaval*. New York: Norton, 2019.

Harvey, David. *The Condition of Postmodernity*. Oxford: Blackwell, 1990.

Harvey, David. *The Urbanization of the Capital: Studies in the History and Theory of Capitalist Urbanization*. Baltimore: Johns Hopkins University Press, 1985.

Hawthorne, Camilla. "Black Matters Are Spatial Matters: Black Geographies for the Twenty-First Century." *Geography Compass* 13, no. 11 (November 2019). https://doi.org/10.1111/gec3.12468.

Hawthorne, Camilla. "In Search of Black Italia." *Transition*, no. 123 (2017): 152. https://doi.org/10.2979/transition.123.1.17.

Hawthorne, Camilla. *"L'Italia meticcia?* The Black Mediterranean and the Racial Cartographies of Citizenship."* In *The Black Mediterranean*, edited by Gabriele Proglio, Camilla Hawthorne, Ida Danewid, P. Khalil Saucier, Giuseppe Grimaldi, Angelica Pesarini, Timothy Raeymaekers, Giulia Grechi, and Vivian Gerrand, 169–98. Cham: Springer International, 2021. https://doi.org/10.1007/978-3-030-51391-7_9.

Hayden, Dolores. *The Grand Domestic Revolution: A History of Feminist Designs For American Homes, Neighborhoods, and Cities*. Cambridge, MA: MIT Press, 1982.

Heidegger, Martin. "Building Dwelling Thinking." In *Poetry, Language, Thought*. New York: Harper Colophon, 1971.

Hemmings, Clare. "Affective Solidarity: Feminist Reflexivity and Political Transformation." *Feminist Theory* 13, no. 2 (August 2012): 147–61. https://doi.org/10.1177/1464700112442643.

Heynen, Nik, Maria Kaika, and Erik Swyngedouw, eds. *In the Nature of Cities: Urban Political Ecology and the Politics of Urban Metabolism*. New York: Routledge, 2006.

Hill Collins, Patricia. "It's All in the Family: Intersections of Gender, Race, and Nation." *Hypatia* 13, no. 3 (1998): 62–82.

Hobart, Hiʻilei Julia, and Tamara Kneese. "Radical Care: Survival Strategies for Uncertain Times." *Social Text* 38, no. 142 (2020): 1–16. https://doi.org/10.1215/01642472-7971067.

Honig, Bonnie. *Antigone, Interrupted*. Cambridge: Cambridge University Press, 2013.

hooks, bell. "Choosing the Margins as a Space of Radical Openness." *Framework: The Journal of Cinema and Media* 36 (1989): 15–23.

hooks, bell. *Outlaw Culture*. New York: Routledge, 1994.

Hopper, Kim. "Commentary: The Counter-reformation That Failed? A Commentary on the Mixed Legacy of Supported Housing." *Psychiatric Services* 63, no. 5 (January 2012): 461–63. https://doi.org/10.1176/appi.ps.201100379.

Hopper, Kim. *Reckoning with Homelessness*. Ithaca, NY: Cornell University Press, 2003. https://www.cornellpress.cornell.edu/book/9780801488344/reckoning-with-homelessness/.

Hunter, Marcus Anthony, and Zandria F. Robinson. *Chocolate Cities: The Black Map of American Life*. Oakland: University of California Press, 2017.

Huron, Amanda. *Carving Out the Commons*. Minneapolis: University of Minnesota Press, 2018. https://www.upress.umn.edu/book-division/books/carving-out-the-commons.

Indigenous Action Media. "Accomplices Not Allies: Abolishing the Ally Industrial Complex." In *Revolutionary Solidarity: A Critical Reader for Accomplices*, 5–16. Flagstaff, AZ: Indigenous Action Media, 2014. https://archive.org/details/RevolutionarySolidarityACriticalReaderForAccomplices/page/n15.

ISTAT. "Bilancio demografico nazionale, anno 2019." Rome: ISTAT, 2020. https://www.istat.it/it/files//2020/07/Report_BILANCIO_DEMOGRAFICO_NAZIONALE_2019.pdf.

ISTAT. "Gli stranieri residenti in famiglia e in convivenza." Rome: ISTAT, 2004. http://dawinci.istat.it/MD/download/com_stranieri_res.pdf.

ISTAT. "Popolazione e famiglie." Rome: ISTAT, 2013. https://www4.istat.it/it/anziani/popolazione-e-famiglie.

ISTAT. "La Povertà in Italia." Rome: ISTAT, 2021. https://www.istat.it/it/files//2021/06/REPORT_POVERTA_2020.pdf.

ISTAT. "Violenza sulle donne." Rome: ISTAT, 2015. https://www.istat.it/it/violenza-sulle-donne/il-fenomeno/violenza-dentro-e-fuori-la-famiglia/numero-delle-vittime-e-forme-di-violenza.

Jazeel, Tariq. "Singularity: A Manifesto for Incomparable Geographies." *Singapore Journal of Tropical Geography* 40, no. 1 (January 2019): 5–21. https://doi.org/10.1111/sjtg.12265.

Johnsen, Sarah, Paul Cloke, and Jon May. "Transitory Spaces of Care: Serving Homeless People on the Street." *Health and Place* 11, no. 4 (December 2005): 323–36. https://doi.org/10.1016/j.healthplace.2004.03.002.

Jolley, Josie. "Embodying Plurality: Becoming More-Than-Homeless." *Transactions of the Institute of British Geographers* 45, no. 3: 635–48. https://doi.org/10.1111/tran.12373.

Kaika, Maria. "Interrogating the Geographies of the Familiar: Domesticating Nature and Constructing the Autonomy of the Modern Home." *International Journal of Urban and Regional Research* 28, no. 2 (2004): 265–86. https://doi.org/10.1111/j.0309-1317.2004.00519.x.

Katz, Cindi. "Revisiting Minor Theory." *Environment and Planning D: Society and Space* 35, no. 4 (August 2017): 596–99. https://doi.org/10.1177/0263775817718012.

Katz, Cindi. "Towards Minor Theory." *Environment and Planning D: Society and Space* 14, no. 4 (1996): 487–99.

King, Peter. *Private Dwelling: Contemplating the Use of Housing.* London: Routledge, 2004.

Klodawsky, Fran. "Home Spaces and Rights to the City: Thinking Social Justice for Chronically Homeless Women." *Urban Geography* 30, no. 6 (August 2009): 591–610. https://doi.org/10.2747/0272-3638.30.6.591.

Kotef, Hagar. *The Colonizing Self: Or, Home and Homelessness in Israel/Palestine.* Durham, NC: Duke University Press, 2020.

Kothari, Miloon. "The Global Crisis of Displacement and Evictions." New York: Rosa Luxemburg Stiftung, 2015. https://www.rosalux.nyc/wp-content/uploads/2020/11/RLS-NYC_displacement_and_evictions.pdf.

Lafazani, Olga. "The Significance of the Insignificant: Borders, Urban Space, Everyday Life." *Antipode* 53, no. 4 (2021): 1143–60.

Lancione, Michele. "Assemblages of Care and the Analysis of Public Policies on Homelessness in Turin, Italy." *City* 18, no. 1 (2014): 25–40. https://doi.org/10.1080/13604813.2014.868163.

Lancione, Michele. "Caring for the Endurance of a Collective Struggle." *Dialogues in Human Geography* 9, no. 2 (2019): 216–19. https://doi.org/10.1177/2043820619850362.

Lancione, Michele. "The City and 'the Homeless': Machinic Subjects." In *Deleuze and the City,* edited by Hélène Frichot, Catharina Gabrielsson, and Jonathan Metzger, 145–60. Edinburgh: Edinburgh University Press, 2016.

Lancione, Michele. "Entanglements of Faith: Discourses, Practices of Care and Homeless People in an Italian City of Saints." *Urban Studies* 51, no. 14 (2014): 3062–78. https://doi.org/10.1177/0042098013514620.

Lancione, Michele. "Giustizia sociale, spazio e città: Un approccio teorico-metodologico applicato a un caso studio." *Rivista Geografica Italiana* 117 (2010): 625–52.

Lancione, Michele. "Homeless People and the City of Abstract Machines: Assemblage Thinking and the Performative Approach to Homelessness." *Area* 45, no. 3 (2013): 358–64. https://doi.org/10.1111/area.12045.

Lancione, Michele. "Inhabiting Dispossession in the Post-socialist City: Race, Class, and the Plan, in Bucharest, Romania." *Antipode* 54, no. 4 (2022): 1141–65. https://doi.org/10.1111/anti.12821.

Lancione, Michele. "Pathways to the Machinic Subject." In *Why Guattari? A Liberation of Cartographies, Ecologies and Politics*, edited by Thomas Jellis, Joe Gerlach, and J.-D. Dewsbury. London: Routledge, 2019.

Lancione, Michele. "The Politics of Embodied Precarity: Roma People and the Fight for the Right to Housing in Bucharest, Romania." *Geoforum* 101 (2018): 182–91.

Lancione, Michele. "Racialised Dissatisfaction: Homelessness Management and the Everyday Assemblage of Difference." *Transactions of the Institute of British Geographers* 41, no. 4 (2016): 363–75. https://doi.org/10.1111/tran.12133.

Lancione, Michele. "Revitalising the Uncanny: Challenging Inertia in the Struggle against Forced Evictions." *Environment and Planning D: Society and Space* 35, no. 6 (2017): 1012–32. https://doi.org/10.1177/0263775817701731.

Lancione, Michele. "The Spectacle of the Poor: Or: 'Wow!! Awesome. Nice to Know That People Care!'" *Social and Cultural Geography* 15, no. 7 (2014): 693–713. https://doi.org/10.1080/14649365.2014.916742.

Lancione, Michele. "Underground Inscriptions." *Cultural Anthropology* 35, no. 1 (2020): 31–39. https://doi.org/10.14506/ca35.1.05.

Lancione, Michele. "Weird Exoskeletons: Propositional Politics and the Making of Home in Underground Bucharest." *International Journal of Urban and Regional Research* 43, no. 3 (2019): 535–50. doi:10.1111/1468-2427.12787.

Lancione, Michele, and Colin McFarlane, eds. *Global Urbanism: Knowledge, Power and the City*. London: Routledge, 2021.

Lancione, Michele, Alice Stefanizzi, and Marta Gaboardi. "Passive Adaptation or Active Engagement? The Challenges of Housing First Internationally and in the Italian Case." *Housing Studies* 33, no. 1 (2018): 40–57. https://doi.org/10.1080/02673037.2017.1344200.

Lancione, Michele, and AbdouMaliq Simone. "Dwelling in Liminalities, Thinking beyond Inhabitation." *Environment and Planning D: Society and Space* 39, no. 6 (2021): 969–75.

Latour, Giuseppe. "Superbonus, trappola prezzi: Nei massimali il costo 'chiavi in mano.'" *Il Sole 24 Ore*, February 11, 2022. https://www.ilsole24ore.com/art/superbonus-trappola-prezzi-massimali-iva-e-costi-extra-AE5RfPDB.

Lazzarato, Maurizio. *Signs and Machines: Capitalism and the Production of Subjectivity*. Los Angeles: Semiotext, 2014.

Le Iene. "Beppe Grillo, il video sull'accusa al figlio di stupro e il commento di Casalino." *Le Iene*, April 27, 2021. https://www.iene.mediaset.it/2021/news/beppe-grillo-video-figlio-stupro-casalino_1039942.shtml.

Lees, Loretta, Sandra Annunziata, and Clara Rivas-Alonso. "Resisting Planetary Gentrification: The Value of Survivability in the Fight to Stay Put." *Annals of the American Association of Geographers* 108, no. 2 (March 4, 2018): 346–55. https://doi.org/10.1080/24694452.2017.1365587.

Lees, Loretta, Hyun Bang Shin, and Ernesto López-Morales, eds. *Planetary Gentrification*. Cambridge: Polity, 2016.

Leogrande, Alessandro. *Uomini e caporali: Viaggio tra i nuovi schiavi nelle Campagne del Sud*. Milan: Feltrinelli, 2016.

Leonardi, Daniela. "Modelli di accoglienza per le persone senza dimora e ruolo degli operatori sociali: Dilemmi, tensioni, vincoli." PhD thesis, University of Turin, 2019.

Lester, Rebecca, and Lauren Cubellis, eds. *Traces of Care*. Durham, NC: Duke University Press, forthcoming.

Liebow, Elliot. *Tell Them Who I Am: The Lives of Homeless Women*. New York: Free Press, 1993.

Löfstrand, Cecilia Hansen, and Kirsi Juhila. "The Discourse of Consumer Choice in the Pathways Housing First Model." *European Journal of Homelessness* 6, no. 2 (2012): 47–68.

Lorde, Audre. "Poetry Is Not a Luxury." In *Sister Outsider: Essays and Speeches*, 36–39. New York: Random House, 2007. First published 1984 by Crossing Press (Freedom, CA).

Lotringer, Sylvère, and Christian Marazzi, eds. *Autonomia: Post-political Politics*. Los Angeles: Semiotext(e), 2007.

Lyon-Callo, Vincent. "Homelessness or the Violence of Poverty and Exploitation: Does It Matter?" *Rethinking Marxism: A Journal of Economics, Culture and Society* 24, no. 2 (2012): 37–41.

Lyon-Callo, Vincent. *Inequality, Poverty, and Neoliberal Governance: Activist Ethnography in the Homeless Sheltering Industry*. Toronto: University of Toronto Press, 2004.

Madden, David, and Peter Marcuse. *In Defense of Housing*. London: Verso, 2016.

Maestri, Gaja. "Are They Nomads, Travellers or Roma? An Analysis of the Multiple Effects of Naming Assemblages." *Area* 49, no. 1 (2017): 18–24. https://doi.org/10.1111/area.12273.

Martinez, Miguel A. "Bitter Wins or a Long-Distance Race? Social and Political Outcomes of the Spanish Housing Movement." *Housing Studies* 34, no. 10 (2019): 1588–611. https://doi.org/10.1080/02673037.2018.1447094.

Massey, Doreen. *For Space*. London: Sage, 2005.

Massey, Doreen. "A Place Called Home?" In *Space, Place, and Gender*, new ed., 157–74. Minneapolis: University of Minnesota Press, 1994. https://www.jstor.org/stable/10.5749/j.cttttw2z.13.

Massey, Doreen. "Power-Geometry and a Progressive Sense of Place." In *Mapping the Futures: Local Cultures, Global Change*, edited by J. Bird, B. Curtis, T. Putnam, G. Robertson, and L. Tickner. London: Routledge, 1993.

Massumi, Brian. *A User's Guide to Capitalism and Schizophrenia: Deviations from Deleuze and Guattari*. Cambridge, MA: MIT Press, 1992.

Matthews, Peter, Christopher Poyner, and Richard Kjellgren. "Lesbian, Gay, Bisexual, Transgender and Queer Experiences of Homelessness and Identity: Insecurity and Home(o)Normativity." *International Journal of Housing Policy* 19, no. 2 (April 3, 2019): 232–53. https://doi.org/10.1080/19491247.2018.1519341.

Maturana, Humberto R., and Francisco J. Varela. *Autopoiesis and Cognition: The Realization of the Living*. Dordrecht: Reidel, 1980.

Mbembe, Achille. "The Universal Right to Breathe." *In the Moment* (blog), April 13, 2020. https://critinq.wordpress.com/2020/04/13/the-universal-right-to-breathe/.

McCann, Eugene J. "Expertise, Truth, and Urban Policy Mobilities: Global Circuits of Knowledge in the Development of Vancouver, Canada's 'Four Pillar' Drug Strategy." *Environment and Planning A* 40, no. 4 (2008): 885–904. https://doi.org/10.1068/a38456.

McCann, Eugene J. "Policy Boosterism, Policy Mobilities, and the Extrospective City." *Urban Geography* 34, no. 1 (2013): 5–29. https://doi.org/10.1080/02723638.2013.778627.

McCarthy, Lindsey. "(Re)Conceptualising the Boundaries between Home and Homelessness: The *Unheimlich*." *Housing Studies* 33, no. 6 (December 6, 2017): 960–85. https://doi.org/10.1080/02673037.2017.1408780.

McElroy, Erin. "Digital Nomads and Settler Desires: Racial Fantasies of Silicon Valley Imperialism." *Imaginations: Journal of Cross-Cultural Image Studies / Revue d'études interculturelle de l'image* 10, no. 1 (July 18, 2019). https://doi.org/10.17742/IMAGE.CR.10.1.8.

McElroy, Erin, and Alex Werth. "Deracinated Dispossessions: On the Foreclosures of 'Gentrification' in Oakland, CA." *Antipode* 51, no. 3 (2019): 878–98. https://doi.org/10.1111/anti.12528.

McFarlane, Colin. *Fragments of the City: Making and Remaking Urban Worlds*. Berkeley: University of California Press, 2021.

McFarlane, Colin. *Learning the City: Knowledge and Translocal Assemblage*. Oxford: Wiley Blackwell, 2011.

McKeithen, Will. "Queer Ecologies of Home: Heteronormativity, Speciesism, and the Strange Intimacies of Crazy Cat Ladies." *Gender, Place and Culture* 24, no. 1 (January 2, 2017): 122–34. https://doi.org/10.1080/0966369X.2016.1276888.

McMordie, Lynne. "Avoidance Strategies: Stress, Appraisal and Coping in Hostel Accommodation." *Housing Studies* 36, no. 3 (2021): 380–96. https://doi.org/10.1080/02673037.2020.1769036.

Meo, Antonella. *Vite in bilico: Sociologia della reazione a eventi spiazzanti*. Naples: Liguori, 2000.

Mezzadra, Sandro, and Brett Neilson. *Border as Method, or, the Multiplication of Labor*. Durham, NC: Duke University Press, 2013.

Mignolo, Walter D. "Epistemic Disobedience and the Decolonial Option: A Manifesto." *Transmodernity* 1, no. 2 (2011): 44–66.

Miller, Daniel, ed. *Home Possessions: Material Culture behind Closed Doors*. Oxford: Berg, 2001.

Mol, Annemarie. *The Logic of Care: Health and the Problem of Patient Choice*. London: Routledge, 2008.

Mudu, Pierpaolo. "At the Intersection of Anarchists and Autonomists: Autogestioni and Centri Sociali." *Acme* 11, no. 3 (2012): 413–38.

Mudu, Pierpaolo, and Sutapa Chattopadhyay, eds. *Migration, Squatting and Radical Autonomy*. London: Routledge, 2016.

Nash, Jennifer C. *Black Feminism Reimagined: After Intersectionality*. Durham, NC: Duke University Press, 2019.

Nast, Heidi J. "Mapping the 'Unconscious': Racism and the Oedipal Family." *Annals of the Association of American Geographers* 90, no. 2 (June 2000): 215–55. https://doi.org/10.1111/0004-5608.00194.

Nast, Heidi J. "Queer Patriarchies, Queer Racisms, International." *Antipode* 34, no. 5 (November 2002): 874–909. https://doi.org/10.1111/1467-8330.00281.

Negri, Antonio. "Domination and Sabotage." In *Autonomia: Post-political Politics*, edited by Sylvère Lotringer and Christian Marazzi, 62–71. Los Angeles: Semiotext(e), 2007.

Nichols, Robert. *Theft Is Property! Dispossession and Critical Theory*. Durham, NC: Duke University Press, 2020.

Novelli, Cecilia Dau. "Matrimonio e famiglia nel magistero dei pontefici del '900." *Rivista di storia della Chiesa in Italia* 71, no. 1 (2017): 131–46.

Omizzolo, Marco. *Sotto padrone: Uomini, donne e caporali nell'agromafia italiana*. Milan: Fondazione Giangiacomo Feltrinelli Editore, 2020.

Osborne, Natalie. "For Still Possible Cities: A Politics of Failure for the Politically Depressed." *Australian Geographer* 50, no. 2 (2019): 145–54. https://doi.org/10.1080/00049182.2018.1530717.

O'Sullivan, Simon. *On the Production of Subjectivity: Five Diagrams of the Finite-Infinite Relation*. New York: Palgrave Macmillan, 2012.

Oswin, Natalie. "The Modern Model Family at Home in Singapore: A Queer Geography." *Transactions of the Institute of British Geographers* 35, no. 2 (April 2010): 256–68. https://doi.org/10.1111/j.1475-5661.2009.00379.x.

Oswin, Natalie. "An Other Geography." *Dialogues in Human Geography* 10, no. 1 (March 2020): 9–18. https://doi.org/10.1177/2043820619890433.

Oswin, Natalie. "Planetary Urbanization: A View from Outside." *Environment and Planning D: Society and Space* 36, no. 3 (June 2018): 540–46. https://doi.org/10.1177/0263775816675963.

Pasquinelli, Carla. *La vertigine dell'ordine: Il rapporto tra sé e la casa*. Milan: Baldini Castoldi Dalai, 2004.

Patton, Paul. *Deleuze and the Political*. London: Routledge, 2000.

Peano, Irene. "Turbulences in the Encampment Archipelago: Conflicting Mobilities between Migration, Labour and Logistics in Italian Agri-food Enclaves." *Mobilities* 16, no. 2 (2021): 212–23. https://doi.org/10.1080/17450101.2021.1885843.

Peck, Jamie. "Geographies of Policy: From Transfer-Diffusion to Mobility-Mutation." *Progress in Human Geography* 35, no. 6 (February 2011): 773–97. https://doi.org/10.1177/0309132510394010.

Peck, Jamie, and Nik Theodore. "Mobilizing Policy: Models, Methods, and Mutations." *Geoforum* 41, no. 2 (March 2010): 169–74. https://doi.org/10.1016/j.geoforum.2010.01.002.

Perry, Keisha-Khan. *Black Women against the Land Grab: The Fight for Racial Justice in Brazil*. Minneapolis: University of Minnesota Press, 2013.

Picker, Giovanni. *Racial Cities: Governance and the Segregation of Romani People in Urban Europe*. London: Routledge, 2018.

Pile, Steve, and Nigel Thrift, eds. *Mapping the Subject: Geographies of Cultural Transformation*. London: Routledge, 1995.

Pleace, Nicholas. "The Action Plan for Preventing Homelessness in Finland 2016–2019: The Culmination of an Integrated Strategy to End Homelessness?" *European Journal of Homelessness* 11, no. 2 (2017): 22.

Pleace, Nicholas. "Housing First." European Observatory on Homelessness, FEANTSA, 2012. https://www.feantsaresearch.org/download/housing_first_pleace3790695452176551843.pdf.

Pleace, Nicholas. "Researching Homelessness in Europe: Theoretical Perspectives Introduction: The New Orthodoxy." *European Journal of Homelessness* 10, no. 3 (2016): 19–44.

Poidimani, Nicoletta. "Ius sanguinis: Una prospettiva di genere su razzismo e costruzione dell'"italianità' tra colonie e madrepatria." In *Quel che resta dell'impero: La cultura coloniale degli Italiani*, 209-34. Milan: Mimesis, 2014.

Polanska, Dominika V., and Grzegorz Piotrowski. "The Transformative Power of Cooperation between Social Movements: Squatting and Tenants' Movements in Poland." *City* 19, no. 2-3 (May 4, 2015): 274-96. https://doi.org/10.1080/13604813.2015.1015267.

Popovici, Veda. "Residences, Restitutions and Resistance: A Radical Housing Movement's Understanding of Post-socialist Property Redistribution." *City* 24, no. 1-2 (2020): 97-111. https://doi.org/10.1080/13604813.2020.1739913.

Porcellana, Valentina. *Dal bisogno al desiderio: Antropologia dei servizi per adulti in difficoltà e senza dimora a Torino*. Milan: FrancoAngeli, 2016. https://www.francoangeli.it/Ricerca/scheda_Libro.aspx?codiceISBN=9788891750655.

Powell, Ryan, and John Lever. "Europe's Perennial 'Outsiders': A Processual Approach to Roma Stigmatization and Ghettoization." *Current Sociology* 65, no. 5 (2015): 680-99.

Power, Emma R., and Kathleen J. Mee. "Housing: An Infrastructure of Care." *Housing Studies* 35, no. 3 (2020): 484-505.

Pullella, Philip. "Gay Marriage a Threat to Humanity's Future: Pope." Reuters, January 9, 2012. https://www.reuters.com/article/us-pope-gay/gay-marriage-a-threat-to-humanitys-future-pope-idUSTRE8081RM20120109.

Purcell, Mark. *The Down-Deep Delight of Democracy*. Chichester: John Wiley and Sons, 2013.

Quirico, Monica. "Lotta Continua and the Italian Housing Movement in the 1970s." *Radical Housing Journal* 3, no. 1 (2021): 149-66.

Quizar, Jessi. "A Logic of Care and Black Grassroots Claims to Home in Detroit." *Antipode* online version (May 2022). https://doi.org/10.1111/anti.12842.

Ramírez, Margaret Marietta. "Take the Houses Back / Take the Land Back: Black and Indigenous Urban Futures in Oakland." *Urban Geography* 41, no. 5 (2020): 682-93. https://doi.org/10.1080/02723638.2020.1736440.

Randazzo, Antonella. *L'Africa del Duce: I crimini fascisti in Africa*. Mario Chiarotto Editore, 2008.

Rawls, John. *A Theory of Justice*. Cambridge, MA: Belknap Press of Harvard University Press, 1971.

RHJ Editorial Collective. "COVID-19 and Housing Struggles: The (Re)Makings of Austerity, Disaster Capitalism, and the No Return to Normal." *Radical Housing Journal* 2, no. 1 (2020): 9-28.

Robinson, Catherine. *Beside One's Self: Homelessness Felt and Lived*. New York: Syracuse University Press, 2011.

Robinson, Cedric J. *Black Marxism: The Making of the Black Radical Tradition*. Chapel Hill: University of North Carolina Press, 2000.

Rodriguez, Akira Drake. *Diverging Space for Deviants: The Politics of Atlanta's Public Housing*. Athens: University of Georgia Press, 2021.

Rolnik, Raquel. *Urban Warfare: Housing under the Empire of Finance*. New York: Verso, 2019.

Rolnik, Raquel, and Michele Lancione. "Building Territories to Protect Life and Not Profit." *Radical Housing Journal* 2, no. 1 (2020): 139-47.

Romeo, Ilaria. "L'editto fascista." *Collettiva*, September 12, 2020. https://www.collettiva.it/copertine/italia/2020/12/09/news/l_editto_fascista-694257/.

Rosa, Elisabetta. "Marginality as Resource? From Roma People Territorial Practices, an Epistemological Reframing of Urban Marginality." In *Rethinking Life at the Margins: The Assemblage of Contexts, Subjects, and Politics*, edited by M. Lancione. Farnham, UK: Ashgate, 2016.

Rosa, Sissi De. "Barilla, no spot con famiglie gay: È polemica sul web." *Ultime Notizie Flash*, 2013. https://www.ultimenotizieflash.com/curiosita/2013/09/26/barilla-no-spot -con-famiglie-gay-e-polemica-sul-web.

Roy, Ananya. "Dis/Possessive Collectivism: Property and Personhood at City's End." *Geoforum* 80 (March 2017): A1–A11. https://doi.org/10.1016/j.geoforum.2016.12.012.

Roy, Ananya. *Poverty Capital: Microfinance and the Making of Development.* New York: Routledge, 2010.

Roy, Ananya. "Racial Banishment." In *Keywords in Radical Geography: Antipode at 50.* New York: Wiley-Blackwell, 2019.

Roy, Ananya. "'The Shadow of Her Wings': Respectability Politics and the Self-Narration of Geography." *Dialogues in Human Geography* 10, no. 1 (March 2020): 19–22. https://doi.org/10.1177/2043820619898899.

Roy, Ananya, and Hilary Malson, eds. *Housing Justice in Unequal Cities.* Los Angeles: Institute on Inequality and Democracy at UCLA, 2019.

Roy, Ananya, Genevieve Negrón-Gonzales, Kweku Opoku-Agyemang, Clare Talwalker, and Abby VanMuijen. *Encountering Poverty.* Berkeley: University of California Press, 2016. https://www.jstor.org/stable/10.1525/j.ctv1wxsk4.

Roy, Ananya, Raquel Rolnik, Terra Graziani, and Hilary Malson. *Methodologies for Housing Justice Guide.* Los Angeles: Institute of Inequality and Democracy at UCLA, 2020.

Ruddick, Susan M. *Young and Homeless in Hollywood: Mapping Social Identities.* New York: Routledge, 1996.

Rybczynski, Witold. *Home: A Short History of an Idea.* New York: Viking Penguin, 1986.

Said, Edward W. *Culture and Imperialism.* New York: Vintage, 1994.

Salerno, Eric. *Genocidio in Libia: Le atrocità nascoste dell'avventura coloniale (1911-1931).* Rome: Manifestolibri, 2005.

Santinello, Massimo, and Marta Gaboardi. "Presentazione del numero: Marginalità estreme." *Psicologia di Comunità*, no. 2 (2015): 5–7.

Saraceno, Chiara. *Mutamenti della famiglia e politiche sociali in Italia.* Bologna: Il Mulino, 2003.

Sgambato, Emiliano. "Il mutuo 'copre' il 65% del valore della casa, 5 anni fa quota al 58%." *Il Sole 24 Ore*, May 29, 2018. https://www.ilsole24ore.com/art/il-mutuo-copre -65percento-valore-casa-5-anni-fa-quota-58percento—AE3vEewE.

Shabazz, Rashad. *Spatializing Blackness: Architectures of Confinement and Black Masculinity in Chicago.* Chicago: University of Illinois Press, 2015.

Sharma, Sarah. *In the Meantime: Temporality and Cultural Politics.* Durham, NC: Duke University Press, 2014.

Sheppard, Eric, Helga Leitner, and Anant Maringanti. "Provincializing Global Urbanism: A Manifesto." *Urban Geography* 34, no. 7 (November 2013): 893–900. https://doi .org/10.1080/02723638.2013.807977.

Silver, Jonathan. *From Homes to Assets: Housing Financialisation in Greater Manchester.* Manchester, UK: Greater Manchester Housing Action, 2018.

Silver, Jonathan, and Simon Marvin. "Powering Sub-Saharan Africa's Urban Revolution: An Energy Transitions Approach." *Urban Studies* 54, no. 4 (March 2017): 847–61. https://doi.org/10.1177/0042098016668105.

Simone, AbdouMaliq. *Always Something Else*. Basel, Switzerland: Basler Afrika Bibliographien, 2016. https://www.jstor.org/stable/j.ctvh9vvoc.

Simone, AbdouMaliq. *Improvised Lives: Rhythms of Endurance in an Urban South*. Cambridge: Polity, 2018.

Simone, AbdouMaliq. *The Surrounds: Urban Life within and beyond Capture*. Durham, NC: Duke University Press, 2022.

Simone, AbdouMaliq. "The Uninhabitable?" *Cultural Politics* 12, no. 2 (2016): 135–54. https://doi.org/10.1215/17432197-3592052.

Simone, AbdouMaliq. "The Urban Poor and Their Ambivalent Exceptionalities." *Current Anthropology* 56, no. S11 (2015): S15–S23. https://doi.org/10.1086/682283.

Simone, AbdouMaliq, and Edgar Pieterse. *New Urban Worlds: Inhabiting Dissonant Times*. Cambridge: Polity, 2017.

Snow, David A., and Leon Anderson. *Down on Their Luck: A Study of Homeless Street People*. Berkeley: University of California Press, 1993.

Somerville, Peter. "Homelessness and the Meaning of Home: Rooflessness or Rootlessness." *International Journal of Urban and Regional Research* 16, no. 4 (1992): 529–39. https://doi.org/10.1111/j.1468-2427.1992.tb00194.x.

Somerville, Peter. "Understanding Homelessness." *Housing, Theory and Society* 30, no. 4 (December 2013): 384–415. https://doi.org/10.1080/14036096.2012.756096.

Sousa Santos, Boaventura de. *Epistemologies of the South: Justice against Epistemicide*. London: Routledge, 2016.

Spivak, Gayatri Chakravorty. "Can the Subaltern Speak?" In *Marxism and the Interpretation of Culture*, edited by C. Nelson and L. Grossberg, 271–313. London: Macmillan, 1988.

Squatting Europe Kollective, ed. *The Squatters' Movement in Europe: Commons and Autonomy as Alternatives to Capitalism*. London: Pluto, 2014.

Stengers, Isabelle. "The Cosmopolitical Proposal." In *Making Things Public: Atmospheres of Democracy*, edited by B. Latour and P. Weibel, 994–1003. Cambridge, MA: MIT Press, 2005.

Stewart, Kathleen. *Ordinary Affects*. Durham, NC: Duke University Press, 2007.

Stierl, Maurice. "A Fleet of Mediterranean Border Humanitarians." *Antipode* 50, no. 3 (2018): 704–24. https://doi.org/10.1111/anti.12320.

Storto, Giancarlo. *La casa abbandonata: Il racconto delle politiche abitative dal piano decennale ai programmi per le periferie*. Rome: Officina Edizioni, 2018.

Summers, Brandi Thompson. "Reclaiming the Chocolate City: Soundscapes of Gentrification and Resistance in Washington, DC." *Environment and Planning D: Society and Space* 39, no. 1 (February 2021): 30–46. https://doi.org/10.1177/0263775820978242.

Summers, Brandi T., and Desiree Fields. "Speculative Urban Worldmaking: Meeting Financial Violence with a Politics of Collective Care." *Antipode* online version (November 2022). https://doi.org/10.1111/anti.12900.

Tadiar, Neferti X. M. "Life-Times of Disposability within Global Neoliberalism." *Social Text* 31, no. 2 (2013): 19–48. https://doi.org/10.1215/01642472-2081112.

Tadiar, Neferti X. M. "Thresholds." *Environment and Planning D: Society and Space* 39, no. 6 (2021): 1111–28. https://doi.org/10.1177/02637758211046959.

Tarde, Gabriel. *Essais et mélanges sociologiques.* Tampa, FL: Elibron Classics, 2005.

Taylor, Affrica, and Carmel Richardson. "Queering Home Corner." *Contemporary Issues in Early Childhood* 6, no. 2 (June 2005): 163–73. https://doi.org/10.2304/ciec.2005.6.2.6.

Tazzioli, Martina. *The Making of Migration: The Biopolitics of Mobility at Europe's Borders.* London: Sage, 2019.

Temenos, Cristina, and Eugene McCann. "Geographies of Policy Mobilities." *Geography Compass* 7, no. 5 (May 2013): 344–57. https://doi.org/10.1111/gec3.12063.

Thieme, Tatiana. "Beyond Repair: Staying with Breakdown at the Interstices." *Environment and Planning D: Society and Space* 39, no. 6 (2021): 1092–1110. https://doi.org/10.1177/02637758211013034.

Thompson, Samantha. "Caring Housing Futures: A Radical Care Framework for Understanding Rent Control Politics in Seattle, USA." *Antipode* online version (September 2022): 1–22. https://doi.org/10.1111/anti.12874.

Tsai, Jack, and Robert A. Rosenheck. "Considering Alternatives to the Housing First Model." *European Journal of Homelessness* 6, no. 2 (2012): 201–8.

Tsemberis, Sam. *Housing First: The Pathways Model to End Homelessness for People with Mental Illness and Addiction.* Center City, MN: Hazelden, 2010.

Tsenkova, Sasha, and Dominika V. Polanska. "Between State and Market: Housing Policy and Housing Transformation in Post-socialist Cities." *GeoJournal* 79 (2014): 401–5. https://doi.org/10.1007/s10708-014-9538-x.

Tulumello, Simone. "The 'Souths' of the 'Wests': Southern Critique and Comparative Housing Studies in Southern Europe and USA." *Housing Studies* 37, no. 6 (2022): 975–96. https://doi.org/10.1080/02673037.2021.1966391.

Turner, John F. C. *Housing by People: Towards Autonomy in Building Environments.* London: Marion Boyars, 1976.

UN-HABITAT. "Forced Evictions: Fact Sheet No. 25/Rev. 1." New York: United Nations Human Rights, 2014. https://www.ohchr.org/Documents/Publications/FS25.Rev.1.pdf.

Unione Inquilini. "Sfratti anno 2018, leggera diminuzione, ma situazione resta drammatica." Unione Inquilini segreteria nazionale, July 8, 2019, http://www.unioneinquilini.it/index.php?id=8763.

Vallerand, Olivier. "Home Is the Place We All Share: Building Queer Collective Utopias." *Journal of Architectural Education* 67, no. 1 (2013): 64–75. https://doi.org/10.1080/10464883.2013.767125.

Vasudevan, Alexander. "The Autonomous City: Towards a Critical Geography of Occupation." *Progress in Human Geography* 39, no. 3 (2015): 316–37. https://doi.org/10.1177/0309132514531470.

Vasudevan, Alexander. "The Makeshift City: Towards a Global Geography of Squatting." *Progress in Human Geography* 39, no. 3 (2015): 338–59. https://doi.org/10.1177/0309132514531471.

Vasudevan, Alexander. *Metropolitan Preoccupations: The Spatial Politics of Squatting in Berlin.* London: Wiley-Blackwell, 2015.

Veness, April R. "Neither Homed nor Homeless: Contested Definitions and the Personal Worlds of the Poor." *Political Geography* 12, no. 4 (1993): 319–40.

Verdicchio, Pasquale. "The Preclusion of Postcolonial Discourse in Southern Italy." In *Revisioning Italy: National Identity and Global Culture*, edited by B. Allen and M. J. Russo, 191–212. Minneapolis: University of Minnesota Press, 1997.

Vieta, Marcelo. "The Stream of Self-Determination and Autogestión: Prefiguring Alternative Economic Realities." *Ephemera: Theory and Politics in Organization* 14, no. 4 (2014): 781–809.

Vilenica, Ana. "Becoming an Accomplice in Housing Struggles on Vulturilor Street." *Dialogues in Human Geography* 9, no. 2 (July 2019): 210–13. https://doi.org/10.1177/2043820619850352.

Vincze, Enikő. "The Ideology of Economic Liberalism and the Politics of Housing in Romania." *Studia Universitatis Babeş-Bolyai Studia Europaea* 62, no. 3 (2017): 29–54. https://doi.org/10.24193/subbeuropaea.2017.3.02.

Vradis, Antonis, Joe Painter, and Anna Papoutsi. *New Borders: Hotspots and the European Migration Regime*. London: Pluto, 2019.

Ward, Colin. *Housing: An Anarchist Approach*. London: Freedom Press, 1976.

Ward, Colin. *When We Build Again: Let's Have Housing That Works!* London: Pluto, 1985.

Watts, Beth, and Suzanne Fitzpatrick. "Capabilities, Value Pluralism and Homelessness." *Housing, Theory and Society* 37, no. 3 (2020): 295–99. https://doi.org/10.1080/14036096.2019.1705388.

Wile, Rob. "A California Gubernatorial Candidate Spent a Week as a Homeless Person." *Business Insider*, July 31, 2014. https://www.businessinsider.com/kashkari-describes-being-homeless-2014-7.

Wilhelm-Solomon, Matthew. "Dispossession as Depotentiation." *Environment and Planning D: Society and Space* 39, no. 6 (2021): 976–93. https://doi.org/10.1177/02637758211036467.

Williams, James. *Gilles Deleuze's Difference and Repetition*. Edinburgh: Edinburgh University Press, 2013. https://www.jstor.org/stable/10.3366/j.ctt1g09x57.

Willse, Craig. *The Value of Homelessness: Managing Surplus Life in the United States*. Minneapolis: University of Minnesota Press, 2015.

Wood, Patricia Burke, and Julie E. E. Young. "A Political Ecology of Home: Attachment to Nature and Political Subjectivity." *Environment and Planning D: Society and Space* 34, no. 3 (June 2016): 474–91. https://doi.org/10.1177/0263775815622787.

Wright, Steve. "Mapping Pathways within Italian Autonomist Marxism: A Preliminary Survey." *Historical Materialism* 16, no. 4 (2008): 111–40. https://doi.org/10.1163/156920608x357747.

Wynter, Sylvia. "Unsettling the Coloniality of Being/Power/Truth/Freedom: Towards the Human, After Man, Its Overrepresentation—an Argument." *CR: The New Centennial Review* 3, no. 3 (2003): 257–337. https://doi.org/10.1353/ncr.2004.0015.

Yiftachel, Oren. *Ethnocracy: Land and Identity Politics in Israel/Palestine*. Philadelphia: University of Pennsylvania Press, 2006.

Young, Iris Marion. *On Female Body Experience: "Throwing Like a Girl" and Other Essays*. Studies in Feminist Philosophy. New York: Oxford University Press, 2005.

Page numbers in italics refer to figures; page numbers in bold refer to tables.

Black feminism, 53–54, 196, 197–99, 224–25

Black Lives Matter movement, 217–18

Blunt, Alison, 10, 27–28, 54

Boano, Camillo, 252n20

body and embodiments of precarity, 16, 37, 54, 101–2, 189–91, 197, 201

borders and bordering practices: definition of, 31–32; faith-based interventions and, 112–13; home(lessness) and, 27, 30–33, 34–35, 38–41, 43–48, 156, 187, 231 (*see also* anthropocentrism); media representations of home(lessness) and, 134, 136, 145–48; migration and, 65, 92–96, 101, 124–25, 224

Brar, Dhanveer Singh, 52

Brickell, Katherine, 10, 28

brigantaggio (brigandage), 87–88

Brothers of Italy (Fratelli d'Italia), 71

Brown, Esther, 189–90

Bryant, Jason, 196

Bucalossi Law (10/1977), 75–76, 77

building amnesty (*condoni edilizi*), 76

Busch-Geertsema, Volker, 62–63

Bush administration (2001–2009), 157–58

Business Insider (news website), 139

Butler, Judith, 11, 35, 36, 37, 59, 188, 236n45

Byrd, Jodi A., 59, 60

Caminiti, Luciana, 90

capability-based approaches, 129–30

capitalism: COVID-19 pandemic and, 167–68; critical urban studies and, 176–77; Deleuze and Guattari on, 15, 40, 57; financialization of housing and, 4, 11, 58, 72–74, 132–34; home(lessness) and, 48 (*see also* capitalization); in Italy, 71, 87–96; neoliberalism and, 5, 9, 45, 76, 104, 162, 177; proprietorship and, 56; Rolnik on, 133. *See also* racial capitalism

Capitalism and Schizophrenia (Deleuze and Guattari), 57

capitalization, 37, 48, 55, 56–60; expulsion and, 224; extraction and, 224; Housing First (HF) and, 162; liberatory politics of home and, 173–74, 197. *See also* racial capitalism

caporalato, 93–94

care and caring: Christian family and, 78–81; as contested and debated notion, 143; Heidegger on, 180; liberatory politics of home and, 6, 17–19, 42, 130, 197–98, 200–206, 210–15,

220–22, 227–28 (*see also* accompliceship); media representations of home(lessness) and, 143–52, **153–54**. See also *agape* (unconditional love); *caritas* (charity)

caritas (charity), 102–3, 107–10, 112–13, 148–51, 206

Castán Broto, Vanesa, 50, 180, 181

"Casti connubii" (Of chaste wedlock) (Pius XI), 82

Catholicism. *See* Roman Catholic Church

Centri di Accoglienza Straordinaria (CAS; Center for Exceptional Reception), 95–96

Centri di Permanenza e Rimpatrio (CPR; Permanence and Repatriation Centers, previously Identification and Expulsion Centers), 96, 106, 124–27

Chapman, Kiera, 245n18

Chattopadhyay, Sutapa, 177

Christian Democracy (Democrazia Cristiana), 70–71

Christianity: caritas (charity) and, 102–3, 107–10, 112–13, 148–51, 206; family and, 78–87, 90 (*see also* patriarchy); Good Samaritan (parable) and, 109–10, 111, 148–50, *150*, 152. *See also* Roman Catholic Church

Church of Saint Anthony of Padua (Turin), 106–10, *107*, 112–14

cisnormativity, 54–55. *See also* patriarchy

civil unions, 9, 86

climate change, 50, 156

Codice Rocco (Rocco Code, 1927), 82

Colau, Ada, 255n69

Colebrook, Claire, 40

colonialism, 43–45, 88–91, 209–10

colonies of home, 43–45; ritornellos of home(lessness) and, 48–61

colonies of home in Italy: overview of, 69–70, 77–78, 96–98; Catholic-infused Left and, 96–97; Centri di Permanenza e Rimpatrio (CPR; Permanence and Repatriation Centers) and, 96, 106, 124–27; faith-based interventions and, 102–3, 105, 106–14, *107–8*, 185; family-communitarian responses and, 104–5; lessness and, 127–30; methods and fieldwork on, 102, 105–6, 192; patriarchy and heteronormalization in, 71, 72, 78–87, 90–91, 96; racial capitalism and, 87–96; sanitation and, 121–24, *122*; state interventions and, 103–4, 105, 106, 114–23, *115*, *122*

www.ingramcontent.com/pod-product-compliance
Lightning Source LLC
Chambersburg PA
CBHW031056280326
41928CB00049B/487